DO NOT WRITE
IN THIS BOOK

D1406394

# This book comes with access to more content online.

## Quiz yourself, track your progress, and score high on test day!

Register your book or ebook at
**www.dummies.com/go/getaccess.**

Select your product, and then follow the prompts
to validate your purchase.

You'll receive an email with your PIN and instructions.

# SAT

10th Edition with Online Practice

## by Ron Woldoff and Geraldine Woods

## SAT For Dummies®, 10th Edition with Online Practice

Published by: **John Wiley & Sons, Inc.**, 111 River Street, Hoboken, NJ 07030-5774, www.wiley.com

Copyright © 2021 by John Wiley & Sons, Inc., Hoboken, New Jersey

Published simultaneously in Canada

For general information on our other products and services, please contact our Customer Care Department within the U.S. at 877-762-2974, outside the U.S. at 317-572-3993, or fax 317-572-4002. For technical support, please visit https://hub.wiley.com/community/support/dummies.

Wiley publishes in a variety of print and electronic formats and by print-on-demand. Some material included with standard print versions of this book may not be included in e-books or in print-on-demand. If this book refers to media such as a CD or DVD that is not included in the version you purchased, you may download this material at http://booksupport.wiley.com. For more information about Wiley products, visit www.wiley.com.

Library of Congress Control Number: 2020948885

ISBN 978-1-119-71624-2 (pbk); ISBN 978-1-119-71625-9 (ebk); ISBN 978-1-119-71626-6 (ebk)

Manufactured in the United States of America

SKY10022404_111120

# Contents at a Glance

# Table of Contents

# Introduction

Years ago, during an early gig as a consultant, I sat at a desk that had a *For Dummies* book on the shelf. The book was something office related, like *SQL For Dummies*. I took a sticky note and wrote the word "Ron" with a black marker, then placed the sticky note over the word "Dummies" on the spine of the book, so it read, "SQL For Ron." It fit nicely.

Since starting my test-prep company, I've had students who would go on to do great things, and many have gone on to have amazingly successful careers. You, too, are in this group of future success stories. How do I know? Because you're on your way to a good school for a college degree, which will open lots of doors, and you're oh-so-close to getting started. You just need to get past this one hurdle called the SAT.

The SAT challenges your ability to conjure up everything you've covered in high school — some stuff you haven't touched in years. Really all you need is a refresher, some strategies, and practice. This book has all that and more: It goes beyond rehashing what you've learned (and forgotten) by providing exam-specific strategies and tips for answering questions quickly and getting through the exam. There are examples, practice questions, and practice exams to help you build your skills, identify areas you need to work on, and build your confidence for test day.

I know deep in my heart that every person I work with can do well on this exam. Right off the bat, I aim for 100 percent with each student. You're a little rusty here, haven't seen that there, could use a few tips, but you'll pick it up fast and do just fine. Succeeding on the SAT is like handling any other task: If you know what to do, and you practice, you'll be fine. I get you started with some review and guidance, and you can take it from there.

## About This Book

*SAT For Dummies*, 10th Edition with Online Practice, is a whirlwind tour of the SAT. This book takes you through each section of the exam, explaining what the test-makers are looking for and how you can deliver it. This book starts at the very beginning to cover all the basic math and verbal concepts, and because you have the capacity, it then challenges you with SAT-level questions. This book also shows you how to approach these questions, avoid making common mistakes, and master the intuitive tricks that help you knock it out of the park.

To earn a top score on the SAT, you have three goals:

1. **Know what's on the exam.**

   That's in this book, so read the whole thing. No matter how well you know a topic, you can discover strategies and avoid common traps, and the SAT has a way of asking a question that's different from what you're used to — or what you learned in the classroom. This book has dozens of tried-and-true strategies so you can cut through the muck and get the most points on the SAT.

2. **Strengthen your weak subject areas.**

   Turn to specific sections for targeted information. This book is organized to make it easy for you to find strategies and practice for specific question types that you have trouble with.

   If you need more help with practice questions, check out *1,001 SAT Practice Questions For Dummies* (also published by Wiley).

3. **Prepare for the test-taking experience.**

   You'll need practice exams to get ready for the experience. Packaged with this book are four online practice exams: two in this book, and all four online. When your exam is around the corner, take one or two practice exams in real-life, dress-rehearsal settings. Flip to Part 6 for ten ways to build your skills from the practice exams.

Basically, this book does it all: It prepares you for the exam by bringing your skills from the basic level to the SAT level. What else is there?

There's vocab.

To help you with vocab, as you read through this book, you'll notice that some words have a style all their own. Each SAT vocabulary word in this text appears in *this font*, followed directly by its meaning. Fortunately, the SAT doesn't hammer vocab like it used to, and most of the vocab on the exam is in context, so it's easier to work with. That said, a good way to learn SAT vocab is to encounter it in a question and see what it means along with how it's used. When you get stuck on a vocab word, write it down. This is an effective complement to studying from a list or flash cards.

## Icons Used in This Book

Icons are those cute little pictures that appear in the margins of this book. They indicate why you should pay special attention to the accompanying text. Here's how to decode them:

**TIP**

This icon points out helpful hints about strategy — what the all-star test-takers know and the rookies want to find out.

**WARNING**

This icon identifies the sand traps that the SAT-writers are hoping you'll fall into as you take the test. Take note of these warnings so you know what to do (and what not to do) as you move from question to question on the real SAT.

**REMEMBER**

When you see this icon, be sure to file away the information that accompanies it. The material will come in handy as you prepare for (and take) the SAT.

**PLAY**

This icon indicates an example practice question within the regular chapter text.

# Beyond the Book

Besides all the ways this book can help you perform well on the SAT, there are even more online, including these:

>> **Cheat Sheet:** At www.dummies.com, type "SAT For Dummies cheat sheet" in the search box and you'll find the book's cheat sheet, which gives you last-minute details that you'll want to have at your fingertips, including a rundown of how to get the most points on each SAT Test.

>> **Nearly 600 practice questions:** You'll find hundreds of SAT-type questions online to help you build your competence and confidence. Focus on areas where you need practice and verify that you're up to speed in other areas. You can select the level of difficulty and answer the questions through untimed and timed quizzes, so you can work at your own speed and gain experience working under pressure.

To gain access to additional tests and practice online, all you have to do is register. Just follow these simple steps:

1. **Register your book or e-book at Dummies.com to get your PIN. Go to** www.dummies.com/go/getaccess.

2. **Select your product from the drop-down list on that page.**

3. **Follow the prompts to validate your product, and then check your email for a confirmation message that includes your PIN and instructions for logging in.**

**TIP**

If you do not receive this email within two hours, please check your spam folder before contacting us through our Technical Support website at http://support.wiley.com or by phone at 877-762-2974.

Now you're ready to go! You can come back to the practice material as often as you want — simply log on with the username and password you created during your initial login. No need to enter the access code a second time.

# Where to Go from Here

Get started! No matter what you do next, start simple. You have exactly what you need right here in your hands, so breathe deep and turn the page.

# 1

# Getting Started with the SAT

**IN THIS PART . . .**

Get the details about what's on the SAT and how your performance is measured.

Figure out how to plan and manage your study time ahead of test day, along with some pointers if you're retaking the exam.

Know what you need to do to prepare for the exam (beyond studying) along with what to expect on test day.

IN THIS CHAPTER

» Thinking about the ACT

» Seeing what the SAT covers

» Scheduling the SAT

» Accommodating special needs

» Doing amazing even if English isn't your first language

» Understanding what the SAT looks for

» Getting the SAT scoring

Chapter **1**

# What to Expect with the SAT

The best and easiest way to reduce your anxiety and own the SAT is to become familiar with it. Knowing what to expect means you can plan for it, so nothing on exam day is a surprise.

In this chapter, you find the basics of the SAT, including when, where, and how often you should take the test. This chapter also tells you what sort of scores you receive, explains how to deal with special needs, and gives you a peek into the structure of the exam itself. If English isn't your first language, there are some tips on how to get the edge over your primarily-English-speaking competition.

## What About the ACT?

Most 11th and 12th graders take one of two giant exams on their way to college. One is the SAT, and the other is the ACT. Most colleges accept both, but you should check with your target schools just to be sure. When you call or email the college admissions office, among your other questions, ask these things:

> » Do you require an exam score with my application?

> » If so, do you accept both the SAT and the ACT?

> » Do you need me to write the exam essay?

The SAT and the ACT are similar in overall difficulty. The math is about 90 percent the same, but SAT math goes more in depth than ACT math, while ACT math covers more topics. (ACT math has logarithms, for example, which SAT math does not.) Some students may find ACT math easier.

The ACT's writing and language questions are about the same as the SAT's, while ACT reading questions are almost the same but don't include evidence-based questions (more on those in Chapter 3). The ACT also has its Science Test, which the SAT does not. To compensate, the SAT has some science-based questions mixed into the Reading Test, but not nearly to the extent of the ACT Science Test. Students who struggle with scientific studies may prefer the SAT.

Each exam has an optional essay question at the end, but the ACT essay assignment is very different. The SAT essay is covered here in Chapter 7, but for more on the ACT essay, and the ACT overall, pick up the latest edition of *ACT For Dummies* by Lisa Zimmer Hatch and Scott A. Hatch (published by Wiley).

There are also the SAT Subject Tests, which specialize in about 20 topics including biology, history, math, and languages. Depending on the school or academic program that you apply to, you may have to take one or more Subject Tests.

Besides contacting your target schools and checking their websites, you can find more on the application requirements by checking a college guide. A *college guide* is a *compendium* (thorough collection) of school listings and admission requirements. Many libraries and bookstores carry college guides, and you can also talk with your college counselor, who may also have one.

If college isn't in your immediate future, you may want to take the SAT just to get it out of the way, while the test topics are still fresh in your head. If your plans include a stint in the armed forces or the Peace Corps before hitting higher education, you can keep your options open by taking the SAT before you go. Then when you're ready to get back into the classroom, you'll have some scores to send to the college of your choice. Note that SAT scores are officially valid for five years (as of this writing), but the college you apply to may require newer scores. Just keep that in mind.

## So What's on the SAT?

What are you getting into here? Well, it's nothing you can't handle, but it helps to know what's coming up. Here is the SAT testing experience, in this order:

>> SAT Reading Test: 52 questions, 65 minutes

>> SAT Writing and Language Test: 44 questions, 35 minutes

>> 10-minute break

>> SAT Math Test, No Calculator Allowed: 20 questions, 25 minutes

>> SAT Math Test, Calculator Allowed: 38 questions, 55 minutes

>> 10-minute break (if you're staying for the essay)

>> SAT Essay (optional), 1 essay question, 50 minutes

# Signing Up Before Sitting Down: Registering for the SAT

The SAT is given at multiple times at select high schools throughout the United States and in English-speaking schools in many other countries. Homeschoolers can also take the SAT. This section explains how and when to register for an exam and acceptable methods of payment.

## How to register

You can register for the SAT online, by mail, or, if you've taken the SAT before, by phone.

Online registration is simple: Go to www.sat.collegeboard.org/register to create an account, sign up, and choose a test center and date. You need a credit card or a PayPal account and a digital photo of yourself ready to upload. Be sure the photo meets the College Board's standards: a head shot where your whole face is visible and you're the only one in the photo. Head coverings are okay if they're religious in nature.

You can also register by mail. At the time of this writing, you have to register by mail if you're younger than 13 or older than 21 or if you need to take the exam on a Sunday for religious reasons. However, also at the time of this writing, the COVID-19 pandemic is changing the rules everywhere, so registration may be different by the time it's your turn.

You can also ask your school guidance counselor for a registration form. If you're homeschooled, call the nearest public or private high school, or call the College Board Customer Service Center for help. If you register by mail, you'll have to attach a photo and enclose registration payment (credit card number, a check from a United States bank, or a bank draft).

The College Board Customer Service line within the U.S. is 866-756-7346 and outside the U.S. is 212-713-7789. Hearing-impaired test-takers can call the TTY Customer Service number, which within the U.S. is 888-857-2477 and outside the U.S. is 609-882-4118. You can also contact the College Board by mail at this address: College Board SSD Program, P.O. Box 8060, Mount Vernon, IL 62864-0060.

**TIP**

However you register, you'll be asked whether you want to sign up for the Student Search Service. Answer yes and fill out the questionnaire. Colleges, universities, and some scholarship-granting organizations receive information about you from this service. Expect lots of emails and letters — a little annoying, perhaps, but it's good to know that the schools are interested in you. You may also discover a school or scholarship that meets your needs perfectly.

**WARNING**

Scammers are interested in you too. Don't send personal or financial information to any organization unless you know it's legitimate. You know this, of course, but exam registration and college application is a new game. Not sure the contact is legit? Call the College Board Customer Service line to check.

## When to take the test

The SAT was typically offered seven times a year, but at the time of this writing, everything is being reworked due to COVID-19. SATs are regularly cancelled and postponed, so by the time you get this book, hopefully the pandemic and quarantine will have passed, but the number of yearly exams may be different.

You can take the exam as often as you want. Ideally, you take it two or three times, but the door is open if you want another chance. Most high-schoolers follow this pattern:

>> **Start in the fall of your sophomore year:** Here you take the PSAT/NMSQT, which is sort of a junior SAT, for the first time. Right now as a 10th grader, this exam doesn't count for much other than a practice and eye-opener of the series of exams to come.

>> **Continue in the fall of your junior year:** Here you take the PSAT/NMSQT again, only this time it counts. If you do well, it opens the door for several scholarship opportunities and special programs. No pressure.

>> **In the spring of your junior year:** Take the SAT as a first run, which serves as a practice test, though you can send in your scores if you're pleased with them. Note you can also practice with an unscored practice exam, but this experience isn't quite the same as the real deal. Some juniors take the SAT twice during the spring.

>> **Again in the fall of your senior year:** The SAT strikes again, but this time you're ready, and you should do well enough to use these scores for your application. You also have the chance for a few tries. If you're an early-decision candidate, you should take the test in October or November.

>> **Finally, in the winter of your senior year:** You have one more chance to get it right, or if you did get it right, you have one more chance to get that scholarship. By now you're a pro, so success should be right in your hands. There may be some juniors in the room with you.

Everyone takes the SAT on Saturday except for those who can't for religious reasons. If you fall into that category, your SAT may be on a Sunday or a Wednesday following a Saturday SAT day. Get a letter from your religious leader on letterhead and mail it in with your registration form.

**TIP**

Register early to select a test site. When you register, you may request a test site, but if it's filled, you get an alternate. So don't delay — send in the form or register online as soon as you know when and where you want to take the exam. In these COVID-19 days, some exams are experimenting with home-based testing, so this may be an SAT option by the time it's your turn. Otherwise, you'll probably want to test at your high school, if possible, where the campus setting is familiar to you.

# Special Needs Considerations

Like many products and services, the SAT stresses fairness and equal access for all students, including those with special needs. Even if you don't think you belong in this category, skim this section. You may discover an option that will help you "show what you know" when it matters most.

## Learning disabilities

If you have a learning disability, you may be allowed to take the SAT under special conditions. The first step is to get an Eligibility Form from your school counselor. (Homeschoolers, call the local high school.) You may also want to ask your college counseling or guidance office for a copy of the *College Board Services for Students with Disabilities Brochure*. If your school doesn't have one, contact the College Board directly or check the testing agency's website (www.collegeboard.org/ students-with-disabilities).

**TIP**

Once you are certified for accommodations on any College Board test (an AP, an SAT Subject Test, or the PSAT/NMSQT), you're certified for all the College Board tests, unless your need arises from something that is temporary. If you fall into that category, see the next section for more information.

File the form well in advance of the time you expect to take the test. If the College Board grants you the accommodation, you'll be eligible for extra time on the SAT, which could mean an extra 50 percent of time for each test. So if a regular test-taker has 50 minutes to write the essay, for example, an extended-timer gets 75 minutes.

## Physical issues

At no additional charge, the SAT also provides wheelchair accessibility, large-print tests, and other accommodations for students who need them. Be sure to submit your Eligibility Form early so that the College Board can request documentation and get things ready for you. You can send paper documentation or file an Eligibility Form online. Check out www.collegeboard.org/students-with-disabilities for details.

If a physical issue (a broken arm, for example,) occurs shortly before your scheduled SAT and you can't easily take the exam at a later date, call the College Board Customer Service, explain the situation, and have your physician fill out the forms requesting whatever accommodation you need.

Questions about special needs? Your high school's counselor or principal can help, or you can check the preceding link or email the College Board (ssd@info.collegeboard.org).

## Financial help

If you need financial help, you can apply for a fee waiver, available to low-income high-school juniors and seniors who live in the United States, Puerto Rico, and other American territories. (United States citizens living in other countries may also be eligible for fee waivers.) The College Board also gives you four extra score reports for free, along with four request forms for college application fee waivers. The College Board does what it can.

If you're worried about paying for school later on, there are loans, grants, scholarships, and other programs to help you achieve success in college and hopefully your career. There are many, many opportunities and places to look, so talk to your school counselor. That's what the counselor is for!

You can also check with your school counselor for fee-waiver applications. (As with everything SAT, if you're a homeschooler, call the local high school for a form.) And be careful to avoid additional fees when you can. You run into extra charges for late or changed registration and for some extras — super-speedy scores, an analysis of your performance, and the like. (See the section "Scoring on the SAT" later in this chapter for more information on score-reporting options.)

# Making the SAT Work for You as a Foreign Student

This is an opportunity for you to stand out among your high-school peers and represent with honors the country where you are a national! A high score on this exam is certainly within your reach, even if English is not your first language, if you know what to do and practice your skills.

For the SAT Reading Test, you may get stuck on some of the academic vocabulary. To work on this, as you practice SAT reading, underline and look up any word you don't know. (More on this in Chapter 3, because every student gets stuck on this, even English-only speakers.) After a while, you'll know enough of the words.

For the SAT Writing and Language Test, you have probably studied the mechanics of English more than your English-born counterparts, so you may have a better academic understanding of sentence structure and verb form than they do. I have observed many, many times in a class with both English-only and non-native English speakers, that after a refresher of the basics of this test, the non-native English speakers often do much better than the English-only speakers!

For the SAT Math Tests, the math doesn't change from language to language, so if you can crack the basic language used to put forth the problem, you should do just fine. There may be some fine differences (for example, 2,345.67 in one language appears as 2.345,67 in another), but the basics are the same, and these differences are easy to master. Just be sure to practice using SAT materials.

Two things that you can do right now:

>> **First, start reading English books.** Pick movies or novels that you love in your own language and read the English versions. You'll be into the story, and you'll know the gist of events well enough to pick up the English style of writing. Most importantly, you'll learn the placement of grammar and the style of expressive writing.

>> **Next, see if there's an SAT Subject Test that tests skills in your native language!** This test should be easy for you, and you'll score far better than your primary-English-speaking counterparts. Include your top-scoring Subject Test score with your application and show the schools how naturally strong you are in a topic (your native language) that so many others struggle with. At the time of this writing, the SAT offers Subject Tests in Spanish, French, Chinese, Italian, German, Hebrew, Japanese, Korean, and even Latin, where you could do well if you speak a number of Latin-based languages. The list changes, so check and see: https://collegereadiness.collegeboard.org/sat-subject-tests/subjects/languages. The College Board page even tells you, "Show your mastery of (this language)."

# Examining Your Mind: What the SAT Really Looks For

The exam attempts to measure the skills you need to succeed in school and in the workplace. It is not a measure of how smart you are, nor is it a measure of how well you do in school. It measures how adaptable you are, and especially how well you prepare for a blockbuster exam.

**TIP**

The college admission essay is a great place to put your scores in perspective. If your SAT score struggles from a special circumstance, such as a learning disability, a school that doesn't value academics, a family tragedy, or any other reason, you may want to explain your situation in an essay. A good essay gives the college a way to interpret your achievement and to see you, the applicant, in more detail. For help with the college admission essay, check out *College Admission Essays For Dummies* by Geraldine Woods (Wiley).

The SAT doesn't test facts you studied in school. You don't need to know when Columbus sailed across the Atlantic or how to calculate the molecular weight of an atom. Instead, the SAT takes aim at your ability to follow a logical sequence, to comprehend what you've read, and to write clearly in Standard English. The math portion checks on the math skills you have picked up during your years in high school. The point is the SAT isn't a giant final exam or a review of high school. It's a test of your *skills*, *not* your knowledge.

Use this to your advantage. The skills for the Reading Test, covered in Chapter 3, are easy to learn and just take practice to master. The details asked in the Writing and Language Test are of a limited scope and fully reviewed in Chapter 5. The skills for the Math Test are also of a limited scope and are captured in Part 4 of this book. In other words, pretty much everything you need to know for the SAT fits into a medium-sized book. There may be an occasional "oddball" question as the SAT steps outside its defined scope of topics, but these questions are very few and very far between.

One *caveat* (disclaimer) to the preceding claim: Everything you need to know for the SAT is right here in this book *assuming* you already have a basic grasp of English and math. This claim assumes that you have certain skills at the basic high-school level: You can read and understand a narrative in English, you can construct a complete sentence in English, and you can execute basic math, which includes long division and adding fractions. If any of these topics is an area where you struggle, there are literally thousands of books and resources available to you, many free online or at a library. You can also check with your school for any type of remedial program, including student tutors. This is something you can easily fix and place into the past.

# Scoring on the SAT

The SAT gives colleges an in-depth look at your skills and performance. If you take the exam more than once, as most students do, you can use the detailed information from your score reports to craft a personalized study program and zero in on the skills you need to fine-tune.

## Types of scores

The redesigned SAT gives you a number of scores. Here's the idea:

>> **Composite score:** This is the score that everyone is worried about. It's the sum of the Reading Test, Writing and Language Test, and Math Tests (400 to 1600 points). The maximum SAT score is 1600, with a top combined score of 800 on the Reading Test and the Writing and Language Test and 800 on Math Tests. The minimum is 400, which you get for showing up.

>> **Essay score:** The optional essay receives separate scores for reading, analysis, and writing, each scored at 2 to 8 points, for a total range of 6 (for showing up) to 24 (for knocking it out).

>> **Cross-test scores:** These scores are determined by questions of a particular type in all three areas of the SAT (Reading, Writing and Language, and Math). You get a score for analysis in history/social studies (10 to 40 points) and another for analysis in science (10 to 40 points). These cross-test scores are a metric of your performance, but not one that schools typically pay attention to.

>> **Subscores:** Here's another way that the SAT slices and dices your performance. On the Reading Test and the Writing and Language Test, there are scores for command of evidence (1 to 15 points) and understanding words in context (1 to 15 points). On the Writing and Language Test, you get scores for expression of ideas (1 to 15 points) and Standard English conventions (1 to 15 points). The Math Tests also do this, giving you 1 to 15 points each for algebra, advanced math, and problem solving/data analysis. Don't worry about these subscores as much. Schools almost always look at your composite score and your essay score.

**TIP**

You can run through the basics of converting your correct answers to a tangible SAT score in Chapter 18, following the practice exams in Part 5.

## Score reporting

The SAT experience includes four score reports which can be sent to your choice of schools. (*Yikes?* Not really. More like, *Yes!*) If you want to send out more reports to more schools, you can do so for a nominal fee. Check the College Board website at www.collegeboard.org for current prices. You can request additional score reports when you sign up for the exam, when you take the exam, or after the fact. At the time of this writing, your scores are good for five years.

After you get your SAT scores, you can order a Question and Answer Service, which shows each question from the exam, which answer you selected, and if applicable, the correct answer. There is a small fee for this, and the fee waiver may apply. If you are planning to retake the SAT, you absolutely *must* order this service: It's like turning on a light to see your exam performance. The bad thing is that this service isn't available for some tests, but the good thing is that it *is* free with your PSAT, so use that!

Score reports arrive in your mailbox and at your high school about five weeks after you take the test, and in your email about a week sooner. The College Board usually posts on its website the date that the test scores will be available.

Last thing. Be sure to create a free College Board account at www.collegeboard.org, where you can check your scores and register for the SAT, PSAT, and any SAT Subject Tests. Here, along with your score, you can find how well you did in comparison to everyone else who took the exam when you did. You can also immediately access the Question and Answer Service and get right to the questions.

**IN THIS CHAPTER**

» Planning your prep time before the SAT

» Getting ready on the night before and morning of your SAT

» Taking control of the testing experience

» Managing your time

» Dealing with adverse conditions

# Chapter **2**

# Strategies for Success

"All things are ready, if our mind be so," wrote William Shakespeare. When you hit test day, your preparation is the key to your success. You know this; it's why you're here. And this chapter outlines the strategies and game plans for you to prepare for the SAT and the opportunities that follow.

SAT prep can start at any point along your high-school path and still be effective. In this chapter are how to plan your studying when the test is a year away, a few months away, and right around the corner. And for those of you who suddenly realize that the test is *next week*, there is a panic-button scenario (and some suggestions on goal planning and time management). Lastly, this chapter tells you what to do the night before and the morning of SAT day, and what to do if you're faced with adverse conditions.

## Starting Early: The Long-Term Phase

You're the person who buys summer clothes in December. (Smart! That's when they're on clearance.) You also plan ahead — way ahead. This is not a bad strategy for long-term success in life and career. When your SAT is roughly a year out, start with these strategies:

» **Sign up for challenging courses in school.** Skip the courses that require papers short enough to tweet and just enough math to figure out how many minutes remain before your next vacation. Go for subjects that stretch your mind. Specifically, stick it out with math at least through Algebra II. If high school is in your rearview mirror, check out extension or enrichment adult-ed courses. Colleges will appreciate this initiative along with your SAT scores.

>> **Get into the habit of reading.** Instagram, Snapchat, and Discord don't do the trick. Instead, take on academic journals, established news sources, and any publication aimed towards an adult audience. The more you read challenging material, the more you build your ability to comprehend it. This will help you in so many ways in life, but on the SAT, it helps you understand vocabulary, analyze reasoning, and deconstruct evidence. Take note of unfamiliar words and check the words online. Also notice how an author makes a point — through description, citing experts, word choice, and so forth. This helps you understand the passages of the Reading Test, recognize the writing methods of the Writing and Language Test, and construct a logical, flowing essay for the optional Essay Test.

>> **Take a critical eye.** Reading the school or local paper, websites, or any publications, look for reasoning techniques. They're everywhere, and once you spot them, you see them all over. Is the sales pitch, persuasive argument, or editorial using statistics, emotion, anecdotes, or humor to make its point? As a side benefit, you learn to see through these tactics and spot the logic.

>> **Revisit your math.** Resist the urge to burn your geometry text the minute the semester is over. Keep your math notebooks and especially your old exams. Revisit the questions, especially the ones you missed, because these are the topics you'll see on the SAT. Research shows that memory improves when concepts are reviewed after a period of time, and this will help you when the SAT asks you to factor a quadratic, which you may not have done for a couple of years.

>> **Take the practice exams in Part 5 of this book.** Work your way through all those questions and then check the answers and explanations to everything you got wrong, skipped, or wobbled on. After you identify your areas where you need to focus, you know what you have to practice. There are also free practice exams at www.collegeboard.org.

>> **Build up your grammar.** The grammar review in Chapter 5 covers *almost* all of what you need for the Writing and Language Test, but the SAT likes to throw the occasional "oddball" grammar curveball that no one is expecting. For a more thorough, in-depth review of English grammar, pick up *English Grammar Workbook For Dummies* or *1,001 Grammar Practice Questions For Dummies* (both authored by Geraldine Woods and published by Wiley).

>> **Take the PSAT/NMSQT.** This "mini-SAT" gives you a chance to experience test conditions. It may also open the door to some robust scholarships, including the National Merit Scholarship (the "NMS" in the title of the test). The PSAT is a good preview of the SAT, and when you get your scores, you get to see the questions you missed along with the right answers — which, as stated in Chapter 1, is like turning on a light to see your exam performance.

This is a good, early start. Now continue on to the medium-range plan as the time before your SAT shortens.

# Moving Along: The Medium-Term Phase

As the SAT moves along its timeline closer to your door — or something like that — here's the medium-term phase of your plan. Don't worry if you didn't start earlier. You have time, and these steps make a huge difference.

>> **Continue sharpening your reading skills.** College-level reading skills matter in all the exam tests (Reading, Writing and Language, and Math). Continue reading college- and adult-level materials and searching up words that you don't know. *Peruse* (read carefully) the daily newspaper, either online or in print, and check out the way that stories are told and statistics appear. Be sure to read the editorials and think about how the author argues a point.

» **Work on your writing.** Send a story in to the school newspaper or send letters or emails to a publication editor. Writing for an audience ups your writing game, because you pay much closer attention to your reasoning and grammar. Do this a few times, and you're a pro! This is especially true with the sort of writing that makes a case for a particular point of view, because that's what you have to read, analyze, and possibly write on the SAT.

» **Get a math study-buddy.** Not a tutor. A tutor is good, but you can also benefit from studying with someone on your own level. You'll get stuck on questions that your friend knows, while your friend will need help that you can provide. The studying process gets a little less tedious, and you'll be glad to know that you're not the only one in the room who doesn't know all the answers.

» **Revisit the practice exams in Part 5 of this book.** Pay special attention to the questions that you missed before, or if this is your first round, mark those missed questions for review later on. Also check any question that puzzled you or took too much time, even if you guessed the right answer! After you know which sort of question is likely to stump you, read the chapters that explain how to answer those questions.

» **Revisit your PSAT/NMSQT.** Just as with the practice exams, you need to revisit your performance on an SAT-style exam, but the PSAT is more relevant because it shows you how you do in an actual exam setting. Plus, you need to make sure that you can handle the topics that you missed on that exam, such as reading passage main idea, verb parallelism, or coordinate geometry.

Keep following this plan, and you'll be in fine shape for the SAT. Now to shift your process for the final stretch.

# Getting Closer: The Short-Range Phase

The SAT is weeks away! Whether you've been following the progression or are starting now, these steps can make a nice difference and add quite a few points to your score.

» **Work or revisit the practice questions in Chapters 4, 6, 8, and Part 4 of this book.** If you can answer the question easily, you're good — but if you struggle with a question, review the chapter pages that show you how to answer it. Then you can find similar questions in *1,001 SAT Practice Questions For Dummies* (also written by coauthor Ron and published by Wiley).

» **Work at least one practice exam from Part 5 or www.collegeboard.org.** Do your diligence and keep practicing! Get your stamina ready for the SAT marathon plus get a sense of what's on the exam. Review your practice exam afterwards, so you know where to focus. Best case, review it with a friend who is also taking the SAT and has taken the same practice. Check out Chapter 20 for good ways to use the practice exam to boost your score.

» **Clear your calendar of all unnecessary activity so you can study as much as possible.** It's time to prioritize, and it's just for a few weeks. Anything that can wait: Let it wait. Right now is crucial, and an hour in the weeks before your exam is worth a *lot* more than an hour in the weeks after. That movie or golf game can wait.

» **Get a wristwatch so you can manage your time.** Now is the time (so to speak) to go to the store or online and get a nice, simple wristwatch that has absolutely no functionality at all except to tell the time. Try it out, make sure it's comfortable, and most of all, *make sure it doesn't beep,* otherwise the proctors will take it. More on the cutting-edge, exam-changing, night-and-day difference that the advantage of having a wristwatch gives you in the upcoming section "It's All You: What to Do the Morning of Your SAT."

# Planning It Out: What to Do the Night Before Your SAT

Your SAT is tomorrow. Scared? That's normal. When you walk into that testing room, *everyone* is scared — except you're more prepared. The fear is normal, so don't deny it. Just accept that tomorrow is a big day and do what you can to control it. More on handling anxiety and taking control coming up in this chapter, but for now, here's what you do on the night before the SAT.

Most important: Don't study anything. Instead, get your rest. You've prepared for months (or weeks), and you've built your skills and addressed your gaps. Right now, you need to build your strength, so *get some rest*. There's always one more thing to review, but now is the time to shift focus from studying to conserving energy.

Don't go out. There'll be another party or game. Stay home and relax, maybe read or watch a movie. (No binge watching! You need your sleep.) Have a good, wholesome dinner and avoid anything intense like sushi or super spicy food. The last thing you need on exam day is an upset stomach.

Resist the urge to contact friends who are also taking the test. If they're nervous too, their anxiety is not going to help you relax. Instead, *mitigate* (reduce the effect of) your anxiety by taking control of the situation. Take control of the morning by setting your phone alarm and asking Mom or Dad to wake you just in case, so you're not worried about oversleeping. Take further control by getting your stuff together (detailed in the next section) and placing it all in one spot, so it's ready to go and you're not worried about forgetting something. As you take more control of the situation, the rest will follow.

# It's All You: What to Do the Morning of Your SAT

Whatever your normal morning routine is, do the same on this day. Along these lines, eat something good that you're used to, that has protein (eggs, cheese, meat, tofu, and so on). Stay away from sugary foods (donuts, sugary cereals, and the like) because sugar gives you a surge of energy and then a chunk of fatigue. You don't want to crash in the middle of the Reading Test.

**REMEMBER**

If disaster strikes — fever, car trouble, uncle's arrest — and you suddenly can't take the SAT, call the College Board and request that they transfer your fee to the next available date.

## Bringing the right stuff

Be sure to have these items with you. Get them together the night before:

» **Admission ticket for the SAT:** Don't leave home without it! If you registered online, print out the ticket. If you registered by mail or phone, make sure you have your ticket. (If your ticket hasn't arrived, check with the College Board, ideally a week or so before the test.) Without your ticket, you can't get in, and you'll have to do this whole routine over again.

» **Photo ID:** The SAT accepts your driver's license, school ID, passport, or almost any other official document that includes your picture. The SAT doesn't accept your Social Security card, library card, or anything without your picture. If you're not sure what to bring, ask your school counselor or check the College Board website at www.collegeboard.org.

» **No. 2 pencils:** Don't guess. Look for the No. 2 on the side of the pencil. Take at least three or four sharpened pencils, and be sure they have usable erasers. You can also bring one of those pink rubber erasers.

» **A calculator:** You don't absolutely need a calculator to take the SAT, but it does help on some questions. A four-function, scientific, or graphing calculator is acceptable, but it cannot make noise and it cannot connect to the internet. There are other rules too, so if you're not sure, check the College Board website (www.collegeboard.org) to see if yours is on the list of acceptable devices. Also, the day before the exam, *check the batteries* or *plug it in.*

» **Some snacks:** Bring some healthy snacks (trail mix, cheese, or other non-candy items) in your backpack. You can eat them during your rest breaks, and your water bottles can keep them cold.

» **Water bottles:** Bring a couple chilled water bottles to drink during your breaks. Don't bring anything sugary like soda or juice, because you'll crash and get even more thirsty. If you want to bring something with electrolytes, such as a smart water, make sure it's a drink that you've tried before: If it gives you a headache, you don't want to discover that on the day of the test.

» **A wristwatch:** You must, must, *must* wear a wristwatch to the exam. Wearing a watch is a huge and easy step for you to manage your time and take control of the testing situation. Dissolve a big part of your anxiety by knowing exactly when each section will end and how much time you have. The worst way to take the SAT is in constant fear of the proctor jarring you with, "Put your pencils down!" Your wristwatch can't beep or be a smartwatch, so on this day, bring something cheap that tells the time and does nothing else.

After you arrive at the test center, take out what you need and stow the rest of the stuff in a backpack under your seat.

**WARNING**

You're not allowed to bring a phone, camera, laptop, or tablet to the testing room. Nor can you bring scrap paper, books, or other school supplies (including rulers, compasses, and highlighters) except for those pencils and your trusty calculator. Leave these other items behind. Also, no portable music devices. If your watch is a smartwatch, leave it home!

## Taking control of the tension

You'll probably feel nervous when you arrive at the test center. This is normal, and it's okay. Try a couple of stretches and head shakes to chase away tension. During the exam, wriggle your feet and move your shoulders up and down whenever you feel yourself tightening up. If you roll your neck, be sure to close your eyes and not to face the other students so you don't risk a charge of cheating. And take a few deep breaths to calm yourself.

**TIP**

Use the tension to boost your score. Before you begin the exam, visualize a time when you were nervous and had a good outcome — say, before riding a roller coaster or just prior to your entrance onstage. Use the tension to bring energy and focus.

## Starting off

The test proctor distributes the booklets with a vindictive thump. Then said proctor instructs you to fill in the top of the answer sheet with your name, date of birth, Social Security number, registration number, and so forth. Your admission ticket has the necessary information. You also have to copy some numbers from your test booklet onto the answer sheet. Be prepared to spend some time filling out these forms before launching your SAT.

**WARNING**

*Don't* open the test booklet early. Wait for the proctor to instruct you to open it! The proctor can send you home, scoreless and SAT-less, for starting early, working after time is called, or looking at the wrong section. A false start in this game is more than a 5-yard penalty — it's the end of the game.

The proctor announces each test and tells you when to start and stop. The proctor probably uses the wall clock or a wristwatch to time you. When the proctor tells you to start a test, write down the test's start and stop times before you dive into the questions. Each test gives the duration at the top of the first page. For example, the Reading Test is 65 minutes, so if you start that test at 8:30, write down, "8:30–9:35." This takes about two seconds, and it's so worth it to know where you are during the test.

## Focusing during the test

Keep your eyes on your own paper, except for quick glimpses at your watch, so you can concentrate on the task at hand. If you glance around the room, you may see someone who has already finished. Then you'll panic: *Why is he done, and I'm only on Question 2?* You don't need this kind of idea rattling around in your head. Besides, that student may have skipped to the end. Also, wandering eyes open you to a charge of cheating.

**TIP**

You aren't given extra scrap paper, but you *are* allowed to write all over the test booklet. Your booklet *is* your scratch paper, so mark it up! This is where you eliminate wrong answers (more on this in Chapter 3) and make notes. If you have two possible answers, circle the ones you're considering, take a guess on the answer sheet, circle the question, and move on. Come back to the question at the end of the section if you have time — but you hardly ever have time, so it's a good thing you took that guess.

**WARNING**

In the Reading Test, where you skip around, the strategy is different and detailed in Chapter 3. However, in the Writing and Language Test and Math Tests, where you go straight through the questions, don't leave an answer blank! Guess an answer, circle the question, and move on. If you get stuck on a question, you lose valuable time and may miss out on five questions at the end! Definitely not worth it, even if you get that one question right. If you leave an answer blank, you could lose track of which answer in the bubble sheet goes to which answer in the exam. I've seen it happen *way* too much. Also, because a wrong answer counts the same as an unanswered one, you may as well throw a mental dart and guess for a chance of getting it right. Since you've circled the question, you can go back to it later — but if time runs out, at least you've taken the guess!

## Pacing yourself

As you progress through the Math Tests, the questions sharply rise from easy to hard. (The Reading and Writing and Language Tests . . . not so much.) As you cut through the math, you may find yourself feeling more and more challenged. When you approach the end, don't worry so much about skipping questions. You get the same points for each right answer to an "easy" question as you do for a "hard" question. If you're stuck on an early question, take a guess, mark the question, and come back to it later. This way, you're sure to reach all the later questions that you're able to answer. Also, during the last minute of each section, bubble in an answer to every remaining question, perhaps choosing one letter and sticking with it for every blank. With no penalty for guessing, you may as well take a shot!

**TIP**

No one gets a perfect score, so don't expect to. All you need to do is score better than many of the other students, and with these strategies and practice, you will! Once you're in college and/or have a scholarship, the SAT doesn't matter anymore. But for now, you're not trying to get *all* of them right — you're trying to get *most* of them right.

# It Isn't You: Testing Under Adverse Conditions

Your test isn't actually given by the College Board. It's given by a proctor qualified by the College Board, and this proctor is required to adhere to certain standards. If something odd happens during the test that you believe negatively affected your score, such as construction noises, no working air conditioning (say in Phoenix), or anything else that shouldn't be the case, register a complaint with the College Board customer service right away for a chance to have those scores cancelled and for you to retake the exam, at no charge. Complaining to the testing center staff does no good: You must communicate directly with the College Board. You don't have much time to register this complaint, so don't delay.

**WARNING**

Schools tend to freeze the heck out of the testing rooms, so being chilly isn't grounds for registering a complaint! It does mean that you should prepare by wearing layers that you can remove if needed. Note that you may not be allowed to wear a jacket or a cap, but a sweater is okay.

## SHOULD YOU TAKE THE PSAT/NMSQT?

The PSAT used to be short for the *Preliminary Scholastic Aptitude Test,* but now PSAT just means *Pre-SAT.* The NMSQT part still stands for something — *National Merit Scholarship Qualifying Test.* Though it has a two-part name, the PSAT/NMSQT is just one test, but it performs both functions of preparing you for the SAT and screening you for a host of available scholarships. If you're a super brain, the PSAT/NMSQT may move you into the ranks of semifinalists for a National Merit Scholarship, a *prestigious* (high-status) scholarship program, or give you entry to other special programs. You don't have to do anything extra to apply for these scholarships and programs. Just take the test, and if you make the cut, the National Merit Scholarship Program and other organizations will contact you. Some students who do not score high enough to become semifinalists will receive a Letter of Commendation, which also looks good on your college applications. Even if you're not sure that you'll win a scholarship or receive a letter, you should still take the PSAT/NMSQT. It mirrors the SAT, and though the PSAT is slightly shorter, it gives you a feel for the SAT itself and your performance on a standardized exam.

# 2

# Mastering the
# SAT Reading Test

# Chapter **3**

# Getting Acquainted with the SAT Reading Test

The SAT Reading isn't like what you're used to. These are college–level journal articles on literature, science, and social studies, and you're asked to identify such mind–bending concepts as the purpose of a phrase or what's implied by a paragraph. The SAT starts with this test, so you're also doing this at eight on a Saturday morning.

**TIP**

If the depth of your regular reading hovers around Instagram and Twitter, you're going to struggle with the nuance and complexity of SAT reading. Ease yourself into this task by reading *Time* magazine, the *New York Times*, the *Wall Street Journal,* or any regular publication aimed at adults, at least once a week, starting now. Your best bet is to get a print edition that you can hold in your hands: Not only are there no online distractions, but you also get used to reading the SAT, which is on paper too. These steps will also ease your transition into college.

## Understanding the Reading Section

The SAT Reading Test consists of five short passages which you read and wrangle for 65 minutes. Here's what to expect on this test:

» **Four 1-part passages:** You see four passages, each 500 to 750 words long, and each with 10 to 11 multiple-choice questions.

» **One 2-part passage:** You see one passage that is split in two parts, also with 10 or 11 multiple-choice questions. These two half-passages typically offer two points of view on the same topic.

» **Content:** You get one passage drawn from a work of literature, two passages from science, and one single plus one two-part passage from social studies.

>> **Purpose:** Passages may present arguments or theories, relate a series of events, describe situations or places, or reveal characters and attitudes.

>> **Graphics:** Some passages, typically science but sometimes social studies, are accompanied by charts, graphs, or diagrams similar to those that appear in textbooks.

# Managing Your Time with Key Strategies

As you cut through the SAT Reading, use these simple, tried-and-true strategies to get the most questions right before running out of time on this section.

## 1. Work the literature passage last.

The literature passage is *always* the first in the group, but work this passage last. The passage itself may be straightforward, but the questions tend to go deep into things like the motivations of characters and the symbolism of situations — things that take time to read and absorb. Work this time-heavy literature passage after the other, faster passages.

## 2. Start with the blurb at the beginning of each passage.

These few lines tell you from a high level what's happening in the passage, whether it's an excerpt from Abraham Lincoln or a study of migrating geese. This vital context provides simple underlying knowledge to help answer the questions. You will read the whole passage, but not right away.

## 3. Start with the line-number questions.

These are the questions that send you to a certain line or lines in the passage. Be sure to read a few lines above and below (within the paragraph), but these are the easiest to answer because you usually don't need to understand the whole passage.

*Note:* We're not talking about questions where you select a line (via line numbers) to support the *previous* answer. Those poodle-bombs are broken down later in this chapter.

## 4. Next work the detail questions.

These questions challenge you to remember certain details about the passage. Don't worry about that. Instead, skim the passage for *keywords* from the question. For example, if the passage is about rearing dogs and the question is about leash training, skim the passage for the keywords "leash training," and you'll usually find that only a small part of the passage — like a paragraph — covers that. Then just read that paragraph and answer the question!

## 5. End with the inference and main-idea questions.

The main-idea question is easy to spot because it asks about the passage as a whole, and the inference question typically asks what *could* have happened or what's implied. These demand a full understanding of the entire passage. Here's the wisdom of this whole chapter summed up into one line. You ready? ***You get an understanding of the full passage by working the line-number and detail questions first.***

*Now* read the whole passage. It goes much faster and easier because you already understand parts of it.

Of course, inference and main-idea questions may be early among the questions — but that's okay: You skip them for now, go to the line-number and detail questions, and then come back to the main-idea questions. Answer the questions in the order that works for you.

If you want to try reading the whole passage before taking on the questions, get a timer and try this out on a practice test. If the passage doesn't make sense to you, you run the risk of getting stuck trying to decipher it. At 65 minutes for the Reading Test, you have about 13 minutes for each passage and its questions. Reading one of these passages to fully understand it can take you upward of 10 minutes! Then you only have a few minutes left for the 10 or 11 questions that follow. Not only do you run out of time, you wear yourself out.

# Getting Each Question Right, Quickly, With More Key Strategies

It's all about the strategies, right? With 65 minutes to answer 52 questions, you have slightly over a minute per question, and the topic is not always easy to understand. That's okay. Use these proven question strategies combined with the preceding, tried-and-true time-management strategies to answer each question correctly:

**1. Cover the answer choices.**

Use your answer sheet to cover the answer choices. *Don't cheat.* Even though the right answer is there, three other trap answers are also there. Dodge these traps and *focus on the question.*

**2. Answer the question yourself.**

Read the question, go to the relevant part of the passage (be it line number, keyword, or the whole thing for inference/main idea), and answer the question *in your own words.*

**3. Cross off the wrong answers.**

Your answer won't match the right answer. That's okay: It doesn't have to. What will happen is that the other answer choices will be so far out in left field that they couldn't possibly be correct. Here's what you do:

**a. Move your answer sheet down just a little to expose Choice (A).**

Your answer sheet is covering the answers, remember? Now move it down a little to peek at the first answer. Based on your own answer, could this be right? The answer is hardly ever *yes.* More often it's either *not a chance* or *I'm not sure.* If it's *not a chance,* cross it off. If it's *I'm not sure,* put a dot next to it. **Don't spend time on it.** Either cross it off or dot it, and *move on.*

**b. Move your answer sheet down a little more to expose Choice (B).**

Here's the thing. Sometimes an answer is so clearly, impossibly wrong that you can cross it off as soon as you read it. If you're not sure, put a dot so you can go back to it. Either way, move quickly to cross off or dot each answer choice.

**c. Now check Choices (C) and (D).**

One at a time, either cross off or put a dot next to each answer. Typically, you'll have three crossed off and one dotted, so go with the dot and get to the next question. If you have two answer choices dotted, check them to see which is more likely. If you can't tell, that's okay: take a guess, circle the question in the test booklet, and come back to it later with the remaining time.

WARNING

**When does this strategy fail?** When you go straight for the answer choices without thinking of your own answer first. What happens then is that you get caught in the trap of wrong answers, where you read each answer and think, "Maybe that's it," and spend all this time going back and forth to the passage. Don't do that.

*Also, don't doubt your own answer when you read the answer choices.* Sure, the correct answer knows the depth and detail better than you — but so do the three wrong answers! *Trust yourself* to answer the question well enough! No matter how far off your answer is, it'll be close enough to cross off three wrong answers.

No one gets a perfect score on the SAT Reading Test, so don't kill yourself trying to. It's okay to miss a question here and there — but it's not okay to spend five minutes on one question.

**REMEMBER**

# Answering the Best-Evidence Questions

Here's one for you. You get a vague inference question. By following the preceding strategies, you answer the question yourself, and then you use your own answer to cross off the three way-wrong answer choices and go with the remaining fourth answer. You don't really trust this fourth answer, but it has to be right, because the other three are so far off. And it is.

Next question. "Which choice provides the *best evidence* for the answer to the *previous* question?" Wait, what? You're supposed to be done with this! Nope. This question has a second part, where you select evidence from the passage. Each answer choice refers to a sentence in the passage, and you pick the sentence that supports your answer to the previous question. It looks like this:

Which choice provides the best evidence for the answer to the previous question?

**PLAY**

**(A)** Lines 32–34 ("The student . . . whole Dummies book.")

**(B)** Lines 43–45 ("On exam day . . . amazingly well.")

**(C)** Lines 68–74 ("Several schools . . . scholarships.")

**(D)** Lines 79–82 ("There was enough . . . a Jeep.")

Each passage has two best-evidence questions, for a total of ten in the Reading Test. Don't worry. There's a strategy for these.

1. **Using the answer choices, mark those sentences in the passage.**

   This is an about-face from the previous strategy of covering the answer choices, but for the second part of the two-part question, it's okay. Go through the passage and mark the four sentences that the answer choices refer to. This way, you can find them easily while you're focusing on the actual question. You don't have to distract yourself by looking for that dang sentence.

   Since each passage has two best-evidence questions, you don't want to get the sentences you marked for the first one mixed with the sentences you marked for the second one. Mark the sentences one way for the first round, say with [brackets], and another way for the second round, such as <u>underline.</u>

   **TIP**

2. **Reread the correct answer to the previous question.**

   With 52 Reading questions, your thoughts start to get slippery. Make sure you're clear on which bit of inference that you're looking to support.

3. **Cross off the wrong sentences.**

   See? This strategy is similar. With that previous answer in mind, go to the passage and cross off the sentences that don't support it. Again, you'll have three that are way off and one that is so-so, and that's what you go with.

**TIP**

Here's an alternate approach: Some students like to work these two-part questions in tandem. They mark the sentences in the passage, then they use these sentence answers from the second question to find the answer to the first question. This is also an effective strategy, so try it out and see what you think.

# Putting the Strategies to Use

Strategies take practice. You're not used to this approach, and it's easy to mess it up the first few times. That's okay. Practice the strategies, get them wrong, forget steps — *before* exam day. That's what practice is for.

## Starting with the line-number questions

Line-number questions aren't always first, but they are the easiest to answer, making these the best and fastest segue to your understanding of the passage as a whole.

**PLAY**

This excerpt is from the science passage *The Dancing Mouse: A Study in Animal Behavior,* by Robert M. Yerkes.

> As a rule the dancing mouse is considerably smaller than the common mouse. All the dancing mice had black eyes and were smaller as well as weaker than the common gray house mouse. The weakness, indicated by their inability to hold up their own weight or to cling to an object, curiously enough does not manifest itself in their dancing; in this they are tireless. Frequently they run in circles or whirl about with astonishing rapidity for several minutes at a time.

Line

(05)

In Line 4, the best definition of "manifest" is

Cover the answer choices! What do *you* think the best definition of "manifest" is as it's used in the passage, based on what the "weakness" doesn't do? How about "appear"? Now cross off wrong answers:

**(A)** emphasize

**(B)** prove

**(C)** discover

**(D)** show

How did you do? Did you cross off Choices (A), (B), and (C)? They're so far out that it *has* to be Choice (D). Here's the logic:

| (A) | emphasize | Cross this off: "Emphasize" refers to something already present, while "appear" refers to something new. |
| (B) | prove | Cross this off: "Prove" also refers to something already present, not something new like "appear." |
| (C) | discover | Cross this off: "Discover" refers to actively finding something, while "appear" refers to being found. |
| (D) | show | Place a dot: "Show" could refer to actively finding something, but it also could refer to being found, like "appear." |

Vocabulary-in-context questions like this one do have a trap. Many of these questions ask for the definition of a word you probably already know. But — the passage may use the word in an odd or unusual way, and the answer choices are usually known definitions of the word. For example, the word *deck* may be "a surface of a ship," "a wooden structure outside a house," "a pack of cards," or "to decorate." In the Christmas carol "Deck the Halls," *deck* matches the last meaning, but outside the song, who uses that meaning? Don't settle for a definition that you recognize: Make sure it matches the context of the sentence.

## Continuing with the detail questions

Detail questions follow the line-number questions in that you can usually get them right without fully absorbing the entire passage. These are also *keyword* questions, where you skim the passage for keywords from the question. In this example, the passage is a single paragraph, so the keyword approach isn't needed, but on the full-length passages, it makes a huge difference.

According to the passage, in what way does the dancing mouse not have a weakness?

Cover them answers. In what way do *you* think the dancing mouse is superior? (Never mind how that sounds.) Reread the paragraph and focus on its abilities. In a full-length passage, you'd skim for the keyword "weakness."

Seems that the mouse only has weakness, but it's tireless in dancing. Keep that in mind now, and cross off the wrong answers:

**(A)** endurance

**(B)** muscle strength

**(C)** visual acuity

**(D)** tenacity

Did you cross off Choices (B), (C), and (D)? They're so impossible that it *has* to be Choice (A). Here's the process:

| (A) | endurance | Place a dot. "Endurance" is in the ballpark of "tireless." |
| (B) | muscle strength | Cross this off: It has nothing to do with "tireless." |
| (C) | visual acuity | Cross this off: It's not even close (though the passage mentions the mouse's eyes, don't misinterpret this). |
| (D) | tenacity | Cross this off: *Tenacity* means "ability to cling," and though it may relate to "tireless," the passage refers to dancing, not clinging. |

The word "tireless" by itself could match "tenacity," like when you're clinging to the handles of a jet ski. Be sure to keep the context in mind when checking the answer choices.

## Ending with the inference and main idea questions

An *inference* is a conclusion that you reach based on evidence, and the SAT Reading section features many of these questions. You get a certain amount of information, and then you have to stretch it a little. The questions may resemble the following:

>> The authors imply which of the following about success and the *SAT For Dummies?*

>> Which of the following statements would the author most likely agree with regarding college and career path?

Inference questions require a certain understanding of the whole passage, so be sure to work these after the line-number and detail questions. Now you read the whole passage, then do what you did before: Cover the answer choices, answer the question yourself, and cross off wrong answers.

Try this inference question, based on these sentences about the westward journey of settlers during the 19th century.

**PLAY**

> The women generally do the driving, while the men and boys bring up the rear with horses and cattle of all grades, from poor weak calves to fine, fat animals, that show they have had a good living where they came from.

With which statement would the travelers described in this passage probably agree?

Cover the answers! Of course, you can't predict "which one," but you *can* think of what the answer *could* be. What do *you* think the travelers' attitude would be like? How about, "The women are sick of driving and the men are sick of handling animals."

Now: Cross off wrong answers.

**(A)** Only healthy animals can survive a long journey.

**(B)** All livestock should be treated equally.

**(C)** Gender distinctions are considerations in assigning work.

**(D)** Many pioneers are motivated by greed.

Did you cross off Choices (A), (B), and (D)? They're so impossible that it *must be* Choice (C). Here's the detail:

| (A) | Only healthy animals can survive a long journey. | Cross this off. |
|-----|--------------------------------------------------|-----------------|
| (B) | All livestock should be treated equally. | Cross this off as well. |
| (C) | Gender distinctions are considerations in assigning work. | Maybe. The men handled animals and the women drove. Place a dot. |
| (D) | Many pioneers are motivated by greed. | This may be true, but it doesn't match your answer and it's not supported by anything in the passage. |

Now for a main idea question from the same short passage. Remember, if this were a longer passage, now would be the time to read the whole thing.

**PLAY**

Which of the following is closest to the main idea of the passage?

Hide those answers. What do *you* think the main idea is? Something like, "The settlers went west." Keep it simple.

Now cross off wrong answers:

**(A)** The cattle varied in quality.

**(B)** The westward journey was slow.

**(C)** Horses brought up the rear.

**(D)** Women were better drivers even then.

Did you cross off Choices (A), (C), and (D)? They're so far out there that it *must be* Choice (B). Here's why:

| (A) | The cattle varied in quality. | Cross this off: It may be true, but it's not the main idea, and it doesn't match your answer. |
|-----|-------------------------------|-----------------------------------------------------------------------------------------------|
| (B) | The westward journey was slow. | Place a dot: It's not far from your answer. |
| (C) | Horses brought up the rear. | Cross this off: Also true, but it's not the main idea, and it also doesn't match your answer. |
| (D) | Women were better drivers even then. | Cross this off: It's true through the ages, but it doesn't match your answer. |

Note a pattern in these main idea answer choices: Even the wrong answers may be true and/or stated somewhere in the passage, but being true or stated doesn't make it the *main idea*.

# Taking On the Reading Passages

SAT Reading passages come in three flavors: Literature, Social Studies, and Science. The Literature passage is always first, but *work it last* because it takes the most time. If you're geared toward science, you could work the Science passages first; or if you're history/humanities oriented, you could start with Social Studies. Either way, Literature goes last.

## Distancing with social studies

You wish it were distant, but it's social. Anyway, if the passage is about social studies (history, anthropology, sociology, education, cultural studies, and so on), keep these tips in mind:

>> **Go for the positive.** The SAT doesn't criticize anyone with the power to sue or contact the media. So if you see a question about the author's tone or viewpoint, look for a positive answer.

>> **Note the structure.** The passages frequently present a claim and support it with sets of facts or quotations from experts. If you're asked about the significance of a particular detail in a passage, the detail is probably evidence in the case that the author is making. In a history passage, *chronology* (order of events) may be particularly important. Sketch a short timeline if the passage seems to focus on a series of linked events.

>> **Identify cause and effect.** History and social studies passages often explain *why* something happens. Search for keywords such as *therefore, hence, consequently,* and others that signal a reason.

>> **Look for opposing ideas.** Experts, including historians, are into criticizing each other's interpretations of archaeological discoveries or important events. (Maybe it's to assert themselves, but anyway . . . ) Many social studies passages present two or more viewpoints, especially in the two-part passages. Look for the opposing sides, or identify the main theory and the objections to it.

Each SAT Reading test has one set of two-part passages, which are almost always Social Studies. These are two half-sized passages that take the space of one regular passage, and they are appropriately named *Passage 1* and *Passage 2*. They sit right next to each other, and they're followed by a few questions on the first passage, then some on the second passage, and then a few more on how the passages fit together. Here's what you do:

1. **Always read the blurb at the beginning.**

   As with any other Reading passage, start with that blurb.

2. **Answer the questions that deal solely with Passage 1.**

   These are always the first three or four questions. Use the same approach as you would with any other passage: Start with the line-number questions, then work the detail questions, and then read the passage and answer the inference and main idea questions.

3. **Answer the questions that deal solely with Passage 2.**

   Rinse and repeat. The Passage 2 questions are always grouped after the Passage 1 questions.

4. **Answer the questions that ask about how the passages fit together.**

   The fit-together questions are always the last of the bunch. Keep an eye out for these common themes:

   1. How would the authors of both passages agree or disagree?

   2. Does one passage give an example of the point made in the other passage?

   3. What would the author of one passage say about something in the other passage?

You can try your hand at the two-part passages in the next chapter and in the practice tests that accompany this book, but for now, try out these questions on this brief history passage taken from *To and Through Nebraska*, by Frances I. Sims Fulton, describing settlers traveling to the West during the 19th century:

> During all this time, and despite the disagreeable weather, emigrants from the cities of the Northeast to the wilderness in the West keep up the line of march, traveling in their "prairie schooners," as the great hoop-covered wagon is called, into which, often are packed their every worldly possession, and have room to pile in a large family on top. Sometimes a sheet-iron stove is carried along at the rear of the wagon, which, when needed, they set up inside and put the pipe through a hole in the covering. Those who do not have this convenience carry wood with them and build a fire on the ground to cook by; cooking utensils are generally packed in a box at the side or front. The coverings of the wagons are of all shades and materials. When oil cloth is not used, they are often patched over the top with their oil-cloth table covers, saving them from the rain.

**PLAY**

The details about the wagon serve to

Cover the answers. In your own words, why does the author describe the covered wagons in so much detail? Probably to give an example of how the travelers are resourceful and clever. Now cross off wrong answers:

**(A)** reveal the convenience of covered wagons

**(B)** emphasize the ingenuity of the travelers

**(C)** show that the travelers were ill-equipped for life on the frontier

**(D)** contrast life in the city with life in the wilderness

Did you cross off Choices (A), (C), and (D), leaving Choice (B) as the only possible answer? Here's the rationale. According to the passage, the travelers pack everything they need into one wagon. Some have more than others, but those who, for example, lack stoves "carry wood with them and build a fire on the ground" (Line 7). They protect themselves from the rain with either a wagon cover or a tablecloth.

**PLAY**

Which of the following best fits the theme of this passage?

Cover the answers. In your own words, what's the passage mainly about? Maybe something like, "Traveling and camping in a covered wagon." Perfect. Now cross off those wrong answers:

**(A)** Cooking on the frontier

**(B)** Chasing the gold rush

**(C)** Traveling in a prairie schooner

**(D)** Economics of the Old West

Cross off Choice (A), because even though cooking is part of it, it's not the main idea. Cross off Choice (B) which, though it may be true, isn't specific enough, and more importantly, doesn't match your answer. Choice (C) gets a dot: Remember "prairie schooner" is what they called the covered wagons. Cross off Choice (D), which isn't even mentioned in the passage. Choice (C) is left, so that's what you go with.

# Blinding me with science

That takes us back. Anyway, the science passages don't rely on your knowledge of the topic: Everything you need to know is in the passage. You are expected to know the basics — for example, the Earth orbits the Sun, water boils when it's hot, cells divide — but there's no need to study any science topics to prepare for these passages. Instead, practice the strategies.

These passages cover such science topics as biology, chemistry, environmental science, physics, experiments, and various phenomena. Try this approach to a science passage:

» **Search out the facts.** Whether describing an experiment, survey, or observation, some information is in the text and some in the graphic element, if the passage is illustrated. Pay attention to numbers, including percentages, populations, and rates of growth or change.

» **Don't worry about technical terms, but do know general science vocabulary.** If you see a strange word, the definition is probably tucked into the sentence. You won't encounter a question based on the definition of *Tephritidae* unless the passage explains what *Tephritidae* is. (It's a type of fruit fly.) Look for these definitions as you read. You should, however, know general terms that pop up frequently in science-related material, such as *control group* (a group that doesn't participate in an experiment and serves as a point of comparison) and *catalyst* (a substance that causes or increases the rate of a chemical process). As you work through practice exams, jot down these definitions from the answer explanations, because you may see them again on exam day.

>> **Identify the argument.** Some SAT science passages present a dispute between two viewpoints. The SAT questions may zero in on the evidence for each scientific theory or hypothesis, and then quiz you about each author's stance.

>> **Notice the examples.** The SAT science passages tend to offer examples both in the text and in the graphics. The questions may ask what the examples prove.

The SAT includes graphic elements in most science and occasional social studies passages. Be sure to follow these guidelines:

>> **Look at everything.** The title; the explanation on the top, bottom, or sides; the labels inside a diagram — *everything*. Don't memorize it, but notice it: Are the numbers on the side in thousands? Is there a pattern or contrast? Imagine a graph with bars reaching the level of 12. You need to know whether this represents 12 actual or 12 thousand.

>> **Note the variables.** The *variable* is the part that changes. Some graphs include more than one — perhaps a solid line showing peanut butter sales and a dotted line tracing jelly sales. Don't worry about the detail — you'll go back to the graph for the detail — but understand the trend or story that the graph is telling.

>> **Note the relationship between the graphic and the text.** Usually these two parts work together. A bar graph may tell you how many test-takers earned scholarships, while the text may explain how many got Jeeps (such a great theme). Together, these statistics paint a clear picture.

Try this visual-elements question:

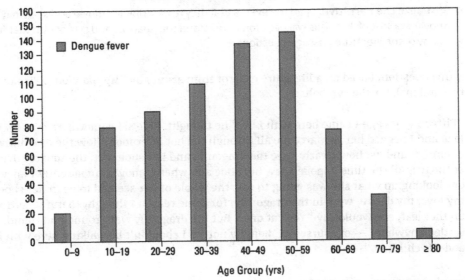

**Cases of Dengue Fever, Confirmed or Suspected, 2010**

*Source: Centers for Disease Control, U.S. Government.*

**PLAY**

Which statement about Dengue Fever is true?

Cover the answers. In your own words, what do you think is up with the Fever? It seems to hit middle-aged folks the hardest. Good thing you're young. Anyway, with this middle-aged point in mind, cross off the wrong answers:

**(A)** Infants are less likely to contract Dengue Fever than the elderly.

**(B)** In 2010, most cases of Dengue Fever occurred in people aged 40 to 60.

**(C)** The risk of catching Dengue Fever rises with age.

**(D)** Dengue Fever is especially dangerous for infants and children.

Choices (A), (C), and (D) are easy targets for crossing off, leaving Choice (B) as the only possible answer. This is because the bars for ages 40 to 49 and 50 to 59 are higher than those for other age groups.

## Saving the literature for last

Literature is the first passage. *Work it last.* Yes this is repeated, but students always forget. When you face this literature passage, keep these tips in mind:

>> **Look for symbolism that relates to the big picture.** SAT literature passages often contain a great deal of description. Often things are symbolic or representative, or they stand out in the author's narrative for a reason. For example, something like "Joan never forgot seeing the keys on the table." What's important about those keys? Pay attention for something later that relates to the keys.

>> **Stay attuned to word choice.** A literature passage is perfectly suited to questions about the author's tone (*bitter, nostalgic, fond, critical*, and so forth). Pay attention to the feelings associated with certain words.

>> **Visualize the narrative.** Read the events as if they're describing a movie and see what the movie would look like. This will help you understand the nuances and symbolism that fuel many of the literature passage questions.

Try this question, based on a literature excerpt from a story by Virginia Woolf. Visualize the narrative and look for the symbolism:

"Fifteen years ago I came here with Lily," he thought. "We sat somewhere over there by a lake and I begged her to marry me all through the hot afternoon. How the dragonfly kept circling round us: how clearly I see the dragonfly and her shoe with the square silver buckle at the toe. All the time I spoke I saw her shoe and when it moved impatiently I knew without looking up what she was going to say: the whole of her seemed to be in her shoe. And my love, my desire, were in the dragonfly; for some reason I thought that if it settled there, on that leaf, she would say "Yes" at once. But the dragonfly went round and round: it never settled anywhere — of course not, happily not, or I shouldn't be walking here with Eleanor and the children."

PLAY

In this passage, the speaker's attitude may best be characterized as

Cover the answers. What do you think characterizes the speaker's attitude? Maybe something like, desperate for the dragonfly to make Lily say yes, but then glad it didn't? Now cross off the wrong answers:

**(A)** mocking

**(B)** confused

**(C)** nostalgic

**(D)** argumentative

Desperate and glad don't connect with Choices (A), (B), or (D), so cross those right off, leaving Choice (C) as the only possible answer. And it's right. Here's why: In this paragraph, the speaker looks at the past, remembering an afternoon when he "begged" (Line 2) Lily to accept his marriage proposal. He's feeling pleasure and sadness at remembering the past, which of course is *nostalgic*, Choice (C). The sadness shows in Lily's refusal, which he now sees "happily" (Line 8). Choice (B), confused, doesn't match because he wasn't confused: He simply changed his mind, and apparently dodged a bullet.

And of course, SAT Literature loves symbolism. Try this one:

PLAY

In this passage, Lily's shoe most likely represents

Cover the answers. What do *you* think her shoe represents? Maybe a counterpart to the dragonfly that will not cooperate and also Lily's feelings. Something like that. Your answer doesn't have to be close. It just has to be something that you think without looking at the answers. Now cross off wrong ones.

**(A)** Lily's desire to protect others

**(B)** Lily's reluctance to settle down

**(C)** Lily's love for the narrator

**(D)** the narrator's attraction to Lily

See? When you think of your own answer, even if it's far out there, it makes the wrong answers *really easy* to cross off. You should have easily crossed off Choices (A), (C), and (D), leaving Choice (B), though iffy, as the only possible answer, and the right one. See dear reader, *that* is how you turn a challenging question into an easy one.

TIP

The answer that you think of hardly ever matches the right answer. That's okay — *it doesn't have to*. Your self-thought answer serves a much more important role: *It makes the wrong answers stand out like weeds in a garden.* Cross 'em off, go with the remaining one, and that's all you have time to do in the roughly one-minute-per-question that you get in the Reading Test.

Now, build your skills, work this strategy, and knock out the practice Reading questions in the next chapter.

# Chapter 4

# Where It Counts: Practicing the SAT Reading Test

N ow you've got the strategies from Chapter 3. No one gets a perfect Reading Test score, but as long as you get a higher score than do most other SAT-takers (which you will, because you're learning the strategies from this book, and other test-takers are not), you'll do well enough to reach or exceed your goals in college admissions. If social studies are your strength, start with those passages, but if science is your forte, you can work those first. Following are two Social Studies, two Science, and one Literature passage.

On the actual exam, you get four one-part and one two-part passage, but in this practice session there are two two-parters: one Social Studies and one Science, so you can practice both. (Literature is never two-part.) Whether one- or two-part, start with the introductory blurb and check the visual element (if present) for helpful information.

Remember the basics:

1. Read the introductory blurb.
2. Start with the line-number questions.
3. Work the detail questions.
4. Read the whole passage.
5. Answer the inference and main-idea questions.

Then for each question (except for the best-evidence questions):

1. Cover the answer choices.
2. Answer the question yourself.
3. Cross off the wrong answers or put a dot if you're not sure, but don't spend time on it.

And for those best-evidence questions:

**1.** **Using the answer choices, mark the sentence answers in the passage.**

**2.** **Reread the correct answer to the previous question.**

**3.** **Cross off the wrong answers.**

Got all that? Now practice the strategies and make your mistakes here so that you make fewer mistakes on the exam.

# Social Studies Passages

**PLAY**

Questions 1–11 are based on the following passage.

This passage is from *Into the House of the Ancestors* by Karl Maier (Wiley).

At first glance, there is little in Bamako, Mali, to suggest anything other than poverty and underdevelopment. The main road into the city from the north is filled with potholes and traffic jams of
(05) creaking minibuses and cars and goats and streams of people who walk the slow but steady pace dictated by the sun of the Sahel, that dry swath of scrub and savannah, which shields the moist West African Coast from the furnace of the Sahara Desert.

(10) Cross the street from the bustling roadside market, walk through the university entrance, and take an immediate left, two flights up to the Department of Epidemiology and Parasitic Infections, and there is the latest equipment: computers, micro-
(15) scopes, scanners, and a host of other machines with jaw-breaking names, such as the Programmable Thermal Controller, which analyzes the malaria parasite's DNA. Unlike those in some other major research centers in Africa, the scientists in Bamako
(20) are Africans, mostly Malian, but with a sprinkling of researchers from neighboring African countries. This is not a case of Europeans and Americans taking a mobile First World lab and setting it up in the African bush. Rather, it is a center of scientific
(25) excellence, which is administered by Malians, and where the most immediate benefits fall to Malians, though the ramifications are invaluable to Africa and the entire world.

The stakes could not be higher. Malaria is the
(30) biggest killer in Africa today, more ruthless than

cholera, yellow fever, and measles, far outdistancing the latest more highly publicized outbreaks, such as the Ebola virus, and even, at least for the time being, overshadowing AIDS. No one in Hollywood ever made a movie about malaria, but in Africa it claims (35) the lives of nearly one million children each year. Ninety percent of the 300 million to 500 million clinical cases that occur each year are in Africa. In some parts of Mali, especially in the rice-growing area on the banks of the Niger River, one out of five (40) children die before the age of five, most of them from malaria.

What sets the center off from most other such bodies is its work in the villages and its close relationship with traditional leaders and healers. Dr. Ogoba- (45) ra Doumbo, head of the Department of Epidemiology and Parasitic Infections at the School of Medicine in Bamako, believes that not only must the research be relevant to the lives of ordinary Malians, but modern science has much to learn from them. "Traditionally (50) in Africa, Western researchers come for a while, secure the information they require, and then they are off. I wanted to create the link between the research and the communities which need health development. It is a philosophy of establishing field doctors (55) in collaboration with the local communities. That is the dynamic that we have created here."

Unselfish as Doumbo's views may seem, they reflect the cold calculation that village communities have as much to teach scientific researchers as (60)

the researchers have to teach the villagers. In effect, the center is attempting to do what so many universities, governments, and professional organizations have failed to do: build a bridge
(65) between the so-called traditional and modern faces of Africa. Only in-depth fieldwork can address some of the key questions that must be answered before there is real understanding of the malaria parasite and the mosquito. From the point of view of pure
(70) research, the villages furnish the center with a constant supply of blood samples from the hottest malarial battlefronts, which allow the scientists to track how the parasite is mutating. By working with community elders, traditional healers, and
(75) especially important target groups, such as women, Doumbo's field workers are able to help people save their children's lives and to set up an unparalleled observation post.

Rural Mali has provided more than a testing ground,
(80) however. Traditional healers have developed their own medicines, and unlike many Western and other African scientists, Doumbo and his colleagues are humble enough to admit that the healers often are way ahead of them. With [the usual drugs] losing
(85) the battle against malaria . . . the Mali center has discovered a traditional remedy. Malaria 5 is a combination of three herbal medicines used for years by Malian healers. Together with the Ministry of Health, the center has tested Malaria 5 and proved
(90) that it has effectively battled malaria strains which [the usual drugs] can no longer fight. This discovery Doumbo cites as an example of cooperation between Western and African medicine.

1. The description of Bamako, Mali, in paragraph one (Lines 1–9) serves primarily to

   (A) explain how challenging it is to work in Bamako

   (B) show the poverty of Mali

   (C) give the reader information about Mali's climate and economy

   (D) create a contrast between the research center and its surroundings

2. Each of these statements about the Department of Epidemiology and Parasitic Infections is true EXCEPT

   (A) The center primarily investigates the Ebola virus, cholera, yellow fever, and measles.

   (B) The center's scientists take blood samples from rural residents.

   (C) The center studies traditional medicines.

   (D) The center uses computers to access research materials.

3. The passage implies that the media

   (A) pay too much attention to illnesses in Africa

   (B) do not focus enough attention on African diseases

   (C) focus on some diseases for a short period of time and then move on

   (D) portray African doctors incorrectly

4. Which choice provides the best evidence for the answer to the previous question?

   (A) Lines 12–18 ("Department of Epidemiology . . . malaria parasite's DNA")

   (B) Lines 18–21 ("Unlike those in some other major research centers . . . neighboring African countries")

   (C) Lines 31–34 ("far outdistancing . . . overshadowing AIDS")

   (D) Lines 43–45 ("What sets the center off . . . leaders and healers")

5. The reference to Hollywood is intended to illustrate

   (A) Western exploitation of Africa

   (B) the power of publicity

   (C) how the media misses important stories

   (D) a universal interest in healthcare

6. The quotation from Dr. Ogobara Doumbo (Lines 50–57) depicts Western researchers as

   (A) interested only in obtaining research data

   (B) better trained than African researchers

   (C) respectful of traditional healers

   (D) committed to extensive periods of research in Africa

7. In the context of Line 57, which of the following is the best definition of "dynamic"?

   (A) energy

   (B) liveliness

   (C) change

   (D) pattern

8. What is the most likely reason the author refers to "so-called" traditional and modern Africa (Lines 55–56)?

   (A) The definitions of the two are not clear.

   (B) Only one of the terms is accurate.

   (C) The "traditional" face of Africa is actually a recent development.

   (D) The author highlights the distinction between the two.

9. The discovery of Malaria 5 is an example that demonstrates

   (A) traditional healers knowing more than research scientists

   (B) the importance of investigating herbal compounds

   (C) the advantages of working with traditional healers

   (D) the idea that malaria will soon be extinct

10. Which choice provides the best evidence for the answer to the previous question?

    (A) Lines 80–84 ("Traditional healers . . . ahead of them")

    (B) Lines 84–86 ("With [the usual . . . traditional remedy")

    (C) Lines 86–88 ("Malaria 5 is . . . Malian healers")

    (D) Lines 88–91 ("Together with . . . no longer fight")

11. The author's attitude toward the Department of Epidemiology and Parasitic Infections may best be characterized as

    (A) laudatory

    (B) critical

    (C) antagonistic

    (D) serious

# Passage I Answers

1. **D.** The author lowers the reader's expectations by taking the reader through "the potholes and traffic jams of creaking minibuses and cars and goats and streams of people who walk" (Lines 4–6). Then, in the second paragraph, the scene changes completely to a high-tech paradise. Contrast is the point here, so Choice (D) is your answer.

2. **A.** Though the diseases listed in Choice (A) are mentioned in the passage, the focus of the center is malaria. Therefore, the center *primarily* deals with that disease. Choice (A) is untrue — and the answer you seek.

3. **C.** The third paragraph declares that malaria is ignored because the media pay attention to "highly publicized outbreaks" (Lines 32), such as Ebola. An outbreak, however terrible, usually lasts for only a short period of time. The passage also states that Ebola "at least for the time being" (Lines 33–34) gets more publicity than AIDS. These statements add up to a "disease of the week" mentality, which is expressed by Choice (C).

4. **C.** As you see in the explanation for Question 3, malaria is a killer "far outdistancing the latest more highly publicized outbreaks, such as the Ebola virus, and even, at least for the time being, overshadowing AIDS" (Lines 31–34). The correct answer is Choice (C).

5. **C.** Because "no one in Hollywood ever made a film about malaria" (Lines 34–35), the disease may not be the first thing that pops into your mind when you think about deadly threats. Yet the passage tells you that nearly a million African children die from malaria each year. One million! That's an important story, and the media misses it. Hence, Choice (C) is the best answer here.

6. **A.** The statement that "Western researchers come for a while, secure the information they require, and then they are off" (Lines 51–53) tells you that the scientists return to their country of origin after obtaining blood samples or whatever other information they need. Opt for Choice (A), and you're right.

7. **D.** *Dynamic* may be a description (an adjective) meaning "fast, energetic," but in Line 57, *dynamic* is a noun. As a noun, a dynamic is a system of behavior — in other words, a pattern, as Choice (D) indicates.

8. **A.** The word *so-called* indicates disagreement. If someone refers to your so-called talent, he or she really means that you have no talent at all. The passage talks about the advantages of both traditional and modern medicine. "The traditional" may be more modern than the term implies, because the passage tells you that a new medicine was synthesized from three herbal medicines. "The modern" may be less than cutting edge, too, because many drugs created solely in labs have lost their effectiveness. All these facts add up to a blurry line between the two terms, and Choice (A) expresses that idea.

9. **C.** The drug Malaria 5 is "an example of cooperation between Western and African medicine" (Lines 92–93). Without the healers, Malaria 5 wouldn't exist. But it also wouldn't exist without the research center, because scientists there figured out how to combine three traditional remedies. Because both are needed, Choice (A) doesn't work. Choice (B) is too broad, and nothing in the passage supports Choice (D). You're left with Choice (C), the right answer.

**10. D.** The entire sentence reads, "Together with the Ministry of Health, the center has tested Malaria 5 and proved that it has effectively battled malaria strains which [the usual drugs] can no longer fight." This tells you that Malaria 5 is "an example of the advantages of working with traditional healers."

**11. A.** Everything about the Department in this passage is positive, so the author is praising it. *Laudatory* means "praising:" It's from the word *laud*, which is also the root of *applaud*. Choice (A) is correct.

**Questions 12–21 are based on the following passages.**

PLAY

Passage 1 is from a history of ancient Egypt. Passage 2 is excerpted from *The Ancient Egyptians For Dummies* by Charlotte Booth (Wiley).

*Passage 1*

Hatshepsut was the daughter of the great warrior king, Thutmosis I, and, according to some historians, was during his later years associated with him in the government. Her father left two sons, as
(05) well as a daughter; and the elder of these, according to Egyptian law, succeeded him. He was, however, a mere youth, of a weak and amiable temper; while Hatshepsut, his senior by some years, was a woman of great energy, clever, enterprising, vindictive, and
(10) unscrupulous. The contrast of their portrait busts is remarkable, and gives a fair indication of the character of each of them. Thutmosis II has the appearance of a soft and yielding boy. Hatshepsut holds her head erect, giving her an air of vigor and resolution.
(15) She took the direction of affairs under her brother's reign, her influence paramount in every department of the government.

The joint reign of Hatshepsut and Thutmosis II did not continue for more than a few years. The king
(20) died while he was still extremely young, and after his death Hatshepsut showed her hostility to his memory by erasing his name wherever it occurred on the monuments, and substituting for it either her own name or that of her father. She appears
(25) also at the same time to have taken full possession of the throne, and to have been accepted as actual sovereign of the Egyptian people. She assumed male apparel and an artificial beard and gave herself on many of her monuments the style and title of a king.
(30) She took the titles of "*son* of the sun," "the good *god*," "*lord* of the two lands," "beloved of Amun, the protector of *kings*." A curious anomaly appears in some of her inscriptions, where masculine and feminine forms are inextricably mixed up; though
(35) spoken of consistently as "the king," and not "the queen," yet the personal and possessive pronouns which refer to her are feminine for the most part,

while sometimes such perplexing expressions occur as "His Majesty herself."

The legal position which Hatshepsut occupied (40) during the sixteen years that followed the death of Thutmosis II was probably that of regent for Thutmosis III, his (and her) younger brother; but practically she was full sovereign of Egypt. It was now that she formed her grand schemes of foreign (45) commerce. She caused to be built a fleet of ships, propelled both by oars and sails, and each capable of accommodating some sixty or seventy passengers. Of these, thirty were the rowers, whose long sweeps were to plough the waves and bring the vessels into (50) port, whether the wind were favorable or not.

*Passage 2*

A spectacular event of the reign of Hatshepsut was a shopping expedition to the city of Punt. The expedition was very profitable for Egypt, and Hatshepsut was remembered for her participation — (55) even though it was an act of a king and not a queen.

The excursion is recorded on Hatshepsut's mortuary temple at Deir el Bahri in Luxor. The location of Punt has been questioned over the years. Many places, from the Indian Ocean to Ethiopia, have been (60) suggested as the location; the only thing that is known is that it was reached via the Red Sea.

The trading expedition was primarily for incense trees. Incense was used extensively in Egypt by the cult of the god Amun as well as by ordinary people (65) as a fumigator. Because incense was not a natural resource of Egypt, it had to be imported. Ever industrious, Hatshepsut wanted to plant the trees in Egypt and make incense a natural resource. She did indeed plant these trees along the causeway leading (70) to her mortuary temple, and some of the pits can still be seen today.

12. In the context of Line 7, what is the best definition of "temper"?

    (A) anger
    (B) annoyance
    (C) nature
    (D) moderation

13. In the context of Line 8, what is the best definition of "senior"?

    (A) older one
    (B) aged person
    (C) retiree
    (D) person of higher rank

14. The information in the second paragraph of Passage 1 (Lines 18–39) serves to

    (A) explain why Thutmosis II died
    (B) show that Thutmosis II was not a good ruler
    (C) illustrate gender roles in ancient Egypt
    (D) defend Hatshepsut's actions

15. Hatshepsut's "fleet of ships" (Line 46) was intended for

    (A) defense
    (B) trade
    (C) luxury travel
    (D) ceremonies

16. Which of the following would best add clarification to the events described in Passage 2?

    (A) a photo of an incense tree
    (B) a diagram of Hatshepsut's mortuary temple
    (C) a map showing sites in ancient Egypt as well as possible locations of Punt
    (D) a family tree showing Hatshepsut's lineage

17. With which statement would the author of both passages agree?

    (A) Hatshepsut overpowered her male relatives.
    (B) Hatshepsut was obsessed with power.
    (C) Hatshepsut recognized the need for trade with other nations.
    (D) Hatshepsut traveled extensively.

18. Which choice provides the best evidence for the answer to the previous question?

    (A) Lines 14–16 ("an air of vigor . . . brother's reign")
    (B) Lines 22–24 ("erasing his name . . . her own name")
    (C) Lines 45–46 ("grand schemes . . . foreign commerce")
    (D) Lines 50–51 ("plough the waves . . . favorable or not")

19. In contrast to Passage 1, Passage 2

    (A) relies more on unproven assumptions
    (B) reflects poorly upon Hatshepsut's assumption of male privileges
    (C) indicates a less favorable opinion of Hatshepsut
    (D) exemplifies a benefit of Hatshepsut's initiatives

20. Which choice provides the best evidence for the answer to the previous question?

    (A) Lines 52–53 ("A spectacular event . . . to the city of Punt")
    (B) Lines 67–69 ("Ever industrious . . . natural resource")
    (C) Line 56 ("act of a king . . . queen")
    (D) Lines 70–72 ("plant these trees . . . seen today")

21. Information about Hatshepsut's character in Passage I and Passage II relies upon all the following types of evidence EXCEPT

    (A) comments from her peers
    (B) a sculpture
    (C) official titles
    (D) items at her burial site

# Passage II Answers

**12. C.** The sentence speaks of Thutmosis II as someone of "weak and *amiable* (friendly) temper" (Line 7). His older sister, on the other hand, is described as "clever, enterprising, vindictive, and unscrupulous" (Lines 9–10), all words that describe her personality or *nature*. Choice (C) is correct.

**13. A.** A *senior* in high school along with a *senior* citizen is someone who is *older*. So perhaps Choices (C) and (D) tempted you. In Passage I, though, Hatshepsut is "senior by some years" (Line 8). The phrase "by some years" tips you toward the real answer, Choice (A).

**14. C.** In this paragraph, you hear that Hatshepsut wore a fake beard and took masculine titles. In other words, she had to take masculine attributes (characteristics) to act as a ruler — indications of the gender roles of ancient Egypt, Choice (C).

**15. B.** Lines 45–46 refers to Hatshepsut's "grand schemes of foreign commerce" and is followed by the statement that she "caused to be built a fleet of ships" (Line 46). The side-by-side placement of these two statements shows you that the fleet was meant for trade, as Choice (B) indicates.

**16. C.** Most of Passage II concerns Hatshepsut's trip to Punt, and the passage also refers to "Deir el Bahri in Luxor" (Line 58). Do you know where these sites are? Many readers wouldn't, so a map would be helpful. Choice (C) is the answer.

**17. C.** Passage I gives you information about Hatshepsut's "grand schemes" (Line 45) and the fleet of ships she had built. Passage II goes into more detail on her "shopping expedition" (Line 53) to Punt. Put these ideas together and you see that she was planning for the future by building boats and trading for the seeds of incense trees. Choice (C) works well here. The other choices are possible, but you don't have enough information to know for sure.

**18. C.** As you see in the explanation for Question 17, Hatshepsut planned ahead by building ships and using them for trade, bringing back seeds of incense trees, as Choice (C) says.

**19. D.** In Passage I, the author calls Hatshepsut "clever, enterprising, vindictive, and unscrupulous" (Lines 9–10). The first two descriptions are positive, but not the last two. Vindictive people hold grudges and seek revenge; unscrupulous people don't spend much time worrying about right and wrong. Nothing in Passage II is negative. The author portrays Hatshepsut's journey to Punt as an attempt to make Egypt less dependent on imported goods, something a good ruler should do. In fact, Passage II calls Hatshepsut "ever industrious" (Lines 67–68). True, the author mentions that Hatshepsut's trip was something "a king and not a queen" would do (Line 56), but you see no evidence that the author opposes this act. Choice (D) is best here.

**20. B.** As the explanation to Question 19 states, the author of Passage 1 drops two negative words into the list of descriptions. Passage 2, on the other hand, calls her "ever industrious" and portrays her more positively. Choice (B) is the answer.

**21. A.** In Lines 10–12 in Passage 1, you see a description of a "portrait bust" (sculpture) of Hatshepsut, which the author says "gives a fair indication of [her] character." Out goes Choice (B). You also learn that she "took the title" of a king (Line 29), so you can rule out Choice (C). In Line 71 of Passage 2, you learn that pits of incense trees may be seen at her "mortuary temple" (tomb), so Choice (D) isn't the answer. You're left with Choice (A), the answer.

# Science Passages

**Questions 22–31 are based on the following passage.**

PLAY    This excerpt is from *Reality's Mirror* by Bryan Bunch (Wiley).

Human beings find some arrangements more appealing than others. When people trim the natural shapes of trees and herbs to produce a pleasing landscape, they are looking for, among other things,
(05) a balance. Putting all the tall delphiniums[1] off center in a border or the large yews[2] on one side of the walk and the small yews on the other just does not seem adequate. The same is true of ideas. When a philosopher, scientist, or mathematician puts ideas forward
(10) as something that will appeal to others in his or her field, it is generally considered good practice to make sure that the ideas have a kind of balance. The balance required, however, is not between large and small ideas; it is more complex yet simpler. Certain
(15) concepts or entities should have similar concepts or entities on the other side of the conceptual walk. Other concepts or entities can exist without requiring this balancing act. Why is this so? Let's look at an example.

(20) A philosopher might think that since Being exists, Nonbeing must also exist; a scientist learns that for every action there is an equal and opposite reaction; a mathematician would be lost without negative numbers as well as positive ones. These are ex-
(25) amples of concepts or entities that exhibit *balance.* The true, the good, and the beautiful all have their opposite partners.

Other concepts or entities, however, have no similar counterparts. For example, scientists have not found
(30) an opposite for mass — no entity that a scientist could label antimass. The need for balance is so strong, however, that some physicists predict that one day antimass will be found.

The nonexistent antimass should not be confused
(35) with the existing antimatter, about which more will be said later. The prediction of the existence of antimatter is one of the most spectacular examples of using mathematics to describe some previously unknown entity. In science, the conclusion that
(40) certain entities must have matching but opposite partners is a direct outcome of interpreting a

mathematical treatment of the entities in question. Antimatter emerges as one of the consequences of equations that describe matter. Specifically, the
equations that tell how the electron behaves imply    (45) the existence of a twin particle that is in some ways the direct opposite of the electron. When scientists found such a particle, the equations had already shown that it must be there.

The belief among scientists in this kind of balance    (50) goes even deeper. If some sort of balanced pairing does not exist, scientists may say that at some earlier time or in some other physical state the balance once did exist. By reaching for a higher energy, for example, it is predicted that the balance will be re-    (55) captured. This line of thinking has led to the development of huge machines that can reach such high energies and temporarily restore the balance.

[1]A type of flower. [2]A type of tree.

**22.** In the first paragraph (Lines 1–19), the author discusses a garden to

(A) explain the attraction of Nature

(B) advocate balance in Nature

(C) show that scientific thought may be applied to commonplace things

(D) provide a concrete image of symmetry

**23.** Which choice provides the best evidence for the answer to the previous question?

(A) Lines 2–5 ("When people trim . . . things, a balance")

(B) Lines 17–18 ("Other concepts or entities . . . balancing act")

(C) Line 8 ("The same is true of ideas")

(D) Lines 12–14 ("The balance required, however, is not between large and small ideas")

24. In the context of Line 8, what is the best definition of "adequate"?

   (A) complete
   (B) satisfactory
   (C) plenty
   (D) permissible

25. According to the passage, with which statement would a philosopher agree?

   (A) No one can define "true" or "good" or "beautiful."
   (B) Good can exist only if evil exists.
   (C) Nature tends toward imbalance.
   (D) Opposites attract.

26. Which choice provides the best evidence for the answer to the previous question?

   (A) Line 8 ("The same is true of ideas")
   (B) Lines 17–18 ("Other concepts or entities can exist . . . balancing act")
   (C) Lines 26–27 ("The true, the good, and the beautiful . . . their opposite partners")
   (D) Lines 50–51 ("The belief among scientists . . . even deeper")

27. According to the ideas expressed in the passage, each of the following is an example of symmetry EXCEPT

   (A) a forest
   (B) a butterfly
   (C) a human face
   (D) armies attacking and defending a fort

28. One reason scientists predict that someday "antimass" (Line 31) will be found is that

   (A) antimatter exists
   (B) some evidence of antimass has already been discovered
   (C) the need for balance is extremely strong
   (D) antimass is a natural quality

29. The author discusses antimatter in order to

   (A) show that mathematics is useful
   (B) explain why some entities appear unbalanced
   (C) focus the reader's attention on scientific theories
   (D) support the idea that Nature seeks balance

30. In the context of Line 39, which of these is the best definition of "conclusion"?

   (A) judgment
   (B) termination
   (C) goal
   (D) end

31. Given "the belief among scientists in this kind of balance" (Line 50), with which of the following statements would scientists also agree?

   (A) A system may be unbalanced only for a limited period of time or under certain conditions.
   (B) Scientific theories are more often wrong than right.
   (C) Balance is always temporary.
   (D) Only the past can predict the future.

# Passage III Answers

**22.** **D.** The first paragraph "shows" the reader a garden that's lopsided, with all the "tall delphiniums off center . . . or the large yews on one side" (Lines 5–6). The garden image is preceded by the statement that "people trim the natural shapes" (Lines 2–3) because of a need for "balance" (Line 5). *Symmetry* means *balance*, so Choice (D) is your answer. Were you fooled by Choice (A)? True, the first paragraph talks about what human beings find "more appealing" (Lines 1–2), but Choice (A) is too vague.

**23.** **A.** Take a look at the explanation for Question 22. You see that all the garden comments support a need for balance, with the garden as an example. Choice (A) is correct.

**24.** **B.** The passage explains that a garden with all the tall plants on one side or all the big trees clumped together "just does not seem adequate" (Lines 7–8), which reads like, "just not good enough." In other words, it's not satisfactory, and Choice (B) is your answer.

**25.** **B.** The second paragraph of the passage (Lines 20–27) is the only one to deal directly with philosophy. The author gives an example of balance in math, with positive numbers requiring the existence of negative numbers. The author also states that "[t]he true, the good, and the beautiful all have their opposite partners" (Lines 26–27). Put those two ideas together — as the author does in paragraph two — and you arrive at Choice (B). The other choices are all the sort of vague statement that philosophers love to debate, but only Choice (B) is justified in the passage.

**26.** **C.** The explanation for the answer to Question 25 points you to the second paragraph, where the concept of balance is illustrated with examples from both math and philosophy. Choice (C) combines these ideas and is the correct answer.

**27.** **A.** The balanced garden of paragraph one (Lines 1–19) is similar to Choices (B) and (C) — both examples of visual symmetry. The passage also discusses balanced actions (Line 22: "an equal and opposite reaction"), so Choice (D) doesn't work. You're left with Choice (A). A forest doesn't necessarily grow in a balanced, patterned way, so it's not an example of symmetry.

**28.** **C.** Antimass is called "nonexistent" in Line 34, but the passage states that "the need for balance is so strong . . . that one day antimass will be found" (Lines 31–33). Sounds like Choice (C)! The prize for runner-up goes to Choice (A), because antimatter balances out matter. However, Choice (C) addresses the balance issue directly, so it's a better answer.

**29.** **D.** The passage explains that by the time the existence of antimatter was proved experimentally, it had already been predicted mathematically because of a fundamental quality of Nature — its tendency to be balanced. Therefore, Choice (D) is your answer.

**30.** **A.** Lines 40–41 describe the way in which scientists put ideas together ("interpreting a mathematical treatment") to reach a "conclusion," or judgment. Choice (A) is your answer.

**31.** **A.** The last paragraph talks about the lack of balance sometimes found in Nature and goes on to say that if balanced pairs don't exist now, "at some earlier time or in some other physical state the balance once did exist" (Lines 52–54). Therefore, Nature tends toward balance, and anything unbalanced now was balanced at some point or is balanced in some other way. This is why Choice (A) is the correct answer.

PLAY

**Questions 32–42 are based on the following passages.**

Passage 1 discusses the relationship between geography and human culture. Passage 2 is an excerpt from *The Secret Life of Dust* by Hannah Holmes (Wiley). The author addresses climate change. (**Note:** An *oviraptor* is a type of dinosaur. Mount Pinatubo was a volcano that erupted in 1991.)

*Passage 1*

Human culture is invariably rooted in the site in which it flourishes. Thus human history is also the study of land and water formations, climate, and characteristics of the physical world. Climate,
(05) of course, is neither a constant nor a sole factor in human development. The earth's climate has undergone many variations in its long history. So too are there shifts in civilizations. Today's fertile soil, verdant forests, and prosperous empire may very
(10) well be tomorrow's ruins, as the fall of classic Mayan civilization following a prolonged drought in the ninth century illustrates.

Acknowledging the influence of climate, scientists today study the gradual rise in average temperature,
(15) preparing for major shifts in trade, population density, and political affinity. Modern science has in some sense inherited the mantle of ancient seers. One historian declared that climatologists have taken up the role of ancient priests — those in
(20) Egypt, for example, whose prayers to the gods were designed to ensure that the annual flood of the Nile River was sufficient for agriculture but not so extensive as to cause damage to settlements.

Yet anyone studying the effect of climate change on
(25) human culture must also take into account the consistency and resiliency of human life. Archaeologists at some sites have found similarities in artifacts and settlement patterns before and after major climate changes. More than 73,000 years ago, for example,
(30) the eruption of Mt. Toba, a volcano in Indonesia, ejected so much dust into the atmosphere that sunlight was dimmed and the earth entered an ice age. If climate change is such a powerful force, how is it that humanity survived this period with its culture
(35) largely intact?

*Passage 2*

One very clear message in the ice is that the Earth's climate is naturally erratic. According to the dust and gases trapped in the ice, the climate is always — always — in flux. If it's not getting warm-
(40) er, it's getting colder. Year to year the shifts may be masked by an El Niño, a La Niña, a Mount Pinatubo,

or some other temporary drama. But decade to decade, century to century, the world's temperature is in constant motion.

On a grand scale, our moderate, modern climate is (45) abnormal. Through most of the dinosaur era the planet's normal state was decidedly steamier. When the oviraptor perished in the Gobi Desert, the world may have been eleven to fourteen degrees hotter, on average. (50)

Then, just 2.5 million years ago, the planet entered a pattern of periodic ice ages, punctuated by brief warm spells. The ice caps, as a result, have taken to advancing and retreating intermittently. The glaciers have ruled for the lion's share of time, with the (55) warm "interglacials" lasting roughly ten thousand years each. We inhabit an interglacial known as the Holocene, which ought to be coming to an end any day now. The thermometer, however, does not seem poised for a plunge. (60)

All things being equal, no climatologist would be surprised if the Holocene persisted for another few thousand years — climate change is that erratic. But all things are not equal. Human industry has wrought profound changes in the Earth's atmos- (65) phere since the last warm period.

**32.** Based on the statements in the first paragraph (Lines 1–12) of Passage 1, which position would that author most likely support?

(A) History is intertwined with geography.

(B) Human beings shape their environment, not the other way around.

(C) Climate and prosperity are completely unrelated.

(D) Dramatic climate changes always cause dramatic cultural shifts.

33. Which choice provides the best evidence for the answer to the previous question?

(A) Lines 1–4 ("Human . . . physical world")

(B) Lines 6–7 ("The earth's climate . . . history")

(C) Lines 8–10 ("Today's fertile soil . . . ruins")

(D) Lines 10–12 ("as the fall of the . . . ninth century illustrates")

34. In the context of Line 8, what is the best definition of "shifts"?

(A) transfers

(B) modifications

(C) swings

(D) adjustments

35. The example of the Mayan civilization serves to

(A) emphasize the importance of water conservation

(B) exemplify how history and climate are related

(C) show that no empire is immune to climate change

(D) reveal how human behavior influences climate

36. Which of the following best expresses the meaning of this statement: "Modern science has in some sense inherited the mantle of ancient seers" (Lines 16–18)?

(A) Much scientific knowledge is as imprecise as magic.

(B) Scientific knowledge isn't accessible to ordinary people.

(C) Science attempts to predict future events.

(D) Scientists today are expected to understand the past.

37. The author mentions Mt. Toba (Line 30)

(A) as an example of human endurance in the face of climate change

(B) to warn of the dangers of natural forces

(C) to show that volcanoes can do damage

(D) as an illustration of the way human behavior changes when climate changes

38. The author of Passage 2 mentions the oviraptor (Line 48) to show

(A) the difference between human and animal responses to changes in climate

(B) how living creatures adapt to changes in climates

(C) a species that became extinct because of climate shifts

(D) an example of something that lived during a warm period

39. Which choice provides the best evidence for the answer to the previous question?

(A) Lines 42–44 ("But decade . . . constant motion")

(B) Lines 45–46 ("On a grand . . . abnormal")

(C) Lines 46–47 ("Though most . . . steamier")

(D) Lines 48–50 ("When the oviraptor . . . on average")

40. Compared to the authors of Passage 1, the author of Passage 2

(A) describes volcanic eruptions as more important factors in climate change

(B) believes that climate change has less effect on human behavior

(C) is more concerned with humans' effect on climate than the effect of climate on humans

(D) sees climate as having greater historical importance

41. Evidence from both passages supports the idea that

(A) climate change is inevitable

(B) human beings cannot withstand radical climate changes

(C) human activity affects climate

(D) climate changes very little

42. The title that best fits both passages is

(A) Global Warming

(B) Natural Climate Change

(C) Volcanoes and Climate

(D) Human Effects on Climate

# Passage IV Answers

32. **A.** Lines 1 through 4 make clear that *the site* (that is, the geography and climate) where people live is a factor in human culture, a belief expressed by Choice (A). Did Choice (C) entrap you? Lines 10–12 refer to the fall of the Mayan Empire because of extreme drought, but Line 3 firmly asserts that climate isn't the *sole factor* determining the stability of a civilization.

33. **A.** Check out the answer explanation to Question 32, and you see that the lines in Choice (A) support the idea that history is intertwined with geography.

34. **C.** Lines 6–8 tell you that "climate has undergone many variations . . . so, too, are there shifts in civilizations." The word *too* tells you that you're looking for a synonym of *variations,* which Choice (C) provides. Choice (B) is close, but a modification usually refers to a small change to an existing thing, and the paragraph describes more extreme changes.

35. **B.** The Mayan empire fell because of a prolonged drought (Lines 10–11), so you can immediately eliminate Choices (C) and (D). To choose between the remaining two answers, examine the whole paragraph, which discusses the effect of climate on human culture. In that context, Choice (B) is the best answer.

36. **C.** Ancient seers tried to predict the future, and Lines 15–16 tell you that today's scientists are "preparing for major shifts in trade, population density, and political affinity" — future trends, in other words. Hence, Choice (C) is correct.

37. **A.** The third paragraph of Passage 1 (Lines 24–35) talks about climate and culture. The passage states that the eruption of Mt. Toba brought on an ice age, but — and this is an important but — human culture survived intact (not damaged or broken). Therefore, Choice (A) is your best answer here.

38. **A.** Choices (A), (B), and (C) are out because the second paragraph of Passage 2 states that "through most of the dinosaur era the planet's normal state was decidedly steamier." This also makes Choice (D) the correct answer.

39. **C.** Lines 46–47 state that "most of the dinosaur era," the earth was warmer, so the climate didn't change and thus affect the oviraptor.

40. **C.** Lines 64–66 state that "human industry has wrought profound changes in the Earth's atmosphere since the last warm period." Thus, the author considers how humans affect climate, not the other way around, as is the case in Passage 1. Go for Choice (C).

41. **A.** Passage 1 makes a point of stating that climate isn't "a constant" (Line 5), and Passage 2 flat out tells you that climate is always changing. Therefore, Choice (A) fits perfectly. Choice (C) may have lured you because the author of Passage 2 does state that human activity is a factor; Passage 1, however, ignores the human effect on the weather.

42. **B.** Choice (A) is out because Passage 1 talks about Mt. Toba, which led to global cooling (not warming). Passage 2 doesn't really deal with volcanoes, so Choice (C) is also out. Passage 1 ignores human effects on climate, so the answer can't be Choice (D). As a result, Choice (B) is the correct answer.

# Literature Passage

**PLAY**

Questions 43–52 are based on the following passage.

In this excerpt from Dickens's 19th-century novel *Great Expectations*, the narrator recalls a Christmas dinner.

I opened the door to the company — making believe that it was a habit of ours to open that door — and I opened it first to Mr. Wopsle, next to Mr. and Mrs. Hubble, and last of all to Uncle Pumblechook. N.B.[1],
(05) I was not allowed to call him uncle, under the severest penalties.

"Mrs. Joe," said Uncle Pumblechook: a large hard-breathing middle-aged slow man, with a mouth like a fish, dull staring eyes, and sandy hair stand-
(10) ing upright on his head, so that he looked as if he had just been all but choked, and had that moment come to; "I have brought you, as the compliments of the season — I have brought you, Mum, a bottle of sherry wine — and I have brought you, Mum, a
(15) bottle of port wine."

Every Christmas Day he presented himself, as a profound novelty, with exactly the same words, and carrying the two bottles like dumb-bells. Every Christmas Day, Mrs. Joe replied, as she now replied,
(20) "Oh, Un-cle Pum-ble-chook! This IS kind!" Every Christmas Day, he retorted, as he now retorted, "It's no more than your merits. And now are you all bobbish[2], and how's Sixpennorth of halfpence[3]?" meaning me.

(25) We dined on these occasions in the kitchen, and adjourned, for the nuts and oranges and apples, to the parlour; which was a change very like Joe's change from his working clothes to his Sunday dress. My sister was uncommonly lively on the present oc-
(30) casion, and indeed was generally more gracious in the society of Mrs. Hubble than in other company. I remember Mrs. Hubble as a little curly sharp-edged person in sky-blue, who held a convention-ally juvenile position, because she had married Mr.
(35) Hubble — I don't know at what remote period — when she was much younger than he. I remember Mr. Hubble as a tough high-shouldered stooping old

man, of a sawdusty fragrance, with his legs extraor-dinarily wide apart: so that in my short days I al-ways saw some miles of open country between them (40) when I met him coming up the lane.

Among this good company I should have felt myself, even if I hadn't robbed the pantry, in a false posi-tion. Not because I was squeezed in at an acute angle of the table-cloth, with the table in my chest, and (45) the Pumblechookian elbow in my eye, nor because I was not allowed to speak (I didn't want to speak), nor because I was regaled with the scaly tips of the drumsticks of the fowls, and with those obscure corners of pork of which the pig, when living, had (50) had the least reason to be vain. No; I should not have minded that, if they would only have left me alone. But they wouldn't leave me alone. They seemed to think the opportunity lost, if they failed to point the conversation at me, every now and then, and stick (55) the point into me. I might have been an unfortunate little bull in a Spanish arena, I got so smartly touched up by these moral goads.

[1] Abbreviation for "note well." [2] Hungry. [3] A small quantity of British money. (60)

43. Which statement about the opening of doors may be inferred from the first paragraph (Lines 1–6)?

(A) The door that the narrator opens is nor-mally locked.

(B) The door that the narrator opens is never used for company.

(C) The narrator is not normally allowed to open the door for visitors.

(D) Certain doors are used on special occa-sions and others for everyday entries.

44. The author's attitude toward Uncle Pumblechook and Mrs. Joe in the second and third paragraphs (Lines 7–24) may best be characterized as

(A) mildly critical

(B) admiring

(C) ambivalent

(D) sharply disapproving

45. Which choice provides the best evidence for the answer to the previous question?

(A) Lines 5–6 ("I was not allowed . . . severest penalties")

(B) Lines 8–10 ("middle-aged slow man . . . upright on his head")

(C) Lines 16–20 ("Every Christmas Day . . . This IS kind")

(D) Lines 28–31 ("My sister was uncommonly . . . than in other company")

46. In the context of Line 9, which of the following is the best definition of "dull"?

(A) boring

(B) blunted

(C) sharp

(D) unattractive

47. The move from the kitchen to the parlour is compared to Mrs. Joe's change of clothes because

(A) Mrs. Joe is uncomfortable with both

(B) both take place only on special occasions

(C) the narrator is confused by each of these actions

(D) Mrs. Joe insists upon both of these changes

48. The details in the last paragraph (Lines 42–58) serve to

(A) show how the author enjoys Christmas dinner

(B) explain the behavior of the dinner guests

(C) describe a 19th-century Christmas celebration

(D) make the case that the narrator is not treated well

49. In the context of Line 48, what is the best definition of "regaled"?

(A) amused

(B) entertained

(C) sold

(D) lavished

50. The metaphor of "an unfortunate little bull in a Spanish arena" (Lines 56–57) means that

(A) the narrator, like a bull in a bullfight, is an involuntary target of teasing attacks

(B) the narrator's table manners are more like those of an animal than a polite child

(C) the narrator did not participate actively in the conversation

(D) the dinner guests were the targets of the narrator's mocking comments

51. The author of this passage would most likely agree with which statement?

(A) Children should be seen and not heard.

(B) The narrator has a happy life.

(C) Holiday gatherings may be joyous occasions.

(D) People often show off during holiday gatherings.

52. Which choice provides the best evidence for the answer to the previous question?

(A) Lines 5–6 ("I was not allowed to call . . . severest penalties")

(B) Lines 6–10 ("a large hard-breathing . . . choked")

(C) Lines 25–30 ("We dined . . . lively on the present occasion")

(D) Lines 53–56 ("They seemed to think the opportunity lost . . . into me")

# Passage V Answers

**43. D.** The first paragraph contains the statement that the narrator was "making believe that it was a habit of ours to open that door." *That door* implies a contrast with another door, so you can rule out Choices (A) and (C). The two remaining choices present no real puzzle. Because company is arriving, Choice (B) can't be correct. Bingo — Choice (D) is your answer.

**44. A.** The description of Uncle Pumblechook clearly shows that Choice (B) won't do, because a mouth like a fish isn't an admiring comment. Choice (C) is possible, but not Choice (D) as the author isn't sharply disapproving and the negative comments are quite tame (*ambivalent* means "of two opinions"). Choice (A) is the best. If Uncle Pumblechook and Mrs. Joe are pretending to do something novel, rather than a ritual repeated each year (giving and receiving the gift of the wine), and they do this again and again, the author is critical of them, but only mildly.

**45. C.** Choice (B) gives comments that are certainly mildly critical, but these comments are only about Uncle Pumblechook. Question 44 asks about the impression of two characters: Uncle Pumblechook and Mrs. Joe, and Choice (C) insults both characters. As you see in the explanation to Question 44, these lines show the false surprise of these two characters.

**46. D.** In the cited line, *dull* refers to Uncle Pumblechook's eyes. The opposite of dull is "sparkling and lively" — qualities that attract attention and admiration. Uncle Pumblechook definitely doesn't have an attractive face; he has a "mouth like a fish" and "hair standing upright on his head" (Lines 8–10). Put it all together, and you arrive at *unattractive*, Choice (D).

**47. B.** Mrs. Joe is *uncommonly lively*, so Choice (A) is out. The passage gives no indication that Mrs. Joe insists on anything, so you can rule out Choice (D). You see no evidence of the narrator's confusion about the move, so Choice (C) doesn't work. The best answer is Choice (B), because Joe's change is referred to as *Sunday dress* and Choice (B) refers to special occasions.

**48. D.** The author is certainly not enjoying dinner, so Choice (A) is out. As is Choice (B), because though the dinner guests' behavior is possible, the details tell you more about how the narrator is treated than about the guests' general behavior. Choice (C) is too general. Choice (D) is the only one to make the cut.

**49. D.** The narrator gets "the scaly tips of the drumsticks" and "obscure corners of pork" (lines 48–50). These don't sound like nice presents, but they are what he is given, so Choice (D) works best here.

**50. A.** The guests are described as unwilling to leave the narrator alone, so you can rule out Choice (D) because the narrator isn't the attacker. Choice (C) is true but has no relationship to the bullfighting image and neither does the statement about table manners. The narrator is, however, described as the target of attacks by the guests' statements, just as the bull faces attacks in a bullfight. Thus, Choice (A) is the correct answer.

**51. D.** The change from one room to another, the use of a special door, the ceremonial exchange of gifts — all these details prove that the characters in this passage are showing off, putting on airs, pretending to be better than they really are, and in general acting like contestants on a reality show.

**52. C.** As the explanation to Question 51 reveals, several details in the passage lead you to believe that these characters are showing off. Of the lines given to you as answer possibilities, only Choice (C) lists some of the ways that the characters *show off*.

# 3

# Conquering the Writing and Language Test and Writing a Killer Essay

# Chapter **5**

# Gearing Up for the SAT Writing and Language Test

Whether you practice Pulitzer-level writing or express yourself with emojis, you have to take on the SAT Writing and Language Test. This test is in two parts. The first part, which is the focus of this chapter, is a set of multiple-choice questions about grammar, style, logic, and structure, all based on passages that are well written but leave room for improvement. The second part is an optional essay, covered further in Chapter 7.

**TIP**

Like the SAT Reading Test, the SAT Writing and Language Test challenges your experience along with your skills. This book helps strengthen your skills, but you can also build your experience outside of studying for the SAT. Constant doses of YouTube and Pinterest don't help you learn to recognize the constructs of grammar, style, and organization that appear in professional and academic writing. Right now, during this time before your SAT, start reading news, science, or anything aimed at an educated audience. The difference between studying grammar and reading an actual publication is like the difference between watching baseball and playing baseball, and this exercise will boost your performance on both the Reading Test and the Writing and Language Test.

## Getting to Know the Writing and Language Test

The SAT Writing and Language Test consists of four passages (like essays) each mixed with 11 multiple-choice questions. The test-makers want to know how you'd revise the passage if you were the author. Here are the details:

» You have 35 minutes to take on four passages. This means you get just about 9 minutes per passage — but more on that later.

>> The topics range from science to history/social studies and some fiction. Unlike the SAT Reading Test, there's no advantage to approaching the fiction passage last or approaching the questions out of order.

>> Of the 44 questions in this test, about 20 cover Standard English conventions of grammar and punctuation, and about 24 address style, or "expression of ideas." This last category is broad and may include proper word choice (selecting the right word for the context), organization of ideas, supporting logic, and effective use of evidence.

**REMEMBER**

Fortunately, the topics appearing in this test are limited to a certain scope: There are certain grammar elements, certain punctuation, and certain style questions that the SAT asks again and again. You don't have to master everything about English! Just a few parts.

# Managing Your Time with Simple Strategies

As you take on the SAT Writing Test, use the following basic, tried-and-true strategies to get the most questions right with the time that you have.

## Answering the easy questions before the hard questions

One question that takes five seconds is worth as much as another that takes three minutes. What if you work the three-minute question, answer it correctly, and then miss out on the last few questions because you ran out of time? Seems like the three-minute question still won.

Don't let this happen. An in-depth style question will take far longer than a simple grammar question. When you get one of these bonkers that takes a while, here's what you do:

1. **Guess an answer.** The idea is that you'll come back to this question, but just in case you don't, you have a chance to get it right. (A wrong answer isn't worse than an unanswered question, so you may as well throw a mental dart.)

2. **Circle the question in your test booklet.** This way, when you go back, you can find the question quickly. You'll have a few to run back to.

3. **Fold the corner of the page in the test booklet.** The Reading Test runs 18 pages, so this speeds up your finding the questions at the end.

## Using the 9-minute rule

With 35 minutes for four passages, you get just under 9 minutes per passage. Managing your time is key to taking control of this section.

1. **Write down the start time of the passage.** The test booklet is your scratch paper, so write down the time you start this test. You *did* put on a wristwatch, didn't you? If you didn't, you might be lucky and have a clock in front of the room. If the clock is on the side or the back of the room, don't look at it! The proctor will think you're cheating. And wear a dang watch.

2. **Write down the halfway point and end point.** This is simple. Just add 18 and 35 to the start time. If you start the section at 9:00 a.m., the halfway point is 9:18, and the end point is 9:35.

**3.** **Check your time at the end of the second passage (Question 22).** If you're ahead of the halfway point, you can go back and answer the circled questions from strategy 1. If you're running behind, forget them and go on to the next passage.

TIP

Try the 9-minute rule on a practice. Get a sense of your pace and whether to skip-and-guess or stop-and-work the sticky questions *before* the actual exam. Your pace on exam day may be different, but you'll still have a sense of how you work, which means you can take control of your approach.

# Nailing the Common Questions

These questions are relatively easy if you know what to look for. Here are the best strategies for the most common types of questions.

## Starting with grammar and punctuation

The SAT Writing and Language Test covers the basic principles of standard English that you are expected to know in college. You see an underlined word or phrase and then decide whether it needs to be corrected. Later, in the "Killing It Softly: The SAT Grammar Review" section, you find a comprehensive review of grammar topics to know for the exam — and for college! But for now, here are the grammar and punctuation issues to look for on the SAT:

>> **Incorrect punctuation:** Apostrophes and commas may be extra, missing, or in the wrong place. The SAT also mixes up colons and semicolons for you to sort out.

>> **Incomplete sentences:** *Run-ons* (having two subjects and two verbs) must be properly joined, and *fragments* (such as a subject but no verb, for example, "The dog.") must be completed.

>> **Misplaced modifiers:** A *modifier*, which is just an adjective in more than one word, must be near the noun that it modifies. For example, "The skier went off the trail, laughing loudly." *Laughing loudly* is the modifier, so it must be near *the skier*, not the *trail,* otherwise the sentence reads as if the *trail* were laughing. Maybe it was.

>> **Wrong homonyms:** Do you turn right or write? Is this tree taller than or taller then the tent? There are many homonyms in English, but the SAT just asks about the common ones.

>> **Wrong-tense verbs:** Make sure that the verb tense expresses the right time for an event or state of being. Also check for subject-verb agreement, which especially appears in parallel structure. Oh right — parallel structure.

>> **Parallel structure:** This means that if one noun has a few verbs, say, "the dog runs, jumps, and pants," the verbs are all in the same tense. It's not always that simple, but it is always that easy.

Besides what *to* look for, here's what *not* to look for. This is the Don't Worry list, shorter than the Worry list, but at least you know what to expect.

>> **Don't worry about spelling.** The SAT doesn't test spelling except for those homonyms.

>> **Don't worry about capitalization.** The SAT very infrequently takes on capitalization. Assume that capital letters are in the right spots unless a glaring mistake jumps out at you.

REMEMBER If you catch a grammar or punctuation mistake, be sure that your answer choice doesn't contain a *different* error. You must be able to plug in the new version and end up with a proper result.

Ready to practice? Try this sample question, excerpted from a science passage.

PLAY

Samples taken every quarter mile along the river show the extent of the problem. The water five miles downstream <u>not only was polluted but also laden with debris</u>, including tires, chunks of wood, and plastic trash bags.

**(A)** NO CHANGE

**(B)** was not only polluted but also laden with debris

**(C)** not only polluted but also debris was laden there

**(D)** not only polluted but also laden with debris

The paired conjunction *not only/but also* should trigger an immediate check for parallel structure. After *not only* is a verb, *was.* After *but also* there is no verb. Choice (D) removes the verb, but now you're left with a fragment. Choice (B) moves the verb. Now *not only* and its partner *but also* join the parallel descriptions *polluted* and *laden.*

TIP

The SAT Writing and Language test has two columns, one with the passage and the other with a set of answer choices (often with no question stem) roughly at the level of the writing issue you're about to address. If there is no question stem, the question is always the same: "How should the underlined words be changed, if at all?" and the first choice, (A), is always *NO CHANGE.* Choices (B), (C), and (D) offer different wordings or punctuation.

*Note:* For a full-scale grammar refresher, take a look at the latest editions of *English Grammar For Dummies* and *English Grammar Workbook For Dummies*, by Geraldine Woods, or *1,001 Grammar Practice Questions For Dummies*, by Ron Woldoff. Each book is published by Wiley.

## Getting vocabulary in context

The SAT doesn't test vocabulary directly, but questions may ask whether you grasp the *nuance*, or shades of meaning, of a word or expression in a particular context. A question may highlight one word — sometimes a fairly sophisticated word — that appears where it doesn't quite fit, and the answer choices offer alternatives. Many words have nearly the same meaning, but nearly isn't good enough when you're writing. For instance, a snowboarder doesn't *flow* between pilons, he or she *slaloms.* Both words could refer to downhill travel, but only one is appropriate for snowboarding.

TIP

As you enhance your SAT prep by reading college-level publications (you *are* doing this, aren't you?), do a quick look-up of any unfamiliar word and jot down (or just think of) what it means. This is easy enough online, where you can right-click or tap on a word; if you're reading print, you can actually say, "Okay Google (or Siri, or Alexa), define *nomenclature.*"

To answer these questions, pay attention to both the definition and the connotation (or feeling and situation) associated with the word. Try this one:

**PLAY**

Few in the community are pleased with the plan to construct a sewage plant on First Street. Opponents <u>detract</u> the proposed facility despite claims that it will bring much-needed jobs to the area.

**(A)** NO CHANGE

**(B)** criticize

**(C)** degrade

**(D)** diminish

*To detract* is "to take value away from," a definition related to *criticize* but not exactly the same. A bow tie may *detract* from your outfit, and if you wear it, someone may *criticize* you, but no one will *detract* you. Go for Choice (B). By the way, *to degrade* is "to disrespect," as in *a dog food advertisement that degrades cats,* and *to diminish* is "to lessen in value or amount," as in *his appetite diminished after he ate all the chips.*

# Writing with style, logic, and organization

A sentence can be grammatically correct, but it may not be relevant to the flow or narrative of the passage. Sometimes you have to determine the best way to support or communicate the intended meaning. You may also be asked whether additional information is needed or whether a sentence should be deleted or moved. If there's a table or graph, expect at least one question on conveying the information in the graphic.

This type of question typically has a question stem that is specific about what should be in the correct answer. *The most common mistake on this type of question happens when the student doesn't read the question stem,* so yes, be sure to read that. The question stem is something like:

"The writer wants to include information . . ."

"The writer wants to support the point that . . ."

"Which choice best maintains the style and tone of the passage?"

"Which choice most effectively completes the explanation that . . ."

"To make the paragraph most logical, which choice . . ."

Usually, each answer choice is grammatically correct, so keep these other points in mind:

» **State something once.** Wrong answers may repeat information, so if one answer choice has far more words than another, check to see whether those extra words are necessary or redundant.

» **Unity is crucial.** Everything in a paragraph should revolve around one idea. If a sentence veers off topic, it has to go.

» **The flow of logic is essential.** Check for smooth transitions between one paragraph and another. The reader should immediately realize why the writer moved in a particular direction. If not, look for an answer choice that reveals the logical thread.

» **Interpret visual information correctly.** The text may refer to information that a chart, graph, or diagram contains. Be sure that the text supports the message in the graphic. If not, look for an answer choice that does.

## Switching transitions

A *transition* establishes the relationship between two clauses, usually a series of events. You'll be asked to pick the transition that makes the most sense. For example, you wouldn't say, "She got in her car *because* she drove away" or "She got in her car and *however* drove away." You would say, "She got in her car and *then* drove away."

Here are some common transitions that you'll find on the SAT:

>> **Contrast:** "He loves ice cream, *but* he hates Rocky Road." Other contrast words include *however, although, otherwise, on the other hand,* and *never/nonetheless.*

>> **Joining:** "She loves music, *and* she loves the blues." Other joining words include *moreover, further, likewise, in addition,* and *besides.*

>> **A results in B:** "He watered the plants, *so* they grew tall." Other "A results in B" words include *therefore, afterwards,* and *consequently.*

>> **B results in A:** "The car was clean *after* she washed it." Other "B results in A" words are *because, since,* and *being that.*

Don't try to memorize these, but rather learn to recognize them. That's easier and more useful. Try it out on this practice question.

**PLAY**

The sequoia, a type of redwood, is the largest species of tree in the world, growing as tall as 280 feet. <u>However</u>, the largest specimen is General Sherman, which can be found in California's Sequoia National Park.

**(A)** NO CHANGE

**(B)** otherwise

**(C)** therefore

**(D)** furthermore

California's General Sherman is an *example* of the giant sequoia, so the contrast transitions *however* and *otherwise* go out. The species didn't *result* in Sherman, so out goes *therefore.* The only choice you're left with is Choice (D), *furthermore,* which is a *joining* transition and supports the example.

## Moving in order

The question may also ask you to move a sentence or paragraph to a different point in the passage. Fortunately, this question type is few and far between, but it's in there. This tends to be time-consuming, so it's a good candidate to circle, guess, and come back to later.

Whether you come back to this question or work it on the first go, pay attention to these logical points of the portion that you're being asked to move:

>> **Does it introduce or conclude something?** If so, this portion may go before or after, respectively, the topic of the paragraph or passage.

>> **Does it clarify something?** If so, it may go after an introduction or description of the topic.

>> **Does it add to the narrative?** If so, place it where it makes sense among the order of events.

>> **Does it offer an exception?** If so, it probably goes after a clarification.

There are many variations of these logical points, but the preceding list will get you started on understanding where the portion goes. Try this one:

PLAY

[1] It was a perfect day for the auto show. [2] After a while, we took a pizza break. [3] The line to get in was short, and the entrance fee wasn't bad. [4] We ended up staying until the show closed for the day.

To make the most sense, Sentence 2 should be placed

(A) where it is now

(B) before sentence 1

(C) after sentence 3

(D) after sentence 4

Sentence 2 adds to the narrative. It almost makes sense where it is, after the group took a break during the auto show, except that Sentence 3 clearly describes them *entering* the auto show. It makes logical sense that the group took a break after entering the show, so Sentence 2 goes after Sentence 3, and Sentence 4 naturally concludes the story. The answer is Choice (C), and here are the sentences ordered properly:

[1] It was a perfect day for the auto show. [3] The line to get in was short, and the entrance fee wasn't bad. [2] After a while, we took a pizza break. [4] We ended up staying until the show closed for the day.

# Killing It Softly: The SAT Grammar Review

This grammar review is quick and painless, and if you're pretty good at grammar, this is a good refresher and heads-up of what to expect. Here are the most commonly tested grammar topics on the SAT.

## Verb matching

Verb matching includes singular to singular, plural to plural, and consistent verb tense.

In terms of agreement, the SAT asks about

>> Subject-verb pairs

>> Pronoun-antecedent pairs

### Subject-verb agreement

A *verb* expresses action or state of being; the *subject* is whoever or whatever is *doing* the action or *in* the state of being. A singular subject takes a singular verb, and a plural subject takes a plural verb. Check out these examples:

"The *snowmobiler chases* James Bond." *Snowmobiler* is a singular subject; *chases* is a singular verb.

"Six more *snowmobilers join* the pursuit." *Snowmobilers* is a plural subject; *join* is a plural verb.

The SAT expands upon this with trickier arrangements, such as the following:

>> **There/here:** These words aren't subjects. The subject comes *after* the verb, like this:

"Here are three calculators." The subject is *calculators,* matching the verb *are.*

>> **Either/or** and **neither/nor:** These words may join two subjects, so match the verb to the closest subject:

"Neither the car nor the tires *are* in the garage." *Tires* is the closest subject, and it's plural, so *are* is the correct verb.

"Neither the tools nor the truck *is* in the shop." *Truck* is the closest subject, so the singular verb *is* is correct.

>> **Interrupters between the subject-verb pair:** If an interrupter, such as a modifier or prepositional phrase, comes between the subject and the verb, it doesn't change the verb form.

"The soda machine, along with the games, *is* perfect for the basement." *Along with the games* is an interrupter, so the singular subject *soda machine* stays with the singular verb *is.* An interrupter could also be set off by dashes: "The dog — after chasing the cats — is chasing a car."

**REMEMBER**

Two singular nouns joined by *and* make a plural. ("The fox and the hound *are* both inside." *The fox* and *the hound* together make a plural subject.)

## Noun-pronoun agreement

The noun that the pronoun refers to is called an *antecedent*. Regardless of what it's called, it's the word that a pronoun replaces. In the sentence "The receiver chased the ball and caught it," *it* is a pronoun, and *the ball* is the antecedent because *it* stands for *the ball*. The rule on antecedents is super simple: Singular goes with singular and plural with plural. You probably already know all the easy applications of this rule. In the *receiver/ball* sentence, you'd never dream of replacing *the ball* with *them*. The SAT-makers, however, go for the tricky combinations:

>> **Pronouns containing *one*, *thing*, or *body* are singular.** Match these pronouns with other singular pronouns.

"Everyone brought his or her cheat sheet to the SAT." *Everyone* is singular because it has *one* in it, and it goes with the singular *his or her*. Same with *none* and *nobody*.

>> **Either, neither, each,** and **every** are singular. These words are sometimes followed by phrases that sound plural (*either of the boys* or *each father and son*), but these words are always singular.

"Neither of the boys has brought his calculator to the SAT." *His* is singular.

**TIP**

What makes a pronoun singular or plural also makes a verb singular or plural.

## Easing verb tension

On the SAT Writing and Language Test, tense isn't just what's happening to your muscles. *Tense* is the quality of verbs that indicates time. Remember these rules:

>> **The helping verbs *has* and *have* connect present and past actions.** When you see these helping verbs, something started in the past and is either still going on or just stopped. ("In this game, Rodney *has been* playing soccer for about 40 minutes, and Julie *had been* watching until her phone rang.")

>> **The helping verb *had* places one past action before another past action.** ("Josephine *had scored* a goal before Rodney did.")

>> **The tense doesn't change for the same subject.** You may see a sentence where the verbs change tense. "Charise *is cooking* dinner and *watches* TV," should be, "*watching* TV." If the second verb has a different tense, it needs a new subject.

**TIP**

Verbs also have a situation where the condition is contrary to the fact. This just means that when a statement isn't true, it's worded differently. (*If I were creating the SAT, I would dump all the grammar questions. If I had known about the grammar, I wouldn't have burned my English textbooks.*) The *if* part of the sentence — the untrue part — gets *were* or *had*, and the other part of the sentence features *would*. The SAT-makers may place *if I would* or *if I was* to trip you up. Your job, of course, is to catch that and mark *if I were*.

# Parallel writing

A favorite SAT question concerns *parallelism*, the way a sentence keeps its balance. The basic premise is simple: Each verb in a sentence that is attached to the same noun *must be* in the same tense. You can't "surf and soak up sun and playing in the sand" because *playing* is a different tense. You can "surf and soak up sun and play in the sand" without any problems — well, without any grammatical problems. Keep these ideas in mind:

>> **Look for lists.** Whenever you have two or three verbs bunched together, they probably have the same noun. Make sure the verbs match.

>> **Look for paired conjunctions.** Conjunctions are joining words. Three common paired conjunctions are *either/or, neither/nor,* and *not only/but also*. When you encounter one of these pairs, make sure the verbs are in the same tense.

>> **Look for two complete sentences joined together: usually the verbs are both active or both passive.** In an active-verb sentence, the subject is doing the action or is in the state of being expressed by the verb. ("Archie flies well." "Archie is happy.") In a passive-verb sentence, the subject receives the action of the verb. ("The window was broken by a high-speed pitch.") A parallel sentence generally doesn't switch from active to passive or vice versa.

# Casing pronouns

Pronouns have *case*, which refers to using *he* versus *him, she* versus *her, they* versus *them, it* versus . . . well, *it* is the same. Anyway, the rule is simple. Use a subject pronoun (*he, she, they*) for a subject and an object pronoun (*him, her, them*) for almost everything else. Here's how you tell the difference:

>> **Identify the subject and the object.** The *subject* is the one that's doing something, and the *object* is the target of the action. For example, if you see, "The referee penalized the player," the *referee* is the subject and the *player* is the object. In pronoun case, this sentence would read, "*He* penalized *him.*"

>> **Isolate the pronoun.** If you see, "The proctor gave the test to three boys and she," you may not notice the error. Cut out "the three boys," however, and you have, "The proctor gave the test to . . . she." Now the error is easier to spot: The sentence should read, "The proctor gave the test to . . . *her.*"

**REMEMBER**

One thing: The pronoun has to be *clear*. Something like, "Mary and Sandy each used the book, and she aced the exam!" won't fly. The sentence has to be clear.

## Using punctuation

Punctuation also appears on the SAT Writing and Language test. These rules are what you need to know:

» **Join sentences legally.** Sometimes a comma and a conjunction (joining word) — *and, or, but,* and *nor,* for example — do the job, and sometimes you need a semicolon. Transition words *(consequently, therefore, nevertheless, however)* look strong enough to join two sentences, but they're not. When you have one of these stuck between two sentences, add a semicolon. More on the semicolon follows.

» **Punctuate descriptions correctly.** If the description is essential to the meaning of the sentence — you don't know what you're talking about without the description — don't use commas. If the description is interesting but nonessential, place commas around it.

Don't place commas around this description, because you need the George part to clarify the sentence: "The play *that George wrote* makes no mention whatsoever of the SAT."

Meanwhile, place commas around this description, because the opening date isn't essential to the point of the sentence: "George's play, *which opened last Friday*, broke records at the box office."

» **Check apostrophes.** You may find a missing possessive form in front of an *-ing* word. You may also find an apostrophe where it doesn't belong, say in a possessive pronoun or in a simple, non-possessive plural.

  • A possessive pronoun (*whose, its, theirs, his, hers, our,* and so on) never has an apostrophe.

  • A conjunction that joins two words (*it's, don't, isn't, aren't*) always has an apostrophe. This is how you tell *it's* from *its*: *It's* joins *it* and *is* and gets an apostrophe; *its* is the possessive of *it* and does not have an apostrophe.

Know that *it's* with an apostrophe is the conjunction of *it* and *is,* as in, "*It's* parked outside." Also, *its* without an apostrophe is the possessive pronoun, as in, "The dog pulled on *its* leash."

» **Know semicolons.** The *semicolon* (;) joins two complete sentences. It takes the place of the *comma + and.* "The dog ran outside*, and* the cat chased it" could also be correctly stated as, "The dog ran outside; the cat chased it." Typically, the SAT has a complete sentence *before* the semicolon — you need to make sure there's a complete sentence *after* it. Also, the semicolon never goes with the word *and* — it takes its place.

» **Use colons.** The *colon* (:) does two things. It joins two complete sentences exactly like a semicolon. Sometimes the second sentence is capitalized, but it doesn't have to be. Any time a semicolon is correct, a colon works just fine. "The dog ran outside: The cat chased it." (You'll never have to pick between a semicolon and a colon if they're both correct.)

The other thing the colon does is begin a list, taking the place of *such as* or *for example.* A sentence like, "There are things on the table, *such as* an SAT, a calculator, and an aspirin" can also be written as, "There are things on the table: an SAT, a pencil, and an aspirin." The list is never capitalized (unless it has proper nouns), and the colon never goes with the words *such as* or *for example* — it takes their place.

## Wording up

The SAT asks about vocabulary in context, so you may see a word that *sounds* right but is completely wrong. These word pairs are frequent fliers on the exam:

- » **Affect and effect:** The SAT *affects* your life. The *effect* of all this prep is a high score. See the difference? The first is a verb and the second a noun. Once in a while, *effect* can be a verb meaning "to bring about" as in "Pressure from the colleges *effects* change," and *affect* can be a noun that means mood, as in "The scholarship brought a wonderful *affect.*" But these are rare.

- » **Fewer and less:** *Fewer* is for stuff you can count (shoes, teeth, cavities) and *less* for stuff you measure (sugar, ability, toothache intensity).

- » **Good and well:** In general, *good* describes nouns, and *well* describes verbs. In other words, a person or thing is *good,* but you do something *well.* The SAT is *good,* and you study *well* for the exam. The ice cream tastes *good,* for example, describes the noun *ice cream.*

- » **Ensure and insure:** You *ensure* something happens or doesn't happen, like practice *ensures* success. You *insure* something when you provide *insurance,* like the agent *insured* your truck and jet ski. That should be easy to remember.

- » **Farther and further:** Take something *farther* if it's literally going the distance, like my horse ran *farther* than your horse. Take it *further* for a matter of extremes, like the lawyer investigated *further.* No one messes this up.

This list obviously doesn't contain all the misused words or expressions you may encounter on the SAT tests, but these are the common offenders.

Here's a mini-sample of a typical writing passage and some questions to go with it.

**PLAY**

Can animals predict earthquakes? Since ancient times, strange or unusual behavior in fish, birds, reptiles, and <u>animals has been reported</u>. In modern times, too, people have noticed
                                                                    1
what they believe to be early warning signals from their pets. In 1975, for example, snakes awoke from hibernation just before a major earthquake in China. The snakes froze to <u>death,</u> the weather was still too cold for them to survive.
        2

[1] Many pet owners firmly believe that their dogs or cats have advance knowledge of the terrifying event that is a major earthquake. [2] Because many animals can see, hear, and smell things beyond the range of human senses, <u>it may be the case that they detect</u> small changes
                                                                                      3
in air pressure, gravity, or other phenomena associated with earthquakes. [3] <u>Animals that</u>
<u>predict earthquakes may be reacting to the *P* wave that humans can't feel.</u> [4] Researchers
        4
know that earthquakes <u>cultivate</u> two types of waves, *P* waves and *S* waves. [5] The *P* wave
                                5
travels faster than the *S* wave, which is stronger and more easily felt.

<u>Each year more and more people die from earthquakes.</u> If animals are indeed able to warn
                                        6
of earthquakes, and if scientists find an effective way to monitor the animals' signals, many lives will be saved.

## Estimated Number of Deaths from Earthquakes, Worldwide, 2008–2019

| 2008 | 2009 | 2010 | 2011 | 2012 | 2013 | 2014 | 2015 | 2016 | 2017 | 2018 | 2019 |
|---|---|---|---|---|---|---|---|---|---|---|---|
| 88,708 | 1,790 | 226,050 | 21,942 | 689 | 1,572 | 756 | 9,624 | 1,297 | 1,012 | 4,535 | 244 |

*U.S. Geological Survey*

1. (A) NO CHANGE
   (B) animals have been reported
   (C) other animals have been reported
   (D) other animals has been reported

2. (A) NO CHANGE
   (B) death;
   (C) death, because
   (D) death, being that

3. Which choice concisely supports the speculative tone of the passage?

   (A) NO CHANGE
   (B) it is possible that they detect
   (C) they may detect
   (D) they detect

4. To make the second paragraph most logical, Sentence 3 should be placed

   (A) where it is now
   (B) before Sentence 1
   (C) after Sentence 2
   (D) after Sentence 5

5. (A) NO CHANGE
   (B) generate
   (C) propagate
   (D) spawn

6. Which of the following, added at this point, is best supported by the data in the table?

   (A) NO CHANGE
   (B) The number of people who die from earthquakes is fairly consistent from year to year.
   (C) The number of people who die from earthquakes is steadily decreasing.
   (D) In 2010, more than 200,000 people died from earthquakes.

# Answers

1. **D.** This question tests your knowledge of two things: comparisons and verb tense. Fish, birds, and reptiles are animals, so the logic of comparing them to animals is faulty. Insert "other" and that problem goes away. Now your choices are narrowed to Choices (C) and (D). Look at the subject, which is *behavior*, a singular word. (The *animals* are part of a phrase beginning with *of*, so they don't count as a subject.) The singular subject requires a singular verb, *has*, making Choice (D) your answer.

2. **B.** The original sentence is actually a *run-on* — two complete thoughts joined by a comma, a grammatical felony. Replace the comma with a semicolon, and you're fine. Choices (C) and (D) correct this, but the extra words *because* and *being that* aren't necessary: Go with Choice (B).

3. **C.** Note the question stem, which asks for the speculative tone of the passage in a concise way. This means use fewer words, but also maintain the original meaning. Each choice is grammatically correct, but Choices (A) and (B) are too wordy, while Choice (D) changes the meaning. Choice (C) is correct as it gets the point across with the fewest words.

4. **B.** *Cultivate* refers to carefully growing, as one would a garden, *propagate* means to create a copy, and *spawn* applies to animals producing offspring. The word you want is *generate*, which means "to cause or produce." The best answer, therefore, is Choice (B).

5. **D.** Sentence 3 clarifies something. It tells you why the *P* wave may be important for the animals' ability to pre-sense an earthquake. Thus, it needs to follow the introduction and definition of the *P* wave in Sentences 4 and 5. Choice (D) is the correct answer.

6. **D.** The table accompanying this passage doesn't show an increase, decrease, or consistent number of annual deaths. One terrible year —2010 — accounted for nearly a quarter million deaths, but other than that, the numbers are all over the place. Choice (D) is best supported by the data. Note that each answer choice to question 6 is grammatically correct.

# Taking It Further

The multiple-choice portion of the SAT Writing and Language Test is usually the easiest score to bring up. Once you know what to look for, it just takes a little practice and time-management to close the gap on this test. Go to the next chapter for that practice, and remember, *this is the time and place for you to make your mistakes.*

# Chapter 6

# Getting It "Write": Practicing the Writing and Language Multiple-Choice Test

Now to try the strategies from Chapter 5. Make your mistakes, lose track of time, miss the parallel verb form — do all those things wrong *here, now,* so that you become aware of your tendency to be human and control this for the big day.

Here are four passages similar to those on the real exam, along with 44 questions divided among them to practice your grammar and style skills. After each passage are the answers and explanations. As you practice, keep track of your strengths and weaknesses. After you find out what tends to stump you, concentrate your attention on those topics. Catch your mistakes to become aware of them, and you'll naturally improve.

TIP

The explanations here will suffice for readers who have studied some grammar, or you can flip back to Chapter 5 for more review. You can also pick up the latest editions of *English Grammar For Dummies* or *English Grammar Workbook For Dummies* by Geraldine Wood, or *1,001 Grammar Practice Questions For Dummies,* authored by me. For more practice taking on the Writing and Language Multiple-Choice Test, check out *1,001 SAT Practice Questions For Dummies.* All these titles are published by Wiley.

## Passage I

Jocelyn Bell says, "that she started by failing." When eleven years old, a standardized na-
   1                                             2
tional exam used in Great Britain to determine a student's academic future proved difficult for

her. Fortunately, her parents believed in her ability to learn. They were also firmly committed

to education. <u>They didn't withdraw her from school. Instead, they enrolled her in boarding school rather than accept an end to her education.</u> Bell went on to earn advanced degrees in
<sub>3</sub>
physics and to make important contributions to her field. Today, she is one of two full-time female professors of physics (out of 150) in Britain.

[1] While she was studying at Cambridge University, Bell, along with her professors and fellow graduate students, <u>has built</u> a radio telescope. [2] Bell's main duty was to analyze data
<sub>4</sub>
from this telescope. [3] She pored over miles of data from the telescope. [4] Her hard work and sharp powers of perception paid off. [5] She discovered some fast and regular bursts of radio waves that she initially called "scruff." [6] <u>She analyzed these radio waves. She ruled out several possible sources, including orbiting satellites and French television broadcasts.</u>
<sub>5</sub>
[7] At one point Bell called them "LGM" — little green men — and considered whether they were signals from alien life forms. [8] Eventually, Bell and her colleagues proved that the "scruff" arose from a particular type of fast-spinning neutron star. [9] The media named the signals, which occurred in predictable patterns, "pulsars." [10] Jocelyn Bell's discovery of the first pulsar, named CP 1919 ("Cambridge Pulsar Number 1919"), was followed by more, some found by Bell herself and others by researchers around the world. [11] <u>A neutron star is a dense mass that comes into existence when an extremely large star explodes.</u>
<sub>6</sub>

In 1974, Jocelyn Bell's professors received the Nobel Prize in Physics, one of the world's most prestigious awards, for their work on pulsars. Because Bell was only a student when she discovered CP 1919, Bell did not share the prize. Some protested this <u>deletion</u>, but Bell did not.
<sub>7</sub>
Student work should not be recognized, she <u>believes</u>, unless there are special circumstances.
<sub>8</sub>
She didn't think that her discovery fell into that category. However, some critics believed that gender bias played a role in the decision to exclude her.

After this early achievement, Jocelyn Bell continued researching and teaching at other universities. <u>She has received many awards in which she studied almost every wave spectrum in astronomy and gained an unusual breadth of experience.</u> At Southampton University,
<sub>9</sub>
she was awarded a grant to study gamma ray astronomy. She also studied and taught X-ray astronomy in London and infrared astronomy in Edinburgh. She currently teaches at the Open University, which enrolls many students who, like Bell, did not pass the traditional exams. <u>Bell's discovery of pulsars was truly impressive.</u>
<sub>10</sub>

**Question 11 asks about the passage as a whole.**

1. **(A)** NO CHANGE
   **(B)** says, "I started by failing."
   **(C)** says "that she started by failing."
   **(D)** started by failing is what she says.

2. **(A)** NO CHANGE
   **(B)** At the age of eleven
   **(C)** When she was eleven years old
   **(D)** When eleven

3. Which of the following best combines the underlined sentences?
   **(A)** Instead of withdrawing her from school, they enrolled her in boarding school rather than accept an end to her education.
   **(B)** Instead of withdrawing her from school and they enrolled her in boarding school and did not accept an end to her education.
   **(C)** They enrolled her in boarding school rather than accept an end to her education.
   **(D)** They enrolled her in boarding school rather than except an end to her education.

4. **(A)** NO CHANGE
   **(B)** built
   **(C)** has been building
   **(D)** have built

5. Which of the following best combines the underlined sentences?
   **(A)** Ruling out several possible sources, including orbiting satellites and French television broadcasts, Bell analyzed these radio waves.
   **(B)** She analyzed these radio waves, she ruled out several possible sources, including orbiting satellites and French television broadcasts.
   **(C)** She analyzed these radio waves, but she ruled out several possible sources, including orbiting satellites and French television broadcasts.
   **(D)** As she analyzed these radio waves, she ruled out several possible sources, including orbiting satellites and French television broadcasts.

6. To make the paragraph most logical, Sentence 11 should be placed
   **(A)** where it is now
   **(B)** after Sentence 7
   **(C)** after Sentence 8
   **(D)** after Sentence 9

7. **(A)** NO CHANGE
   **(B)** exemption
   **(C)** exception
   **(D)** omission

8. **(A)** NO CHANGE
   **(B)** believed
   **(C)** had believed
   **(D)** is believing

9. **(A)** NO CHANGE
   **(B)** Receiving many awards, studying almost every wave spectrum in astronomy and gained an unusual breadth of experience.
   **(C)** She studied almost every wave spectrum in astronomy and gained an unusual breadth of experience, receiving many awards.
   **(D)** She has received many awards and studied almost every wave spectrum in astronomy and gained an unusual breadth of experience.

10. Which of the following best concludes the passage?
    **(A)** NO CHANGE
    **(B)** Indeed, Jocelyn Bell has had a great career.
    **(C)** The young girl who started by failing now helps others achieve success.
    **(D)** Bell should have received a prize for her work.

    **Think about the passage as a whole as you answer question 11.**

11. To lend clarity to the passage, which of the following additions, if any, should be made to the first paragraph?
    **(A)** NO CHANGE
    **(B)** information about the careers of Bell's parents
    **(C)** a detailed description of the exam Bell failed
    **(D)** a history of radio astronomy

# Passage I Answers

1. **B.** Ms. Bell probably didn't say "that she" as part of her quote, so out go Choices (A) and (C). Choice (D) is a run-on sentence, making the correct answer Choice (B).

2. **C.** Who or what was eleven years old? Remember, the modifier goes *near* the noun that it modifies. So if the national exam were 11 years old at the time, the sentence as is would be correct, but it's probably talking about Jocelyn, so it's wrong. Choice (C) correctly includes the word *she,* which clarifies who was 11.

3. **C.** Choice (A) has no grammatical errors, but it's repetitive. *Instead of withdrawing her from school* means exactly the same thing as *rather than accept an end to her education.* One of these statements has to go. Choices (C) and (D) solve the repetition problem, but Choice (D) incorrectly substitutes *except* for *accept.*

4. **B.** The present perfect tense, which is formed with the helping verb *has* or *have,* connects the past to the present. The second paragraph mentions several activities, all in the past. They don't continue into the present, so *has built* is the wrong tense. The simple past tense, *built,* is what you want, making Choice (B) the correct answer.

5. **D.** Choice (A) starts with a *participle* (a verb form used as a description), which is often a fine way to tuck ideas into a sentence. However, Choice (A) doesn't express the same meaning as the original. Choice (B) is a run-on (two complete sentences linked by only a comma), so it's out. Choice (C) is legal in Standard English, but the conjunction *but* signals a change in direction and makes no sense in this sentence. Go for Choice (D), which places two events at the same time with the conjunction *as.*

6. **C.** Sentence 11 defines a neutron star, so it goes best right after Sentence 8, where the term is introduced. This makes Choice (C) the best answer.

7. **D.** Bell wasn't named, so what happened to her wasn't a deletion, which is what you do when you cross out or erase. Because she was never on the prize list, *omission* (the term for something that's overlooked or left out) is a better word.

8. **B.** This event occurred in the past, and even if Bell believes this today, the narrative describes her belief in 1974. "Had believed" is wrong because the sentence doesn't include an event in the past that happened after this.

9. **C.** The original sentence doesn't quite make sense because of the phrase *in which.* To fix the sentence, you have many options. Choice (B) doesn't work because it's not a complete sentence. Choice (D) strings together a bunch of ideas with the word *and.* Choice (C) is the best.

10. **C.** The best addition to the end of the passage is Choice (C). The passage comes full circle with this added sentence, a nice bookend to *she started by failing* in the first paragraph.

11. **A.** The passage focuses on Bell and her achievements. Her parents played a role in Bell's life, of course, but they're not the stars of this piece. Therefore, you can rule out Choice (B). The fact that Bell failed a standardized test (she didn't have this book) is an interesting detail, but it isn't important enough to warrant more on the exam, so Choice (C) is out. Radio astronomy is Bell's field, but because the focus at this point is Bell's achievement, you don't need to know anything beyond the fact that she made a significant discovery.

# Passage II

[1]

The prevalence of screens may be a contributing factor to the epidemic of sleep disorders we are now witnessing. According to one researcher, "The higher use of these potentially sleep-disruptive technologies among younger generations may have serious consequences for physical health, cognitive development, and other measures of well-being." Artificial light, including glowing screens, <u>suppress</u> melatonin, a hormone that aids sleep. When a person
12
looks at a screen during the hour before bedtime, <u>they may</u> become more alert and find it
13
harder to fall asleep.

[2]

<u>Sleep deprivation is a problem. Sleep deprivation has been linked to a number of health issues, such as obesity, high blood pressure, irregular heartbeat, cancer, and diabetes.</u> Lack of
14
sleep also damages the immune system, which protects the body from infection. Tired people are more likely to have car accidents or make mistakes at work; many medical errors and industrial disasters <u>are the result of</u> sleep deprivation. One study found that drivers
15
<u>younger than 25</u> were more likely to fall asleep while behind the wheel, a particularly
16
<u>exciting</u> number given that these drivers may not be able to react from instinct if they sud-
17
denly awake in a dangerous traffic situation. Students don't learn as well if they lack sufficient rest. <u>Research subjects, who slept after learning a new task, retained</u> the knowledge
18
and scored higher on tests than those who did not sleep. Scientists say that this "memory consolidation" takes place during sleep; for this reason babies, who learn at a phenomenal rate, need more sleep than adults. According to the National Institutes of Health, elementary school children need at least 10 hours of sleep a night, teens 9 to 10 hours, and adults 7 to 8 hours. Yet in a recent year, nearly 30% of adults reported that they slept less than 6 hours a night, and only 31% of high school students got at least 8 hours of sleep on an average week-day night.

[3]

Sleep deprivation is caused by many factors. A condition called apnea is <u>another</u>. Someone
19
with apnea stops breathing while asleep and wakes up gasping for air many times each night. Work schedules, which may <u>swing</u>, and the assumption that employees will check e-mail or
20
be on call even when they're not physically at the office are also problems. Working more, though, is not the same as working efficiently. Researchers in Finland studied 4,000 men and

women for a period of 7 years. The number of sick days was remarkably higher for those who slept less than 6 hours or more than 9 hours a night. Researchers caution that underlying illness may cause lack of sleep or superfluous sleep, not the other way around. <u>Consequently,</u>[21] sleeping an adequate amount of time is clearly important.

**Question 22 asks about the passage as a whole.**

## Percentage of Adults in the United States Reporting Sleep Behaviors

| Age (in Years) | Fell Asleep Unintentionally During the Day at Least Once During the Past Month | Fell Asleep while Driving in the Past Month |
|---|---|---|
| 18 to 25 | 43.7 | 4.5 |
| 25 to 35 | 36.1 | 7.2 |
| 35 to 45 | 34.0 | 5.7 |
| 45 to 55 | 35.3 | 3.9 |
| 55 to 65 | 36.5 | 3.1 |
| 65 and up | 44.6 | 2.0 |

*Source: Centers for Disease Control*

12. **(A)** NO CHANGE
    **(B)** has suppressed
    **(C)** suppresses
    **(D)** are suppressing

13. **(A)** NO CHANGE
    **(B)** he or she may
    **(C)** you may
    **(D)** one may

14. How should the underlined sentences be combined?
    **(A)** Sleep deprivation is a problem; sleep deprivation has been linked to a number of health issues, such as obesity, high blood pressure, irregular heartbeat, cancer, and diabetes.
    **(B)** Sleep deprivation is a problem, and sleep deprivation has been linked to a number of health issues, such as obesity, high blood pressure, irregular heartbeat, cancer, and diabetes.
    **(C)** Sleep deprivation, a problem, which has been linked to a number of health issues, such as obesity, high blood pressure, irregular heartbeat, cancer, and diabetes.
    **(D)** Sleep deprivation is a problem that has been linked to a number of health issues, such as obesity, high blood pressure, irregular heartbeat, cancer, and diabetes.

**15.** **(A)** NO CHANGE
   **(B)** result from
   **(C)** are the results from
   **(D)** result when there is

**16.** Which of the following is best supported by the data in the table?
   **(A)** NO CHANGE
   **(B)** between 25 and 35
   **(C)** between 35 and 55
   **(D)** older than 55

**17.** **(A)** NO CHANGE
   **(B)** agitating
   **(C)** disturbing
   **(D)** moving

**18.** **(A)** NO CHANGE
   **(B)** Research subjects who slept after learning a new task retained
   **(C)** Research subjects, who slept after learning a new task retained
   **(D)** After learning a new task and sleeping, research subjects

**19.** **(A)** NO CHANGE
   **(B)** another one
   **(C)** one
   **(D)** an additional one

**20.** **(A)** NO CHANGE
   **(B)** fluctuate
   **(C)** adapt
   **(D)** reorganize

**21.** **(A)** NO CHANGE
   **(B)** However
   **(C)** Nevertheless
   **(D)** As a result

**22.** To make the passage most logical, Paragraph 2 should be placed
   **(A)** where it is now
   **(B)** before Paragraph 1
   **(C)** after aragraph 3
   **(D)** DELETE the paragraph.

# Passage II Answers

**12. C.** The subject of the sentence is *light,* not *screens.* Because *light* is singular, it pairs with the singular verb *suppresses.* Choices (B) and (C) are singular, but the simple present tense (Choice [C]) is best for an ongoing action.

**13. B.** In the first part of this sentence, *a person* is a singular, third-person expression. (*Third person* means talking about someone.) The pronoun *they* is plural, so it doesn't match *a person.* Choice (B) substitutes the singular pronouns *he or she* and is the correct answer. The pronoun *you* or *one* don't match *a person.*

**14. D.** Choices (A) and (B) are grammatically correct but unnecessarily repeat *sleep deprivation.* Choice (C) eliminates the repetition but isn't a complete sentence. Choice (D), the best answer, eliminates the repetition and creates a complete sentence.

**15. B.** Short, sweet, and complete — these are the qualities you want in writing, and Choice (B) provides them.

**16. B.** Look at the table and stick with the column on the right, which shows the percentage of drivers who reported falling asleep while behind the wheel: 7.2 percent of drivers ages 25 to 35, which is the highest of the ranges listed. This matches Choice (B).

**17. C.** The thought of all those drivers snoozing at 65 miles an hour would certainly keep anyone up at night, so it's *disturbing. Exciting* is for something good, *agitating* refers to bringing about anger (which may be relevant but doesn't fit here), and *moving* suggests emotion (also relevant but not in this sentence).

**18. B.** Not all *research subjects retained* knowledge, only those *who slept after learning a new task.* The description *who slept after learning a new task* is essential to your understanding of the sentence and shouldn't be surrounded by commas, so Choice (B) is correct.

**19. B.** Paragraph 1 discusses one cause of sleep problems (too much screen time), Paragraph 3 returns to the topic of causes, and Paragraph 2 covers the consequences of sleep deprivation. The logical flow improves when you place Paragraphs 1 and 3 next to each other. Choice (B) does so by moving Paragraph 2 to the beginning of the passage.

**20. C.** The first sentence of the paragraph refers to *many factors.* Because no *factor* is cited, *another* makes little sense. *One* (Choice [C]), on the other hand, simply introduces the concept of *apnea.*

**21. B.** If you were inserting a word into the sentence to replace *swing,* you might choose *change,* because here you need a general word that allows for different times of day, days of the week, and number of hours. *Swing* involves movement and change, but it works better for physical motion. Choice (B), *fluctuate,* is a synonym for *change* and is the answer you seek.

**22. C.** At this point, a *joining* transition is best, not a *resulting* or *contrast* transition.

# Passage III

On the stage, the actor bowed his head. The setting was a prison cell. <u>The actor began to tell his fellow inmates a story. The story was about a man, a man from the region of La Man-cha, Spain.</u>
23
Soon the set <u>reformed</u> into a country inn and the character, Don Quixote, came
24
to life.

Don Quixote is the central figure in *Man of La Mancha*, a Broadway play. The character is based on the novel *Don Quixote*, written by Miguel de Cervantes in the 16th century. The novel is loosely based on Cervantes' life story. <u>Having been born</u> in 1547 in Alcala de Henares, a
25
small city near Madrid, Cervantes grew up in poverty. Little is known of Cervantes' education, though some say he attended the University of Salamanca. Around 1570 Cervantes enlisted in the Spanish navy and <u>soon after</u> was wounded in the Battle of Lepanto. In his autobiography,
26
Cervantes wrote that he "had lost the movement of the left hand for the glory of the right," a pun based on the fact that <u>Cervantes he believed that</u> he was fighting for what was right.
27
He added, "If my wounds have no beauty . . . they are, at least, honorable in the estimation of those who know where they were received, for the soldier shows to greater advantage dead in battle than alive in flight."

After Lepanto, Cervantes <u>fought battles</u> and was captured by pirates and taken to Algiers,
28
where he was enslaved for five years. He was freed after ransom was paid, and he <u>returned to Spain and devoting</u> much of his time to writing while he worked as an accountant and tax
29
collector. He died in 1616; his novels and plays were only moderately successful. <u>His book *Don Quixote* is his most well-known novel.</u>
30

Today Miguel de Cervantes is recognized as one of the first great novelists. *Don Quixote*, <u>noted</u> a masterpiece, has inspired generations of writers and many modern reinterpretations,
31
such as Broadway's *Man of La Mancha*. The title character is a country gentleman obsessed with the age of chivalry. He puts on rusty armor, mounts a broken-down old horse, <u>and riding</u> off in search of adventure with a peasant, Sancho Panza, as his squire. Don Quixote
32
lives in a world of illusion, seeing windmills as murderous giants and a shaving basin as a gold helmet. Cervantes intended his novel as a satire of chivalric romances, a style of writing popular in his time. For centuries, <u>though</u>, *Don Quixote* has been a symbol of the human need
33
for idealistic heroes, willing to risk their lives to do what is right.

23. How should the underlined sentences best be combined?

    (A) The actor began to tell his fellow inmates a story about a man from La Mancha, Spain.

    (B) The actor began to tell his fellow inmates a story, which was about a man, and the man from the region of La Mancha, Spain.

    (C) Telling his fellow inmates a story, the actor spoke about a man who was from the region of La Mancha, Spain.

    (D) The actor began to tell his fellow inmates a story, that was about a man, from the region of La Mancha, Spain.

24. (A) NO CHANGE
    (B) transformed
    (C) dissolved
    (D) redesigned

25. (A) NO CHANGE
    (B) Being born
    (C) Born
    (D) He was born

26. (A) NO CHANGE
    (B) soon after he had enlisted
    (C) more time went by when he
    (D) after

27. (A) NO CHANGE
    (B) Cervantes believed that
    (C) Cervantes, what he believed was that
    (D) DELETE the underlined portion.

28. (A) NO CHANGE
    (B) was fighting battles
    (C) went on to battles, where he fought
    (D) fought other battles

29. (A) NO CHANGE
    (B) returning to Spain and devoting much of his time
    (C) returned to Spain where he was devoting much of his time
    (D) returned to Spain and devoted much of his time

30. Which of the following best supports the logic and flow of the passage?

   **(A)** NO CHANGE

   **(B)** Cervantes never knew the recognition that he and his works would achieve.

   **(C)** The ransom paid for his release was significant.

   **(D)** The Ottoman Empire suffered a defeat in the Battle of Lepanto.

31. **(A)** NO CHANGE

   **(B)** regarded

   **(C)** seen

   **(D)** deemed

32. **(A)** NO CHANGE

   **(B)** he rides

   **(C)** and he rides

   **(D)** and rides

33. **(A)** NO CHANGE

   **(B)** therefore

   **(C)** moreover

   **(D)** afterwards

# Passage III Answers

23. **A.** The first three choices are grammatically correct, but Choice (A) is the most concise. Choice (D) has unnecessary commas.

24. **B.** The set changed completely, or *transformed*, from a jail cell to a country inn, so Choice (B) is correct. The original word, *reformed*, refers to something *repaired*, and *dissolved* is an artificial visual effect that doesn't happen during a live performance. Choice (D) fails because the set isn't being *redesigned* during the show. The design process took place before the play began.

25. **C.** The introductory verb form, a *participle*, gives you information about Cervantes. The simple participle, *born*, is better than *having been born* or *being born*. The more complicated forms imply a time line (*Having sealed the envelope, Kerinna couldn't insert the photo*) or a cause-and-effect relationship between the statements in the sentence (*Being forgetful, Kerinna relied on her planner to track her appointments*). You don't need either situation here, because the events of Cervantes' youth (birth and growing up in poverty) are simply listed. The order is understood (how can you grow up before you're born?), and one event didn't cause the other.

26. **A.** The original phrase establishes the order of events clearly and concisely, so no change is needed.

**27. B.** The original is faulty because the pronoun *he* should replace the noun *Cervantes*, not sit next to it in the sentence. Choices (B) and (D) both solve the problem. Dropping the whole expression, though, changes the meaning — something you shouldn't do on the SAT. *Cervantes believed* is important information, because those he fought may have had an entirely different view of the situation.

**28. D.** The passage says that Cervantes fought in the Battle of Lepanto, but the statement that he *fought battles* implies a new activity. Add *other*, as in Choice (D), and the situation becomes clear.

**29. D.** In this parallel expression, the verbs must be in the same tense. The original has *returned* and *devoting*, so that's out. Changing *devoting* to *devoted*, as Choice (D) does, solves the problem. Are you wondering why you can't change *returned* to *returning*, as Choice (B) offers? The new version of an underlined portion of the sentence must fit smoothly with everything else in the sentence. *He returning* doesn't work as a subject-verb pair.

**30. B.** The paragraph describes Cervantes's career, and Choice (B) concludes this thought by mentioning his posthumus recognition. Choice (A) introduces *Don Quixote*, but this isn't needed until the next paragraph. Choices (C) and (D) are both extraneous and out of place: The detail isn't needed for this narrative, and discussions of both the ransom and the battle were concluded earlier in the passage.

**31. D.** The concept you need here is *judged* or *considered*. Those aren't answer choices, but a synonym, *deemed*, is, so Choice (D) is your answer. Did you fall for Choices (B) or (C)? Those words include the right idea, but they need the word *as* (*regarded as, seen as*) to work.

**32. D.** In this parallel sentence, each verb must match. The three verbs in the original (*puts, mounts, riding*) don't match, so *riding* has to go. You don't want a subject for the third verb, because they're all paired with the initial *he*. If you stick another *he* in front of *rides*, your list is *he puts, mounts, he rides*, which has other problems.

**33. A.** This sentence describes a *contrast* between Cervantes' intention and the actual effect of his novel. The word *though* is a *contrast* transition signaling a change in direction.

# Passage IV

On October 16, 1962, the United States Secretary of State informed President John F. Kennedy that American spy planes <u>discovered</u> a construction site in Cuba. Analysts determined
34

that it was a base to launch long-range nuclear missiles <u>capable of reaching all of the United</u>
35

<u>States</u>, much of South America, and most of Canada. <u>Cuba a communist country about 90</u>

<u>miles from the southern tip of Florida was</u> an ally of the Soviet Union, which at the time was
36

engaged in a cold war with the United States.

For one week the President and his advisors debated several possible potential strategies. The U.S. could invade Cuba, bomb the missile bases, establishing a naval blockade around the island, or deal with the Soviet Union diplomatically. Within a few days, aerial photographs showed more missile launching sites, with 16 to 32 missiles in place.

Alternately, Kennedy called Nikita Khrushchev, the Soviet leader, to tell him that the United States was surrounding Cuba with warships, and creating a ring around the island. He told Khrushchev, "I have not assumed that you or any other sane man would, in this nuclear age, deliberately plunge the world into war, which it is crystal clear no country could win and which could only result in catastrophic consequences to the whole world, including the aggressor." Kennedy informed the American public on October 22nd of the missiles and the United States' demand that they be stripped. The next day, Soviet submarines moved toward Cuba, also most ships carrying building material for the bases stopped en route. One ship, an oil tanker, continued its journey.

[1] The world waited. [2] What if a Soviet ship challenged the blockade and fired on an American vessel? [3] Would full-scale war break out? [4] No ships fired, but in Cuba construction work continued. [5] At least some of the missiles were launch-ready. [6] On October 27, Robert Kennedy, the Attorney-General and brother of the President, met secretly with the Soviet ambassador. [7] They reached an agreement, the United States promised not to invade Cuba, and the Soviet Union agreed to remove its missiles from Cuba. [8] The U.S. agreed to remove some of its missiles from Turkey, a country close to the Soviet Union. [9] As Kennedy noted in his conversation with Khrushchev, no one could have won a nuclear war.

The blockade was lifted, and the world breathed a sigh of relief. Nuclear war had been averted. In June 1963, Kennedy referred to the crisis, saying, "In the final analysis, our most basic common link is that we all inhabit this small planet. We all breathe the same air. We all cherish our children's future. And we are all mortal."

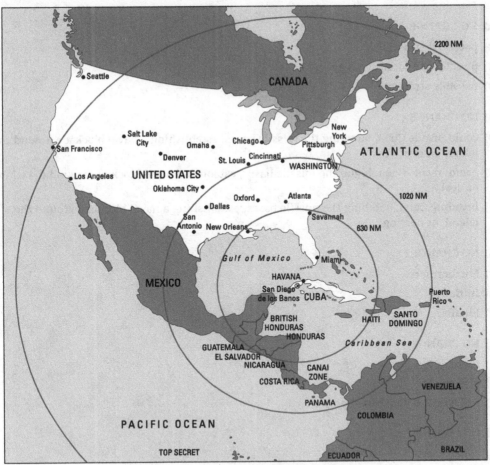

*Circles show the range of various missiles based in Cuba*

Source: JFK Library

34. (A) NO CHANGE
    (B) had discovered
    (C) have discovered
    (D) did discover

35. Which of the following is best supported by the information in the graphic?

    (A) NO CHANGE
    (B) capable of reaching most of the United States
    (C) capable of reaching some of the United States
    (D) not capable of reaching the United States

36. (A) NO CHANGE
    (B) Cuba was a communist country about 90 miles from the southern tip of Florida was
    (C) Cuba a communist country about 90 miles from the southern tip of Florida, was
    (D) Cuba, a communist country about 90 miles from the southern tip of Florida, was

37. **(A)** NO CHANGE

   **(B)** potential strategies

   **(C)** possible potential strategy

   **(D)** possible strategy

38. **(A)** NO CHANGE

   **(B)** could invade Cuba, bombing the missile bases, establishing a naval blockade around the island, or deal

   **(C)** could invade Cuba, bomb the missile bases, establish a naval blockade around the island, or deal

   **(D)** invading Cuba, bombing the missile bases, establishing a naval blockade around the island, or dealing

39. **(A)** NO CHANGE

   **(B)** Furthermore

   **(C)** Initially

   **(D)** Finally

40. **(A)** NO CHANGE

   **(B)** thereby

   **(C)** effectively

   **(D)** DELETE the underlined portion

41. **(A)** NO CHANGE

   **(B)** consequently

   **(C)** but

   **(D)** furthermore

42. **(A)** NO CHANGE

   **(B)** They reached an agreement; the United States promised not to invade Cuba, and

   **(C)** Reaching an agreement where the United States promised not to invade Cuba, and

   **(D)** They reached an agreement. The United States promised not to invade Cuba,

43. **(A)** NO CHANGE

   **(B)** crisis, and he said

   **(C)** crisis, at which time he said

   **(D)** crisis, and took the opportunity to say

44. To best support the logical flow of the paragraph, Sentence 9 should be placed

   **(A)** where it is now

   **(B)** before Sentence 1

   **(C)** after Sentence 3

   **(D)** after Sentence 7

# Passage IV Answers

**34.** **B.** The past action *discovered the site* happened before the past action *informed the President*, so the helping verb *had* correctly places this. *Have* in Choice (C) suggests that the spy planes were discovering the site right until the Secretary informed the President.

**35.** **B.** The map shows that most, but not all, of the United States was in range of Cuban missiles. The Pacific Northwest lies beyond the edge of the largest circle. Only Choice (B) accurately reflects this.

**36.** **D.** The information that Cuba is *a communist country about 90 miles from the southern tip of Florida* is interesting, but it's not essential. In grammar terms, an *essential* element identifies what it describes. You already know the passage is about Cuba. *Nonessential* elements should be set off from the rest of the sentence by commas, as in Choice (D).

**37.** **B.** *Possible* and *potential* are synonyms, so you don't need both. The word *several* indicates that you need *strategies* (plural), not *strategy* (singular). Choice (B) works best.

**38.** **C.** When you see a list, think about *parallelism.* The original list of verbs *(invade, bomb, establishing, deal)* is faulty. *Establishing* doesn't fit. Change that verb to *establish,* as in Choice (C), and you're fine. Did you select Choice (D)? The list matches, but changing everything to the *-ing* form creates another problem, because then the sentence has no subject-verb pair.

**39.** **D.** The transition *finally* places the action — Kennedy calling Khrushchev — as the final step of the U.S. response to the discovery of the missiles. The narrative after this shifts to the Soviet action.

**40.** **D.** The original sentence creates a run-on sentence, with no subject to the verb *creating.* The other three answer choices fix this, but they all say the same thing — with Choice (D) using the fewest words. Always go for the fewest words if the meaning of the sentence stays intact.

**41.** **C.** The Soviet submarines moved toward Cuba, which is one action, while the ships carrying building materials stopped, which is another action. The contrast transition "but" works best here.

**42.** **B.** The original is a run-on, with one complete sentence tacked onto another with just a comma. To solve the problem, change the comma to a semicolon. Did Choice (D) catch your eye? That selection illustrates the importance of reading carefully. The period after *agreement* solves one problem, but the deletion of *and* from the end creates another run-on.

**43.** **A.** The original is concise and correct. No changes needed.

**44.** **C.** The sentence goes best after the rhetorical question, *Would a full-scale war break out?* It transitions from the world waiting suspensefully to the actions that followed.

IN THIS CHAPTER

» Determining whether to tackle the essay

» Understanding what the essay scorers look for

» Planning and writing your essay for maximum points

» Looking at writing techniques

» Evaluating your essay according to SAT standards

# Chapter 7

# Preparing for the Essay

The SAT ends with an optional essay assignment. You can add 50 minutes to the end of your SAT by writing the essay, or you can stop and go home. By the way, your words will probably flow from a No. 2 pencil onto paper. The College Board has toyed with computer-based testing, but as of this writing, it's almost all on paper. In this chapter, you find information on the standard SAT essay format and the best approach to this section, along with a sample question and answers.

## Deciding Whether to Actually Write the Essay

Why in the world would you write this? The exam alone is four hours of prison, with check-in and breaks, on an early Saturday morning. It'll be afternoon by the time you get to the essay assignment. Who would want to add an hour of writing? With a pencil!

Here's why: Your target school may require the essay. Does it? It's up to you to find out. Check with the admissions office, or try this link: https://collegereadiness.collegeboard.org/sat/register/college-essay-policies.

If you're using the print edition of this book to supercharge your SAT skills (as opposed to an e-version where you can click or tap the link), just do a search on Collegboard.org for the college essay policies. This link takes you to a page listing most major schools and whether they recommend or require the essay. Some schools ignore it, but others won't accept your application without it.

# Knowing the Assignment

The essay instruction doesn't change. It's split into two parts, one before and one after a passage that is about 700 words long. You basically get instructions, then a passage to read, then more instructions. The passage is typically an opinion piece, making an argument for a particular point of view or to take a certain action on a real-life situation.

Before the passage is a box with the first part of the instructions, which reads something like this (except with the name of the author in place of "Author"):

As you read the passage, consider how Author uses

- Evidence, such as facts or examples, to support the claims

- Reasoning to develop ideas and to connect claims and evidence

- Stylistic or persuasive elements, such as word choice or appeals to emotion, to add power to the ideas expressed

Then comes the passage, 700 or so words of the author's persuasive argument. Usually it's a plea for funding or for you to take social or ethical responsibility. Your task is *not* to discuss whether you agree or how you feel about the passage. Instead, you discuss *how well* the author makes his or her point. More on that later.

Following the passage is another box with instructions. It looks like this, only the author's name replaces "Author" and a brief recap of the narrative replaces the blank:

Write an essay in which you explain how Author constructs an argument to persuade the reader that _____. In your essay, discuss how Author uses one or more of the elements of style listed above, or other elements, to strengthen the logic and persuasiveness of Author's argument. Focus on the most important features of the passage. Do not explain whether you agree or disagree with Author's ideas. Instead, concentrate on how Author builds a persuasive case.

This two-part prompt looks complicated, but it's not. Your job is to analyze the author's argument and, most important, to discuss the writing techniques the author employs to convince readers of his or her point of view. Don't worry about reading the prompt on the exam. Read it now. It doesn't really change, and neither does your approach.

# Knowing What the Essay Scorers Look For

The SAT has a cadre of English teachers who specialize in scoring the essays. It's probably a sizeable lineup — about 2.2 million SATs are given each year — but these teachers look for specific points in your writing. An image of each essay is also posted on the web, where colleges that you apply to can view it. (One reason it's so important to write neatly.)

Two scorers independently evaluate each essay. If their assessments differ, then a third scorer chimes in, but this isn't likely because what they look for is specific — which is good! If you know what they look for, and how to write to it, then the essay is something you can do well. Anyway, each grader awards 1 to 4 points in each of three categories, giving you a range of 2 to 8 points per category, for a max of 24 points overall:

>> **8 points for Analysis:** You evaluate the author's use of evidence, logic, and persuasive techniques. In other words, can you explain how well the author makes his or her point? Describe this by citing specific lines from the passage.

>> **8 points for Reading:** You comprehend the main idea of the passage, noting details and their relationship to the main idea and grasping the structure of the passage. Basically, do you understand what the author is getting at? Show this by describing the big-picture impact of what the author is describing.

>> **8 points for Writing:** Support your statements in a well-organized essay that employs evidence (from the passage) and shows mature writing style (varied sentence patterns, consistent tone, grammatically correct sentences) and higher-level vocabulary. Basically, can you write at the college level? Practice this by writing the practice essay assignments from this book and reviewing feedback on your AP essays, which also evaluate this skill.

Here are more details to help you understand what SAT–graders are looking for:

>> **Do you understand the subtleties of the passage?** Most people get the main idea, but to rise to the top of the scoring chart, you have to dig into the small stuff. Graders look for at least three or four specific points about the author's argument. Check for exceptions to the principle the author argues for. Note the time frame (in modern society, in the last two years, looking to the future, and so forth). Examine the context: what special situation(s) the author describes (within a family, worldwide, and everything in between; person-to-person or on social media, and the like). If the passage expresses a disagreement with a popular position, where exactly does the author's stance fall, and why?

>> **Can you analyze how each element of style contributes to the message?** The scorers don't want a list; they want an analysis. If you've explained how word choice or an anecdote or metaphor affects the reader, you're doing well. For example, if the author compares a happy memory to a diamond, the memory is precious and never goes away. A memory compared to a fluffy cloud suggests beauty and haziness, meaning it may drift from consciousness. These observations bring points to your essay.

>> **Is your essay organized, moving logically from one idea to the next?** Make sure that when you write, one paragraph leads clearly to the next. A middle-of-the-road essay doesn't have good flow, and a poor essay leaves readers wandering around without a clue. Transitions strengthen the logical chain. If you begin a paragraph with *however, nevertheless,* or a similar word, you signal an exception to the point you just made. *Also, then, moreover,* and the like tell the reader that you're building on an idea you just expressed. Transitions are easy to use and provide helpful markers for your graders.

>> **Is your vocabulary at the college level?** Academic writing is formal, so stay away from slang. Your word choice should show variety, and try using some college-level words. Good words to tuck away for the essay are *antipathy* (a strong dislike of people), *adroit* (skilled and clever), *discrete* (separate and isolated), *egregious* (totally inappropriate), *laudatory* (praiseworthy), and *paragon* (peak of excellence). You don't need that many words — just a few good ones like some Frisbees on a roof.

>> **Is your writing fluent, with varied sentence structure?** An excellent essay matches sentence structure and meaning. Less important ideas, for example, show up in subordinate clauses, and main ideas appear in independent clauses. An acceptable but unremarkable essay strays only occasionally from the usual subject-verb-object pattern. In a poor essay, the sentences are short and choppy.

>> **Is your writing grammatical, with good spelling and punctuation?** This one is simple: Follow the rules of Standard English, and your score rises. Some mistakes are okay — the scorers know this is a rough draft — but too many mistakes would be *egregious* (defined in the fourth bullet). Also: If you don't know how to spell a word, *use a different word.* And if grammar isn't your strong point, turn to Chapter 5 for help.

**REMEMBER**

No one writes a perfect essay, especially as a rough draft, and certainly not under the pressure of a high-stakes exam. The essay scorers understand this. They're looking for a good first draft with thoughtful and accomplished writing. Relax and write what makes sense to you based on the guidance and strategies in this chapter, and your essay will be fine.

# Getting Started

The silver lining is that to write two to three pages, the SAT gives you 50 minutes, which is plenty of time. Be sure to plan and sketch an outline before you begin. As long as you hit the points that the essay scorers look for, your essay will do well, and hitting those points is easy if you know what to do. At this point you will have endured four hours of SAT, so you'll need to know these steps fairly well, which means, yes, practice. Start with about five minutes to prepare your notes and outline. The exam booklet is your scratch paper, so use this to mark up the passage and take your notes. Nothing you write on the test booklet or the passage counts toward your score, so go crazy and mark it up. Here's what to do:

**1.** **Read the passage while marking it up and making notes.**

You're looking for two things:

- **Any type of persuasive element:** Underline any visual imagery (a story about puppies), empirical evidence (Earth's population is 9 billion), predictions (Earth's population will reach 12 billion), reasoning (Billy *must* have taken the cookies), or any other instrument that the author uses to drive an idea into your head. You'll use these elements to collect your Analysis points.

- **Any type of big-picture impact:** Circle anything that could go beyond what the author describes. If the author writes that there are too many puppies, circle that and write a note off to the side that they will grow into dogs that chase all the cats. If the author writes that earth's population is growing, circle that and note that there's plenty of space in the Midwest. If the author writes that Billy took all those cookies, circle that and note that he'd better exercise or he'll get diabetes. You'll use these elements to show that you understand the passage and collect your Reading points.

Here's how to do this well:

- **Stay within the idea of the passage.** If the passage is about funding space exploration, and you circle the part about breathing technology, don't note that it helps scuba divers. That's out of scope. Note instead that the breathing technology may reduce allergies in space.

- **Focus on the main points.** Avoid expanding on the small details. If you're not sure, circle and note it anyway, because you don't have to use it. But keep in mind you're looking for key ideas, not minutiae.

- **Don't echo what the author has already written.** If the author writes that breathing technology has further benefits such as reducing illnesses in space, you can't use that too — you have to think of something else. The purpose is to demonstrate that you fully understand what the author is getting at, not that you can copy the ideas.

- **You may note more than you use.** This is a good thing. As you write, in the next step, you'll pick and choose the best points for your essay.

2. **Make an outline.**

At this point, you understand the essay well enough to know mostly what you're going to write. Think of how you'd explain to someone the method that the author is using to make a point. Jot down the persuasive elements that you underlined and number them. You may also number them in the passage instead of jotting them down.

3. **Write the introduction.**

The first word can be the hardest to write, but in the words of that athletics company: *Just do it.* It doesn't have to be fancy. Just tell the story. Restate the author's main point, including whatever is happening that drove the author to write this piece and propose a solution. You can also mention that the author uses certain persuasive elements.

4. **Start the first body paragraph for Reading points.**

Now you scoop up all the parts of the passage that you circled and annotated! Each paragraph that you write is based on one or two paragraphs from the passage. Start by paraphrasing the author's ideas that you circled and describe the notes you made on the impact of those ideas. Cite the passage by using the numbered paragraphs: "In Paragraph 2, the author says This, which may lead to That." Boom: Reading points.

5. **Add to that body paragraph for Analysis points.**

Next you harvest the parts of the passage that you underlined. Describe the persuasive elements that the author uses to drive home the ideas that you just wrote about. Are there metaphors and analogy, visual imagery, empirical evidence, predictions, and appeals for reasoning? Describe both the author's persuasive method and the effect it may have on the audience. Cite the passage. Bam: Analysis points.

6. **Keep writing the paragraph.**

If you struggle to get more than a few lines from the previous two steps, add a couple lines on why the author's point is so important and what could go wrong if the ideas aren't followed. For example, if the author writes about the importance of bringing water on a hike, add a few lines on enjoying the hike and not being distracted by dehydration.

**REMEMBER**

You're not supposed to agree or disagree with the author's perspective: You're supposed to analyze the presentation. When you expand on the author's idea, don't make it sound like your own take on it! Instead, write something like, "The author would probably consider that . . ." or "agree that . . ."

7. **Write the other body paragraphs.**

Rinse and repeat Steps 4 through 6 for your Reading and Analysis points, and use the guidance earlier in this chapter for your Writing points.

8. **At 12 minutes to go: Write the conclusion.**

A conclusion restates the introduction, so basically copy and reword the introduction. By now you know the essay better, so you can write a more robust conclusion.

9. **At 7 minutes to go: Proof your essay.**

Read through your essay and make sure your writing is clear. Also check your grammar. Look for misspelled words, wordy sentences, repetition, and anything else that should be corrected. Correct each mistake by crossing it out *neatly,* placing a caret (^), and writing the correction above it or to the side. If you want to add a phrase, place an asterisk (*) where the phrase would go and write the phrase at the bottom, with another asterisk to connect it. If you add more phrases, just use different marks. Don't worry about the essay scorers frowning at your markups: They'll appreciate that you took the time to check your work, and your essay will be better! This step *will* improve your score.

**REMEMBER**

You don't have time to rewrite anything. Just clean it up before the clock runs out. Also, whatever you add on proofing has to go within the writing box on each page of the essay answer sheet. Anything outside that box isn't captured.

**TIP**

No one writes a perfect essay, so don't try to. Just hit all the points and write clearly, and you'll do fine. Practice these steps, and you'll be able to write this essay even while under pressure at the end of a four-hour exam session.

# Identifying Other Writing Techniques in the Passage

Certain techniques are common in persuasive writing. Here are more things to look for when you mark up the passage.

## Appeals to logic, authority, and emotion

Ancient Greeks, who valued the art of persuasion, named three general strategies for argument:

» **Logos** is an appeal to logic or reason. Factual evidence and examples may be part of logos. Perhaps the writer cites statistics on the rate of car crashes when the speed limit is lowered and refers to accident rates in neighboring areas with different traffic laws.

» **Ethos** relies on the character and qualifications of the writer (perhaps a highway patrol officer who regularly handled crash sites), or, in some cases, quotations from experts (perhaps urban planners). Look for references to authorities on the subject if you suspect that the writer is relying on *ethos* to make a point.

» **Pathos** hits the emotions. The writer may present a story about one particular accident victim, hoping to tug the readers' heartstrings.

You can probably find these in the SAT passage.

## Diction and tone

*Diction*, or word choice, may have a huge effect on the reader's reaction. Consider the difference between "privacy" and "loneliness" in an essay about solitude. One of those words (privacy) creates a positive impression, and the other (loneliness) a negative one.

*Tone* is influenced by the way the words are put together (*syntax*, in English-teacher terminology). Sophisticated vocabulary and sentence structure tells you that the writer sees the reader as educated and aware; simpler vocabulary and shorter, more straightforward sentences may create a "just us folks" impression of innocence. Irony contributes to tone also. If the writer says one thing, knowing that the reader receives the opposite impression, the tone may be sarcastic or mocking. Check for tone by "hearing" the passage in your mind.

**TIP**

As you read the passage for main ideas and persuasive elements, also mark any words or sentences that indicate the aforementioned Greek strategies or diction and tone. In your essay, mention the style and any variations, along with any effect these may have on the reader.

# Organization

A good author always has a plan to organize the arguments — and SAT essay passages come from good authors. Your job is to figure out the underlying structure, or organizing principle, for the material. Mark these techniques if you see them in the passage:

>> **Comparison:** In an argument about lowering the speed limit, you may see accident rates in Germany compared to those in the United States, a paragraph describing differing driving patterns or laws, and so forth.

>> **Cause and effect:** You may find a paragraph (or an entire passage) about the consequences of a particular action. Continuing the speed limit example, you would see that a law was passed changing the speed limit from 65 to 55 miles per hour, and statistics on the decrease in traffic fatalities.

>> **Observations and conclusions:** You may read seemingly random facts that gradually forge a chain of logic drawing the reader to the writer's point of view.

>> **Chronological order:** The author describes series of events, in order, perhaps extrapolating into the future. This organizational tactic may be coupled with cause and effect or observations and conclusions.

>> **Concession and reply:** This tactic appears when the author assumes that the reader doesn't agree with the argument. This writing technique acknowledges and responds to the opposing point of view. Using the speed-limit example mentioned in the first bullet point, the author may concede that driver inattention has more influence on the accident rate than speed limits do. Then the writer will go on to argue that lower speed limits save *some* lives and are therefore still desirable.

# Other techniques

Keep your pencil out for these style points, which show up often in arguments:

>> **Repetition:** Normally, writers avoid repetition. When you see repetition of words or a set of strikingly similar expressions, figure out what the writer is emphasizing. For example, a section of the Declaration of Independence lists the actions of King George III that the colonists object to. The writer uses the expression "he has" more than 20 times. The result resembles a criminal indictment. Each time you read "he has," the King seems more and more nefarious.

>> **Parallel structure:** When a string of similar elements makes an appearance, the items on the list have equal weight and importance. The same holds true for comparisons.

>> **Figurative language:** Imaginative comparisons add depth to the writer's arguments. In his magnificent "I Have a Dream" speech, Martin Luther King Jr. refers to "the bank of justice" and a check returned from the bank marked "insufficient funds" as a metaphor of the unmet demands for equal rights.

If you run across any of these techniques, mark them accordingly so that you can discuss them in your essay and analyze their impact on the reader.

# Trying Out a Sample Essay Question

In this section, you find a sample essay question along with a grid to score the response. You also see examples of a poor, medium, and great answer, so you have a sense of how the graders evaluate a response. It's not a bad idea to write your own essay, and there's a rubric for you to grade it. Don't peek at the answers and explanations until you're finished. If you want to conserve your strength, simply read the question along with the answers and analysis. When you're ready for practice, turn to Chapter 8.

## The question

As you read the passage, consider how Keith Sawyer uses

- Evidence such as facts or examples to support his ideas

- Logic to develop the argument and link claims and supporting evidence

- Style choices — appeals to emotion, figurative language, word choice, and so forth — to add to the persuasive power of the argument

*The following passage is taken from* Zig Zag: The Surprising Path to Great Creativity *by Keith Sawyer (Wiley).*

(1) Most successful creativity comes through the process you begin without knowing what the real problem is. The parameters aren't clearly specified, the goal isn't clear, and you don't even know what it would look like if you did solve the problem. It's not obvious how to apply your past experience solving other problems. And there are likely to be many different ways to approach a solution.

(2) These grope-in-the-dark situations are the times you need creativity the most. And that's why successful creativity always starts with asking.

(3) It's easy to see how business innovation is propelled by formulating the right question, staying open to new cues, and focusing on the right problem. But it turns out the same is true of world-class scientific creativity. "The formulation of a problem is often more essential than its solution," Albert Einstein declared. "To raise new questions, new possibilities, to regard old problems from a new angle, requires creative imagination and marks real advances in science." Einstein went on to say, "For the detective the crime is given," he concluded. "The scientist must commit his own crime as well as carry out the investigation."

(4) If the right "crime" — the right puzzle or question — is crucial for business and scientific breakthroughs, what about breakthroughs in art or poetry or music? A great painting doesn't emerge from posing a good question — does it?

(5) The pioneering creativity researcher Mihaly Csikszentmihalyi of the University of Chicago decided to answer that question. He and a team of fellow psychologists from the University of Chicago spent a year at the School of the Art Institute of Chicago, one of the top art schools in the United States. "How do creative works come into being?" they wanted to know. They set up an "experimental studio" in which they positioned two tables. One was empty, the other laden with a variety of objects, including a bunch of grapes, a steel gearshift, a velvet hat, a brass horn, an antique book, and a glass prism. They then recruited thirty-one student artists and instructed them to choose several items, position them any way they liked on the empty table, and draw the arrangement.

(6) After observing the artists, Csikszentmihalyi was able to identify two distinct artistic approaches. One group took only a few minutes to select and pose the objects. They spent another couple of minutes sketching an overall composition and the rest of their time refining, shading, and adding

details to the composition. Their approach was to formulate a visual problem quickly and then invest their effort in solving that problem.

(7)     The second group could not have been more different. These artists spent five or ten minutes examining the objects, turning them around to view them from all angles. After they made their choices, they often changed their minds, went back to the table, and replaced one object with another. They drew the arrangement for twenty or thirty minutes and then changed their minds again, rearranged the objects, and erased and completely redrew their sketch. After up to an hour like this, the students in this group settled on an idea and finished the drawing in five or ten minutes. Unlike the first group — which spent most of the time *solving* a visual problem — this group was *searching* for a visual problem. The research team called this a "problem-finding" creative style.

(8)     Which artists' work was more creative: that of the problem solvers or that of the problem finders? Csikszentmihalyi asked a team of five Art Institute professors to rate the creativity of each drawing. With few exceptions, the problem finders' drawings were judged far more creative than the problem solvers' — even though their exploratory process left them much less time to devote to the final image, which was all the judges (who knew nothing of the process involved) were evaluating.

(9)     *The most creative artists were those who focused on asking the right question.*

(10)    Six years after the students graduated, the most successful of the students had become well known in the art world, with work in leading New York galleries and even in the permanent collections of famous museums. And these successful artists were by and large the problem finders back when they were in art school. They were the artists who focused on asking the right question.

Write an essay in which you explain how Sawyer constructs an argument to persuade the reader that creativity comes from asking the right question. In your essay, discuss how Sawyer uses one or more of the elements of style listed previously, or other elements, to strengthen the logic and persuasiveness of his argument. Focus on the most important features of the passage. Do not explain whether you agree or disagree with Sawyer's ideas. Instead, concentrate on how he builds a persuasive case.

## The answer

Many paths lead to a good answer to this essay question. Here are some possible ideas you might mention in your essay, broken down into three categories, and some loose guidelines for awarding points. *Note:* Sample graded responses follow the general points listed here.

### Reading

The essay graders check to see whether you understood everything in the passage. This passage centers on one idea, developed in several ways:

>> "Formulating the right question" is crucial to creativity.

>> Your "past experience" may not help you with a new problem.

>> When you're confused, in a "grope-in-the-dark" situation, creativity matters most.

>> The "real advances" that Einstein mentions come only when you're open to "new questions, new possibilities."

- » The author states that this idea holds true for business, where he says that "it's easy to see" that innovation comes with the correct question, "staying open to new cues, and focusing on the right problem."

- » The author extends the idea to science with the quotation from Einstein.

- » Creativity in art also comes from "a problem-finding creative style."

Give yourself 8 points for this category if you mentioned six or seven of these items. If you hit only four or five items, give yourself 6 points. If you discussed two or three items in the bulleted list, award yourself 4 points. If all you did was restate the main idea, give yourself 2 points.

## Analysis

SAT graders also want to see a good analysis of the argument in which you explain *how* the author makes his or her case. Here are some points about this passage:

- » The author provides no proof for his assertions about business. His statements in that regard are untested assumptions and overall weaken the author's case.

- » Appeal to ethos: The essay quotes Albert Einstein, a widely known genius who came up with startling new ideas about the nature of space and time. He shows up in a paragraph about the need for scientists to formulate questions. Einstein was a scientist, so his opinion is *authoritative* (reliable, from a trusted source).

- » Appeal to logos: The art experiment is factual, explaining how the artists worked and how their creations were evaluated. The use of a factual example is classic *logos*. You can argue with opinions, but it's much harder to *contest* (fight) the results of a well-designed experiment.

- » The essay structure moves logically from point to point. Right in the first paragraph, Sawyer explains the problem — which is that you often don't know what the problem actually is. Next Sawyer moves to Einstein's views on creativity and finally to the art experiment, both of which confirm that the most creative people fiddle around with the question before they seek the answer.

- » The crucial point appears as a single sentence that itself is a single paragraph: "The most creative artists were those who focused on asking the right question." To add emphasis, Sawyer places that line in italics.

- » Sawyer's diction is simple and straightforward; few words are above elementary-school level, though the concepts Sawyer discusses are fairly sophisticated. He speaks directly to readers with the second-person pronoun *you*. The result is a recommendation that any reader can understand and adopt.

- » By mentioning "business innovation," Einstein, and art, Sawyer underlines the universality of his view of creativity.

Scoring yourself on analysis is similar to scoring your reading. Give yourself an 8 if you wrote something resembling six or seven of the points in the bulleted list or a point we didn't mention that you're sure is relevant. If you discussed only four or five points, give yourself a 6. If you hit two or three points in the bulleted list, award yourself 4 points. If your essay mentions only one idea about the author's writing style, give yourself 2 points.

## Writing

This category is the toughest one to self-score, because you have to step back and examine your own work as if a stranger had written it. (If you can, show your essay to an English teacher or a friendly adult. A pair of expert eyes can evaluate your work more effectively.) You, as well as your helper if you have one, should check these factors:

>> **Structure:** Does your essay have a solid, logical structure? One possibility is to work in order from the first paragraph of the passage, where the author states the thesis and then move through paragraph after paragraph until you reach the end of the passage. A more mature organization of ideas might begin by stating Sawyer's views on creativity in greater detail. An analysis of *logos* and *ethos* could be grouped in Paragraph 2. A discussion of Sawyer's structure, including the single-sentence paragraph, forms the main idea of the third paragraph. Finally, examples of simple diction and second-person point of view create a fourth paragraph.

>> **Evidence:** Do you back up every statement you make with quotations or specific references to the passage? Count how many times you zeroed in on details. You should have at least two in every paragraph you write and maybe more.

>> **Language:** Does your essay sound formal, as if a teacher were explaining the passage? If you lapsed into slang or informal word choice, your essay is weaker.

>> **Mechanics:** English teachers group grammar, spelling, and punctuation in this category. As you reread, underline any sentence fragments or run-ons, misspelled words, and faulty commas or quotation marks.

Adding up points to evaluate your writing is tricky. In general, give yourself 2 points (up to a total of 8) for each category in the bulleted list in which you excelled. If you stumbled slightly in a category (say, three or four grammar mistakes or slightly drifted off topic), give yourself 1 point. If you feel your performance in one of these categories was poor (say seven or eight grammar errors or went way off topic), put 0 points but pay attention to how you could have written this better. That's the point of the practice: Make your mistakes here, now, when it *doesn't* matter.

## Scoring your own essay

You probably aren't a professional grader. You can, however, get a fair idea of how your essay measures up to College Board standards if you fill in this grid.

| Category | Reading | Analysis | Writing |
|---|---|---|---|
| **Number of Points** | | | |

The results are your essay reading, analysis, and writing scores.

## Examining graded responses

To help you evaluate your work, here are three sample responses illustrating poor, average, and great essays.

## Response 1: A "poor" essay

Keith Sawyer said, "creativity comes from asking the right question". He talked about how you don't really know what the answer is unless you ask the right question. Creative people ask the right question. If they struggle for a while sometimes.

Keith Sawyer appeals to your emotions because everyone wants to be creative. If you are in business, you want to sell products. Creativity is important in business. If you are an artist, they want to make art. Art is creative. Keith Sawyer did an experiment where artists had to use some things to make a painting. Some artists worked with a plan. Others erased again and again, like me writing an essay. The second group did better. Sawyer wrote about the experiment so you would feel what the artists felt. The example shows how you have to ask the right question.

The words in Keith Sawyer's writing are simple, mostly. He quotes Albert Einstein, who is famous for being a genius. This quote shows that Einstein agrees with Keith Sawyer. He thinks that you have to commit a crime to be creative, which is to ask the question. The word "crime" shows that it can be dangerous to be creative.

Keith Sawyer tells you to take a chance, and he uses examples (like the artists), authorities like Einstein, and simple words to convince you that "creativity comes from asking the right question."

Here are the scores for this essay:

» **Reading:** 2 points. The writer understands the main idea — that creativity comes from asking the right question — but not much else. The writer makes a couple of reading-comprehension errors. Keith Sawyer did not do the experiment at the University of Chicago; a professor named Csikszentmihalyi did. Einstein did refer to a crime, but he did not see creativity as dangerous. Instead, the "crime" is the puzzle to be solved, the question to be asked.

» **Analysis:** 2 points. The writer mentions the appeal to authority (Einstein) but doesn't explore the way that scientific authority might influence the reader. Neither does the writer discuss the way the example of the art experiment adds to Sawyer's argument. The writer also discusses the *metaphor* (imaginative comparison) of the crime but misinterprets its purpose. The quotation ("Creativity comes from asking the right question") comes from the prompt, not from the passage.

» **Writing:** 4 points. The essay could be better — much better! — but the spelling and grammar are fairly good. The sentences are complete, with the exception of "If they struggle for a while sometimes." The sentences are short and show little variety. The writer has some immature habits, such as labeling evidence ("___ shows that").

The total scores for this essay are 2 (Reading), 2 (Analysis), and 4 (Writing).

## Response 2: A "medium" essay

"The most creative artists were those who focused on asking the right question." Keith Sawyer places this sentence alone in a paragraph, in different letters, to show how important the idea is. In this passage, Sawyer talks about how creative artists, business people, and scientists are creative.

First Sawyer explains the problem is what you want to find. He says that there are many ways to find a solution. "Grope in the dark" is a metaphor, so the reader connects to the experience of trying to find something without the benefit of visual clues. This connects to the idea that what you knew in the past may not help you. Sawyer makes his point broad when he mentions business. He appeals to authority, the scientist Albert Einstein to back up his idea. If a genius thinks that it is important "to raise new questions, new possibilities, to regard old problems from a new angle," then regular people should think so too. Plus, most people think of science as factual, not an opinion that you can argue about. Scientific fact becomes part of Sawyer's argument this way.

Next Keith Sawyer explains an experiment with artists at the University of Chicago. The artists who spent most of their time defining a problem by starting and then restarting to draw did better than those who made a plan and could not give up the plan. He even talks about the success of these artists after school. The group that had to make a question first did better. This example convinces the reader that questioning and creativity go hand in hand together. The experiment has a factual outcome, how successful the artists are. Again, you can't say that Sawyer's main idea is just an opinion. It was tested in a scientific way. The results were real.

The experiment takes up most of the passage, so you can see that it is really important to Sawyer's argument. He wants you to imagine you in a way that you are a problem solver. He wants you to see success for yourself. He makes the experiment real, he makes the reader understand that questioning is real and possible. Some people may think that the people in the experiment were not creating questions the way Sawyer said they were, but his explanation is believeable.

All over the passage, the evidence is found. Sawyer makes his point, and he convinces you that questions are more important than anything else.

Here are the scores for this essay:

>> **Reading:** 6 points. The writer got the main idea (creativity comes from asking the right questions) and some of the smaller points about "past experience," Einstein's references to "new possibilities," and the broadening of the argument from business to science and the arts. The writer correctly interprets the experiment and its importance in the essay.

>> **Analysis:** 4 points. The writer interprets the significance of the single-sentence paragraph in italics and the importance of the experiment's being described at length. The writer also understands what the quotation from Einstein adds to the argument. The discussion of "grope in the dark" is fairly well done, too.

>> **Writing:** 4 points. This essay isn't very well organized, and at times the writer repeats information or ideas. The essay doesn't show mature style and includes very few quotations from the passage. However, you see few grammar mistakes.

The total scores for this essay are 6 (Reading), 4 (Analysis), and 4 (Writing).

## Response 3: A "great" essay

Albert Einstein, the epitome of genius in most people's minds, said that "to raise new questions, new possibilities, to regard old problems from a new angle, requires creative imagination." Einstein's authority adds weight to Keith Sawyer's examination of the relationship between questioning and creativity. Sawyer's analysis takes into account business, science, and art, hitting the topic from several angles so that one is sure to relate to the reader's own experience.

Sawyer's discussion of business is not supported by ample evidence. In paragraph 3, he states that "business innovation is propelled by formulating the right question," but he gives no examples from marketing or the creation of a new gadget or company. This weakness in his argument, though, is more than made up for by his lengthy discussion of an experiment with art students at the University of Chicago. Faced with the chance to create something from a limited number of objects, one group made a plan and stuck to it. The more successful group, that was judged by outside experts and by success in their careers later in life, spent most of the time deciding what to create, experimenting with the creation of the "question," in Sawyer's interpretation. This factual example supports the main point and brings the reader along. The experimental design can be criticized, but not the results, and certainly not the idea from paragraph 10 that "six years after the students graduated . . . these successful artists were by and large the problem finders back when they were in art school." Sawyer emphasizes the connection with his final sentence: "They were the artists who focused on asking the right question."

Sawyer's enthusiastic tone comes across with italicized statements and words. The reader's eye is pulled to the single sentence paragraph, "The most creative artists were those who focused on asking the right question." The passage revolves around that striking effect. Sawyer's figurative language, such as his reference to "grope-in-the-dark," evoke strong reactions from the reader. The "dark" can be a scary place, the unknown. Yet the dark can also hide mistakes and encourage risk, an element of creativity. In the same way, quoting Einstein's reference to a detective and a crime brings in another element of risk, and another element of creativity.

Sawyer's simple vocabulary and use of the second person (you) connects his ideas to the reader's experience, showing that anyone can be creative, as long as they are "focused on asking the right question."

Here are the scores for this essay:

>> **Reading:** 8 points. The writer grasped the main idea and many nuances of Sawyer's argument.

>> **Analysis:** 8 points. The essay discusses the appeal to authority (Einstein), the lack of evidence for the relationship between creativity and business, and the role of the art experiment. The essay also touches on tone, word choice, paragraph structure, and figurative language ("grope-in-the-dark" and "crime").

>> **Writing:** 6 points. The essay is fairly well organized, though the points analyzed could be grouped together more logically. The writing shows a mature style and is nearly error-free.

The total scores for this essay are 8 (Reading), 8 (Analysis), and 6 (Writing). Not bad! Now try the practice prompts in the next chapter.

# Chapter **8**

# Practicing Essays

I f you're reading this chapter, and especially if you're trying your hand at any of the three practice SAT essay questions it contains, you've probably decided to write the optional, 50-minute essay. Good for you! But if you're going to do it, do it well. Simulate real test conditions. Lock the cat in the garage. Plop your little sister in front of the television with enough snacks to last an hour. Turn off the phone. Set a timer for 50 minutes and tear out four sheets of lined paper from a notebook. (Loose-leaf is also acceptable.) Sharpen a No. 2 pencil. (The SAT doesn't allow you to write with a pen, and so far, computerized testing is available only in a tiny percentage of testing sites. Unless you know for sure that your SAT location has computer-based testing, stay away from screens and keyboards.)

**TIP**

We suggest you write your essay(s) after reading Chapter 7. Once you complete an essay, take a break and then evaluate it, measuring your work against the scoring guidelines in the answer section.

## Practice Essay I — Momentum: Igniting Social Change

Are you constantly holding your phone or tablet while staring at a computer screen? Do you want to change the world? If so, this question is for you.

### The question

Read this excerpt from *Momentum: Igniting Social Change* by Allison Fine (Wiley 2007).

As you read the passage, consider how Fine uses

- Evidence such as facts or examples to support her ideas

- Logic to develop the argument and link claims and supporting evidence

- Style choices — appeal to emotion or authority, word choice, and so forth — to add to the persuasive power of the argument

(1) In 1999 the ruler of Kuwait, Sheikh Jabir al-Ahman al-Jabir as-Sabah, issued a decree granting women full political rights. Advocates of women's suffrage in this small Arab country were hopeful that legislation would soon follow to codify the decree. Six years passed in vain while legislation stalled. Suddenly, in May 2005, the Kuwaiti legislature voted by a surprisingly large margin of 35 to 23, with one abstention, to remove the word *men* from Article One of the election laws, thereby guaranteeing women the right to vote and the opportunity to run for elected office. Who voted for the legislation was clear. Why they voted for it was something of a mystery. So what happened? Privately, often beneath their burkas (the full-length robes often worn by women in conservative Muslim countries), women used their Blackberries and cell phones to send text and email messages urging legislators to vote in favor of full women's suffrage. Kuwaiti legislators learned that emails don't wear skirts or burkas.

(2) In the click of a mouse or the touch of a screen, we have traveled from the Information Age to the Connected Age, from silent majorities to connected activism. The passion for social change is colliding with the reality that we are increasingly connected to one another through social media. Social media are important not only for their wizardry but because they are inexpensive and accessible and can make interactions, and therefore social change, massively scalable. Connectedness does not come from technology but is facilitated and strengthened by it. Being successful in the Connected Age means using technology to achieve an end. All people, in every aspect of their work, will have to know how and when to use various tools to inform and unite people and to fuel collective action.

(3) Digital technology continues to develop at a ferocious pace, and whether and how we embrace these developments will determine how successful we are as activists. The policies that are debated and the decisions that are made will determine how open or closed our society will be. Do we believe that personal privacy trumps the needs and interests of the government and corporations? How do we view common spaces in cyberspace: as opportunities to meet and exchange ideas and things or as potential places for theft and deceit?

(4) Perhaps the gravest barrier to participation in the Connected Age is the ongoing threat to our security and privacy caused by the aggregation, and in some cases the outright theft, of our personal information. The dampening effect of privacy concerns, including the ongoing onslaught of spam, cannot be underestimated, and neither can the damage it can cause to broad participation and the use of social media to effect social change. The process of developing societal and legal norms for privacy and communal behavior in the Connected Age will be messy, even maddening at times. It will range from simple social interactions (When and how can one use cell phones in public?) to far more serious issues (Who owns my health care information?). A tug of war among industries, consumers and their advocates, and governments around the world is unfolding, and activists must be a part of it. Activist organizations must participate in this public-policy debate, and they must inform and educate their members to ensure that the overall direction is toward open access and away from closed and proprietary tendencies.

(5) We must move with a sense of urgency to incorporate connected activism into social-change efforts. We need to get better at taking a few problems off the table before new problems get crowded onto it. . . . As long as we have social problems to solve, we need to keep searching for a better way. Broad, positive, sustainable change is possible in the Connected Age. Kaliya Hamlin, an activist, advocate, and blogger, perhaps put it best when she said, "Social change is happening. People are exchanging ideas, learning from one another and learning to trust one another in new and different ways, particularly . . . strangers. This process will lead to new and different ways of tackling existing problems. We don't have to come with solutions; we just have to get out of the way of passionate people and good ideas will emerge."

Write an essay in which you explain how Allison Fine constructs an argument to persuade the reader that social media can bring about constructive change. In your essay, discuss how Fine uses one or more of the elements of style listed above, or other elements, to strengthen the logic and persuasiveness of her argument. Focus on the most important features of the passage. Do not explain whether you agree or disagree with Fine's ideas. Instead, concentrate on how Allison Fine builds a persuasive case.

## The answer

Allison Fine raises many important issues in her essay and argues persuasively for her view that social media can *effect* (bring about) positive change.

Showing that you grasped these points contributes to your "reading" score:

» Fine mentions texts and email but also refers to "digital technology." She sees these means of communication as powerful tools.

» The women of Kuwait, who normally have fewer rights than men, employed social media to obtain *suffrage* (the right to vote).

» Social media gives voice to people who would otherwise not be heard because these tools are "inexpensive and accessible."

» Social media is also a means of communication between activists, what Fine calls "the Connected Age."

» Activists *not* using social media are at a disadvantage.

» Privacy concerns are real (though Fine doesn't give details), and figuring out "societal and legal norms for privacy and communal behavior" is tough. Activists must play a part in this debate.

» Regardless of how "messy" the debate is, the movement should be toward "open access."

» Social media isn't going away, so activists and others must deal with it.

How did you do? If you mentioned six or seven of the bullet points, give yourself an 8 for "reading." If you hit four or five of the points, take 6 points for reading. Only two or three? Award yourself 4 points. If you stayed on the main idea, take 2 points for reading.

**REMEMBER**

These guidelines are flexible. If you discussed these ideas in different terms, or if you came up with something we didn't mention, take credit — and points — for reading.

Now consider Allison Fine's writing style. All these ideas (and some we didn't list here) may be part of your "analysis" score:

» Beginning with an anecdote draws the reader into a real situation, one that gives a positive spin to the effect of social media. The women of Kuwait can vote! This success story sets the scene for Fine's *advocacy* (promotion of) social-media activism. Because the story is somewhat emotional, this may be labeled *pathos*.

» The first paragraph ends with a dramatic statement: "Kuwaiti legislators learned . . . burkas." The reference to *burkas,* robes that cover a woman's head and body, powerfully illustrates the old order (women without power) and the new (the activism through email).

» The second paragraph sets up several parallel sentences creating comparisons: "from the Information Age to the Connected Age, from silent majorities to connected activism." The parallel structure gives them equal historical importance. Fine implies that the forward movement is inevitable; there's no going back.

» The third paragraph raises questions that the reader (and society) must answer: "Do we believe . . . corporations? How do we view . . . deceit?" The questions set up opposing ideas — "open or closed," "personal privacy" versus "needs and interests of the government and corporations," "exchange of ideas" versus "theft and deceit."

» Paragraphs 4 and 5 are an example of concession and reply. Fine acknowledges the dangers and disadvantages of new media, but she sees as crucial the "overall direction . . . toward open access."

» The final paragraph is an example of *ethos,* as Fine quotes an "activist, advocate, and blogger" who presumably knows the power of social media.

» The diction is often extreme: Fine mentions "barrier" and "threat" in Paragraph 5.

Evaluate your analysis. If you mentioned five or six of the bullet points, give yourself an 8 for "analysis." If you hit three or four, take 6 points for analysis. Only two? Award yourself 4 points. If you discussed only one technique, take 2 points for analysis.

**REMEMBER**

These guidelines are flexible. If you discussed other style points or grouped several together, adjust your analysis score.

Your final category is writing and applies to your own essay. Evaluating your own writing may be difficult. If you can find a friendly teacher or a helpful adult, ask for assistance in checking your grammar and style. Pay attention to these factors:

» **Structure:** Does your essay have a solid, logical structure? One possibility is to work in order from the first paragraph of the passage, where the author states the *thesis* (idea to be proved), and then move through paragraph after paragraph until you reach the end of the passage. Another possibility is first to examine Fine's ideas on social media, including her acknowledgement of the problems associated with it. Then you might discuss her appeal to pathos (the Kuwaiti example) and ethos (the blogger quotation). Finally, examples of extreme diction and parallel structure create a third paragraph.

» **Evidence:** Do you back up every statement you make with quotations or specific references to the passage? Count how many times you zeroed in on details. You should have at least two in every paragraph you write and maybe more.

» **Language:** Does your essay sound formal, as if a teacher were explaining the passage? If you lapsed into slang or informal word choice, your essay is weaker.

» **Mechanics:** English teachers group grammar, spelling, and punctuation in this category. As you reread, underline any sentence fragments or run-ons, misspelled words, and faulty commas or quotation marks.

Adding up points to evaluate your writing is tricky. In general, give yourself 2 points (up to a total of 8) for every category in the bulleted list in which you excelled. If you stumbled slightly in a category (say, three or four grammar or drifted off topic), give yourself 1 point. If you feel your performance in one of these categories was poor (perhaps you made seven or eight grammar errors or went way off topic), take 0 points.

For sample graded responses that may assist you in your grading, turn to Chapter 7.

## Scoring your essay

To get a fair idea of how your essay measures up to College Board standards, fill in this grid.

| Category | Reading | Analysis | Writing |
|---|---|---|---|
| **Number of Points** | | | |

The results are your essay scores.

# Practice Essay II — Addressing Mathematical Innumeracy

*Innumeracy* is the mathematical equivalent of *illiteracy*. The first term refers to ignorance of math and the second, to the inability to read and write. Here's a passage that explores why so many Americans are clueless when faced with a number — any number!

## The question

Read the following excerpt from *200% of Nothing* by A.K. Dewdney (Wiley).

As you read the passage, consider how Dewdney uses

- Specific statements to develop his ideas

- Logic to develop the argument and link claims and supporting evidence

- Style choices — appeal to emotion, figurative language, word choice, and so forth — to add to the persuasive power of the argument

(1) What if you are already a mathematician and don't know it? We all use logic (of a largely unconscious kind) to take us through everything from business meetings to family dinners. If only we could be good *conscious* mathematicians!

(2) At the conscious level, too many of us are still innumerate, the mathematical twin of illiterate, the term for people who cannot read. Because we are innumerate, we cannot deal with fractions, large numbers, percentages, and other relatively simple mathematical concepts. Meanwhile we are beset more than ever by the abuses that stem from this innumeracy. And those who abuse and misuse mathematics also abuse us. We become prey to commercial trickery, financial foolery, medical quackery, and numerical terrorism from pressure groups, all because we are unable (or unwilling) to think clearly for a few moments. In almost every case, the mathematics involved is something we learned, or should have learned, in elementary school or high school.

(3) Suppose you grant that we are all mathematicians in some sense of that, at a very minimum, we all have this innate, largely unconscious logical ability. Why, then, do we continue to exhibit such awful innumeracy and why, for that matter, is mathematics education in such a crisis? The answer is already implicit in what I have said about mathematics in life. Mathematics itself is too simple!

(4) By this I don't mean that the subject is simple. Far from it! No subject of human thought has anything like the stunning depth and complexity of mathematics. But the elements of mathematics, primary concepts like numbers, sets, relations, and even functions, are really quite simple. Paradoxically, it is only this simplicity (and clarity) that makes the complexity of mathematics possible.

(5) Those of us with little or no familiarity with formal mathematics are nevertheless used to thinking complex thoughts about complex subjects, namely other people. When we come to study mathematics, we find it hard, perhaps, because we cannot get used to thinking about such simple subjects. It's much harder, for a mind that readily analyzes Aunt Mary's strange behavior at the reception, to realize that A, B, and C have no character or personality whatever.

(6) In mathematical concepts, all unnecessary details have been stripped away by the process of abstraction. The naked idea stands before you and your first temptation is to clothe it with some detail, even if it means missing the whole point of the concept. Deep down you want A, B, and C to have human dimensions. Instead, they simply stand for numbers, sets, or some other apparently barren concept. . . .

(7) As Sheila Tobias, author of *Overcoming Math Anxiety,* has pointed out, people who are introduced to mathematical problem solving for the first time routinely try to add dimensions to the problem that simply aren't there. Used to bringing an enormous array of data to the mental table, they simply aren't ready for the utter simplicity of it all. They may attempt to fill in enough lifelike elements to make the characters real and, therefore, manageable by a mind used to more complex situations. Otherwise, the terrain is all too alien.

(8) If mathematics is so hard for people, it may not be due to a lack of innate ability at all, but rather to a cognitive style that demands a certain level of complexity that just isn't there! If this idea holds any truth at all, it may help people learn mathematics better by inspiring them with a sense of confidence. Sometimes expectation paves the way to a completely new learning experience. If the theory holds water, it suggests that the best way to teach mathematics, at least to students encountering it for the first time, is to move gradually toward simple, abstract situations from complicated, real-life ones. Not apples and oranges at the supermarket shelf nor transactions at the cash register, but the shoppers themselves, and the logic of their social interactions.

Write an essay in which you explain how Dewdney constructs an argument to persuade the reader that math education is poorly designed. In your essay, discuss how Dewdney uses one or more of the elements of style listed above, or other elements, to strengthen the logic and persuasiveness of his argument. Focus on the most important features of the passage. Do not explain whether you agree or disagree with Dewdney's ideas. Instead, concentrate on how he builds a persuasive case.

# The answer

A. K. Dewdney argues that math is too simple for human beings to understand. This *premise* (hypothesis, idea to be proved) leads Dewdney to the conclusion that math education must change. Okay, that's the main idea, but Dewdney's argument is more complicated. Discussing these ideas in your essay contributes to your "reading" score:

>> Dewdney believes that everyone can be a mathematician; *innate* (inborn) ability isn't the problem.

>> Mathematical ability is largely "unconscious"; we all do math without realizing it.

>> When math becomes conscious, as in a school or test problem, we overcomplicate the issue.

>> Too many Americans suffer from "innumeracy," a complete misunderstanding of mathematical concepts, when they approach math with preconceived notions.

>> People think about people, and people are complicated. Faced with a simple math problem, solvers apply the same sort of thinking to math as they do to other human beings. This technique doesn't work well.

» We tend to take an abstract idea and "clothe it with some detail." Unnecessary detail makes solving the math problem much more difficult, if not impossible.

» Confidence is key. If people expect to fail, they will. If they expect to succeed, they have a greater chance of doing so. (Remember this as you approach the SAT!)

» Beginning with real-life situations and gradually moving toward simpler, more abstract math problems is easier.

» The more math is related to people and personality, the easier it is.

Time for the math. Add up the number of ideas from the bulleted list. If you mentioned seven or eight of the bullet points, give yourself an 8 for reading. If you hit four, five, or six points, take 6 points for reading. Only got two or three? Award yourself 4 points. If you stayed on the main idea, take 2 points for reading.

REMEMBER

These guidelines aren't set in stone. If you discussed the ideas in different terms, or if you discovered something in the passage that we overlooked, add more points to your reading score.

Now consider A.K. Dewdney's writing style. Here are some ideas that may be part of your "analysis" score:

» The passage begins with a rhetorical question — a question with an answer the author anticipates. As Dewdney asks, "What if you are already a mathematician and don't know it?" he sets you up for a "yes." Then he goes on to prove the answer true.

» The second paragraph lists details of innumeracy — fractions, large numbers, and percentages — that most people can't deal with. This list gives an idea of the scope of the problem.

» Next, Dewdney explains the consequences — "commercial trickery, financial foolery, medical quackery, and numerical terrorism from pressure groups." These parallel items are all terrible, and Dewdney uses this structure to emphasize the importance of this problem.

» Dewdney uses an extreme word, "abuse," to describe how math is used improperly. The diction here takes the problem to a new and more serious level.

» Two pairs appear in the second paragraph: "unable (or unwilling)" and "learned or should have learned." The second half of each pair places responsibility on the person. This structure supports Dewdney's point that math ability can be developed.

» The passage as a whole is organized as a straight, logical line, leading the reader from one idea (you can do math) to another (math teachers make it harder) and then to still another (math should be taught differently).

» Using the pronouns "we" and "us" links the author to the reader.

» In the sixth paragraph, Dewdney ventures into figurative language. A "naked idea" is something you want to "clothe in some detail." Dewdney illustrates the concept he's discussing. He personifies the process of thinking, just as people personify math.

» With the example of "Aunt Mary," Dewdney takes his abstract concept and makes it real.

» The reference to Sheila Tobias stems from ethos, an appeal to authority.

» Mentioning "cash registers" and "the shoppers" illustrates Dewdney's recommendations for a better way to teach math.

How did you do? If you mentioned eight to ten of the eleven bullet points, give yourself an 8 for "analysis." If you hit six to eight points, take 6 points for analysis. If you discussed three to five ideas, take 4 points. Fewer than three? Give yourself 2 points for analysis.

**REMEMBER**

If you discussed other style points or grouped several together, adjust your analysis score.

Your final category is writing and applies to your own essay. Grading your own work is like performing your own dentistry — hard to do! If you can enlist a teacher or other educated adult, do so. Check these factors:

» **Structure:** Does your essay have a solid, logical structure? One possibility is to work in order from the first paragraph of the passage, where the author asks whether you are "already a mathematician," and then move through the logical thread of his argument. Another way to organize your thoughts is to devote a paragraph to Dewdney's structure, another to the examples and appeals to ethos, and another to diction and parallel structure.

» **Evidence:** Do you back up every statement you make with quotations or specific references to the passage? Count how many times you zeroed in on details. You should have at least two in every paragraph you write, and maybe more.

» **Language:** Does your essay sound formal, as if a teacher were explaining the passage? If you lapsed into slang or informal word choice, your essay is weaker.

» **Mechanics:** English teachers group grammar, spelling, and punctuation in this category. As you reread, underline any sentence fragments or run-ons, misspelled words, and faulty commas or quotation marks.

To evaluate your writing, try to see the big picture. Then give yourself 2 points (up to a total of 8) for each category in the bulleted list in which you excelled. If you stumbled slightly in a category, give yourself 1 point. If you feel your performance in one of these categories was poor, take 0 points.

## Scoring your essay

To get a fair idea of how your essay measures up to College Board standards, fill in this grid.

| Category | Reading | Analysis | Writing |
|---|---|---|---|
| **Number of Points** | | | |

The results are your essay scores.

# Practice Essay III — Nonsexist Language

Are you a fan of grammar? How do you feel about stereotypes? Take a look at this essay by Margaret Spicer to see if your views match hers.

## The question

As you read the passage, consider how Spicer uses

- Specific statements to develop her ideas

- Logic to develop the argument and link claims and supporting evidence

- Style choices — exaggeration, figurative language, word choice, and so forth — to add to the persuasive power of the argument

(1) Today's paper has a full-page ad for a type of investment product I've been considering for some time. The advertisement, which must have cost several thousand dollars, detailed why I should leave my current financial advisor and switch to the guy whose smiling photo appears in a sidebar. I was halfway to writing "follow up on this" on my to-do list when I crashed into a recommendation about what I should "ask the salesman when evaluating his product." Excuse me? No females sell investment products? I could accept this sentence if it referred to Smiling Guy's company, because presumably he'd know the gender composition of his sales force. However, the recommendation was to ask *my* advisor. My advisor could be anywhere and therefore could be anyone, including a female.

(2) I imagine that Smiling Guy (or his copy editor) was taught that a masculine pronoun includes both men and women. This principle, the "masculine universal," was in effect for many years. In fact, in the 19th century, the British Parliament passed a law stating that masculine references were understood to include females. This quirk of language, though, has practical effects. Studies show that children hearing about careers tend to accept and apply stereotypes if language reinforces traditional gender roles. Job advertisements referring to both "he and she" tend to attract men and women in more or less equal numbers; those referring only to one gender draw far fewer responses from the gender that was omitted. Plus, inclusiveness costs nothing and brings huge advantages. Leaving out half the human race (notice that I didn't say "mankind") isn't good business. This fact I know for sure, as there's no way I'm giving my money or time to Smiling Guy, because to him I don't exist. I'd rather speak with a *broker, investment counselor,* or *agent* (all gender-neutral words) than with a company that attaches the word *sales* only to a *man* and *his* product.

(3) The problem Smiling Guy faces is rooted in Standard English grammar. One unbreakable rule, agreement, holds that singular forms must be paired with singular forms and plural with plural. A *table* has stains on *its* legs; *tables* have stains on *their* legs. The singular noun *table* pairs up with the singular pronoun *its,* and the plural noun *tables* pairs with the plural pronoun *their.* So far, so good, because *its* is neither masculine nor feminine, but "neuter," in grammar terminology. The plural pronoun *their* wins the hospitality award, because this useful pronoun pairs with plurals of nouns that are masculine, feminine, and neuter.

(4) *Their* was once considered a good match for both singular and plural nouns, and it still is in conversation. In formal writing, though, *their* is plural only. Until a few decades ago, most grammarians saw no problem with the masculine universal; the proper match for a noun such as *student* was *he* (singular, masculine), and any females in the vicinity were expected to understand their supposed inclusion in that pronoun.

(5) Enter feminism, sometime in the late '60s and early '70s. It became obvious that Standard English, when dealing with a singular noun that could apply to either gender, had a pronoun problem. Some radicals urged the adoption of *per* or other manufactured words to replace, for example, *his* or *her*. Other grammarians opted for *their,* arguing that this now firmly plural term should revert to its singular/plural, all-inclusive nature. Still others urged a 50-50 split, alternating the masculine universal with the feminine universal (*she* and *her,* referring to both sexes), paragraph by paragraph. Personally, I find it jarring to read about giving a baby *his* bottle and changing *her* diaper shortly thereafter. Most English teachers adopted this rule: Use *his or her* or *he or she* when you refer to a mixed group of males and females or when you don't know which genders are represented in the group. That's the solution I prefer.

(6) Smiling Guy, avoid sexist language, and perhaps your company will appear on my to-do list after all.

Write an essay in which you explain how Spicer constructs an argument to persuade the reader that avoiding sexist language is important. In your essay, discuss how Spicer uses one or more of the elements of style listed above, or other elements, to strengthen the logic and persuasiveness of her argument. Focus on the most important features of the passage. Do not explain whether you agree or disagree with Spicer's ideas. Instead, concentrate on how she builds a persuasive case.

# The answer

The main idea of this blog post is that sexist language is a problem with serious consequences. Beyond that central *contention* (argument), here are other reading points from the passage that you might mention in your essay:

>> Spicer reacts negatively to an advertisement that refers only to males and refuses to do business with a company that uses sexist language.

>> The advertisement is based on an assumption, but its wording stems from a problem with the English language.

>> Studies show that language influences perception and has "practical effects" (reinforcing stereotypes and gender roles, gaining or losing customers or job applicants).

>> Grammar rules call for singular pronouns, but English has no gender-neutral singular pronouns for people, only the masculine *he* or the feminine *she.*

>> The pronoun problem can be solved in several ways, none of which is clearly superior.

>> Historically, females were represented by masculine words, a practice confirmed by law.

>> Many people, including Spicer, now see the "masculine universal" as sexist.

>> Movement toward gender-inclusiveness can have positive effects, such as increased sales.

How did you do? If you mentioned six or seven of the bullet points, give yourself 8 points for reading. If you hit four or five, take 6 points for reading. Only got two or three? Award yourself 4 points. If you stayed on the main idea, take 2 points for reading.

REMEMBER

You probably found things we haven't listed, and you may have discussed these ideas in different terms. Take credit — and points — for every accurate idea you grasped from this reading.

Now consider Margaret Spicer's writing style. All these ideas (and some we didn't list here) may be part of your analysis score:

>> The opening anecdote draws the reader into a real-life situation.

>> Although the passage refers to a real person, whose photo appears in the advertisement, Spicer calls him "Smiling Guy," making his attitude and personality more universal. The implication is that other advertisements or situations include sexist language.

>> Within the anecdote lies an appeal to logos, or logic. Spicer reasons that "my advisor could be anywhere and therefore could be anyone, including a female."

>> The appeal to logos continues with an explanation of the effects of gendered language in children and job applicants. Because these statements come from "studies," the implication is that the findings are factual and not simply opinions. The studies, however, aren't cited specifically.

>> *Juxtaposing* (placing next to each other) the terms "human race" and "mankind" shows that nonsexist terms can easily replace the masculine universal.

>> In the third and fourth paragraphs, Spicer gives a short grammar lesson on pronouns and gender. This information explains why avoiding sexist pronoun usage is difficult.

» In the fifth paragraph, you see some historical background and possible solutions. Taken together with the two preceding paragraphs, you have a "problem/solution" structure, which is a variation of the "cause-and-effect" pattern of organization.

» The third, fourth, and fifth paragraphs also create a concession and reply. The concession to opposing arguments is that English lacks a singular, nonsexist pronoun for people. The reply is the suggestion to return *they* and *their* to singular and plural status or to use *him or her* or *he or she* as needed.

» The passage comes full circle with a reference to "Smiling Guy" and the initial advertisement. The single-sentence paragraph adds emphasis to the point.

Evaluate your analysis. If you mentioned seven or eight of the bullet points, give yourself an 8 for analysis. If you hit five or six, take 6 points for analysis. If you settled on three or four ideas, take 4 points. If you discussed only one or two techniques, give yourself 2 points for analysis.

**REMEMBER**

If you discussed other style points or grouped several together, adjust your analysis score.

Your final category is writing and applies to your own essay. Ask any educated adult with a good grasp of grammar and style to help you, if you can. Check these factors:

» **Structure:** Does your essay have a solid, logical structure? One possibility is to work in order from the first paragraph of the passage, where the author's anecdote sets forth the problem, and then move through paragraph after paragraph until you reach the end of the passage. Another possibility is first to examine Spicer's ideas on nonsexist language, including her acknowledgement of the grammar problems associated with pronouns. Then you might discuss her appeal to logos (reference to her rejection of the investment and studies on children and job applicants). Next up could be a discussion of concession and reply, coupled with an examination of the problem/solution structure of the passage.

» **Evidence:** Do you back up every statement you make with quotations or specific references to the passage? Count how many times you zeroed in on details. You should have at least two in every paragraph you write, and maybe more.

» **Language:** Does your essay sound formal, as if a teacher were explaining the passage? If you lapsed into slang or informal word choice, your essay is weaker.

» **Mechanics:** English teachers group grammar, spelling, and punctuation in this category. As you reread, underline any sentence fragments or run-ons, misspelled words, and faulty commas or quotation marks.

Give yourself 2 points (up to a total of 8) for each category in the bulleted list in which you excelled. If you stumbled slightly in a category, give yourself 1 point. If you feel your performance in one of these categories was poor, take 0 points.

## Scoring your essay

To get a fair idea of how your essay measures up to College Board standards, fill in this grid.

| Category | Reading | Analysis | Writing |
|---|---|---|---|
| **Number of Points** | | | |

The results are your essay scores.

# 4

# Owning the SAT Math Tests

# Chapter **9**

# Meeting Numbers Head-On: The SAT Math Tests

O n to the math. After two hours of SAT, you're doing great! You've practiced and applied the strategies from this book. Now you have to run for another two hours of math. You can do this too.

There are two math tests, back to back. The first math test features 20 questions for 25 minutes, with no calculator allowed. The second math test has 38 questions for 55 minutes, and you are allowed to use a calculator. Other than that, the two tests are basically the same. One thing to note is that the questions tend to start out at a low level of difficulty, which increases as you progress through the test.

Difficulty is relative. A question that's easy for you may be challenging for your friend, and vice versa. It doesn't matter anyway, because if you know how to approach the question, it's easy no matter what. The SAT determines difficulty by the number of students who missed the question during a trial, not by the question itself. So a "difficult" question to the SAT is simply one where more students didn't know how to approach it. If you know how to approach the question, which you will in about five chapters, the question is easy.

Furthermore, if you know how to approach an SAT math question, then it takes less than a minute to answer. This means that if you know what to do, you can answer all the questions in the SAT Math tests easily and without rushing. And this leads to the first two bits of wisdom:

» **Make each question easy by knowing what you're doing.** There aren't that many topics on SAT Math. There are a few, and they're all topics that most students see in high school *and* are recapped in the following chapters. There are plenty of math topics that you don't see, such as matrices, which only appear on the ACT.

» **Don't rush, because you'll make all kinds of mistakes.** Instead, to speed up your progress through the test, make sure you don't get stuck. The way you don't get stuck is by *knowing what you're doing.* Then you'll answer all the questions easily with time to spare.

Here are more bits of wisdom (also known as Math Test Strategies) along those same lines:

>> **Don't take more than a minute on any one question.** If you don't know what to do and you get stuck, that's okay. Take a guess and move on:

- Take a guess in your answer sheet.
- Circle the question in your booklet.
- Fold the corner of the page in your booklet.
- Move on to the next question.
- Come back to this question at the end of the section.

>> **If you find yourself working a lot of math, you missed what the question is asking.** An SAT Math question is more like a puzzle than a math problem. It never takes a lot of math, but it may take a strategic approach. If you understand the question and set it up correctly, all the fractions cancel and everything lands nicely and neatly. If you don't understand what it's asking, you start working a lot of math, so step back and follow the preceding strategy: Take a guess, move on, and come back to this question at the end of the section. You'll probably spot how to work the question on this second look.

>> **Treat each question like it's worth the same number of points.** A question that goes fast is worth the same points as one that takes forever. So work the fast questions first! Then go back to the time-consumers.

>> **Use the test booklet as your scratch paper.** Write your calculations in the extra blank space, but take time to bubble in your answers. Even though the proctor collects the test booklet, your notes and figuring don't affect your score.

>> **If you're almost out of time, bubble 'til the end.** Really, this shouldn't happen. If you practice the skills taught in the next few chapters, you'll be fine — but things happen! Worst case, take the plunge and guess through the end of the test. A wrong answer is no worse than an unanswered one, so you may as well take a shot at getting it right.

>> **Bubble your answer after each question.** Don't wait until the end and then go back and bubble them all. What could possibly go wrong?

# Starting with Formulas

The first page of each Math Test has a set of formulas to help you solve the problems. By the time you're on the second page of the test, you'll probably forget it's there — almost everyone does — but these formulas, shown in Figure 9-1, are still good to know.

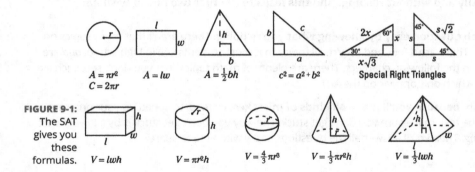

$A = \pi r^2$
$C = 2\pi r$

$A = lw$

$A = \frac{1}{2}bh$

$c^2 = a^2 + b^2$

**Special Right Triangles**

**FIGURE 9-1:** The SAT gives you these formulas.

$V = lwh$

$V = \pi r^2 h$

$V = \frac{4}{3}\pi r^3$

$V = \frac{1}{3}\pi r^2 h$

$V = \frac{1}{3}lwh$

# Just Gridding

Of the 58 Math Test questions, most are good ol' multiple choice, but 13 (five in the first Math Test and eight in the second) ask you to provide your own answers and bubble them into a grid.

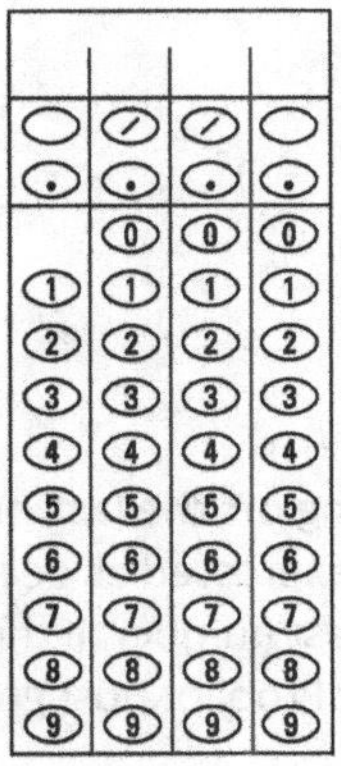

**FIGURE 9-2:**
A blank grid-in.

These questions are known as **grid-ins**. Figure 9-2 shows a sample blank grid-in.

The grid-in problems are normal math questions but with certain rules:

» **Write your answer and then darken the ovals.** The little boxes to write your answer are just there to help you grid the answer properly. You have to darken the circles for the scanner to read it.

» **You can't grid in negative numbers.** No answer is negative, so each answer must be positive or zero.

» **Don't grid in a mixed number.** If you come up with $5\frac{1}{2}$ as your answer, **don't** grid in $51/2$, because the scanner will read "51 over 2," not "five and one-half." Instead, convert your answer to an improper fraction. Grid in $11/2$ (11 over 2), as shown in Figure 9-3, or grid in a decimal: 5.5.

» **You can start from the left, right, or middle.** Just be sure that you have enough boxes for the whole answer.

» **If there is more than one correct answer, pick one and go with it.** If it turns out that the answer can be either 4 or 5, just pick one and grid it in. Don't worry about the *other* answer: The system will accept either one. That also goes for a range: If your answer is between 3 and 7, then any number between 3 and 7 is considered correct.

» **Check whether the answer needs to be rounded.** If you find that the answer is between 6 and 12, check and see whether the answer must be an integer. A lot of times when the answer is a decimal, the question specifies that it should be rounded to a certain number of decimal places.

For example, if you correctly compute an answer of 1.75, and the question specifies that the answer needs to be rounded to *one* decimal place, then a gridded answer of 1.75 is considered incorrect, while the rounded answer of 1.8 is considered correct.

» **Don't place zeroes before a decimal point.** If your answer is .5, darken the oval for the decimal point and the five, as in .5, not 00.5. See Figure 9-3.

FIGURE 9-3:
Three
grid-ins,
properly
filled in.

>> **If your answer is a repeating decimal, fill in all the boxes, rounding off the last number only.** In other words, darken the ovals for .333 or .667 (1 / 3 and 2 / 3 expressed as decimals), not .3 or .67 (see Figure 9-2c). Note that you don't have to round the last number: If the answer is 2 / 3, you can grid that, or .666 or .667: any of those three is correct. Probably just grid the fraction.

REMEMBER

Don't worry if you get more than one possible answer. Some grid-in questions have several possible right answers. (Usually those problems read something like, "what is one possible value of . . .") Just pick one answer and you're set.

# Getting Familiar with the Math Tests

Worried? Don't be. The most important thing to know — that phrase is used a lot, but it's always true — is that *certain math topics are on the SAT, and certain math topics aren't.* If you know what these topics are, and the way that the SAT asks about them, then each answer in the Math Tests is within your reach. These topics are listed here and explored in the following chapters.

TIP

The SAT throws the occasional curveball question in its Math Tests. There may be some unusual topic just on the edge or outside the scope of SAT Math. These are few and far between, but if you encounter one, you know what to do: Circle it, take a guess, and come back to it later. So. Here's the wisdom of this entire book summed up into one line. (That claim is just as true in Chapter 3 as it is here. Guess it's more than one line. Anyway . . .) You ready? *If you know how to answer most of the math questions, you can answer them quickly and have time left over to focus on the harder questions.* That means *you.*

What are those math topics? Glad you asked.

>> **Numbers and operations:** These are about a quarter of the Math Test questions. Basically, anything that doesn't involve an *x* or a drawing falls into this category, which includes whole number operations, fractions, ratios, exponents, and radicals. Of these, ratios and exponents are typically the most commonly occurring.

>> **Algebra and functions:** These are just under half of the Math Test questions and include anything with an *x* or any other letter that represents a number. The most commonly occurring algebra questions include linear equations, systems of equations (which are basically two linear equations), and parabolas.

>> **Geometry and trigonometry:** These are about a quarter of the Math Test questions and include the typical circles and trapezoids along with 3-D shapes such as cubes and cylinders. There's some subtracting the areas or volumes of shapes, and just a little trig. The most common questions in this group involve triangles and parts of circles (such as half of a wheel) along with trig.

>> **Statistics and probability:** These are just a few of the Math Test questions and involve averages and graphs, including scatterplots. The most common questions in this group are definitely the graphs.

So there you are. You now know the secrets of the SAT Math Tests. Nice! Note that whether a group of questions is about a quarter or half of the Math Test questions, or whether certain topics are more common than others, varies from exam to exam. The preceding assessments, along with the estimated priority of each math topic in the following chapters, are based on the review of countless SATs with students. Each exam is different, and yours may not have a quarter of this question type or half of that one. But it'll be close.

## CALCULATING THROUGH IT

So you can use a calculator on part of the math. Big deal. The SAT-makers declare that you can solve every problem on the test with brainpower alone, and they're right. But there's nothing wrong with a little help. A calculator isn't the number-one requirement for doing well on the second Math Test — your preparation is — but it's good to have. Here's a secret of success: Make sure your calculator works, has fresh batteries, or is plugged in the *night before* your exam.

You're allowed to bring a scientific calculator, which lets you figure out stuff like square roots, combination problems involving $\pi$, and more. Many also calculate fractions, which speeds up adding $1/4$ to $1/2$. Be careful though: You can't bring anything with a QWERTY keyboard, a touchscreen, or an internet connection. That also means you can't use your phone. Also, it can't beep or make any kind of noise. (For more on calculators that are or aren't allowed on the SAT, go to www.collegeboard.org.)

You can bring a graphing calculator, which can be useful on some of these questions. If you have one that you like, bring it! If you don't, and you decide to buy one, be sure to get it well in advance so you can practice using it. You don't want to learn how it works *while* you're taking the SAT. Otherwise, don't sweat it. If you're ready for the SAT Math Tests, which you will be after going through the next few chapters, you'll be able to answer all the SAT Math questions without a graphing calculator. Or even without any calculator.

Knowing when *not* to use a calculator is also important. It works the numbers, but it doesn't help you see the pattern, logic, or underlying concept of the question. For a solid math score, you have to understand how the question works, not how the numbers add together, and for this, the calculator doesn't help. Really, it's all you, and that's *more* than good enough.

Also, don't use the calculator for each simple step. Trust yourself! A top-scoring, 4.2 GPA 98-percentile SAT student was preparing for her next exam, and to divide 10 by 2, she typed it into her calculator and came up with 20! Didn't even faze her: She wrote down 20 and kept right on working. True story.

*Tip:* If you don't own a calculator, don't worry about that either. Although the SAT doesn't supply calculators, some schools do provide loaners to students who don't have their own. Talk with your math teacher. (Homeschoolers, call the local high school to inquire about access to their supply.) You can also pick up a cheap calculator that doesn't draw graphs but does handle the basic functions you'll need on the SAT.

Also, unlike the Reading Test and Writing and Language Test, where you learn strategies to take on 11 questions at a time, the Math Test strategies focus on one question at a time. For this reason, in this book, the math practice questions are mixed into the chapters instead of in their own separate chapters. You find out how to work a math topic, practice with a few SAT-style questions, and go to the next topic. Go on — four chapters, and you so got this.

Chapter **10**

# Numbers and Operations

N ow for the first step in your SAT Math review. Not only do the topics in this chapter comprise about a quarter of your SAT Math questions, but also they are the foundation of the questions on other SAT Math topics. For example, you need to understand exponents and radicals, covered in this chapter, before you take on parabolas and trigonometry, covered in the following chapters.

## Starting with the Basics

Different types of numbers work in different ways, so here is a review of the basics and how numbers work together. In the same way that this chapter is the foundation of the other math chapters, this section is the foundation of the other sections in this chapter.

### Checking out types of numbers

The SAT Math Tests refer to defined numbers such as *rational* or *imaginary* in their questions. Here's what they are:

» **Whole numbers:** A *whole number* is any number that that doesn't include a fraction or a decimal and isn't negative. 0 is considered a whole number.

» **Factors:** A *factor* is any whole number that divides neatly into another whole number. For example, 16 can be divided by 1, 2, 4, 8, and 16, so those numbers are all factors of 16. Note that every number is a factor of itself: 5 is a factor of 5. To factor a negative number, factor out a –1 also, even though –1 isn't a whole number. For example, –6 factors into –1, 1, 2, 3, and 6.

» **Multiples:** A *multiple* is any whole number multiplied by any other whole number. For example, multiples of 4 include 4, 8, 12, and so on. Note that every number is a multiple of itself: 7 is a multiple of 7.

» **Prime numbers:** A *prime number* is any number that has exactly two factors: itself and 1. All prime numbers are positive, and all are odd *except* for 2, which is prime. 0 and 1, however, aren't prime numbers.

» **Composite numbers:** Any whole number with more than two factors (in other words, not prime) is *composite*. If you can divide a number by a smaller whole number (other than 1) without getting a remainder, it's a composite number. Note that any composite number can be divided down to its primes. For example, 30, which is composite, can be divided down to its primes: $30 = 2 \times 3 \times 5$.

TIP

Speaking of divisibility, know these points:

● Any number whose digits add up to a multiple of 3 is also divisible by 3. For example, the digits of 789 add up to $24 (7 + 8 + 9 = 24)$; because 24 is divisible by 3, so is 789.

● Same goes for multiples of 9. If the digits of a number add up to a multiple of 9, you can divide the number itself by 9. For example, the digits of 729 add up to $18 (7 + 2 + 9 = 18)$; because 18 is divisible by 9, so is 729.

● Any number ending in 0 or 5 is divisible by 5.

● Any number ending in 0 is also divisible by 10.

Consider the number 365. It's not even, so it can't be divided by 2. Its digits add up to 14, which isn't divisible by 3 or 9, so it's not divisible by either 3 or 9. Because 365 ends in 5, it's divisible by 5. Because it doesn't end in 0, it's not divisible by 10.

» **Integers:** Any whole number or any negative whole number is an *integer*. You see integers on the number line, as in Figure 10-1. You also see non-integers on the number line, but not as often.

TIP

The farther to the right on the number line a number is, the greater it is. For example, –3 is greater than –5, because –3 is to the right of –5 on the number line.

» **Consecutive numbers:** *Consecutive* means "one after another," so *consecutive numbers* are numbers that are, well, one after another. Typically, they're just integers lined up, as in 12, 13, 14, but they can be defined and categorized. For example, consecutive *odd* numbers include 9, 11, 13, while consecutive *even* numbers of course include 6, 8, 10. If a question were to ask about 5 consecutive numbers starting with 7, you would write 7, 8, 9, 10, 11.

» **Rational numbers:** Any integer, along with any number that can be written as a fraction — proper or improper — or as a terminating or repeating decimal, is a *rational number*. Examples of rational numbers include $\frac{2}{3}$, a *proper fraction*; $\frac{3}{2}$, an *improper fraction*; 1.2, a *terminating decimal*; and $1.\overline{09}$ (the decimal for $\frac{12}{11}$), a *repeating decimal* (1.090909 ... ).

» **Irrational numbers:** An *irrational number* has decimals that never repeat or end. Practically speaking, you need to worry about only two kinds of irrational numbers:

● Radicals (such as $\sqrt{2}$ and $\sqrt{3}$)

● $\pi$, which you've seen from working with a circle

FIGURE 10-1:
The number
line.

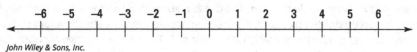

John Wiley & Sons, Inc.

You'll typically see an irrational number in its radical form or as $\pi$, hardly as an unwieldy decimal, but the SAT may expect you to know what it is.

» **Real numbers:** A *real number* is any number that appears on the number line and includes each type of number described previously, including those rational and irrational.

» **Imaginary numbers:** An *imaginary number* is the opposite of a real number. It doesn't appear on the number line, and though there are plenty in applied mathematics, there is only one that may appear on the SAT: the square root of –1, also known as *i*. This is further explored later in this chapter.

» **Undefined numbers:** An *undefined number* is an expression that does not have meaning. The most common undefined number, and the only one that you have to consider for the SAT, is a number divided by zero. You don't actually work with this, but if the question shows $\frac{2}{3-x}$, then somewhere in there, it's guaranteed to show $x \neq 3$ just to *make sure* that you're not dealing with that undefined number.

Here's a sample SAT question based on the concept of number basics:

PLAY

If $x$ and $y$ are both integers where $x$ is greater than 3 and $y$ is less than 2, then $x - y$ *could* be

(A) 3

(B) 2

(C) 1

(D) –1

If $x$ is an integer greater than 3, it must be at least 4. If $y$ is an integer less than 2, it must be at most 1. To find $x - y$, just place those numbers: $4 - 1 = 3$, so Choice (A) is correct. Note that making $x$ bigger or $y$ smaller makes $x - y$ greater than 3, so all the other choices are impossible.

## Remembering the order of operations

How many times has your mom told you to put away your phone and start your homework because you "have to get your priorities straight"? No comment on that, but here are operations priorities in math.

Consider the problem $3 + 4 \times 2$. If you add 3 and 4 first, the result is different from if you multiply 4 by 2 first. You know *PEMDAS*, remembered by, "Please Excuse My Dear Aunt Sally," but actually meaning, "Parentheses Exponents Multiply Divide Add Subtract," which describes the *order of operations*. When faced with a multipart problem, just follow this order.

1. **Do everything in parentheses.**

2. **Calculate all exponents.**

3. **Multiply and divide, from left to right.**

4. **Add and subtract, from left to right.**

The SAT doesn't give you ambiguous math problems such as $3 + 4 \times 2$, but you still should remember to work anything in parentheses first — usually. In Chapter 11, there are examples of questions where you leave the parentheses alone. Don't worry about it — you'll see how it fits together — but be aware of the intended *order of operations* in a given math problem.

# Simplifying Numbers and Operations

Now that you're refreshed on the basics, here's a dive into the actual math questions that the SAT asks.

# Simplifying prime numbers

As defined in the previous section, a *prime number* is any number that has exactly two factors: itself and 1. It's always positive, and the only even prime number is 2 (whose factors are 1 and 2). Any other even number has more than two factors and isn't prime. For example, 4 is divisible by 1, 2, and 4. 0 isn't prime because it isn't positive, and 1 isn't prime because it has exactly one factor: 1.

The secret to working with prime numbers is just knowing that they're limited to a very specific set of numbers. You almost never will be asked to work with prime numbers greater than 20, so just know the first bunch: 2, 3, 5, 7, 11, 13, 17, 19. If you're not sure, make sure the number is *odd* (except 2 of course), and try dividing it by other odd numbers, starting with 3. If you can't divide it evenly, then the number is prime.

**PLAY**

If $c$ is the smallest prime number greater than 5 and $d$ is the largest prime number less than 15, then the value of $c + d$ is

(A) 11

(B) 13

(C) 19

(D) 20

The answer is Choice (D), 20. The smallest prime number greater than 5 is 7, and the largest prime number less than 15 is 13. Add 7 to 13 for the answer of 20.

**PLAY**

If a number $n$ is the product of two distinct primes, $x$ and $y$, how many factors does $n$ have, including 1 and itself?

(A) 2

(B) 3

(C) 4

(D) 5

A prime number has only two factors: 1 and itself. Pretend in your problem that $x = 5$ and $y = 7$. Then $n = 5 \times 7 = 35$. The factors of 35 are 1, 5, 7, and 35. Because you can't break down 5 or 7, there are no other factors. As long as you pick prime numbers for $x$ and $y$, you'll always get four factors for $n$. Choice (C) is correct.

Prime number questions aren't that common in SAT Math, but they're worth knowing and understanding.

# Simplifying percents

*Percent* literally translates to *per cent*, which if you remember your Latin, means *per 100*. That's why 50 percent is 50 out of 100, or one half.

Taking the percent of a number is simple if you're using a calculator with a "%" button, but one of the SAT Math Tests doesn't allow a calculator, so there goes that shortcut. To turn a number into a percent, simply move the decimal point two spaces to the right and add the % symbol: 0.5 becomes 50, and with the % symbol it represents 50%. You can also turn a percent into a decimal by moving the decimal point two spaces to the left and dropping the % symbol, as in 60% = 0.60. (Other examples of percents to decimals include 12.5% = 0.125, 0.4% = 0.004, and so on.) Or you can turn the percent into a fraction, so 60 percent literally means, "60 per 100," or 60/100.

To take the percent of a percent, simply multiply the percents, or convert them back to fractions or decimals and then multiply. For example, if 50% of the chocolates are dark chocolate, and 40% of the dark chocolates have almonds, then what percent of the chocolates are dark with almonds? To multiply as percents, go with $50\% \times 40\% = 20\%$. To multiply as decimals, convert the percents to decimals and use $0.5 \times 0.4 = 0.2$, and as fractions, go with $\frac{50}{100} \times \frac{40}{100} \rightarrow \frac{5}{10} \times \frac{4}{10} = \frac{20}{100}$ or $\frac{1}{2} \times \frac{2}{5} = \frac{2}{10} \rightarrow \frac{20}{100}$. Any way you cut it, the answer is 20%.

For other percentage questions, fall back on the formula you mastered in grade school:

$$\frac{is}{of} = \frac{\%}{100}$$

Suppose you're asked "40% of what number is 80?" The number you're looking for is the number you're taking the percent *of*, so $x$ will go in the *of* space in the formula:

$$\frac{80}{x} = \frac{40}{100}$$

Now cross-multiply: $40x = 8,000$. Dividing by 40 gives you $x = 200$.

You can also consider that the percent of the whole equals the part. In other words, 40% of $x$ is 80. Set up the equation and solve for $x$:

$$40\% x = 80$$
$$0.4x = 80$$
$$x = \frac{80}{0.4}$$
$$x = 200$$

One subtopic of percentages is a problem that involves a percent increase or decrease. A slight variation of the percentage formula helps you out with this type of problem. Here's the formula and an example problem to help you master it:

$$\frac{\text{amount of change}}{\text{starting amount}} = \frac{x}{100}$$

**PLAY**

The value of your investment in the winning team of the National Softball League increased from $1,500 to $1,800 over several years. What was the percentage increase of the investment?

**(A)** 300

**(B)** 120

**(C)** 50

**(D)** 20

The correct answer is Choice (D). The key here is that the number 1,800 shouldn't be used in your formula. Before you can find the *percent* of increase, you need to find the *amount* of increase, which is $1,800 - 1,500 = 300$. To find the percentage of increase, set up this equation:

$$\frac{300}{1,500} = \frac{x}{100}$$

First reduce the fraction:

$$\frac{300}{1,500} = \frac{3}{15} = \frac{1}{5}$$

Then cross-multiply and divide by 5:

$$\frac{1}{5} = \frac{x}{100}$$
$$5x = 100$$
$$x = 20$$

The SAT-makers often try to confuse you by asking about something that doesn't appear in the original question, as in this example:

**PLAY**

At one point in the season, the New York Yankees had won 60 percent of their games. The Yanks had lost 30 times and never tied. (As you know, there are no ties in baseball.) How many games had the team played?

**(A)** 12

**(B)** 18

**(C)** 50

**(D)** 75

The answer is Choice (D). Did you find the catch? The winning percentage was 60 percent, but the question specified the number of losses. What to do? Well, because ties don't exist, the wins and losses must have represented all the games played, or 100 percent. Thus, the percentage of losses must be 100% − 60%, which is 40%. Put the formula to work:

$$\frac{30}{x} = \frac{40}{100}$$

Now cross-multiply: $40x = 3,000$ and $x = 75$

**PLAY**

If you invest $2,000 for one year at 5% annual interest, the total amount you would have at the end of the year would be

**(A)** $100

**(B)** $2,005

**(C)** $2,100

**(D)** $2,500

Solve the question like this: 5% = 0.05, so 5% of $2,000 = 0.05 × $2,000 = $100. But wait! Before you choose $100 as your answer, remember that you still have the $2,000 that you originally invested, so you now have $2,000 + $100 = $2,100. Choice (C) is correct.

Questions solely on percents aren't that common, but this concept underlies many other questions on the SAT Math Tests.

## Simplifying ratios

A *ratio* compares the items of a group as a reduced fraction. For example, if there are 15 trees and 10 hammocks, then the ratio of trees to hammocks is 3:2, because the fraction $\frac{15}{10}$ reduces to $\frac{3}{2}$. Here are some further points to remember about ratios:

> » A ratio is written as $\frac{of}{to}$ or of:to.
>   - The ratio *of* skis *to* poles is $\frac{skis}{poles}$.
>   - The ratio *of* boats *to* trailers = boats:trailers.
> » A possible total is a multiple of the *sum* of the numbers in the ratio.

You may have a ratio question like this on the SAT Math Test:

At an auto show, the ratio of classic cars to concept cars is 4:5. What could be the total number of classic and concept cars at the auto show?

To answer this question, add the numbers in the ratio: $4 + 5 = 9$. The total must be a multiple of 9, such as 9, 18, 27, 36, and so on. Or think of it another way: The sum must divide evenly into the total of 9. So the total can be 27, which divides evenly by 9.

Here's an example in the form of a grid-in:

**PLAY**

To make the dough for her signature wood-fired pizzas, Julia uses 7 cups of flour for every 5 cups of water, and she only uses whole cups. If she uses at least 10 but not more than 20 cups of water, what *could* be the total number of cups of flour and water that goes into the dough?

The answer can be 24, 36, or 48. Add the numbers in the ratio: $7 + 5 = 12$, so the total must be a multiple of 12. If Julia uses at least 10 but not more than 20 cups of water, then she uses 10, 15, or 20 cups, so multiply the multiple of 12 by 2, 3, or 4. Any answer 24, 36, or 48 is considered correct, so go with one and you're good.

Another form of the ratio question gives you the ratio and the total, and then it asks for one of the numbers. Solve it like this:

**1.** Put an *x* by each number in the ratio.

**2.** Set up an equation where these *x* numbers add up to the total.

**3.** Solve for *x*.

**4.** Place the number for *x* back into the equation.

Go through this once and it makes perfect sense.

**PLAY**

A salad uses 2 Campari tomatoes for every 3 artichoke hearts, for a total of 20. How many tomatoes and artichoke hearts are in this salad?

**1.** 2 to 3 becomes $2x$ and $3x$

**2.** Set up the equation as $2x + 3x = 20$

**3.** Solve for *x*:

$$2x + 3x = 20$$
$$5x = 20$$
$$x = 4$$

**4.** Place 4 in for *x* in the equation:

$$2x + 3x = 20$$
$$2(4) + 3(4) = 20$$
$$8 + 12 = 20$$

So, there are 8 tomatoes and 12 artichoke hearts.

PLAY

Given that there are 30 days in April, the ratio of rainy days to sunny days during the month of April could *not* be

(A) 5:3

(B) 3:2

(C) 5:1

(D) 4:1

The rule for ratios states that the total must be divisible by the sum of the numbers in the ratio. Because $5 + 3 = 8$, and 30 isn't divisible by 8, Choice (A) is correct. Just to be sure, check that all the other possible sums do go into 30.

A ratio question doesn't always approach the ratio directly. Sometimes you have to spot that a ratio is involved, like in this one:

PLAY

A party supplier charges a flat rate plus a certain amount per person. If supplies for 12 people cost $140 and supplies for 20 people cost $180, then supplies for 40 people would cost

(A) $220

(B) $280

(C) $300

(D) $360

First, find the cost per person. If 12 people cost $140 and 20 people cost $180, then the additional cost of 8 people is $40 (because $20 - 12 = 8$ and $180 - $140 = $40$). Divide $40 by 8 for a person-to-cost ratio of 1 : $5. Now take the 20-person cost and add the cost of 20 more people. You know that 20 people cost $180 and that 20 additional people cost $100 (because $20 \times $5 = $100$), so add the two together: $180 + $100 = $280$, and the answer is Choice (B).

Ratio questions are fairly common on the SAT Math Tests.

## Simplifying conversions

*Conversions* refers to going from one unit of measurement to another. For example, if a mile is 5,280 feet, and there are 3 feet in a yard, how long is a mile in yards? Working with conversions is simply multiplying or dividing the total number by the conversion.

In this case, because you're converting feet to yards, and there are 3 feet in a yard, divide the 5,280 feet by 3 for the number of yards:

$$\frac{5,280 \text{ feet}}{3 \text{ feet}} = 1,760 \text{ yards}$$

Here's another.

PLAY

If each quarter-inch on the map represents one mile, how much distance is represented by a 3-inch segment on the map?

(A) 3 miles

(B) 4 miles

(C) 9 miles

(D) 12 miles

If each quarter inch is one mile, then one inch is four miles. The 3-inch segment thus represents 12 miles, for Choice (D).

Conversion questions are fairly common on the SAT Math Tests, and they can be varied.

## Simplifying exponents

*Exponents* is one of the most commonly asked topics on the SAT Math. Following are the basics, and later on, this chapter explores the SAT variations.

The *base* is the big number (or letter) on the bottom. The *exponent* is the little number (or letter) in the upper-right corner.

>> In $x^5$, $x$ is the base and 5 is the exponent.

>> In $3^y$, 3 is the base and $y$ is the exponent.

**Any base to the zero power equals one.**

>> $x^0 = 1$

>> $129^0 = 1$

**A base to the first power is just the base.** In other words, $4^1 = 4$.

**A base to the second power is the base times itself:**

>> $x^2 = x \cdot x$

>> $5^2 = 5 \times 5 = 25$

**The same is true for bigger exponents.** The exponent tells you how many times the numbers are multiplied together. For example, $3^4$ means that you write 3 down four times and multiply them all together. So $3^4 = 3 \times 3 \times 3 \times 3 = 81$.

**A base to a negative exponent is the reciprocal of the base to a positive exponent.** A *reciprocal* is the upside-down version of a fraction. For example, $\frac{4}{3}$ is the reciprocal of $\frac{3}{4}$. An integer (except 0) can also have a reciprocal: $\frac{1}{3}$ is the reciprocal of 3. When you have a negative exponent, just put base and exponent under a 1 and make the exponent positive again.

>> $x^{-4} = \frac{1}{x^4}$

>> $5^{-3} = \frac{1}{5^3} = \frac{1}{125}$

The answer isn't negative. When you flip it, you get the reciprocal, and the negative goes away. Don't fall for the trap of saying that $5^{-3} = -5^3$ or $-125$.

Also, if a number or variable with a negative exponent, such as $x^{-4}$, appears in the denominator of a fraction, such as $\frac{2}{3x^{-4}}$, you can make the exponent positive and move it to the numerator, like this: $\frac{2x^4}{3}$. Just reciprocate the part with the exponent, in this case $x$, not the other parts of the fraction, in this case 2 and 3.

**To multiply like bases, add the exponents.**

» $x^3 \cdot x^2 = x^{(3+2)} = x^5$

» $5^4 \times 5^9 = 5^{(4+9)} = 5^{13}$

» $p^3 \cdot p = p^3 \cdot p^1 = p^{(3+1)} = p^4$

» $129^3 \times 129^0 = 129^{(3+0)} = 129^3$

TIP

You can't multiply numbers with *unlike* bases. (Actually, you can, by making the exponents the same, but that's not something you do on the SAT.)

» $x^2 \cdot y^3$ stays $x^2 \cdot y^3$

» $5^2 \times 7^3$ stays $5^2 \times 7^3$ (unless you actually work it out)

**To divide like bases, subtract the exponents.** You can divide two bases that are the same by subtracting the exponents.

» $x^5 \div x^2 = x^{(5-2)} = x^3$

» $5^9 \div 5^3 = 5^{(9-3)} = 5^6$

» $x^3 \div x^7 = x^{(3-7)} = x^{-4} = \frac{1}{x^4}$

» $129^2 \div 129^0 = 129^{(2-0)} = 129^2$

(That last one should make sense if you think about it. Any base to the zero power is 1. Any number divided by 1 is itself.)

TIP

Did you look at $5^9 \div 5^3$, and think that it was $5^3$? Falling into the trap of dividing instead of subtracting the exponents is easy, especially with numbers just begging to be divided, such as 9 and 3. Keep your guard up.

**You should know the common powers of 2, 3, 4, and 5:**

| | | | |
|---|---|---|---|
| $2^2 = 4$ | $3^2 = 9$ | $4^2 = 16$ | $5^2 = 25$ |
| $2^3 = 8$ | $3^3 = 27$ | $4^3 = 64$ | $5^3 = 125$ |
| $2^4 = 16$ | $3^4 = 81$ | | |
| $2^5 = 32$ | | | |
| $2^6 = 64$ | | | |

**Multiply exponents of exponents, like this:**

» $\left(x^2\right)^3 = x^{(2\cdot3)} = x^6$

» $\left(5^4\right)^3 = 5^{(4\times3)} = 5^{12}$

**You can use the common powers to give numbers like bases:**

If you have $9^5 = 3^x$, meaning what exponent of 3 equals $9^5$, turn the 9 into $3^2$, and solve it like this:

$$9^5 = 3^x$$
$$\left(3^2\right)^5 = 3^x$$
$$3^{10} = 3^x$$

And $x = 3$. Try this one:

PLAY

In the expression $16^3 = 2^x$, the value of $x$ is:

**(A)** 4

**(B)** 8

**(C)** 12

**(D)** 16

Give each side the same base. In this expression, 2 probably works the best:

$$16^3 = 2^x$$
$$\left(2^4\right)^3 = 2^x$$
$$2^{12} = 2^x$$
$$x = 12$$

This matches Choice (C).

Here is a variation of the theme:

PLAY

In the expression $25^x = 5^6$, what is the value of $x$?

**(A)** 2

**(B)** 3

**(C)** 5

**(D)** 7

Give each side the same base, which in this case should be 5:

$$25^x = 5^6$$
$$\left(5^2\right)^x = 5^6$$
$$5^{2x} = 5^6$$
$$2x = 6$$
$$x = 3$$

This matches Choice (B). Note that in these two example SAT-type questions, the actual math is very simple. You're not crunching huge numbers; you're using your understanding of the math to simplify and solve these fast.

**You can count bases with exponents if the bases and exponents are the same.** Remember, the base is the number or letter tied to the exponent. For example, with $x^3$, the base is $x$, and the exponent is 3.

>> $x^3 + x^3 = 2x^3$. This works the same way as $x + x = 2x$. You're just counting them.

>> $37x^3 + 10x^3 = 47x^3$. Because the bases are the same and the exponents are the same, just add the numbers (also known as numerical coefficients) to count the instances of $x^3$: $37 + 10 = 47$.

>> $15y^2 - 10y^2 = 5y^2$. Just subtract the numbers to count the instances of $y^2$: $15 - 10 = 5$.

TIP

You can't count bases with different exponents or different bases. In other words, $13x^3 - 9x^2$ stays $13x^3 - 9x^2$, and $2x^2 + 3y^2$ stays $2x^2 + 3y^2$. The bases and exponents must be the same for you to combine them.

There's your refresher of basic exponents, but no SAT Math question asks about exponents like that. Here is what you need to know to take on an exponent question on SAT Math:

>> **You can apply the exponent to terms multiplied together.** If $x$ and $y$ are multiplied together, as $xy$, and the exponent is applied to them, as in $(xy)^3$, this is the same as $x^3 \cdot y^3$.

● You can multiply bases that have the same exponent: $a^4 \cdot b^4 = (ab)^4$.

● Try it with real numbers:

$$2^2 \times 3^2 = 6^2$$
$$4 \times 9 = 36$$

>> **You can multiply a base with an exponent by expressions in parentheses:** Distribute the base with the exponent by each term in the parentheses. It's easier than it sounds:

● To simplify $x^2(x^3 + 1)$, distribute (which means "multiply") $x^2$ among $x^3$ and 1 separately for an answer of $x^5 + x^2$.

● To simplify $a^3(a^4 + a^5)$, first multiply $a^3$ by $a^4$ (to get $a^7$) and then by $a^5$ (to get $a^8$) for a final answer of $a^7 + a^8$.

>> **You can factor a base with an exponent from a pair of like bases with different exponents.** This is simply the reverse of the previous step.

To factor $n^5 - n^3$, divide both $n$'s by the same $n$ with an exponent.

● You could divide by $n$ (which is the same as $n^1$): $n(n^4 - n^2)$.

● You could divide by $n^2$: $n^2(n^3 - n)$.

● You could divide by $n^3$: $n^3(n^2 - 1)$.

Factor the expression according to the SAT Math Test question. For example, say $n^5 - n^3$ were to appear in a question, like this:

PLAY

The expression $\dfrac{(n^5 - n^3)}{(n^2 - 1)}$ is equivalent to:

**(A)** $n^3$

**(B)** $n^2$

**(C)** $n$

**(D)** 1

You can factor $n^5 - n^3$ one of the three ways shown before. Which one do you use? Well, only one of them produces a factor that cancels with $n^2 - 1$: $n^3(n^2 - 1)$.

Now factor $n^5 - n^3$ into $n^3(n^2 - 1)$ and revisit the question:

$$\frac{\left(n^5 - n^3\right)}{\left(n^2 - 1\right)}$$

$$\frac{n^3\left(n^2 - 1\right)}{\left(n^2 - 1\right)}$$

Cancel the $(n^2 - 1)$ from the top and bottom, and you're left with $n^3$, which matches Choice (A).

*That* is how you see exponents in SAT Math. With some practice, you'll spot the trick and answer each of these in under a minute. Here are a couple for you to try. It takes longer than a minute at first:

**PLAY**

If $x - y = 3$, what is the value of $\frac{2^x}{2^y}$?

**(A)** 2

**(B)** 4

**(C)** 8

**(D)** 16

Suppose you had to find the value of $\frac{2^7}{2^4}$. It's 2 with an exponent of $7-4$, or $\frac{2^7}{2^4} = 2^{7-4} = 2^3$, like you've been doing all along. So here it's the *same thing*, only with $x$ and $y$ instead of 7 and 4: $\frac{2^x}{2^y} = 2^{x-y}$. *Okay, Mr. Smart Instructor*, you're probably thinking, *what the #&%! am I going to do with* $2^{x-y}$? Then — snap your fingers — the question tells you that $x - y = 3$. Oh. $2^{x-y} \rightarrow 2^3 = 8$. The answer is Choice (C).

Here's another one like it. Now that you know what you're doing, your challenge is to answer this one in under a minute. Ready?

**PLAY**

If $b - a = 2$, what is the value of $\frac{3^b}{3^a}$?

**(A)** 3

**(B)** 9

**(C)** 27

**(D)** 81

Start with $\frac{3^b}{3^a} = 3^{b-a}$. The question tells you that $b - a = 2$, so solve it like this: $3^{b-a} \rightarrow 3^2 = 9$, for answer Choice (B). How long did that take? It's the *same exact question*, but you know what you're doing, so it takes *less than a minute*.

One more. This is a prime example of how the SAT Math questions *aren't math problems: they're puzzles. If you start doing a lot of math, you missed what the question is asking.* There is almost *no math* to this question.

**PLAY**

If $(2g - 3h)^3 = 27$, then $(2g - 3h)^{-2} =$

**(A)** $\frac{1}{9}$

**(B)** $\frac{1}{6}$

**(C)** 6

**(D)** 9

Forget the values of $g$ and $h$. Look at the first equation: $(2g - 3h)^3 = 27$. Think about it like a puzzle. If something cubed is 27, what could it be? It has to be 3. So place 3 for $(2g - 3h)$ in the second equation:

$$(2g - 3h)^{-2}$$
$$(3)^{-2}$$
$$\frac{1}{(3)^2}$$
$$\frac{1}{9}$$

Choice (A) is correct.

These questions show the many, many variations of exponent questions based on the basic rules, *each of which you can just as easily handle after working through it once.* Exponents is a common topic on the SAT Math Tests, so be sure to practice.

**TIP**

The exponent affects only what it's touching. For example, $5x^2$ is equivalent to $5 \cdot x \cdot x$. You may wonder why the 5 isn't also squared: It's because the exponent is only touching the $x$. If you want to square the 5 also, put the expression in parentheses with the exponent on the outside: $(5x)^2 = 5 \cdot x \cdot 5 \cdot x = 25x^2$. This is also true with the negative sign: Put $-5^2$ in the calculator, and it returns $-25$. This is because the calculator reads $-5^2$ as $-(5 \cdot 5) = -25$. In other words, it squares the 5 and places the negative on it: $-25$. To square the entire $-5$, place it in parentheses and square it, like $(-5)^2$. The calculator reads this as $(-5) \times (-5)$ and returns the answer you were expecting: 25.

## Simplifying square and cube roots

A *square root* refers to a quantity that, when squared, yields the starting quantity. For example, $\sqrt{16} = 4$, because $4^2 = 16$. A *cube root* is similar, except the quantity is cubed to yield the starting quantity. For example, $\sqrt[3]{8} = 2$, because $2^3 = 8$.

In math-speak, a *radical* is a root as well as the symbol indicating a root, $\sqrt{\phantom{x}}$. Although most numbers have square roots that are decidedly not pretty, ($\sqrt{2}$, for example, equals approximately 1.41), most of the radicals you encounter on the SAT will either simplify nicely (such as $\sqrt{25} = 5$) or can be left in the radical form (such as $\sqrt{2}$ or $3\sqrt{5}$).

A square root always yields a positive number because a quantity times itself is never negative. The square root of any negative number is therefore not a real number and is referred to as $i$ for *imaginary*. Whereas $\sqrt{25} = 5$ represents a real number, $\sqrt{-9} = \sqrt{9} \times \sqrt{-1} = 3i$ and is imaginary, covered later in this chapter.

**TIP**

When $x^2 = 16$, $x$ can equal either 4 or $-4$, because you're not taking the square root of $x^2$ or 16: you're finding values of $x$ that satisfy the equation $x^2 = 16$. $\sqrt{16}$ can only be 4, and not $-4$, because a square root can only be a positive number. The $x^2$ variation is covered further in Chapter 11.

A cube root, on the other hand, may yield a positive or negative number, because a quantity times itself three times may be positive or negative. For example, $\sqrt[3]{64} = 4$ and $\sqrt[3]{-64} = -4$, because $(-4)(-4)(-4) = -64$.

Multiplying and dividing radicals is simple, as long as they're the same type of root (in other words, square or cube). Just multiply and divide the numbers as if there's no radical: $\sqrt{5} \times \sqrt{6} = \sqrt{30}$ and $\sqrt{14} \div \sqrt{7} = \sqrt{2}$. Note that you can't add or subtract radicals. For example, $\sqrt{3} + \sqrt{5}$ stays $\sqrt{3} + \sqrt{5}$. You can, however, count radicals if they're the same: $\sqrt{3} + \sqrt{3} = 2\sqrt{3}$, in the same way that $x + x = 2x$.

To take the square root of a fraction, take the square roots of the numerator and denominator as separate numbers. For example, to take the square root of $\sqrt{\frac{4}{25}}$, take the square roots of 4 and 25 separately: $\frac{\sqrt{4}}{\sqrt{25}} = \frac{2}{5}$

If the numerator and denominator don't square root easily, try simplifying the fraction first: $\sqrt{\frac{50}{2}} = \sqrt{25} = 5$

You can break down any radical by factoring out a perfect square and simplifying it, like these:

$$\sqrt{27}$$
$$\left(\sqrt{9}\right)\left(\sqrt{3}\right)$$
$$3\sqrt{3}$$

and

$$\sqrt{12}$$
$$\left(\sqrt{4}\right)\left(\sqrt{3}\right)$$
$$2\sqrt{3}$$

A root can also be shown as a fractional exponent. For example, $3^{\frac{1}{2}} = \sqrt{3}$ and $5^{\frac{1}{3}} = \sqrt[3]{5}$. The denominator of the fraction becomes the *index number* (the small number outside the radical), and the numerator of the fraction stays as the exponent. For example, $7^{\frac{3}{5}} = \sqrt[5]{7^3}$.

Now try some practice:

PLAY

Which is equivalent to $5\sqrt{18}$?

**(A)** $15\sqrt{2}$

**(B)** $12\sqrt{3}$

**(C)** $10\sqrt{5}$

**(D)** $8\sqrt{6}$

Simplify $5\sqrt{18}$ by factoring out the perfect square.

$$5\sqrt{18}$$
$$5\left(\sqrt{9}\right)\left(\sqrt{2}\right)$$
$$5(3)\left(\sqrt{2}\right)$$
$$15\sqrt{2}$$

And the answer is Choice (A).

PLAY

Which of the following is equivalent to $x^{\frac{n}{p}}$ for all values $x$, $n$, and $p$?

**(A)** $\sqrt[n]{x^p}$

**(B)** $\sqrt[p]{x^n}$

**(C)** $\sqrt[n]{x^{\frac{1}{p}}}$

**(D)** $\sqrt[p]{x^{\frac{1}{n}}}$

See, if you know what to do, the question takes less than a minute. When the exponent is a fraction, the denominator of the fraction (in this case, $p$) becomes the *index number* (the small number outside the radical), and the numerator of the fraction (in this case, $n$) stays as the exponent. And of course, the base (in this case, $x$) stays the base. The correct answer is thus Choice (B).

PLAY

$3\sqrt{x} + 5 = 17$

What value of $x$ satisfies the above equation?

Start by isolating the $\sqrt{x}$:

$$3\sqrt{x} + 5 = 17$$
$$3\sqrt{x} = 12$$
$$\sqrt{x} = 4$$

Now don't make the mistake of thinking that $x$ should be 2; $\sqrt{2}$ doesn't equal 4. Instead, square both sides, and $x = 16$.

Square roots are fairly common on the SAT Math Tests, as are cube roots to a lesser extent.

## Simplifying imaginary *i*

An *imaginary* number is a number that can't exist in real math. There are plenty in applied mathematics, but the only one that you see on the SAT results from the square root of a negative number.

A square root always yields a positive number because a quantity times itself is never negative. The square root of any negative number is therefore not a real number and *imaginary*, written as $i$. Whereas $\sqrt{4} = 2$ represents a real number, $\sqrt{-9} = \sqrt{9} \times \sqrt{-1} = 3i$. The italic $i$ specifically refers to the square root of $-1$, so you'll see $i$ defined either as $i = \sqrt{-1}$ or $i^2 = -1$. The two equations tell you exactly the same thing.

The most common mistake while working with $i$ is mixing up whether the result is positive or negative. Here's a summary of how $i$ works, but *don't memorize* this table. Instead, *understand* it.

| $i$ | result |
|-----|--------|
| $i$ | $i$ |
| $i^2$ | $-1$ |
| $i^3$ | $-i$ |
| $i^4$ | $1$ |
| $i^5$ | $i$ |

And it repeats. Because $i^4 = 1$, any power higher than 4 is simply 1 times one of the above results. What is $i^{10}$? Remember you multiply exponents by adding them, so it's like this:

$$i^{10} = \left(i^4\right)\left(i^4\right)\left(i^2\right)$$
$$= (1)(1)(-1)$$
$$= -1$$

Work with $i$ the same way that you work with $x$. As these are true with $x$:

$$2x + 3x = 5x$$
$$(3)4x = 12x$$

They are also true with $i$:

$$3i + 5i = 8i$$
$$(2)3i = 6i$$

One other thing. The SAT Math typically presents $i$ in the form of a quadratic, where you multiply the expressions using the FOIL method. Quadratics are covered further in Chapter 11, but for now, here's a refresher on that ol' FOIL.

FOIL stands for First Outer Inner Last, which basically means multiply everything in one expression by everything in the other. To multiply these expressions:

$$(x+2)(x-3)$$

Start with the First terms, $x$ times $x$, for $x^2$.

Now the Outer terms, $x$ times $-3$, for $-3x$.

Next the Inner terms, 2 times $x$, for $2x$.

Then the Last terms, 2 times $-3$, for $-6$.

Finally, add the pieces for a final quadratic result of $x^2 - x - 6$.

On these questions, you do this with terms containing $i$ instead of $x$, but it works exactly the same way, only $i^2$ becomes $-1$. Here's how the SAT offers it. You ready?

PLAY

For $i = \sqrt{-1}$, what is the value of $(4-3i)(2+i)$?

**(A)** $6-2i$

**(B)** $8+2i$

**(C)** $11-2i$

**(D)** $13+3i$

Don't get mad. FOIL it:

$$(4-3i)(2+i)$$
$$8+4i-6i+3$$
$$11-2i$$

Which piece by piece is:

$$(4)(2)=8$$
$$(4)(i)=4i$$
$$(-3i)(2)=-6i$$
$$(-3i)(i)=3$$

That last one, $(-3i)(i)$, is where you need to be sure it's 3 and not $-3$. Work it step by step:

$$(-3i)(i)$$
$$(-3)(i)(i)$$
$$(-3)(-1)$$
$$3$$

Now that you're sure, add them up for $11-2i$, which matches Choice (C).

Here's another one:

PLAY

If $i^2 = -1$ and $2x = 3i$, what is the value of $4x^2$?

**(A)** $-3$

**(B)** $-4$

**(C)** $-6$

**(D)** $-9$

$4x^2$ is simply $(2x)(2x)$. Because $2x = 3i$, it's also $(3i)(3i)$:

$$(3i)(3i)$$
$$(3)(3)(i)(i)$$
$$(9)(-1)$$
$$-9$$

which matches Choice (D).

You're almost guaranteed to see at least one $i$ question on the SAT Math Tests. There are more $i$ questions tied to conjugates, covered further in Chapter 11.

# Simplifying projections

A *projection* is a scenario where you predict a future state based on a math formula. For example, if today the orange tree is 12 feet tall, and each year it grows 3 more feet, then how tall will it be in 5 years? If $t$ is the unit of time, in this case a year, then in $t$ years the tree will grow $3t$ feet. If today the tree is 12 feet tall, its future height, called $h$, can be projected with this formula:

$$h = 12 + 3t$$

How tall will this tree be in 5 years? Place in 5 for $t$ and simplify it:

$$\begin{aligned} h &= 12 + 3t \\ &= 12 + 3(5) \\ &= 12 + 15 \\ &= 27 \end{aligned}$$

And the orange tree will be 27 feet tall.

The SAT may ask you what the 3, the 12, or the $t$ of the formula represent:

> The 3 represents the additional number of feet per year, so that each year counted by $t$ adds 3 feet to its height.

> The 12 represents the starting height of the tree.

> The $t$ represents the time, in years, that is measured by the formula.

The SAT may also ask how the formula may change. Suppose the tree only grows 2 feet per year, instead of 3. How would you change the formula? Make the 3 into a 2, so that each year $t$ only adds 2 feet to the tree's height:

$$h = 12 + 2t$$

That's a simple projection, and you'll see more of these with linear equations in Chapter 11. The SAT also gives a notoriously complex-looking projection formula, which is actually very simple once the shock factor wears off. This is the epitome of the SAT Math question that looks like madness but (1) *is workable in less than a minute* **if you know what to do,** and (2) *takes simple math* **if you don't fall for the trap.**

The formula in a projection usually has an exponent that's a fraction, and that's the part that makes you jumpy. Don't be. The fraction *always* cancels out, and the rest of the formula *always* becomes simple.

Next to the orange tree is a pomegranate tree. This tree is 5 feet high, and its height is projected with this formula:

$$h = 5 + \frac{10^{\frac{t}{2}}}{t}$$

Do you think the SAT will ask you to project the tree's height in 9 years, or 11 years? No. It'll ask you to project 2 years, or 4 years, or some number that *cancels the fraction exponent* and *keeps the math simple.*

How tall will the pomegranate tree be in 4 years? Place 4 in for $t$:

$$h = 5 + \frac{10^{\frac{t}{2}}}{t}$$

$$= 5 + \frac{10^{\frac{(4)}{2}}}{(4)}$$

$$= 5 + \frac{10^2}{4}$$

$$= 5 + \frac{100}{4}$$

$$= 5 + 25$$

$$= 30$$

And the tree will be 30 feet tall.

**TIP**

Forget the calculator! You don't need it. In fact, the calculator makes this worse, because it takes you down a complex calculation path — the *trap* — that is *way off* from what you need to answer this question. Remember the wisdom from Chapter 9: *If you find yourself working a lot of math, check your approach.*

**PLAY**

$$f(d) = 100 + \left(2^{\frac{d}{2}} + \frac{d}{3}\right)100$$

This equation is a model of the projected number of seed pods given off by a certain Eucalyptus tree in the spring, where $d$ represents the number of days after the start of pollination and $f(d)$ represents the projected number of seed pods. According to the model, what is the projected number of seed pods at the end of the sixth day?

Don't be scared by the equation! Remember, the SAT gives you a number to place in that makes all the fractions cancel out. In this case, place in 6 for $d$, and it's almost too simple:

$$f(d) = 100 + \left(2^{\frac{d}{2}} + \frac{d}{3}\right)100$$

$$= 100 + \left(2^{\frac{(6)}{2}} + \frac{(6)}{3}\right)100$$

$$= 100 + \left(2^3 + 2\right)100$$

$$= 100 + \left(8 + 2\right)100$$

$$= 100 + \left(10\right)100$$

$$= 100 + 1{,}000$$

$$= 1{,}100$$

Here's another one.

**PLAY**

The population of a certain city can be modeled by the function $p(y) = 20,000 \left( 2^{\frac{y}{20}} \right)$, where $p(y)$ represents the population and $y$ measures years since 1990. Based on this function, the projected population of the city in 2030 is

**(A)** 40,000

**(B)** 60,000

**(C)** 80,000

**(D)** 100,000

Put away your calculator. SAT projections are simple, even if they look mad. The expression $2^{\frac{y}{20}}$ isn't so bad when $y$ is a multiple of 20, and in this case it's 40 (the number of years from 1990 to 2030). This means that $2^{\frac{y}{20}}$ is really just $2^{\frac{40}{20}}$, or $2^2$, which of course equals 4. So the answer is 20,000(4), which equals 80,000, or Choice (C). Who needs a calculator? And — how long did this one take? Guessing Less. Than. A. Minute.

Projection questions are common on the SAT Math Tests, so practice until you're comfortable with them.

# Chapter **11**

# Algebra and Functions

*lgebra and functions* are an extension of the numbers and operations covered in Chapter 10. Topics in this chapter comprise about half of the SAT Math Test questions, and while numbers and operations generate only about a quarter of the SAT Math Test questions (as if that's not enough), it's important to understand the concepts in Chapter 10 before moving on to Chapter 11. The topics that follow here build upon the foundation set in the previous chapter.

## Solving for *X*

Solving for $x$ is just that: Turning something like $2x + 3 = 5$ into $2x = 2$ and finally $x = 1$. Simple, right? But the SAT, being what it is, varies this idea in ways you haven't seen before and won't see again until your graduate admissions GMAT or GRE. But that's another story.

The SAT, still being what it is, stays within its predefined scope of math topics and sets the questions up for easy answering if you know how to answer them. This chapter takes you through these SAT-level topics and shows you how to answer each question in less than a minute.

### Solving for *x* with a number

To solve for $x$ or any other variable that the question asks for, move that variable to one side of the equation, and divide both sides of the equation by the coefficient. For example, where $4x = x + 6$, subtract $x$ from both sides of the equation for $3x = 6$. Divide both sides by 3, for $x = 2$, and the solution is 2.

A common SAT trap is where it gives the equation $4x = x + 6$, but instead of asking you to solve for $x$, it asks you to solve for $3x$. Working this problem is just as simple, but you fall back on your tendency to solve for $x$ instead of what the question is asking. Of course, $3x = 6$, but how many test-takers fall for the trap and respond that $x = 2$, which is correct but the wrong answer?

Try this one:

**PLAY**

$$2x + 8 = 12$$

In the above equation, what is the value of $x + 3$?

**(A)** 4

**(B)** 5

**(C)** 6

**(D)** 7

Your reflex is to solve for $x$, which is fine, but be sure to adjust your answer for the value of $x + 3$ and answer Choice (B):

$$2x + 8 = 12$$
$$2x = 4$$
$$x = 2$$
$$x + 3 = 5$$

Practice this so you get used to spotting the trap. You don't want to lose these easy points by sticking with a process that has been correct since grade school, which is solving for $x$ by itself.

## Solving for $x$ with a $y$

The SAT keeps this up by trying to confuse you further. Just as with the projections questions in Chapter 10, these questions appear menacing but are actually simple *if you know what to do.*

The SAT gives you an equation with two unknowns, such as $3x + 4y = 18$ asks you to solve for $x$, and tells you what $y$ is: $y = 3$. Just place in 3 for $y$ and solve for $x$.

$$3x + 4y = 18$$
$$3x + 4(3) = 18$$
$$3x + 12 = 18$$
$$3x = 6$$
$$x = 2$$

The first time you see one of these, you might get stuck putting it together. Of course, the letters aren't always $x$ and $y$. Try this one:

**PLAY**

If $a - b = 1$ and $\frac{b}{3} = 1$, what is the value of $a$?

**(A)** 4

**(B)** 5

**(C)** 6

**(D)** 7

Start with $\frac{b}{3} = 1$. Multiply both sides by 3, and you know that $b = 3$. There! That's the hard part. Now place 3 in for $b$ and solve that puppy:

$$a - b = 1$$
$$a - (3) = 1$$
$$a = 4$$

And the answer is Choice (A), just like that. If this question took you longer than a minute, that's okay. That's why you're here.

# Solving for $x$ in a radical

Another common question type that the SAT presents, which is also just as solvable in a minute if you know what to do, is an equation where an expression with $x$ is embedded within a radical. Just go through it once, practice a few, and you'll have these down for the exam.

Take an equation like this:

$$\sqrt{2x^2 + 7} - 4 = 1$$

Start by keeping everything under the radical on one side of the equal sign, and move everything not in the radical on the other. In this case, add 4 to both sides:

$$\sqrt{2x^2 + 7} = 5$$

Now that one side is completely under the radical, and the other side is not, square both sides:

$$2x^2 + 7 = 25$$

And solve for $x$ the way you usually do:

$$2x^2 + 7 = 25$$
$$2x^2 = 18$$
$$x^2 = 9$$
$$x = 3, -3$$

Here, try one:

**PLAY**

If $\sqrt{3x^3 + 1} - 2 = 3$, what is the value of $x$?

**(A)** 2

**(B)** 3

**(C)** 5

**(D)** 7

You're not laughing. You should be! Each step is simple, and you know where to start. First add 2 to both sides to get rid of the $-2$, then square both sides, and the rest just falls into place:

$$\sqrt{3x^3 + 1} - 2 = 3$$
$$\sqrt{3x^3 + 1} = 5$$
$$3x^3 + 1 = 25$$
$$3x^3 = 24$$
$$x^3 = 8$$
$$x = 2$$

Of course, there are other variations, but if you can manage this, the others won't faze you. Keep in mind that the math is always simple, and the SAT sets its questions up to work out neatly.

# Solving for $x$ in a fraction

The SAT places $x$ (or another variable) into a fraction, like this:

$$\frac{2}{15}x = \frac{2}{3}$$

First thing: When $x$ is outside the fraction, move it to the top of the fraction:

$$\frac{2}{15}x \rightarrow \frac{2x}{15}$$

The basic approach is to cross multiply:

$$\frac{2x}{15} = \frac{2}{3}$$
$$(2x)(3) = (15)(2)$$
$$6x = 30$$
$$x = 5$$

If one side of the equation is a fraction and the other side isn't, then multiply both sides by the denominator of the fraction:

$$\frac{2x}{5} = 4$$
$$(5)\frac{2x}{5} = 4(5)$$
$$2x = 20$$
$$x = 10$$

If both sides have the same denominator, you can just eliminate the denominator (which is the same as multiplying both sides by that denominator).

$$\frac{x}{7} = \frac{43}{7}$$
$$x = 43$$

If $\frac{x-2}{4} = \frac{x+3}{5}$, what is the value of $x$?

PLAY

**(A)** 12

**(B)** 22

**(C)** 24

**(D)** 30

Cross multiply and find your answer:

$$\frac{x-2}{4} = \frac{x+3}{5}$$
$$(x-2)(5) = (4)(x+3)$$
$$5x - 10 = 4x + 12$$
$$x = 22$$

And the answer is Choice (B).

Cross multiplying always works, but sometimes there's a simpler way to solve the problem. See if you can find it with this question:

In the equation $5 - \frac{2x+2}{x+1} = \frac{9}{x+1}$, $x$ is equal to

**(A)** 0

**(B)** 1

**(C)** 2

**(D)** 3

PLAY

Note that the two fractions have common denominators, which means they can be easily combined. In this case, add the clunky $\frac{2x+2}{x+1}$ to both sides:

$$5 - \frac{2x+2}{x+1} = \frac{9}{x+1}$$
$$5 = \frac{9}{x+1} + \frac{2x+2}{x+1}$$
$$5 = \frac{9+2x+2}{x+1}$$
$$5 = \frac{11+2x}{x+1}$$

Now, multiply $x+1$ on both sides and solve for $x$:

$$5 = \frac{11+2x}{x+1}$$
$$(x+1)5 = 11+2x$$
$$5x+5 = 11+2x$$
$$3x = 6$$
$$x = 2$$

And Choice (C) is correct.

Sometimes cross multiplying produces a quadratic (meaning you get an $x^2$ along with an $x$), but the practice questions with quadratics are held for later in this chapter.

## Solving for $x$ in a reciprocal fraction

The SAT presents you with a fraction and asks you to reciprocate it to the other side. In its simplest form, the question looks like this:

If $y = \frac{2}{3}x$, what is $x$ in terms of $y$?

The most effective way to do this is to separate the fraction $\frac{2}{3}$, reciprocate it to $\frac{3}{2}$, and place it on the other side.

$$y = \frac{2}{3}x$$
$$y = \left(\frac{2}{3}\right)x$$
$$\left(\frac{3}{2}\right)y = x$$
$$\frac{3}{2}y = x$$

Technically this is multiplying both sides by the reciprocal, but the separate-and-reciprocate approach is faster with some of the complex fractions that appear on the SAT. Also, the SAT likes to muddle the question. It presents something absurd, like $y = x\frac{2\sqrt{3g}h^4}{5k}$, and asks for $x$ in terms of $y$, which means $x = y(\text{something})$. Note that the answer choices are all in that form. The SAT doesn't just ask for that, though — it presents the question like this:

**PLAY**

If $y = x\dfrac{2\sqrt{3g}h^4}{5k}$, what is $x$ in terms of $g$, $h$, $k$, and $y$?

**(A)** $x = y\dfrac{2\sqrt{3g}h^4}{5k}$

**(B)** $x = y\dfrac{5k}{2\sqrt{3g}h^4}$

**(C)** $x = 2y\sqrt{3g}h^4$

**(D)** $x = 10y\sqrt{3g}h^4 k$

Now you *could* multiply both sides by the reciprocal, $\dfrac{5k}{2\sqrt{3g}h^4}$, and that *will work*, but isn't it easier to just take the reciprocal and move it to the other side? That gives you Choice (B) in . . . 20 seconds?

Does this always work? No. You need to make sure that the fraction is set up to work this way, because *sometimes* you have to break apart the fraction. But first check; *maybe* you can just reciprocate and move it over. Before you step into the complex math, see whether you can just reciprocate and move the fraction.

If the question presents you with $y = x(\text{something})$ and asks for $x$ in terms of $y$, make sure that the $x$ that you're separating out is both in the numerator of the fraction and isn't squared or in a radical. Of course, the question could use any set of letters, but the process is the same.

Remember that $\dfrac{2}{3}x$ and $\dfrac{2x}{3}$ are the same, as are $y = x\dfrac{\sqrt{3g}h^4}{5k}$ and $y = \dfrac{x\sqrt{3g}h^4}{5k}$.

Try it out. Make your mistakes here, now, in practice, so you get it right on the real thing.

# Solving for More Than One *X*

So far, solving for $x$ has meant, for the most part, that you find *one* value for $x$. If $3x = 15$, then you know $x = 5$, and you're good. But many questions on the SAT Math tests ask what $x$ *could* be if it has more than one possible value, such as $x^2 = 9$. In this case, $x$ equals either 3 or $-3$, and you don't know which one. Note that this is usually written as $x = 3, -3$, and it's understood that $x$ has *one* of the two possible values, but not both. These multiple values are also called the *solutions* to the equation.

## Solving an absolute value

*Absolute value* means the distance from 0 on the number line. Because distance is always positive, absolute value is also always positive. The number or value has bars on either side, like this: $|-15|$. Because $-15$ is 15 away from 0, the absolute value of $-15$ is 15, written in math as $|-15| = 15$.

A positive number works the same way. The absolute value of 3 is written $|3|$, which equals 3, because it's 3 away from 0 on the number line. The absolute value of $-5$ is written $|-5|$, which equals 5, because it's 5 away from 0 on the number line.

Be sure to simplify any expression inside the absolute value bars first. If you're working with $|3-4|$, calculate that first, for $|3-4|=|-1|$, and only *then* take the absolute value, which in this case is 1.

If you have an $x$ or other unknown inside the absolute value expression, it means that the expression is that distance from 0 on the number line, and typically could be in two separate places. For example:

$$|x|=7$$

This tells you that $x$ is 7 away from 0 on the number line, but you don't know whether it's on the positive side or negative side, which means that the $x$ could equal 7 or −7. A couple points to glean here:

>> Any $x$ has *one* value: You don't know which one it is without more information. (With $|x|=7$, something like $x > 0$ would do the trick.)

>> Any absolute value is always *positive*. A number cannot be a negative distance from 0, so an equation like $|x|=-5$ is impossible, or in math, has *no solutions*.

With an expression like $|x+2|=5$, you know that $|x+2|$ is 5 away from 0 on the number line, but you don't know whether it goes positive or negative. Therefore, you actually have two equations: $x+2=5$ and $x+2=-5$. Solve them separately for the two possible values of $x$:

$$x+2=5 \quad \text{and} \quad x+2=-5$$
$$x=3 \qquad\qquad x=-7$$

Given $|x+2|=5$, you know that $x$ could equal either 3 or −7. Now try one.

**PLAY**

In the equation $|x-4|=3$, $x$ could equal:

If $|x-4|$ is 3 away from 0, solve this as two separate equations:

$$x-4=3 \quad \text{and} \quad x-4=-3$$
$$x=7 \qquad\qquad x=1$$

Grid in either 1 or 7, and you got this one right.

**REMEMBER**

The value of $x$ can't be both 7 *and* 1. $x$ has *one* value, and that's why the question reads, "$x$ *could* equal."

# Solving a quadratic

A *quadratic* is an equation having an $x^2$ and often an $x$, such as $x^2 + 2x - 15 = 0$. Quadratics are one of the most commonly occurring SAT Math Test questions, and on the SAT, they are simpler than the ones you encounter in Algebra II. Here are some notes:

>> With a quadratic, $x$ usually, but not always, has two possible values.

>> A quadratic results from any equation where $x$ is multiplied by itself. For example, cross multiplying the fractions $\frac{2}{x} = \frac{x}{2}$ results in a quadratic. (In this example, the fractions cross multiply to $x^2 = 4$, so $x = 2$ or $x = -2$.)

>> When $x$ appears more than one time in a single equation or set of equations, all the $x$'s have the *same* value at one time. If an $x$ changes (as in a graphed equation), all the $x$'s change with it.

>> You may need to know what $a$, $b$, and $c$ are from a quadratic equation. These are simply the coefficients from the equation when it equals 0. In the equation $x^2 + 2x - 15 = 0$, $a$, $b$, and $c$ are 1, 2, and –15, respectively (because $x^2$ times 1 is $x^2$, $x$ times 2 is $2x$, and 1 times –15 is, of course, –15).

>> On the SAT, *most* quadratics are simple enough to solve without the Quadratic Formula. You *rarely* need this, but if you do, just place $a$, $b$, and $c$ as described earlier into the formula:

$$x = \frac{-b \pm \sqrt{b^2 - 4ac}}{2a}$$

>> When you draw the graph of any quadratic equation, including $y = x^2 + 2x - 15$, in the $xy$-coordinate plane, the graph results in a parabola, covered later in this chapter.

There are two parts to working with quadratics. The first part is multiplying the expressions, and the second part is factoring them. You multiply expressions using the FOIL method, covered in Chapter 10 and reviewed here:

FOIL stands for First Outer Inner Last, which basically means everything in one expression is multiplied by everything in the other expression. To multiply these expressions:

$$(x + 2)(x - 3)$$

Start with the First terms, $x$ times $x$, for $x^2$

Now the Outer terms, $x$ times –3, for $-3x$

Next the Inner terms, 2 times $x$, for $2x$

Then the Last terms, 2 times –3, for –6

Finally add the pieces for a final quadratic result of $x^2 - x - 6$.

Try this one:

PLAY

The expression $(x - 3)^2$ is equivalent to

(A) $x^2 - 9$

(B) $x^2 + 9$

(C) $x^2 + 6x - 9$

(D) $x^2 - 6x + 9$

The exponent 2 means that $(x-3)$ is multiplied by itself, telling you that this is one to FOIL. (You also know this because you read about the FOIL method not even a page ago.) Set it up to FOIL and go through the steps:

$$(x-3)(x-3)$$
$$x^2-3x-3x+9$$
$$x^2-6x+9$$

And the answer is Choice (D).

More common than *multiplying* expressions is *factoring* them. The numeric part of factoring is always simple: The trick is knowing the concept.

For example, given $x^2+2x=15$, solve for $x$.

**1.** **Set the equation equal to 0.**

It *usually* will already be equal to 0, but just in case:

$$x^2+2x-15=0$$

**2.** **Set up your answer by drawing two sets of parentheses:**
$$(\quad)(\quad)=0$$

**3.** **To get $x^2$, the *first* terms are $x$ and $x$. Fill those in:**
$$(x\quad)(x\quad)=0$$

**4.** **Look now at the *middle* and *last* terms of the equation.**

What two numbers add to 2 and multiply to –15? Remember that on SAT Math, *this part will be simple*. How about 5 and –3?

$$(x+5)(x-3)=0$$

**5.** **If you're not sure, FOIL it back out.**

Just takes a second, and it's worth knowing you did this right:

$$(x+5)(x-3)$$
$$x^2-3x+5x-15$$
$$x^2+2x-15$$

Nice! So how does $(x+5)(x-3)=0$ tell you what $x$ could be? Treat it like two separate equations:

$$(x+5)=0$$
$$(x-3)=0$$

Meaning that $x$ could equal either 3 or –5. In math that's written as $x=3,-5$, and it's understood that $x$ has only one of these two values. Also, when you graph the equation $y=x^2+2x-15$, the resulting parabola crosses the $x$-axis at 3 and –5.

The SAT likes to explore variations of the quadratic. Here are a few:

PLAY

What are the solutions to the equation $2x^2 - 2x = 24$?

**(A)** 3,–4

**(B)** 4,–3

**(C)** 6,–8

**(D)** 8,–6

First set the equation equal to 0: $2x^2 - 2x - 24 = 0$. What next? Divide both sides by 2: $x^2 - x - 12 = 0$. *Now* you can factor it:

$$x^2 - x - 12 = 0$$
$$(x-4)(x+3) = 0$$
$$x = 4,-3$$

for an answer of Choice (B).

Here's another variation:

PLAY

If $x > 0$, what are the solutions to the equation $x^4 - 13x^2 + 36 = 0$?

**(A)** 2,3

**(B)** 4,9

**(C)** 8,18

**(D)** 16,36

Factor this one like a regular quadratic, only with $x^2$ instead of $x$:

$$x^4 - 13x^2 + 36 = 0$$
$$(x^2 - 4)(x^2 - 9) = 0$$
$$x^2 = 4,9$$

And if $x^2$ is 4 or 9, then $x$ is 2 or 3, for Choice (A). Good thing $x > 0$, or this one would have four solutions: the regular 2 and 3 along with –2 and –3.

Crazy, isn't it? That question is *so simple* looking back at it. Here's another:

PLAY

What are the solutions to the equation $x - 9\sqrt{x} + 20 = 0$?

**(A)** 2,3

**(B)** 4,5

**(C)** 16,25

**(D)** 25,81

Yep. Factor it out. It works exactly the same way; just keep in mind that $x$ factors to $\sqrt{x}$ times $\sqrt{x}$.

$$x - 9\sqrt{x} + 20 = 0$$
$$(\sqrt{x} - 4)(\sqrt{x} - 5) = 0$$
$$\sqrt{x} = 4,5$$
$$x = 16,25$$

Thus, the correct answer is Choice (C).

Here's the strategy for this one:

When a perfect square equals a perfect square, take the square root of both sides, and make the numeric side both positive and negative. You know this: $x^2 = 16 \rightarrow x = 4, -4$. Here's the SAT variant:

What are the solutions to the equation $(x-3)^2 = 25$?

**(A)** 4,3

**(B)** 5,2

**(C)** 6,–5

**(D)** 8,–2

The point of this question is that you don't always set it equal to 0 and factor. You could, but here it's faster to take the square root of both sides:

$$(x-3)^2 = 25$$
$$x - 3 = 5, -5$$
$$x = 8, -2$$

In that last step, you're adding 3 to both 5 and –5, for the answers 8 and –2, which match Choice (D).

When you take the root of $(x-3)^2 = 25$, *don't* use ± and write it as $x - 3 = \pm5$. While this is technically true, you need to add 3 to both 5 and –5, and by using ±, you lose the negative answer. Take the extra second and write both 5 and –5.

These are just some of the ways that SAT Math varies the quadratic. First you get stuck, then you work through the answer, and then you totally understand the question. Get stuck on these questions *here, now*, when it *doesn't* matter — and have them for breakfast on Exam Day. Quadratics are among the most commonly asked topics on the SAT Math Tests — you might see five of these — so practice all the variations.

## Solving the difference of squares

A *difference of squares* is a specific quadratic where a perfect square is subtracted from a perfect square, as in $a^2 - b^2$. This expression factors to $(a-b)(a+b)$, so remember it like this:

$$a^2 - b^2 = (a-b)(a+b)$$

Of course, it could be any letters, but it doesn't matter. You don't find out what $a$ and $b$ are, but you don't need to. Think of it like this: $(a+b)$ times $(a-b)$ equals $a^2 - b^2$. So if $(a+b)$ is 8, and $(a-b)$ is 3, what is $a^2 - b^2$? Why, it's 24.

Note that if you foil out $(a-b)(a+b)$, there's no middle term: it's simply $a^2 - b^2$.

In its simplest form, the SAT asks about the difference of squares like this:

If $c^2 - d^2 = 15$ and $c + d = 5$, what is the value of $c - d$?

**(A)** 2

**(B)** 3

**(C)** 4

**(D)** 5

Set it up and place the values that you know:

$$c^2 - d^2 = (c-d)(c+d)$$
$$(15) = (c-d)(5)$$
$$c - d = 3$$

Now the SAT doesn't ask about the difference of squares *quite* like that. That would be too easy! For you, it'll *still* be too easy. Anyway, the SAT embeds the difference of squares into other math topics. Try this one:

If $y^2 - x^2 = 16$ and $y + x = 8$, what is the value of $\frac{2^y}{2^x}$?

**(A)** 2

**(B)** 4

**(C)** 8

**(D)** 16

Start with the $\frac{2^y}{2^x}$ as you would any other divided exponent. The same way that $\frac{2^5}{2^3} = 2^{5-3}$, $\frac{2^y}{2^x} = 2^{y-x}$. Remember doing these in Chapter 10? Anyway, if $y^2 - x^2 = 16$ and $y + x = 8$, you know that $y - x = 2$, so place 2 in for $y - x$ in that exponent: $2^{y-x} \rightarrow 2^2 = 4$ for an easy, less-than-a-minute answer, Choice (B).

The difference of squares is also useful for rationalizing a fraction. *Rationalizing* means making the denominator into a rational number, which is the key to solving certain SAT fraction questions. For example, the fraction $\frac{\sqrt{5}}{\sqrt{3}}$ isn't rationalized. To rationalize it, multiply the top and bottom by $\sqrt{3}$, like this:

$$\frac{\sqrt{5}(\sqrt{3})}{\sqrt{3}(\sqrt{3})} = \frac{\sqrt{15}}{3}$$

The numerator isn't rational, but that's okay — the denominator is, and the fraction is rationalized.

When a polynomial expression is in the denominator, as in $\frac{2 - \sqrt{5}}{4 - \sqrt{5}}$, rationalize it by multiplying the top and bottom by *something* that eliminates the radical on the bottom. The denominator is $4 - \sqrt{5}$, so multiply top and bottom by $4 + \sqrt{5}$, like this:

$$\frac{(2 - \sqrt{5})(4 + \sqrt{5})}{(4 - \sqrt{5})(4 + \sqrt{5})}$$
$$\frac{8 + 2\sqrt{5} - 4\sqrt{5} - 5}{16 - 5}$$
$$\frac{3 - 2\sqrt{5}}{11}$$

The top still has the irrational $\sqrt{5}$, but that doesn't matter. The bottom is fully rational, and the fraction is thus rationalized.

Try this one:

**PLAY**

Which of the following is equivalent to the expression $\frac{2-3i}{3-i}$? Note that $i^2 = -1$.

(A) $\frac{9-7i}{10}$

(B) $\frac{9+7i}{8}$

(C) $\frac{9+7i}{10}$

(D) $\frac{9-7i}{8}$

Rationalize this one: The denominator is $3 - i$, so multiply top and bottom by $3 + i$, like this:

$$\frac{(2-3i)(3+i)}{(3-i)(3+i)}$$

$$\frac{6+2i-9i+3}{9+1}$$

$$\frac{9-7i}{10}$$

And the answer is Choice (A).

Difference of squares questions revisit topics from earlier in this chapter and Chapter 10, like old friends, including exponents, radicals, quadratics, imaginary $i$, and fractions, but with the difference of squares mixed in, like a new friend.

## Solving an expression

An *expression* in math is a set of values grouped together. It's another way that the SAT packages a simple concept as a challenging question. If you cut through the façade, the actual question is simple. Sound familiar?

Say you're solving for $x$: $2x = 6$ becomes $x = 3$, and you know what $x$ is because it's isolated. Do you *always* have to isolate the $x$? No. You can leave it in the expression. Try another one: $12^x = 12^7$. You know that $x = 7$ without isolating it. Okay, here's the concept again, but on a level higher. Find the value of $c$:

$$x^2 - 9x + 20 = x^2 - 9x + c$$

And $c = 20$, which you know for sure even though you didn't *isolate* it. Sometimes it helps to isolate the $c$, by crossing off $x^2$ and $-9x$ from both sides, but you don't *have* to.

And there you have the basics of this topic: Two expressions equal each other, and where there's a number on one side, there's an unknown on the other, and you find the value of the unknown. Sometimes you have to factor one side, or manipulate the equations somehow, but because this is the SAT, *you know it'll be simple even if it looks tricky.*

**PLAY**

In this equation, where $k$ is a constant, what is the value of $k$?

$$x^2 - 8x + 15 = (x-3)(x-k)$$

(A) 5

(B) 15

(C) 25

(D) 45

Factor the polynomial on the left so it matches the one on the right:

$$x^2 - 8x + 15$$
$$(x-3)(x-5)$$

Now it looks like this: $(x-3)(x-5) = (x-3)(x-k)$.

And you know that $k$ is 5 for an answer of Choice (A).

Here's another variation:

**PLAY**

In this equation, where $k$ is a constant, what is the value of $k$?

$$3(x^2 - 5x + 6) = 3x^2 - 15x + 6k$$

**(A)** 2

**(B)** 3

**(C)** 6

**(D)** 18

Looks menacing, doesn't it? How are you going to isolate that $k$? Wait — you *don't* isolate it — just divide both sides by 3. The 3 on the left cancels, and the expression on the right divides evenly by 3:

$$\frac{3(x^2 - 5x + 6)}{3} = \frac{3x^2 - 15x + 6k}{3}$$
$$x^2 - 5x + 6 = x^2 - 5x + 2k$$

You now know that $2k = 6$ making $k = 3$, for answer Choice (B). Now be honest: *How long did that question take you?*

Another variation is where you form a quadratic and find the values of $a$, $b$, and $c$. You remember $a$, $b$, and $c$ from the discussion of quadratics all those pages ago, don't you? Copied straight from there: These are simply the coefficients from the equation when it equals 0. In the equation $x^2 + 2x - 15 = 0$, $a$, $b$, and $c$ are 1, 2, and –15, respectively (because $x^2$ times 1 is $x^2$, $x$ times 2 is $2x$, and 1 times –15 is –15).

**PLAY**

Given this equation, what is the value of $a + b + c$?

$$2x(x+3) + 4(x-1) = ax^2 + bx + c$$

**(A)** 12

**(B)** 10

**(C)** 8

**(D)** 6

By now this should be second nature — for *you*, because you're getting the hang of fielding the SAT tricks. Work with the polynomial on the left so it matches $ax^2 + bx + c$, and you have your a, b, and c!

$$2x(x+3) + 4(x-1) =$$
$$2x^2 + 6x + 4x - 4 =$$
$$2x^2 + 10x - 4 = ax^2 + bx + c$$

You now know that $a$, $b$, and $c$ are 2, 10, and $-4$, respectively. $2 + 10 - 4 = 8$ for an answer of Choice (C).

You good? This is a fairly common topic on the SAT Math, so be sure to practice.

# Setting Up Equations

*Setting up equations* is a style of word problem where it describes a scenario, whether a story or a set of numbers, and you set up an equation to model that scenario. Sometimes you get a numeric answer, and sometimes you get an answer in terms of an unknown.

## Setting up a story

A *story* is a word problem that describes a scenario, and you use this to set up an equation. For example, if Harvey handed out twice as many Twix bars this Halloween as he did last Halloween, and last year he handed out 52 bars, you know that this year he handed out 104 bars. Or, if last year Allison handed out $n$ apples, and this year she handed out three times as many as she did last year, you know that she handed out $3n$ apples. One instance gives you a numeric answer, and the other gives you an answer in terms of an unknown.

The secret to setting up an equation is finding the verb *is*, which can be in other tenses, including *has, had, will have*, and so on. When you find that verb *is* — in whatever tense — *write down an equal sign.* That gets you started.

For example: Billy *is* 3 inches taller than Henry. You can write down, $b = h + 3$. If you're not sure where to put the $+3$, just ask yourself, "Who's taller: Billy or Henry? (Snap fingers.) *Billy* is taller!" So add 3 to Henry.

Now try a simple one.

PLAY

The number of marbles in Box X is three times the number of marbles in Box Y. Which of the following equations is true?

**(A)** $3x = y$

**(B)** $3y = x$

**(C)** $xy = 3$

**(D)** $\dfrac{y}{x} = 3$

Translate the sentence, "The number of marbles in Box X is three times the number of marbles in Box Y" into "$x$ equals 3 times $y$," or "$x = 3y$," which matches Choice (B).

The SAT may include the equation and ask about changing it. Try this one:

PLAY

At her job, Julia's salary, $s$, can be represented by the equation $s = dh$, where she earns $d$ dollars per hour for each of $h$ hours that she works each week. If Julia gets an <u>additional</u> $r$ dollars per hour this week, which of the following equations represents her salary this week?

**(A)** $s = dhr$

**(B)** $s = (d + r)h$

**(C)** $s = d(h + r)$

**(D)** $s = dh + r$

If Julia earns *d* dollars per hour during a usual week and an <u>extra</u> *r* dollars per hour this week, then this week she earns *d* + *r* dollars per hour. Multiply that by *h* for her weekly pay for answer Choice (B).

These are good to know, so have another:

**PLAY**

A copying service charges $2.50 to copy up to 20 pages plus 5 cents per page over 20. Which formula represents the cost, *c*, in dollars, of copying *p* pages, where *p* is greater than 20?

**(A)** $c = 2.50 + 5p$

**(B)** $c = 2.50 + 0.05p$

**(C)** $c = (2.50)(20) + 0.05p$

**(D)** $c = 2.50 + 0.05(p - 20)$

The first 20 pages cost $2.50, so that has to be in the equation. To count the pages after 20, use the expression $(p - 20)$, and multiply this by 0.05 for the charge. This matches Choice (D).

Setting up equations is up there with quadratics as one of the most commonly asked topics on the SAT Math Tests. You're bound to see three questions on this, and they can be varied and challenging, so you need to practice these to keep your under-a-minute average.

## Setting up a sum of numbers

A *sum of numbers* refers to a specific type of "setting up equations" question that students tend to get stuck on, and it's commonly asked, so it's separated out here as its own topic. Basically, the SAT describes a set of numbers, gives you the total, and asks you for one of the numbers.

The question reads something like this: The sum of two numbers is 60. The first number is twice the second number. What is the smaller number?

The secret is, don't use *x* and *y*. Setting it up as $x + y = 60$ won't help you. Instead, just use *x*. If the second number is twice the first number, then that one is $2x$, and the equation becomes this:

$$x + 2x = 60$$
$$3x = 60$$
$$x = 20$$

**PLAY**

The sum of five numbers is 60. The first number is four times the total of the other four numbers. What is this first number?

**(A)** 12

**(B)** 24

**(C)** 36

**(D)** 48

Call the first number *x*. If *x* is four times the total of the other four numbers, then the total of those four numbers is $\frac{x}{4}$. Now set up the equation:

$$x + \frac{x}{4} = 60$$
$$\frac{5x}{4} = 60$$
$$5x = 240$$
$$x = 48$$

And the answer is Choice (D).

Here, try another one:

**PLAY**

Ms. Tan and Mr. Davis teach history and algebra at Brandeis. If together they have 290 students, and Ms. Tan has 30 more students than does Mr. Davis, how many students does Ms. Tan have?

Say Ms. Tan works with $x$ students. If Mr. Davis works with 30 fewer students, then he works with $x - 30$ students. Now set up the equation:

$$x + x - 30 = 290$$
$$2x - 30 = 290$$
$$2x = 320$$
$$x = 160$$

And you bubble in 160.

# Setting up interest

*Interest* refers to the percent of return on a loan or investment. If you place $100 into a savings account, and in 12 months that investment is worth $105 (assuming you didn't touch it), then the additional $5 is *interest*. Start by knowing these terms:

» **Present value (PV) or principal:** This is the starting amount of money, or the $100 in the preceding example.

» **Future value (FV):** This is the value of the investment or loan at some future state. In SAT Math, the future value assumes no other transaction has taken place: no fees, withdrawals, and so forth. This is the $105 in the preceding example.

» **Interest:** This is the actual money that was earned on the investment, or $5 from the preceding example.

» **Interest rate, or $i$:** This is the percent of the principal that becomes interest each term, usually a year. In the preceding example, this is 5 percent. Note that if $i = 5\%$, calculate it as $i = 0.05$.

» **Simple versus compound:** In the second year, is the 5 percent interest rate calculated on the original $100, making it *simple* interest, or the new $105, making it *compound* interest? Finance classes get carried away with this concept, but on the SAT it stays relatively straightforward: Compound means that the interest earns its *own* interest, while simple means it doesn't.

Now to see this in action. Hopefully throughout your life, you put these concepts to work *for* you, where you save or invest money that earns interest that you *own*, rather than *against* you, where you borrow money that accumulates interest that you *pay*. Digressing slightly, but the mindset of planning ahead and preparing for success with money is right in line with planning ahead and preparing for success on the SAT. Here's how it works:

## Simple interest

Simple interest is calculated like this:

$$FV = PV(1+i)$$

Or using the preceding example:

$$\$105 = 100(1+.05)$$

It's easier to memorize if you *understand* it. If you start with $100, how does it multiply to $105? If you multiply the $100 by the interest rate, 5 percent or 0.05, you just get the amount of interest, $5. You need to add 1 to the 0.05, so that when you multiply this by $100, you have the total *future value* of $105.

Here's a trick. The SAT expects you to know the formula for simple interest but not compound interest. If the SAT asks a compound interest question and doesn't provide the formula, just use the simple interest formula more than once. *Usually* the interest compounds only twice, so the question doesn't take long at all.

It goes something like this:

**PLAY**

If you place $100 into a savings account that earns 10% interest compounded annually, how much is in the account at the end of the second year, assuming the account has no other activity?

**(A)** $100

**(B)** $110

**(C)** $120

**(D)** $121

Don't worry about knowing compound interest. With only two cycles, use the simple interest formula twice. Start with the formula and place the numbers from the question to find the value of the account at the end of the *first* year:

$$FV = PV(1+i)$$
$$FV = (\$100)(1+0.10)$$
$$FV = \$100(1.1)$$
$$FV = \$110$$

Now do it again for the *second* year, which starts at $110:

$$FV = PV(1+i)$$
$$FV = (\$110)(1+0.10)$$
$$FV = \$110(1.1)$$
$$FV = \$121$$

And the answer is Choice (D).

## Compound interest

The compound interest formula is streamlined for the SAT. Here's the thing. *Don't memorize it.* Instead, *understand it.* The SAT questions on compound interest don't expect you to come up with the formula. Instead, the answer choices will be four variations of the formula, and if you *understand* it, you can spot the three wrong variations and cross them off.

Interest that compounds once a year (that only exists on the SAT) is calculated like this:

$$FV = PV(1+i)^t$$

It's exactly the same as the simple interest formula, only the $t$ exponent stands for *time*. Note that this variation exists only on the SAT. Real interest compounds more often, so that formula looks like this:

$$FV = PV\left(1+\frac{i}{n}\right)^{nt}$$

where $n$ is the number of times per year that the interest compounds. For example, if the interest compounds monthly, the formula looks like this:

$$FV = PV\left(1+\frac{i}{12}\right)^{12t}$$

The $i$ is divided by 12 because it's the *annual* interest divided monthly. The $12t$ is because the interest compounds 12 times per year.

Note that $n$ represents the number of times that the interest compounds during the time that $i$ interest accumulates. If the interest rate is *monthly*, say 0.6% per month (which is 0.006), and the interest compounds once per month, then $i$ isn't divided by 12 and $t$ isn't multiplied by 12: The formula would look like $FV = PV(1+i)^t$, showing a monthly cycle that accumulates $i$ interest.

Here's an example. See if your *understanding* is sufficient to answer the question:

**PLAY**

The money in a savings account increases 0.8% each month. Which of the following equations shows the future value, $FV$, of the money in the account based on the present value, $PV$, after a period of $m$ months?

**(A)** $FV = PV(0.008)^m$

**(B)** $FV = PV(1.008)^m$

**(C)** $FV = \left(\dfrac{PV}{0.008}\right)^m$

**(D)** $FV = \left(\dfrac{PV}{1.008^m}\right)$

It's not a math problem, remember. It's a *puzzle*. Say you start with $100, so $PV = \$100$. If $i$ is 0.8 percent, then use 0.008 (because 0.8% = 0.008, per Chapter 10). Which equation would lean in the direction of $FV = \$100 \times 1.008 = \$100.80$ after the first month? *Don't* do a lot of math. Instead, *estimate and eliminate.* If you have two or more answers that seem close, *then* do the math. But you won't.

Choice (A): $FV = \$100(0.008)^m$. No matter what $m$ is, this won't lead to $100.80, so cross it off.

Choice (B): $FV = \$100(1.008)^m$. If $m$ is 1, as it would be after the first month, then this leads to $100.80. Leave it — if you need to calculate further, you can always come back and do so.

Choice (C): $FV = \left(\dfrac{\$100}{0.008}\right)^m$. Not a chance. Run it through your calculator with $m = 1$ (in other words, the first month) and you'll see why.

Choice (D): $FV = \left( \dfrac{\$100}{1.008^m} \right)$. This is closer, but here's the thing. Because the denominator is slightly greater than 1, each month the value of the account goes *down* slightly, not up. If a swimming pool has a slow leak, this type of equation would model the diminishing amount of water.

So — what's left? Choice (B). And how much math did you do? Not much, right? You stopped after calculating the first month. *That's why this question takes about a minute.* And here's the thing, which is true for pretty much all the SAT Math. *If you understand the question, the math is simple.* It's easy to fall into the trap of doing a lot of math, so if that happens, and sometimes it does, *stop working on it, move on, and come back to it later.*

Interest rate questions aren't that common, but they help you understand the rate-of-change topic that follows, so they're worth practicing.

## Setting up rates of change

A *rate of change* question is a spin on the interest rate question from the previous section, where a quantity slowly changes over time, like an account with compound interest. The situation can be more complicated, and you typically get two or three questions based on a single scenario. The scenarios and equations are also similar to the projections questions from Chapter 10, only with more depth — and more questions.

A rate of change question describes something that grows, like the population of a city or the revenue of a business. The scenario typically provides an equation to model the rate of change, similar to the compound interest formula. Don't memorize the formula, because it changes based on the question. Instead, *understand* it.

Just look for the *starting point* and the *rate of change*. For a simple example, say that a tree is 5 feet tall and grows 3 feet each year. The SAT asks questions like these:

1. **Which equation models the tree's height after *t* years?**

   The tree's starting point is 5 and its rate of change is 3, so its height is modeled by the equation $h = 3t + 5$.

2. **What is the tree's height after 4 years?**

   $$h = 3(4) + 5$$
   Place 4 in for *t*:  $= 12 + 5$
   $$= 17$$

3. **If the tree actually grows 6 feet per year, not 3, how should the equation be changed?**

   Change the $3t$ to $6t$.

A simple example indeed, but it shows the SAT questions on a rate-of-change scenario. Apply your understanding of calculating interest and the perspective of these simple questions to this example:

**PLAY**

**Questions 1–3 are based on the following information:**

Micah has a 50-pound drum of semolina in his pantry. Each week, he uses 10% of the semolina in the drum for baking.

**1.** Which of the following equations models the amount of semolina, $s$, in pounds, remaining in the drum after $w$ weeks?

(A) $s = 50(1.1)^w$

(B) $s = 50(0.1)^w$

(C) $s = 50(0.9)^w$

(D) $s = 50(1.9)^w$

**2.** At this rate, how many pounds of semolina will remain in the drum at the end of the second week?

(A) 50.1

(B) 45.3

(C) 40.5

(D) 35.7

**3.** If Micah instead obtains a 100-pound drum and uses 20% per week, then he will use exactly half of the drum

(A) in fewer weeks than he would using 10% weekly of the 50-pound drum.

(B) in more weeks than he would using 10% weekly of the 50-pound drum.

(C) in the same number of weeks that he would using 10% weekly of the 50-pound drum.

(D) never, because at this rate he will not use half of the drum.

**1.** **Per** the scenario, Micah uses 5 pounds of semolina in the first week, because 10 percent of 50 is 5. Try out each equation to see which leaves him with 45 pounds when $w = 1$. See, the beauty of this approach is that $w$ is an exponent, so when it equals 1, *it goes away.* You understand the question, you make it simple, you work it in *less than a minute.*

Choice (A): $s = 50(1.1)^w$. This increases the semolina to 55 pounds. Cross it off.

Choice (B): $s = 50(0.1)^w$. This leaves 5 pounds. Micah *uses* 5 pounds and should have 45 left over. Cross it off.

Choice (C): $s = 50(0.9)^w$. This leaves 45 pounds. Looks good. Don't work more math — check the next answer.

Choice (D): $s = 50(1.9)^w$. This increases the semolina to 95 pounds. Cross it off!

And the answer is Choice (C).

**2.** **You** already know how much semolina Micah has after the first week, plus you know the correct equation, so plug 45 in and run it again with $w$ as 1. Or leave the 50 in there and set $w$ as 2. Either way works. Here's the first way:

$$s = 45(0.9)^1$$
$$= 40.5$$

for an answer of Choice (C).

**3.** **You** could math this one out, but why? Instead, just *understand* it. If you have two drums of semolina, *regardless of the volume,* and you consume one at 10 percent per week and the other at 20 percent per week, which one will reach the halfway point first? Why, the 20 percent drum, so Choice (A) is correct.

SAT Math questions in general, but rate-of-change questions in particular, test your *understanding* of a concept more than your ability to punch numbers. This is why the calculator isn't necessarily your friend. It helps a little, as with Question 2, but if you tried answering Question 3 with the calc, you'd *probably* get it right, but it would take a while.

Interest and rate-of-change questions borrow concepts from coordinate geometry, where you track how one number changes (such as time) and causes another number to change (for example, value or amount). This is a good question topic to end setting up equations and begin coordinate geometry.

# Graphing Coordinate Geometry

*Coordinate geometry* refers to a drawing that results from one or more equations. You know the basic equation $y = mx + b$ that makes a line, and that squaring the $x$ makes a parabola, and so on. If you forgot how this works, that's okay; it's all reviewed in this chapter.

Coordinate geometry questions are about a quarter of the SAT math questions, so of the 58 questions on the two Math Tests, you're likely to see 14 or 15. That estimate, of course, varies from exam to exam, but regardless, you'll see plenty of these on the SAT.

On the SAT, coordinate geometry is always two-dimensional (though in geometry there are 3-D shapes). It exists on the *x-y rectangular grid*, also known as the *coordinate plane*. This is a two-dimensional area defined by a horizontal $x$-axis and a vertical $y$-axis that intersect at the *origin*, which has coordinates $(0,0)$, and form *Quadrants I, II, III,* and *IV*.

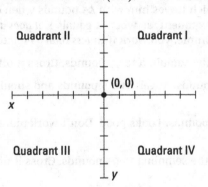

Any point on the grid has an $(x, y)$ value, with the $x$ indicating the horizontal position and the $y$ indicating the vertical position. For example, this point has the coordinates $(4,5)$:

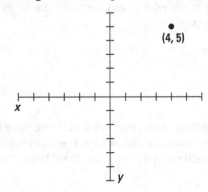

# Graphing a line

A line is graphed by a *linear equation*, which is any equation with $x$ and $y$ and no exponents, such as $y = 2x + 1$. It can use other letters, but they're typically $x$ and $y$. The equation has infinite solutions, because for any value of $x$, there's a matching value of $y$. For example, with $y = 2x + 1$, when $x = 0$, $y = 1$; when $x = 1$, $y = 3$; and so on. These $x$- and $y$-values form a line, and each $x$-value and matching $y$-value falls on the line:

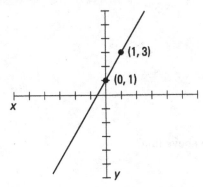

A linear equation is usually given in the *slope-intercept* form $y = mx + b$, where $m$ is the slope and $b$ is the $y$-intercept, which is the $y$ value when $x = 0$ and the line crosses the $y$-axis. Above, with the line $y = 2x + 1$, the slope is 2 and the $y$-intercept is 1.

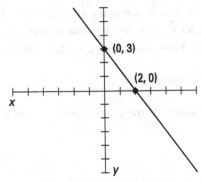

Look at the second drawing above. How do you find the equation from the line itself? Place the slope and $y$-intercept as the $m$ and $b$, respectively, into the equation $y = mx + b$. Start with the $y$-intercept, which is where the line crosses the $y$-axis. In the drawing, the line crosses the $y$-axis at 3, making $b = 3$, so place that into the equation: $y = mx + 3$.

Now for the $m$, which is the slope. This can be found using *rise over run*: The line rises 3 and runs 2, and because it goes down, the slope is negative, so $m = -\frac{3}{2}$. Place that into the equation, and you have the answer: $y = -\frac{3}{2}x + 3$

The slope can also be found using the *slope formula*, $m = \frac{y_2 - y_1}{x_2 - x_1}$. This captures the *rise over run* from any two points on the line. $y_2 - y_1$ refers to one $y$-coordinate minus the other, and $x_2 - x_1$ refers to one $x$-coordinate minus the other. Place these $x$- and $y$-values into the formula:

$$m = \frac{y_2 - y_1}{x_2 - x_1}$$
$$= \frac{0 - 3}{2 - 0}$$
$$= -\frac{3}{2}$$

And you have the same result: $m = -\frac{3}{2}$.

Try this one:

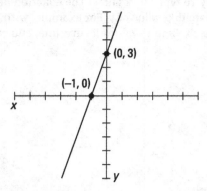

PLAY

Which of the following is the equation of the above line?

(A) $y = \frac{1}{3}x - 3$

(B) $y = -3x + 3$

(C) $y = -\frac{1}{3}x - 3$

(D) $y = 3x + 3$

Start with the bare-bones equation $y = mx + b$. The line crosses at 3, so that's the $b$: $y = mx + 3$. Using *rise over run*, the line rises 3 and runs 1, for $\frac{3}{1}$, or 3, and because it goes upwards from left to right, the 3 is positive. Place that for $m$, and you have the equation $y = 3x + 3$ for answer Choice (D).

A couple notes before you dive into the practice questions.

>> **Parallel lines have the same slope.** They may cross the *y*-axis at different points, but if they have the same slope, they're parallel.

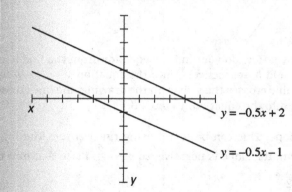

» **Perpendicular lines have the negative reciprocal slope.** Take the slope, reciprocate it, multiply it by –1, and the resulting line is perpendicular. The $y$-intercepts don't matter, even though in this drawing, they match.

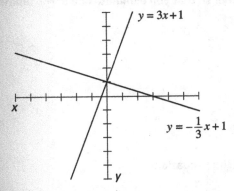

» **Linear equations don't have to use the *slope-intercept* form.** The slope intercept form is your friend $y = mx + b$, but an equation such as $3x + 2y = 6$ is also a line. To convert it to the *slope-intercept* form and find the slope and $y$-intercept, just solve for $y$:

$$3x + 2y = 6$$
$$2y = -3x + 6$$
$$y = -\frac{3}{2}x + 3$$

» **Linear equations don't need *both* x and y.** They can have just one or the other. If there's just an $x$, as in $x = 3$, then the line goes straight up and down, crossing the $x$-axis at 3 (and the slope is undefined). If there's just a $y$, as in $y = 5$, then the line is flat, crossing the $y$-axis at 5 (and the slope is 0).

» **Linear equations don't have to use *x* and *y*.** They can use any letters. Remember the tree example from the section "Setting Up Equations"? The tree is 5 feet tall and grows 3 feet each year: $h = 3t + 5$. If you graph this, the line would have a $y$-intercept of 5 and a slope of 3.

» **If it has a radical or an exponent, it's not a line.** The exponent or radical introduces a curve. In applied math it could be many things, but on the SAT it's typically a parabola or a circle.

Practice working with linear equations, because you'll see plenty of these on the SAT. Also, this topic is the foundation to understanding the other topics in the "Graphing Coordinate Geometry" section, so it's worth practicing.

## Graphing two lines

An SAT question may present two linear equations, representing two graphed lines, and ask you to find the point where the lines cross. Like everything else on this exam, especially the math, it's remarkably simple if you know what to do. Also, this is one of the most commonly asked questions on the exam. You'll see a few of these.

The SAT asks, *which ordered pair satisfies* the equations, or *what is/are the solution(s)* to the equations. Take the equations $y = 2x + 1$ and $y = -x + 4$. Find the solutions in three steps:

1. **Subtract one equation from the other so that you eliminate one of the unknowns.**

$$
\begin{array}{r}
y = 2x + 1 \\
-(y = -x + 4) \\
\hline
0 = 3x - 3
\end{array}
$$

2. **Solve for the remaining unknown.**

$$0 = 3x - 3$$
$$-3x = -3$$
$$x = 1$$

3. **Place that value into one of the original equations.**

$$y = 2x + 1$$
$$= 2(1) + 1$$
$$= 3$$

And you have the answer: $x = 1$ and $y = 3$. This means that when you graph the two lines, they cross at the coordinates $(1, 3)$:

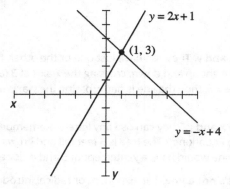

A couple notes:

>> The equations have *infinite solutions* if they both draw the same line, because there are infinite pairs of *x, y* coordinates that work for both equations. If you try to solve this one, you end up with a linear equation, (in this case, $y = 2x + 1$,) which means that any value of *x* has a corresponding value of *y*.

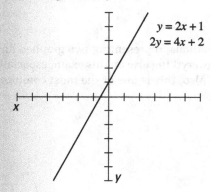

» The equations have *no solutions* if they're parallel, because there is no pair of $x$, $y$ coordinates that works for both equations. If you try to solve this one, you end up with something like $0 = 1$, which means that no value of $x$ has a corresponding value of $y$.

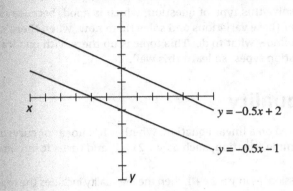

**Try one:**

PLAY

What is the solution to the equations $y = 2x + 3$ and $y = 3x + 7$?

**(A)** $(4, 5)$

**(B)** $(4, -5)$

**(C)** $(-4, -5)$

**(D)** $(-4, 5)$

Set them up and subtract them:

$$y = 2x + 3$$
$$-(y = 3x + 7)$$
$$\overline{0 = -x - 4}$$
$$x = -4$$

Then place $-4$ back into one original equation:

$$y = 2x + 3$$
$$= 2(-4) + 3$$
$$= -8 + 3$$
$$= -5$$

And you have your answer: $(-4, -5)$, for Choice (C).

Another variation of this question is where the SAT presents a scenario, such as two trees growing at different rates, and asks at what point the trees will be the same height. One tree has a height projected as $h = 3t + 5$, and the other is a sapling, smaller but growing faster, whose height is modeled as $h = 4t + 2$. This sapling is 2 feet tall but grows 4 feet per year.

The SAT then asks you at what year the two trees will be the same height. You need to solve for $t$. You could use the method described earlier, but there's another way. When the $h$ of one equation equals the $h$ of the other, it means that the *rest* of one equation, $3t + 5$, equals the *rest* of the other, $4t + 2$. So set those equal to each other and solve for $t$:

$$3t + 5 = 4t + 2$$
$$-t = -3$$
$$t = 3$$

Note that a question like this always has a positive answer because it's based on a real-life scenario. A tree wouldn't be negative 3 years old.

So now you have two ways to solve this type of question, which is good, because the SAT varies this topic many ways. Encounter these variations and solve them now, when there's no pressure, so when the pressure's on, you know what to do. This topic is up there with quadratics as one of the most commonly asked question types, so learn this well.

## Graphing an inequality

*Graphing an inequality* can be based on a linear equation. Whether it's linear or curved, the concept is the same. The SAT takes a simple equation, such as $y = 2x + 1$, and turns it into an inequality.

>> If $y$ is *greater* than the expression, as in $y > 2x + 1$, then the inequality includes the region *above* the line, regardless of the slope.

>> If $y$ is *less* than the expression, as in $y < 2x + 1$, then the inequality includes the region *below* the line, again regardless of the slope.

>> If it is an *or equal* inequality, as in $y \geq 2x + 1$ or $y \leq 2x + 1$, then the region *includes* the line, and the line is solid; otherwise, with > or <, the region does *not* include the line and the line is dashed.

>> If it is a *horizontal* line that is *greater* than the expression, as in $y > 3$, then the inequality includes the region *above* the line; and if the horizontal line is *less than* the expression, as in $y < 2$, then the inequality includes the region *below* the line.

>> If it is a *vertical* line that is *greater* than the expression, as in $x > 5$, then the inequality includes the region *to the right* of the line; and if the vertical line is *less than* the expression, as in $x < 4$, then the inequality includes the region *to the left* of the line.

The SAT doesn't expect you to measure anything carefully. Like most other topics, these questions are based on your understanding of the concepts. The SAT presents you with a scenario and asks you which inequality models it best.

For example, try one with the new sapling:

PLAY

Bill plants a two-foot-tall sapling that is expected to grow *at least* 4 feet per year. Which of the following inequalities best models its growth?

**(A)** $h > 4t + 2$

**(B)** $h < 4t + 2$

**(C)** $h \geq 4t + 2$

**(D)** $h \leq 4t + 2$

Cross off the wrong answers. If each year the sapling grows 4 feet or more, its height wouldn't be *less than* the expression, so eliminate Choices (B) and (D). If it grows *at least* 4 feet, then it *could* grow 4 feet, or it could grow more, so the greater-than sign is out, taking with it Choice (A). This leaves Choice (C), with the appropriate greater-than-or-equal-to sign.

Graphing inequalities aren't that common, but the scenario can be intricate. As complex as the scenario gets, remember the underlying concept is always simple. Any time you choose from equations, you *always* find the right answer by *crossing off wrong answers*.

# Graphing a parabola

A *parabola* is a U-shaped curve that results from an equation where $x$ is squared. For example, this is the graph of $y = x^2$:

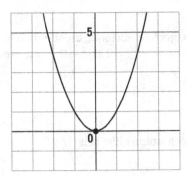

The parabola's *vertex* is the bottom center. If you were to drop a ball bearing into the U-shape, the vertex is where the ball bearing would rest. In the preceding drawing, the vertex is $(0,0)$. The official formula for a parabola is $y = a(x - h)^2 + k$, where these rules apply:

>> The vertex is at the coordinates $(h, k)$.

>> The larger the $a$, the narrower the parabola. Don't worry about the $a$ much — it's rarely asked on the SAT, but know the concept.

For example, here's the parabola graph of the equation $y = 3(x - 2)^2 + 1$:

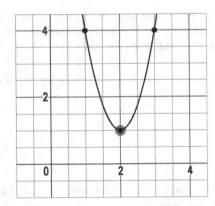

Note that it's narrower than the graph of $y = x^2$, and its vertex is $(2,1)$. Also, the $h$ appears negative in the equation. This parabola may also appear in the form of $f(x) = 3(x - 2)^2 + 1$, where $f(x)$ takes the place of $y$. Variations of $f(x)$ are covered later in this chapter under "Graphing a function," but for now just treat it like this: $f(x) = y$.

The equation of a parabola has three forms:

>> The *vertex form*, $y = (x - 2)^2 - 1$, where the $xy$-coordinates of the vertex are in the equation. For example, here you know that the coordinates of the vertex are $(2, -1)$, because the $x$ coordinate appears negative, but the $y$ coordinate appears as is.

>> The *standard form*, $y = x^2 - 4x + 3$, which you get from multiplying out the vertex form:

$$y = (x-2)^2 - 1$$
$$= (x^2 - 4x + 4) - 1$$
$$= x^2 - 4x + 3$$

>> The *factored form*, $y = (x-3)(x-1)$, which you get from factoring the standard form. This form tells you the *x*-intercepts of the graph, which occur when $y = 0$, and in this case are 1 and 3:

$$y = x^2 - 4x + 3$$
$$= (x-3)(x-1)$$

These are three forms of the same equation, which graphs like this:

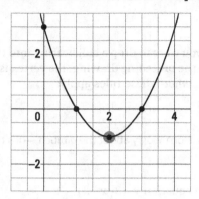

One key thing to remember is that the *factored form* gives you the *x*-intercepts. If the SAT asks for the *x*-intercepts, you can convert the standard form to the factored form by factoring it just as you would a quadratic, covered earlier in this chapter. Try this one:

**PLAY**

At what two points does the graph of the equation $y = x^2 - 3x - 28$ cross the *x*-axis?

**(A)** $(3,0)$ and $(7,0)$

**(B)** $(4,0)$ and $(7,0)$

**(C)** $(-3,0)$ and $(7,0)$

**(D)** $(-4,0)$ and $(7,0)$

The graph crosses the *x*-axes where $y = 0$, so place 0 for *y* and factor it out. Remember when factoring a quadratic, you're looking for two numbers that add to −3 and multiply to −28.

$$0 = x^2 - 3x - 28$$
$$0 = (x+4)(x-7)$$

$y = 0$ when $x = -4$ and $x = 7$, for answer Choice (D).

Here's a common variation on the theme:

**PLAY**

At what two points does the graph of the equation $y = x^2 - x - 2$ cross the line where $y = 4$?

**(A)** $(2,4)$ and $(3,4)$

**(B)** $(-2,4)$ and $(3,4)$

**(C)** $(2,4)$ and $(-3,4)$

**(D)** $(-2,4)$ and $(-3,4)$

Place 4 for $y$ and solve it as you would a quadratic, meaning you set the equation equal to 0, factor it out, and find the values of $x$.

$$y = x^2 - x - 2$$
$$4 = x^2 - x - 2$$
$$0 = x^2 - x - 6$$
$$0 = (x - 3)(x + 2)$$

$y = 4$ when $x = -2$ and $x = 3$, for answer Choice (B).

The SAT may give you a quadratic (another word for parabola) equation in the *standard form* and ask for the vertex. There are two ways to find this. The first is by converting the standard form to the vertex form by *completing the square*, like this:

**1.** **Start with the standard form.**

For example, $y = x^2 - 4x - 5$.

**2.** **Divide the *x*-coefficient by 2.**

In this case, divide –4 by 2, for –2.

**3.** **Place *x* and the result of Step 2 into parentheses squared.**

$(x - 2)^2$

**4.** **Take the square of the result from Step 2 and subtract it from the number without the *x* in the original equation.**

The –2 squared becomes 4, and you subtract this from –5 in the original equation for –9.

**5.** **Set *y* equal to the results of Step 4 and Step 3.**

You have $(x - 2)^2$, so place the –9 to the right, for a result of $y = (x - 2)^2 - 9$.

Here are the steps as a single set:

$$y = x^2 - 4x - 5$$
$$= (x - 2)^2 - 4 - 5$$
$$= (x - 2)^2 - 9$$

And you know that the vertex of this parabola is $(2, -9)$.

The second method involves finding the *axis of symmetry*, which is basically the $x$-value of a line that goes down the middle of the parabola, and placing that $x$ into the equation to find $y$. Both methods are useful depending on the variation of the question, but the axis of symmetry is simpler for just finding the vertex:

**1.** **Start with the standard form.**

In this case, $y = x^2 - 4x - 5$.

**2.** **Set up $\frac{-b}{2a}$.**

In this example, this is $\dfrac{-(-4)}{2(1)} = \dfrac{4}{2} = 2$ –4 by 2, for –2, so the axis of symmetry is $x = 2$.

**3.** **Place this value of $x$ into the equation.**

$$y = x^2 - 4x - 5$$
$$= (2)^2 - 4(2) - 5$$
$$= 4 - 8 - 5$$
$$= -9$$

And you again know that the vertex is $(2,-9)$. Finding the axis of symmetry is easier, but completing the square can be useful on some variations.

The parabola is extremely common on the SAT, but converting from standard to vertex form is not nearly as common. This process becomes easy *fast* with just a little practice, and you'll need it for certain graphing-circles questions in the next section.

Try this one.

**PLAY**

In the quadratic equation $y = x^2 + 2x - 8$, what are the coordinates of the vertex of the parabola?

**(A)** $(-1,-9)$

**(B)** $(-1,9)$

**(C)** $(1,-9)$

**(D)** $(1,9)$

Try this by completing the square:

$$y = x^2 + 2x - 8$$
$$= (x+1)^2 - 1 - 8$$
$$= (x+1)^2 - 9$$

From the vertex form of the equation, you know that the vertex is $(-1,-9)$, but also try this by finding the axis of symmetry:

$$\frac{-b}{2a} = \frac{-(2)}{2(1)} = -\frac{2}{2} = -1$$

And placing the $x$ value into the equation:

$$y = x^2 + 2x - 8$$
$$= (-1)^2 + 2(-1) - 8$$
$$= 1 - 2 - 8$$
$$= -9$$

Either way, you find that the vertex is $(-1,-9)$, for answer Choice (A).

**TIP**

When graphing an equation, the *solutions* are the values of $x$ that cause $y$ (or $f(x)$, covered later) to equal 0 and make the graph touch or cross the $x$-axis.

You'd better believe that parabolas are common on the SAT Math Tests, so practice them.

## Graphing a circle

Many shapes can be graphed from equations, but almost all the graphed shapes that appear on the SAT are the line, the parabola, or the circle.

## Standard form

This is the *standard form* of the equation of a circle:

$$(x-h)^2 + (y-k)^2 = r^2$$

In this equation, the $h$ and the $k$ are the $x$ and $y$ coordinates of the center, and $r$ is the radius. Say you have a circle with a center at coordinates $(3, -2)$ and a radius of 4. Its equation is $(x+3)^2 + (y-2)^2 = 4^2$ or $(x+3)^2 + (y-2)^2 = 16$:

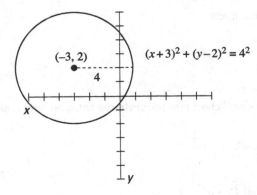

**TIP**

The $r^2$ at the end is one place the SAT tries to trip you up. If the equation of a circle is $(x+3)^2 + (y-2)^2 = 16$, the radius is 4, not **16**.

Here's one for you to try.

**PLAY**

Which of the following is the equation for the graph of a circle having a center of $(-1, -7)$ and a radius of 6?

**(A)** $(x-1)^2 + (y-7)^2 = 6$

**(B)** $(x+1)^2 + (y+7)^2 = 6$

**(C)** $(x-1)^2 + (y-7)^2 = 36$

**(D)** $(x+1)^2 + (y+7)^2 = 36$

If the center of the circle is $(-1, -7)$, then inside the parentheses should be +1 and +7, so cross off Choices (A) and (C). Next, if the radius is 6, then the end of the equation should have a 36, so cross off Choices (A) again and (B). You're left with Choice (D), which is the right answer.

## General form

So far you've been working with the *standard form* of the equation of a circle. There's also the *general form*, which is just taking the standard form and multiplying everything out.

$$(x+3)^2 + (y-2)^2 = 5^2$$
$$(x^2 + 6x + 9) + (y^2 - 4y + 4) = (25)$$
$$x^2 + y^2 + 6x + 9y + 13 = 25$$
$$x^2 + y^2 + 6x + 9y = 12$$

The general form of the same circle is $x^2 + y^2 + 6x + 9y = 12$. Unlike the standard form, which tells you the secrets of the circle's center and radius, the general form doesn't offer much in the way of clear information about the circle.

The SAT gives you the general form of a circle, say $x^2 + y^2 - 2x + 6y = 6$, and asks for the coordinates of the center, or the radius, or something about the circle that's obvious in the standard form but obscured in the general form. You need to convert the equation back to the standard form.

The way to convert the equation from the general form to the standard form is to complete the squares separately for the $x$ part and the $y$ part. Completing the square is introduced in the previous section, "Graphing a parabola," and continued here.

**1.** **Start with the general form of the circle:**

$x^2 + y^2 - 2x + 6y = 6$

**2.** **Place the $x$'s and $y$'s together:**

$x^2 - 2x + y^2 + 6y = 6$

**3.** **Place the single $x$ and half the $x$-coefficient into parentheses squared, and subtract the square of that number.**

Square the –1 and subtract the result: $(x-1)^2 - 1$

**4.** **Do the same with the $y$.**

Square the 3 and subtract the result: $(y+3)^2 - 9$

**5.** **Move the numbers to the right side of the equation.**

In this case, add 1 and 9 to both sides:

$$(x-1)^2 - 1 + (y+3)^2 - 9 = 6$$
$$(x-1)^2 + (y+3)^2 = 16$$

**6.** **Convert the number on the right to its squared form:**

The 16 becomes $4^2$.

Here are the steps as a single set:

$$x^2 + y^2 - 2x + 6y = 6$$
$$x^2 - 2x + y^2 + 6y = 6$$
$$(x-1)^2 - 1 + (y+3)^2 - 9 = 6$$
$$(x-1)^2 + (y+3)^2 = 16$$
$$= 4^2$$

Ready to try one? This variation is somewhat common and appears on about one out of two SAT exams.

PLAY

Which of the following are the center and radius of the graph of the equation $x^2 + y^2 - 6x + 10y = -18$?

**(A)** $(4,-6)$ and 3

**(B)** $(3,-5)$ and 4

**(C)** $(6,-10)$ and 16

**(D)** $(5,-8)$ and 18

Convert the equation from the general form to the standard form, and you can find the center and radius:

$$x^2 + y^2 - 6x + 10y = -18$$
$$x^2 - 6x + y^2 + 10y = -18$$
$$(x-3)^2 - 9 + (y+5)^2 - 25 = -18$$
$$(x-3)^2 + (y+5)^2 = 16$$
$$= 4^2$$

From the standard form of the equation, you know that the center is $(3, -5)$ and the radius is 4, for answer Choice (B).

You will probably see at least one graphed circle on your SAT, so prepare for it.

## Graphing a function

A *function* is any kind of graphed equation that uses $f(x)$ instead of $y$. The equation $y = 3x - 5$ is exactly the same as $f(x) = 3x - 5$, and the value of $x$ goes into the parentheses. So, if $x = 4$, the equation looks like this: $f(4) = 3(4) - 5$. Also, a function may use different letters, such as $g(h)$.

The SAT doesn't always give you the equation for a function. It may give you just a few values in a table, like this:

| x | f(x) |
|---|------|
| 2 | 3 |
| 3 | 8 |
| 4 | 5 |
| 5 | 11 |

The values may not have a pattern, so don't worry about finding one. Just know that when $x = 2$, $f(x) = 3$, and when $x = 5$, $f(x) = 11$. You won't be asked what happens when $x$ is 3.5 or 6 or anything like that: Just stick with what's in the table.

Try this one:

PLAY

For which value of $x$ shown in the table is $f(x) = g(x)$?

| x | f(x) | g(x) |
|---|------|------|
| 2 | 3 | 6 |
| 3 | 8 | 14 |
| 4 | 5 | 5 |
| 5 | 11 | 2 |

(A) 2

(B) 3

(C) 4

(D) 5

When $x = 4$, both $f(x)$ and $g(x)$ equal 5, making $f(x) = g(x)$ for answer Choice (C).

Here's another one:

PLAY

What is the value of $g(f(2))$?

| $x$ | $f(x)$ | $g(x)$ |
|---|---|---|
| 2 | 3 | 6 |
| 3 | 8 | 14 |
| 4 | 5 | 5 |
| 5 | 11 | 2 |

**(A)** 2

**(B)** 5

**(C)** 6

**(D)** 14

From the table, when $x = 2$, $f(x) = 3$, so replace $f(2)$ with 3 in the equation. Now with the $f(2)$ out of there, you have $g(3)$, which per the table is 14. It goes like this:

$$g(f(2))$$
$$g(3)$$
$$14$$

The answer is Choice (D).

The SAT takes it one level higher. Here's how the topic works. Say you have this function:

$$f(x) = x^2 + x - 12$$

From quadratics all those pages ago, you know that the equation factors into this:

$$f(x) = (x + 4)(x - 3)$$

This means that $(x + 4)$ and $(x - 3)$ are *factors* of $f(x) = x^2 + x - 12$. It also means that when $x = 3$ or $x = -4$, $f(x) = 0$. This is also written as $f(3) = 0$ and $f(-4) = 0$.

So put all these together:

» $f(x) = x^2 + x - 12$

» $f(x) = (x + 4)(x - 3)$

» $f(3) = 0$ and $f(-4) = 0$

» $(x + 4)$ and $(x - 3)$ are *factors* of the equation.

Understand this concept back and forth, and you'll quickly answer correctly a question that everyone around you gets stuck on and finally gets wrong.

Try this one based on the equation that you just explored, $f(x) = (x + 4)(x - 3)$.

PLAY

For the function $f(x)$, the value of $f(3)=0$. Which of the following must be true?

**(A)** $(x-3)$ is a factor of $f(x)$

**(B)** $(x+3)$ is a factor of $f(x)$

**(C)** $x$ is a factor of $f(x)$

**(D)** 3 is a factor of $f(x)$

If $f(3)=0$, then the function $f(x)$ must look something like this: $f(x)=(x-3)(\text{something})$. The something part doesn't matter, but the $(x-3)$ causes the function to work like this when $x=3$:

$$f(x)=(x-3)(\text{something})$$
$$f(3)=(3-3)(\text{something})$$
$$=(0)(\text{something})$$
$$=0$$

If the function looks like $f(x)=(x-3)(\text{something})$, then $(x-3)$ is a factor of $f(x)$, for answer Choice (A).

Here's another one based on a new equation but the same concept:

PLAY

For the function $f(x)$, the value of $f(-5)=0$. Which of the following must be true?

**(A)** $(x-5)$ is a factor of $f(x)$

**(B)** $(x+5)$ is a factor of $f(x)$

**(C)** $x$ is a factor of $f(x)$

**(D)** 5 is a factor of $f(x)$

If $f(-5)=0$, then the function $f(x)$ must look something like this: $f(x)=(x+5)(\text{something})$, making $(x+5)$ a factor of $f(x)$ for answer Choice (B).

The second question is repetitive, but you'll be glad it's repetitive when you see its twin on the exam and answer it in . . . 20 seconds? Placing bets here. But the SAT offers this in different forms, so try one more:

PLAY

Given the function $f(x)=\dfrac{5x}{x^2-4x+4}$, which is not a possible value of $x$?

**(A)** 4

**(B)** 2

**(C)** 0

**(D)** $-2$

The denominator $x^2-4x+4$ factors to $(x-2)(x-2)$, which means that $x=2$ makes the denominator 0 and 2 can't be a value of $x$. Choice (B) is correct.

That last question is the same idea as in the previous two questions but packaged differently. That shouldn't stop you. The $f(x)$ question is on the Top Ten SAT Math Topics list, so be ready.

**IN THIS CHAPTER**

» **Understanding how the SAT packages geometry questions**

» **Practicing how to quickly and easily answer these questions**

» **Recognizing the common tricks and traps in SAT Geometry**

» **Seeing patterns to simplify questions**

» **Getting the answers right**

# Chapter **12**

# Geometry and Trigonometry

The geometry and trigonometry on the SAT Math Tests, like the other topics on these tests, go fairly in depth but have limited scope. There are topics you could see, and topics you won't see, and this boundary stays consistent with little exception.

Keep in mind that each SAT Math Test opens with a box of formulas and information, like this:

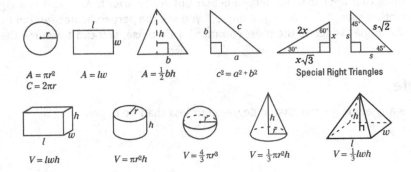

$A = \pi r^2$
$C = 2\pi r$

$A = lw$

$A = \frac{1}{2}bh$

$c^2 = a^2 + b^2$

Special Right Triangles

$V = lwh$

$V = \pi r^2 h$

$V = \frac{4}{3}\pi r^3$

$V = \frac{1}{3}\pi r^2 h$

$V = \frac{1}{3}lwh$

There are 360 degrees of arc in a circle.

The number of radians of arc in a circle is $2\pi$.

There are 180 degrees in the sum of the interior angles of a triangle.

The triangle ratios are especially good to know. Of course, no one ever remembers that the formulas are there, so in this chapter are tips and tricks to remember them.

# Drawing Basic Shapes

*Basic shapes* include squares; trapezoids; triangles, which get particularly complex with side-length ratios; and circles, which get tricky but manageable with arcs and sectors. Simple strategies and some memorization are the keys here, and they're all contained in this section.

## Drawing angles

Any two lines or segments that meet or cross make an *angle*, which is the space between the lines. Understanding angles is easy when you know the different types of angles and a few key concepts.

Finding an angle is usually a matter of simple addition or subtraction. In addition to the rules in the following sections, these three rules apply to angles:

>> Angles can't be negative.

>> Angles can't be 0° or 180°.

>> Fractional angles, such as $44\frac{1}{2}$ degrees or 179.5 degrees, are rare on the SAT. Angles are typically round and whole numbers. If you're placing a number for an angle, use a whole number, such as 30, 45, or 90.

### Right angle

*Right angles* equal 90 degrees and are represented by perpendicular lines with a small box where the two lines meet.

**TIP**

Watch out for lines that appear to be perpendicular but really aren't. An angle is a right angle *only* if the description says, "This is a right angle," you see the perpendicular symbol (⊥), or you see the box in the angle (which is the most common). Otherwise, you can't assume the angle is 90 degrees.

### Acute angle

An *acute angle* is any angle greater than 0 degrees but less than 90 degrees.

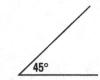

**TIP**

*Acute* means sharp or perceptive, so an acute angle is sharp.

## Obtuse angle

An *obtuse angle* is any angle greater than 90 degrees but less than 180 degrees.

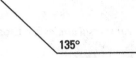

135°

**TIP**

*Obtuse* doesn't mean the opposite of *sharp* in a physical sense, so a dull knife wouldn't be *obtuse*, but it does mean the opposite of perceptive, so an obtuse person is . . . well, not sharp.

Angles around a point total 360 degrees, no matter how many angles there are.

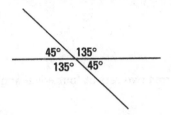

45°    135°
135°    45°

## Complementary angles

*Complementary angles* together form a right angle: 90 degrees.

## Supplementary angles

*Supplementary angles* together form a straight line: 180 degrees.

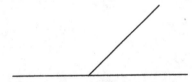

**TIP**

Just remember that *c* stands for both *corner* (the lines form a corner) and *complementary*; *s* stands for both *straight* and *supplementary*.

## Vertical angles

*Vertical angles* are the opposite angles where two lines cross. Vertical angles have equal measures.

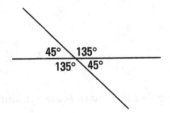

45°    135°
135°    45°

**TIP**

Vertical angles are across the *vertex* (the point where intersecting lines cross) from each other, regardless of whether they're side by side or one above the other.

## Transversal angles

A *transversal* is a line that cuts through two other lines. *Transversal angles* are those that are formed where the transversal intersects with the other two lines.

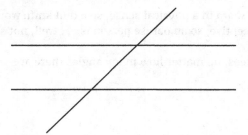

**TIP**

A transversal cutting through two parallel lines forms two sets of four equal angles. This is also relevant to the *parallelogram* later in this section.

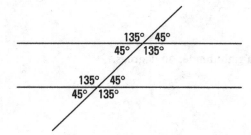

Angle concepts are mixed into other geometry and trigonometry topics, but angle-only questions come in two basic flavors. One is based on supplemental angles totaling 180°, and the other is based on angles around a point totaling 360° with the vertical angles being equal. Here they are:

**PLAY**

In the following image, the angles are supplementary. What is the value of $x$?

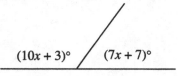

**(A)** 3

**(B)** 7

**(C)** 10

**(D)** 14

Supplementary angles total 180°, so set up an equation where the two angles total 180, forget the degree symbol, and solve for $x$:

$$(10x + 3) + (7x + 7) = 180$$
$$17x + 10 = 180$$
$$17x = 170$$
$$x = 10$$

And that makes Choice (C) the correct answer. Remember SAT math is always simple if it's set up correctly.

**PLAY**

In this drawing, if $a + c = 100°$, what is the value of $e$?

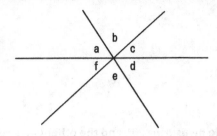

**(A)** 60°

**(B)** 80°

**(C)** 100°

**(D)** 120°

Supplementary angles total 180°, and vertical angles are equal. Find angle $b$, and you know angle $e$:

$$a + c + b = 180$$
$$100 + b = 180$$
$$b = 80$$

Because $b = e$, each is 80 for Choice (B).

Questions on drawing angles aren't that common on the SAT Math, but this concept underlies almost all the other topics in this chapter.

## Drawing triangles

These are some standard types of triangles:

» An *equilateral* triangle has <u>three</u> equal sides and angles.

Equilateral

» An *isosceles* triangle has <u>two</u> equal sides and angles.

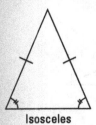

Isosceles

» A *right* triangle has one angle measuring 90°, which appears as a right-angle box in the drawing.

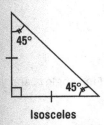

» An *isosceles right* triangle has one angle measuring 90°, and the other two angles each measure 45°.

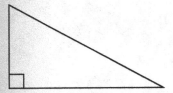

**Isosceles**

» **In any triangle, the largest angle is opposite the longest side.** Similarly, the smallest angle is opposite the shortest side, and the medium angle is opposite the medium-length side.

*Note:* In a right triangle, this largest angle is the right angle because the other two angles total 90 degrees and are thus each less than 90 degrees. The longest side is the *hypotenuse,* which is always opposite the right angle.

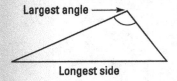

» **In any triangle, the sum of the lengths of two sides must be greater than the length of the third side.** This is written as $a + b > c$, where $a$, $b$, and $c$ are the sides of the triangle.

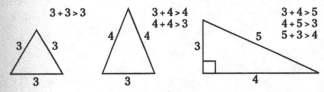

» **In any type of triangle, the sum of the interior angles is 180 degrees.**

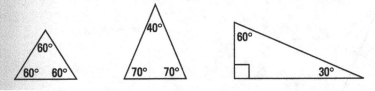

>> *Similar* triangles have the same angles but are different sizes.

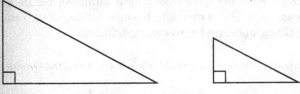

This also means that the side-length ratios are the same. Note that the term *similar* may also apply to other shapes:

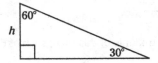

## Calculating the area of triangles

Find the area of a triangle with $A = \frac{1}{2}bh$, where $b$ is the *base* and $h$ is the *height*, also called the *altitude*. The *height* is the distance from any angle to the opposite base. It may be a side of the triangle, as in a right triangle:

The height may also be inside the triangle, in which case it's often represented by a dashed line and a 90-degree box:

The height may also be outside the triangle, also represented by a dashed line and a 90-degree box:

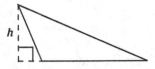

## Using the Pythagorean Theorem

The *Pythagorean Theorem* states that you can find the length of any one side of a right triangle with the side lengths of the other two sides by using the formula $a^2 + b^2 = c^2$, where $a$ and $b$ are the shorter sides and $c$ is the hypotenuse, opposite the 90-degree angle and the longest side of the triangle. Note that this theorem *only* works on a right triangle.

## Saving time with common right triangles

Certain right triangles have commonly used side-length ratios, so before you place two side lengths into the Pythagorean, see whether this right triangle fits one of the ratios. Note that these triangles and ratios are in that graphic that starts each Math Test.

» **3:4:5 triangle.** In this triangle, the two shorter sides are 3 and 4 and the hypotenuse is 5.

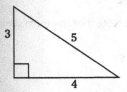

This is a ratio, so the sides can be any multiple of these numbers, including 6:8:10 (2 times 3:4:5) and 9:12:15 (3 times 3:4:5).

» **45-45-90 triangle, also known as an isosceles right triangle.** This is basically a square cut from corner to corner, resulting in triangles having angles 45°, 45°, 90° and a side-length ratio of $1:1:\sqrt{2}$.

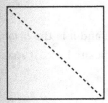 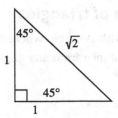

The side lengths of this triangle may appear as any multiple of this ratio, such as $5:5:5\sqrt{2}$.

» **30-60-90 triangle.** This is basically an equilateral triangle cut perfectly in half, resulting in triangles having angles 30°, 60°, 90° and a side-length ratio of $1:2:\sqrt{3}$.

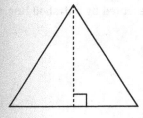 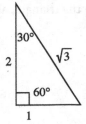

The 30-60-90 makes a regular appearance on the SAT. Just keep in mind that the hypotenuse is twice the length of the smallest side, and if you forget, it's right there in the graphic at the start of the Math Test. If a math question reads, "Given a 30-60-90 triangle of hypotenuse 20, find the area" or "Given a 30-60-90 triangle of hypotenuse 100, find the perimeter," you've got this because you can find the lengths of the other sides:

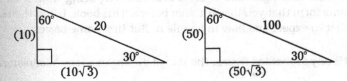

Also, if an SAT question mentions the height of an equilateral triangle, you can use the 30-60-90 triangle to solve it.

**TIP**

All right, enough talking . . . er, writing. Try these:

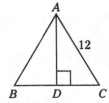

**PLAY**

In this equilateral triangle, the length of segment *AD* is

**(A)** 6

**(B)** 9

**(C)** $6\sqrt{2}$

**(D)** $6\sqrt{3}$

In the 30-60-90 triangle formed by *ABD*, the hypotenuse is 12 and the base is 6 because it's half the hypotenuse. Segment *AD* is the height, which is $6\sqrt{3}$, Choice (D), according to the ratio.

Try another one.

**PLAY**

The measure of one angle of an isosceles triangle is 80°. What *could* be the measure, in degrees, of one of the other two angles?

An isosceles triangle has one unique angle and two twin angles, for a grand total of 180°. If the 80° angle is the unique angle, then the other two angles are 50° and 50°. *Or*, if the 80° is one of the twin angles, then the other twin is also 80° and the third angle is 20°. Which is it? Doesn't matter. Enter either 20, 50, or 80 to get this one right. Don't worry about gridding in the degree symbol.

Triangles are among the most common math topics on the SAT, plus these concepts underly other upcoming math topics, including trapezoids and trigonometry.

# Drawing rectangles and squares

Of course, you know what rectangles and squares are. The SAT, being what it is, still brings you this basic topic in some form that you haven't seen before. This book, being the remedy for these tricks, shows you what to expect and how to handle it. But first some basics:

» **A *quadrilateral* is any four-sided figure.** The sum of the angles of any quadrilateral is 360 degrees.

» **A *rectangle* is a quadrilateral with four right angles,** which makes the opposite sides equal. The area of a rectangle is *length* × *width*, where *length* is the longer side and *width* is the shorter side. The area can also be found with *base* × *height*, where *base* is the bottom and *height* is, well, height, regardless of which is longer.

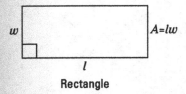

Rectangle

» **A *square* is a rectangle with four equal sides.** The area of a square is $s^2$, where *s* refers to a side length.

» **A *regular* shape is any shape having equal sides and angles.** For example, an equilateral triangle is a regular triangle, and a square is a regular quadrilateral.

Simple, right? Here's what the SAT does with this topic:

**PLAY**

In a certain rectangle, if the length and width were both reduced by 50%, how would the area of the rectangle change?

**(A)** The area would decrease by 25%.

**(B)** The area would decrease by 40%.

**(C)** The area would decrease by 50%.

**(D)** The area would decrease by 75%.

Draw a rectangle and give the side lengths simple numbers, preferably even ones since you'll be dividing them by half, such as $8 \times 10$. Observe the area is 80. Now perform said division by half, so the new side lengths are $4 \times 5$, and the new area is 20, which is a 75% decrease from the original area. The answer is Choice (D).

# Drawing trapezoids and parallelograms

You know these shapes as well, but here's a review of how they work and how to manage them on the SAT.

>> A *parallelogram* **is a quadrilateral where opposite sides and angles are equal, but the angles aren't necessarily right angles.** It's like a rectangle that got stepped on. The area of a parallelogram is *base × height*, where the *base* is the top or bottom (same thing) and the *height* is the distance between the two bases. As in a triangle, the height is represented by a dashed line with a right-angle box.

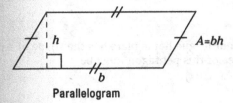

**Parallelogram**

>> A *rhombus* **is a parallelogram with four equal sides.** It's like a square that also got stepped on. The rhombus is measured by the distance between the angles, known as *d* for *diagonal*. The area of a rhombus is $\frac{1}{2}diagonal_1 \times diagonal_2$, or $\frac{1}{2}d_1d_2$ for short.

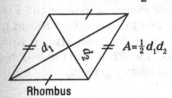

**Rhombus**

>> A *trapezoid* **is a quadrilateral where two sides are parallel and two sides are not.** The area of a trapezoid is $\frac{1}{2}(base_1 + base_2) \times height$, or $\frac{1}{2}(b_1 + b_2)h$, where the bases are the two parallel sides, and the height is the distance between them. If you're not sure how to remember this, it's just base times height, but you average the bases first. Or you can check the graphic at the beginning of the Math Test.

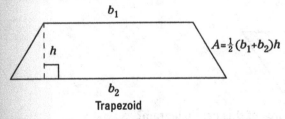

**Trapezoid**

>> **Other polygons that you may see include the** *pentagon*, **the** *hexagon*, **and the** *octagon*, having five, six, and eight sides respectively. If you have to measure the area, just cut these into smaller shapes. The SAT always gives you enough detail to solve the problem.

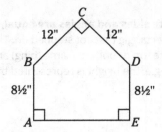

**PLAY**

As shown in the diagram, an official major league home plate has the shape of a pentagon. Given the measurements shown, the area of this pentagon must be

**(A)** $144 + 12\sqrt{2}$

**(B)** $96 + 12\sqrt{2}$

**(C)** $84 + 96\sqrt{2}$

**(D)** $72 + 102\sqrt{2}$

The secret is to split the pentagon into two separate shapes: a triangle and a rectangle. Look at the triangle, *BCD*. Because angle *C* is a right angle, and the two sides adjacent to *C* are the same length, *BCD* is an isosceles right triangle, also known as a 45-45-90 triangle, with the side-length ratio $s:s:s\sqrt{2}$. Therefore, the hypotenuse *BD* is $12\sqrt{2}$, which is also the length of the rectangle. Now find the areas of these separate shapes and add them together.

The triangle's base and height are each 12. Sure, it's rotated, but that doesn't matter: $\frac{1}{2}(12)(12) = 72$. The rectangle has a base and height of $12\sqrt{2}$ and $8\frac{1}{2}$, respectively, which multiply to $\left(12\sqrt{2}\right)\left(8\frac{1}{2}\right) = 102\sqrt{2}$. Fortunately, that matches an answer: Choice (D). Note that the SAT doesn't make you calculate the exact answer.

Here's another one.

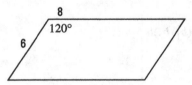

**PLAY**

Which of the following is the area of this parallelogram?

**(A)** 24

**(B)** 48

**(C)** $24\sqrt{3}$

**(D)** $48\sqrt{3}$

How does the 120° help you? If you draw a line from that top corner straight down to the bottom of the shape, you introduce a 30-60-90 triangle. Told you triangles are mixed into everything.

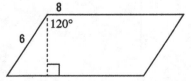

The area of a parallelogram is *base × height*. You know the base is 8, and with the 30-60-90 triangle side-length ratio of $1:2:\sqrt{3}$, you now know the height is $3\sqrt{3}$ (because this new triangle has side lengths $3:6:3\sqrt{3}$). Multiply these together: $8 \times 3\sqrt{3} = 24\sqrt{3}$, for answer Choice (C).

As you can see, these questions are absolute puzzles, and the actual math is simple.

# Drawing circles

Of course, you know circles, but the SAT varies these up too. Like everything else SAT, and so repeated because it's so always true, any trick is easy for you to handle if you've seen the trick before. But first, some basics:

» **The _radius_ goes from the center of the circle to its outer edge.** It's the same length no matter which point of the circle it touches.

Radius

» **Two _radii_ create an isosceles triangle.** This makes sense because an isosceles triangle has two equal sides.

» **A _chord_ is a line segment that goes through the circle.** A chord goes all the way through the circle.

» **The _diameter_ is a chord that goes through the _center_ of the circle.** It's also twice the length of the radius.

Diameter

» **The _circumference_ is the distance around the circle.** Find the circumference, _C_, by using either $C = 2\pi r$, where _r_ is the radius, or $C = \pi d$, where _d_ is the diameter, because the diameter is twice the radius.

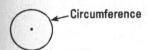

Circumference

» **_Pi_, shown by the Greek letter $\pi$, is the ratio of the circumference to the diameter.** If you take the circumference of any circle and divide it by its diameter, the result is always $\pi$, which equals approximately 3.14.

» **Don't memorize the value of $\pi$.** Just know that it's slightly more than 3.

» **The _area_ of a circle is $A = \pi r^2$.** If you forget any of these equations, check the graphic at the start of each Math Test.

$A = 16\pi$

>> A *tangent* is a line or other shape that touches the circle at exactly one point. A tangent line and the radius of the circle form a 90-degree angle.

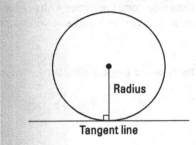

Radius

Tangent line

You know these concepts, and now you've refreshed how they work. The secret is to be fluid in converting one measure to another, such as a radius to circumference or area. Here's an SAT-style question on circles:

PLAY

The radius of circle *A* is twice the radius of circle *B*. How many times greater than the area of circle *B* is the area of circle *A*?

**(A)** Two times greater

**(B)** Three times greater

**(C)** Four times greater

**(D)** Six times greater

Pick a radius for circle *A*, such as 6. If that's twice the radius of circle *B*, then circle *B* has a radius of 3. Now find the areas. Place 6 and 3 for the radii of the two circles to find their areas: $\pi r^2 = \pi (6)^2 = 36\pi$ and $\pi r^2 = \pi (3)^2 = 9\pi$. Because $36\pi$ is four times greater than $9\pi$, the answer is Choice (C).

It's a basic concept that the SAT turns sideways to throw you off. Of course, any question like this one is easy for you now.

## Drawing overlapping shapes

The SAT places two shapes, with one overlapping the other, like a dinner plate resting on a placemat.

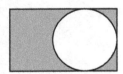

The SAT then asks you for the area of the placemat not covered by the dinner plate, or in SAT terms, the area of the shaded portion of the drawing. The way that you solve this is so simple that you need to try not to laugh out loud when you see this on the exam.

1. **Find the areas of the two shapes, separately.**

2. **Subtract the smaller area from the larger area.**

3. **Leave your answer in terms of $\pi$.**

The question will give you the numbers that you need to answer this one. For example, it'll tell you that the rectangle above is $4 \times 7$. You can derive that the circle has a diameter of 4, for a radius of 2, because it's touching the edges of the rectangle. Now to go through the steps:

**1.** The rectangle area is, $4 \times 7 = 28$ and the circle area is $\pi r^2 = \pi(2)^2 = 4\pi$.

**2.** Subtract the shapes for $28 - 4\pi$.

**3.** And you're done.

You'll hardly ever have to calculate the actual value of $4\pi$ to subtract from 28. Instead, just pick $28 - 4\pi$ from the list of answers, stop laughing, and go on to the next question.

Try this one:

**PLAY**

A circle of radius 3 is surrounded by a square. What is the area of the shaded region?

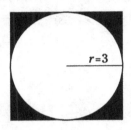

**(A)** $36 - 3\pi$

**(B)** $36 - 6\pi$

**(C)** $36 - 9\pi$

**(D)** $36 - 12\pi$

If the circle has a radius of 3, its diameter is thus 6, meaning the side of the square is also 6. Yes, the next part is even easier. The area of the square is $6 \times 6 = 36$ and that of the circle is $\pi r^2 = \pi(3)^2 = 9\pi$. Subtract them for $36 - 9\pi$, which looks nicely like answer Choice (C).

Overlapping shapes are somewhat common on the SAT math, so make sure you have this topic down by practicing.

# Drawing parts of circles

To draw a part of a circle, just draw the whole circle and take the fraction of the circle. Here are the basics and the exact steps:

» An *arc* is part of the circumference, like the word *arch*. The degree measure of an arc is the same as its central angle, which originates at the center of the circle.

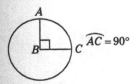

» A *sector* is part of the whole circle, like a slice of pizza. The *arc* is the leftover crust of the pizza (if you don't eat it), and the *sector* is the slice itself. The degree measure of a sector is the same as that of an arc.

Here's how you find the length of an arc:

**1.** Find the <u>circumference</u> of the entire circle.

**2.** Put the degree measure of the arc over 360 and reduce the fraction.

**3.** Multiply the circumference by the fraction.

Here's how you find the area of a sector:

**1.** Find the <u>area</u> of the entire circle.

**2.** Put the degree measure of the sector over 360 and reduce the fraction.

**3.** Multiply the area by the fraction.

Finding the area of a sector is exactly like finding the length of an arc, except for that first step. Now try a couple.

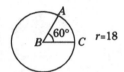

PLAY

Find the length of minor arc *AC*.

**(A)** $36\pi$

**(B)** 60

**(C)** $18\pi$

**(D)** $6\pi$

Start with the circumference of the whole circle: $2\pi r = 2\pi(18) = 36\pi$. Don't multiply $36\pi$ out. Next, put the degree measure of the arc over 360: $\frac{60°}{360°} = \frac{1}{6}$. Finally, multiply the circumference by the fraction: $36\pi \times \frac{1}{6} = 6\pi$, for answer Choice (D).

TIP

The *degree measure* of the arc is not the *length* of the arc. The length is always a portion of the circumference, typically with $\pi$ in it, and always in linear units. If you chose Choice (B) in this example, you found the degree measure instead of the length.

PLAY

If point *B* is at the center of the circle, what's the area of the shaded sector?

**(A)** $\frac{1}{4}\pi$

**(B)** $16\pi$

**(C)** $32\pi$

**(D)** $64\pi$

Start with the area of the whole circle: $\pi r^2 = \pi(8)^2 = 64\pi$. Next, put the degree measure of the sector over 360: $\frac{90°}{360°} = \frac{1}{4}$. Finally, multiply the area by the fraction: $64\pi \times \frac{1}{4} = 16\pi$, which matches answer Choice (B).

You got this, right? Parts of circles are fairly common on the SAT, so be sure you have this down, along with its fine variations.

# Drawing 3-D Shapes

Almost every SAT has a couple questions dealing with a box, cylinder, sphere, or cone. The equations for these 3-D shapes are included in the graphic at the start of each Math section, but here's a review of what you need — because everyone forgets the graphic is there.

## Drawing rectangular solids and cubes

Any rectangular solid — also known as a *rectangular prism* — on the SAT is a perfect shoebox: Each side is a rectangle, and each corner is 90°. This keeps it easy.

**»** **Volume of a rectangular solid:**

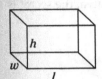

Rectangular solid

The same way that the area of a rectangle is *length × width*, the volume is the area multiplied by the height, for *length × width × height*, or $V = l \cdot w \cdot h$.

**»** **Surface area of a rectangular solid:**

The official equation, where *l* is length, *w* is width, and *h* is height, is $2\left[(l \times w) + (l \times h) + (w \times h)\right]$. Have fun memorizing that one. Instead, *understand* it. A rectangular solid is six rectangles, so measure the surface area of each rectangle. The front and back are the same, so measure one and multiply by two. Same goes for the top and bottom and left side and right side. Fortunately, rectangular solid surface area questions are rare, so don't worry about that equation.

**»** **Volume of a pyramid:**

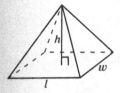

A pyramid has a square base and four identical triangular sides. Like a rectangular solid, find the volume by multiplying the length, width, and height, but with a pyramid, you divide all this by 3: $\frac{1}{3}lwh$.

**»** **Surface area of a pyramid:**

There is no sensible formula for finding the surface area of a pyramid, and fortunately these questions are practically nonexistent. If you do get one, you know what to do: Find the areas of each triangle and the square base, and add 'em up.

>> **Volume of a cube:** $V = s^3$

**Cube**

A cube is exactly like a rectangular solid, only the *length, width,* and *height* are the same, so they're called *edges,* or *e.* Technically the volume of a cube is the same as a rectangular solid, *length × width × height,* but because they're all edges, it's *edge × edge × edge,* or $e^3$.

>> **Surface area of a cube:**

Cube surface area questions are more common, and fortunately, simpler. Say a cube has an edge length of 2, so each side has an area of 4 (because it's a square), and with six sides, the total surface area is $6 \times 4$, which is 24. This is also known as $6e^2$.

What's also common is that the SAT gives you the volume of a cube and asks you for the surface area, or vice versa. Whether you get the volume or the surface area, the secret is to backsolve and get the *edge,* then calculate what the question is asking.

**PLAY**

A certain cube has a volume of 27. What is its surface area?

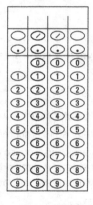

If the volume is 27, backsolve this to get the edge:

$$e^3 = 27$$
$$e = 3$$

Now place the edge length of 3 into the surface area equation:

$$A = 6e^2$$
$$= 6(3)^2$$
$$= 54$$

And the answer is 54.

A certain cube has a surface area of 24. What is its volume?

If the surface area is 24, backsolve this to get the edge:

$$6e^2 = 24$$
$$e^2 = 4$$
$$e = 2$$

Now place the edge length of 2 into the volume equation:

$$V = e^3$$
$$= (2)^3$$
$$= 8$$

And the answer is 8.

The SAT of course goes into more variations than can be explored here, but they're all based on the same concept and just as easily learned.

## Drawing cylinders and cones

You may be asked to find the volume of a cylinder or cone, but rarely the surface area. A question asking for the surface area also provides the surface area equation, and your task will simply be to place the numbers into the equation. The volume questions, however, are more common, and the equations are in the graphic starting each SAT Math Test.

### Volume of a cylinder

Cylinder

A cylinder on the SAT is also called a *right circular cylinder*, where it's like a can of soda or an energy drink. Each base is a circle, and each angle is 90°. The volume of a cylinder is simply the area of the circle — one of its bases — times its height. The area of a circle is $\pi r^2$, times the height $h$, making the volume $\pi r^2 h$.

### Volume of a cone

A cone has a circular base and sides that taper to a point. Its volume is the same as the cylinder, only divided by 3: $\frac{1}{3}\pi r^2 h$.

If a cylinder has a radius of 3 and a height of 4, you can place these into the equation and find its volume:

$$V = \pi r^2 h$$
$$= \pi (3)^2 4$$
$$= 36\pi$$

What's more common is that the SAT gives you the volume and radius and asks for the height, or it gives you the volume and height and asks for the radius. Either way, just take the numbers from the question and place them into the equation.

PLAY

What is the radius of a cylinder having a volume of $48\pi$ and a height of 3?

**(A)** 3

**(B)** 4

**(C)** 6

**(D)** 8

Take the volume equation and place the numbers that the question gives you:

$$V = \pi r^2 h$$
$$(48\pi) = \pi r^2 (3)$$
$$16\pi = \pi r^2$$
$$16 = r^2$$
$$4 = r$$

And the answer is (B).

These questions are no more challenging than any you've seen so far, except that the arrangements are different. Once you get used to the arrangements, taking on these questions is no problem.

## Drawing spheres

Like the cylinder and cone, most questions about the sphere entail volume and rarely involve surface area. The volume equation is given in the beginning graphic, and the surface area equation, if needed, is given with the question.

A *sphere* is a perfectly round ball, like a basketball. Like a circle, it has a radius, so for its volume, simply place the radius into the equation: $\frac{4}{3}\pi r^3$.

Here are two to try.

PLAY

Which of the following is the volume of a sphere that has a radius of 3?

**(A)** $72\pi$

**(B)** $54\pi$

**(C)** $36\pi$

**(D)** $18\pi$

Place the radius into the volume equation. Remember, on the SAT, the math is always simple:

$$V = \frac{4}{3}\pi r^3$$
$$= \frac{4}{3}\pi (3)^3$$
$$= \frac{4}{3}\pi 27$$
$$= 4\pi 18$$
$$= 72\pi$$

And the answer is Choice (A).

Here's another one because you haven't had enough already. Just like on the real exam.

**PLAY**

$$A = 4\pi r^2$$

The surface area of a sphere can be found with the above equation. What is the surface area of a sphere that has a radius of 5?

**(A)** $25\pi$

**(B)** $50\pi$

**(C)** $75\pi$

**(D)** $100\pi$

Place the radius into the surface area equation:

$$A = 4\pi r^2$$
$$= 4\pi (5)^2$$
$$= 4\pi 25$$
$$= 100\pi$$

And the answer is Choice (D). Even if you haven't worked a sphere surface area question, which is most people except those who often engage the SAT, this question took you less than a minute, right? Be honest.

Sphere questions are like any other on the SAT Math Tests: They look challenging but are simple to answer, especially with practice.

# Solving Trigonometry Problems

Unlike the ACT, which typically has at least five trig questions among its 60 Math Test questions, the SAT usually has one or two trig question in its 58 Math Test questions. This means that the scope of trigonometry is narrower, and this is a topic that you can move lower on your priority list. That said, if you got this far, you'll have no problem with these topics. This section covers what you need to know, even if you've never studied trigonometry.

# Solving right triangles with SOH CAH TOA

*SOH CAH TOA* stands for

$$\text{Sine} = \frac{\text{Opposite}}{\text{Hypotenuse}}$$

$$\text{Cosine} = \frac{\text{Adjacent}}{\text{Hypotenuse}}$$

$$\text{Tangent} = \frac{\text{Opposite}}{\text{Adjacent}}$$

*Opposite*, *adjacent*, and *hypotenuse* refer to the sides of a right triangle in relation to one of the acute angles. For example, consider this right triangle:

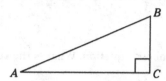

As you know, side *AB* is the *hypotenuse* (opposite the right angle and the longest side of the right triangle). For angle *A*, side *BC* is *opposite*, and side *AC* is *adjacent*. For angle *B*, they switch: Side *AC* is opposite, and side *BC* is adjacent.

Use SOH CAH TOA to quickly find the sine, cosine, or tangent of any acute angle in the right triangle.

» **To find sin *A* (the sine of angle *A*), use the SOH part of SOH CAH TOA.** Place the length of the side opposite angle *A* (in this case, side *BC*) over the hypotenuse (side *AB*).

$$\sin A = \frac{\text{Opposite}}{\text{Hypotenuse}}$$

$$\sin A = \frac{\overline{BC}}{\overline{AB}}$$

» **To find cos *A* (the cosine of angle *A*), use the CAH part of SOH CAH TOA.** Place the length of the side adjacent to angle *A* (in this case, side *AC*) over the hypotenuse (side *AB*).

$$\cos A = \frac{\text{Adjacent}}{\text{Hypotenuse}}$$

$$\cos A = \frac{\overline{AC}}{\overline{AB}}$$

» **To find tan *A* (the tangent of angle *A*), use the TOA part of SOH CAH TOA.** Place the length of the side opposite angle *A* over the side adjacent to angle *A*.

$$\tan A = \frac{\text{Opposite}}{\text{Adjacent}}$$

$$\tan A = \frac{\overline{BC}}{\overline{AC}}$$

**TIP**

SOH CAH TOA only works with a *right triangle* and only with an *acute angle*, not the right angle.

Because sine and cosine are a shorter side over the longer hypotenuse, sine and cosine can never be greater than 1. Tangent, however, can be greater than 1. You don't need to know the common values of sine and cosine, but these can be handy:

sin 90° = 1 and sin 0° = 0

cos 90° = 0 and cos 0° = 1

**PLAY**

Find the sine of angle *A* in the right triangle that follows:

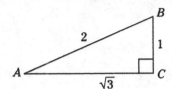

**(A)** 2

**(B)** $\sqrt{3}$

**(C)** 1

**(D)** $\frac{1}{2}$

Using the SOH in SOH CAH TOA, you know that the sine of angle *A* comes from the opposite (1) over the hypotenuse (2), for an answer of $\frac{1}{2}$ which matches Choice (D).

Three additional ratios appear less frequently than sine, cosine, and tangent but are just as easy to find. These are cosecant (csc), secant (sec), and cotangent (cot). Basically, you find the sine, cosine, or tangent and take the reciprocal to find cosecant, secant, or cotangent. The angle is usually represented by the Greek letter theta, $\theta$:

$$\csc\theta = \frac{1}{\sin\theta}$$

$$\sec\theta = \frac{1}{\cos\theta}$$

$$\tan\theta = \frac{1}{\cot\theta}$$

**TIP**

If you get mixed up as to whether cosecant or secant is the reciprocal of sine or cosine, just remember this tip: *C* in *cosecant* goes with *S* in *sine*. *S* in *secant* goes with *C* in *cosine*.

Using the same right triangle, find the cotangent of angle *A*:

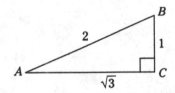

**PLAY**

**(A)** 3

**(B)** 2

**(C)** $\sqrt{3}$

**(D)** 1

Using the TOA in SOH CAH TOA, you know that the tangent of angle *A* comes from the opposite (1) over the adjacent ($\sqrt{3}$), for a tangent of $\frac{1}{\sqrt{3}}$. Take the reciprocal to find the cotangent, $\sqrt{3}$, for answer Choice (C).

Here's another:

For this right triangle, if $\tan B = \frac{4}{3}$, find $\cos A$.

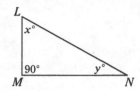

**(A)** $\frac{4}{3}$

**(B)** $\frac{5}{4}$

**(C)** $\frac{3}{4}$

**(D)** $\frac{4}{5}$

Choice (D) is the answer. If $\tan B = \frac{4}{3}$ and tangent is opposite over adjacent (the TOA from SOH CAH TOA), then draw the triangle like this:

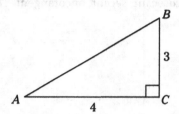

Spotting this as one of the common right triangles (covered earlier in this chapter), you automatically throw down 5 for the hypotenuse:

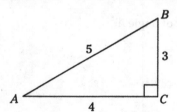

Cosine is CAH, which is adjacent over hypotenuse. Therefore, $\cos A = \frac{4}{5}$.

## Solving unit circles and radians

The *unit circle* is a circle drawn on the x-y graph with a center at the origin — coordinates $(0,0)$ — and a radius of 1.

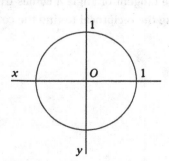

Starting with the radius of the circle at $(1,0)$, the angle $\theta$ is measured going counterclockwise.

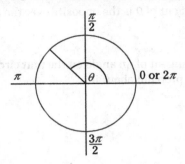

In this drawing, $\theta = 135°$. However, the angle isn't always measured in degrees; rather, it's in *radians*, which means that it's in terms of $\pi$, where $\pi = 180°$.

An angle measuring 45° also measures $\frac{\pi}{4}$ radians. An angle measuring 270° also measures $\frac{3\pi}{2}$ radians. More importantly, or the way it's used on the SAT, you can tell which quadrant an angle is in from the range of radians. In other words, an angle between $\frac{\pi}{2}$ and $\pi$ is in the second quadrant. For the angle $\theta$,

» $0 < \theta < \frac{\pi}{2}$ places the angle in the first quadrant.

» $\frac{\pi}{2} < \theta < \pi$ places the angle in the second quadrant.

» $\pi < \theta < \frac{3\pi}{2}$ places the angle in the third quadrant.

» $\frac{3\pi}{2} < \theta < 2\pi$ places the angle in the fourth quadrant.

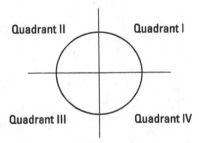

When SOH CAH TOA is applied to an angle in the unit circle, it's always for the angle $\theta$, which comes from the radius of the circle. The *hypotenuse* is this radius, the *adjacent* is the $x$-value, and the *opposite* is the $y$-value. Consider this example, where $\theta = 60°$ and the radius meets the circle at $\left(\frac{1}{2}, \sqrt{3}\right)$, where on the $xy$ graph, $x = \frac{1}{2}$ and $y = \sqrt{3}$.

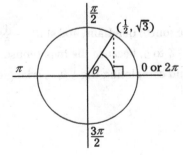

The sine of $\theta$ is the opposite over the hypotenuse, which in this case is $\frac{\sqrt{3}}{2}$. The cosine of $\theta$ is the adjacent over the hypotenuse, $\frac{0.5}{1}$, or $\frac{1}{2}$. The tangent of $\theta$ is the opposite over the adjacent, which is $\frac{\sqrt{3}}{1}$, or $\sqrt{3}$.

Knowing the quadrant and the sine, cosine, or tangent of an angle on the unit circle, you can find exactly where the angle is and solve almost any problem about it.

PLAY

If $\frac{\pi}{2} < \theta < \pi$ and $\cos\theta = -\frac{3}{5}$, what is $\sin\theta$?

(A) $-\frac{4}{5}$

(B) $-\frac{3}{5}$

(C) $\frac{3}{5}$

(D) $\frac{4}{5}$

The first expression, $\frac{\pi}{2} < \theta < \pi$, places the angle in the second quadrant, and $\cos\theta = -\frac{3}{5}$ means the ratio of the $x$-value of the endpoint to the radius is $-\frac{3}{5}$. Because the hypotenuse (or radius) is always positive, the $x$-value is negative. The $\sin\theta$, being the opposite over hypotenuse, is therefore $\frac{4}{5}$, and the correct answer is Choice (D).

Try another.

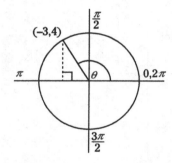

PLAY

If $\frac{3\pi}{2} < \theta < 2\pi$ and $\sin\theta = -\frac{4}{5}$, what is $\cos\theta$?

(A) $\frac{4}{5}$

(B) $\frac{3}{5}$

(C) $-\frac{3}{5}$

(D) $-\frac{4}{5}$

The expression $\frac{3\pi}{2} < \theta < 2\pi$ places the angle in the fourth quadrant, and $\sin\theta = -\frac{4}{5}$ means that the ratio of the $y$-value to the hypotenuse is $-\frac{4}{5}$, or $-4$ to $5$, because the hypotenuse is always positive. This means that drawn on the unit circle, and completing the 3-4-5 triangle, angle $\theta$ looks like this:

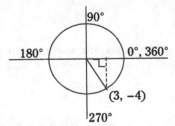

To find $\cos\theta$, place the adjacent ($x$-value) over the hypotenuse, for $\frac{3}{5}$ which matches Choice B).

To convert from $\pi$ radians to degrees, remove the $\pi$ and multiply by 180:

$$\pi = 180°$$
$$3\pi = 520°$$

And, to convert from degrees to $\pi$ radians, do the opposite: Divide by 180 and place the $\pi$:

$$360° = 2\pi$$
$$90° = \frac{\pi}{2}$$

Use that to answer an SAT Math question.

PLAY

If an engine rotates 1,800 degrees per second, what is its rotation per second in $\pi$ radians?

**(A)** $8\pi$

**(B)** $10\pi$

**(C)** $12\pi$

**(D)** $14\pi$

Convert the 1,800 degrees per second into $\pi$ radians by dividing it by 180 and placing $\pi$:

$$1,800° \div 180° = 10 \rightarrow 10\pi \text{ for Choice (B).}$$

## Solving trigonometric equations

You see many more of these equations in Algebra II and Trig, but there are only a few that you need on the SAT. Try these on this right triangle:

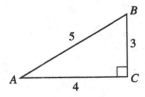

1. $\dfrac{\sin x}{\cos x} = \tan x$

Take angle $A$ for example. Using SOH CAH TOA, you know that $\sin A = \frac{3}{5}$, $\cos A = \frac{4}{5}$, and $\tan A = \frac{3}{4}$. Now prove this equation by placing these values:

$$\frac{\sin x}{\cos x} = \tan x$$
$$\frac{\frac{3}{5}}{\frac{4}{5}} = \frac{3}{5} \times \frac{5}{4} = \frac{3}{4}$$

**2.** $\sin x = \cos(90 - x)$ or $\sin A = \cos B$

Remember, the two non-right angles total 90°, so 90° minus one angle equals the other angle. With the triangle above, $\sin A = \frac{3}{5}$ equals $\cos B = \frac{3}{5}$.

**3.** $\sin^2 x + \cos^2 x = 1$

Back to the 3-4-5 triangle above. $\sin A = \frac{3}{5}$ and $\cos A = \frac{4}{5}$. First square these: $\sin^2 A = \left(\frac{3}{5}\right)^2 = \frac{9}{25}$ and $\cos^2 A = \left(\frac{4}{5}\right)^2 = \frac{16}{25}$. Now add them: $\frac{9}{25} + \frac{16}{25} = \frac{25}{25} = 1$.

The SAT asks these in a conceptual form. If you understand these three equations, and more importantly, *recognize* them in the question, you save yourself a lot of math work and give yourself a lot of laughter as you answer the question in well under a minute. Try this one:

**PLAY**

If $\cos a° = n$, which of the following must be true for all values of $a$?

**(A)** $\sin^2 a = n$

**(B)** $\cos(90 - a)° = n$

**(C)** $\sin(90 - a)° = n$

**(D)** $\tan(90 - a)° = n$

Knowing that $\sin x = \cos(90 - x)$, because you just read it a second ago, you know that $\cos a° = \sin(90 - a)°$. Because these each equal $n$, the answer is Choice (C).

See? No math. Practice these concepts and learn to recognize them *quickly*.

IN THIS CHAPTER

» Understanding common ways to define a group of numbers

» Recognizing common tricks and knowing how to get around them

» Calculating probability and how the SAT spins it

» Recognizing standard arrangements in the SAT questions

# Chapter 13

# Statistics and Probability

The topic of statistics and probability builds on numbers and perations covered in Chapter 10. Like every other math topic on the SAT, the numeric part is always simple, and knowing how to set up the solution is key. This chapter reviews SAT-style questions on sets-of-number topics that include averages (also known as arithmetic mean), median, mode, and range, along with probability and reading graphs.

## Defining the Mean, Median, and Mode

Of all the methods to quantify or measure a set of numbers or data, the most common — and what you see on the SAT — involves the *mean*, *median*, and *mode*. Your job is to look past the tricky way that the SAT sets up the question and see the simple underlying concept.

### Defining the mean

Sometimes the SAT gives you a group of numbers and asks you to find the *average* (also called the *mean* or *arithmetic mean*). To find the average, just add up the numbers and divide that total by the count of numbers you just added. For example, to find the average of 2, 4, and 9, add those numbers and divide by 3, because there are three numbers. It looks like this:

$$\begin{aligned} a &= \frac{2+4+9}{3} \\ &= \frac{15}{3} \\ &= 5 \end{aligned}$$

If you have the average and *some* of the numbers, set up the equation with x as the missing number. If the average of 3, 6, 14, and some unknown number is 7, use x as the unknown number:

$$7 = \frac{3+6+14+x}{4}$$

$$7 = \frac{23+x}{4}$$

$$28 = 23+x$$

$$x = 5$$

This type of question usually looks like this:

**PLAY**

A student has taken three tests, with an average (arithmetic mean) of 88. What grade must he receive on his next test in order to have an overall average of 90 and get his A?

**(A)** 90

**(B)** 94

**(C)** 96

**(D)** 98

Set up the equation with x as the upcoming test. You don't know the other three test scores, but you know they average 88, so use 88 for each one:

$$90 = \frac{88+88+88+x}{4}$$

$$90 = \frac{264+x}{4}$$

$$360 = 264+x$$

$$x = 96$$

He needs 96 on this next test for that A. He'll get it. The correct answer is Choice (C).

One variation of the averages question is average driving speed. To solve this, place the total distance in miles over the total time in hours. For example, if you drive the 140 miles from Phoenix to Flagstaff in 2 hours, divide 140 by 2 for your average speed of 70 miles per hour.

**PLAY**

If Sally drove the 120 miles from San Diego to Long Beach in 1.75 hours, and then drove back to San Diego in 2.25 hours, what was her average speed, in miles per hour?

**(A)** 50 miles per hour

**(B)** 60 miles per hour

**(C)** 70 miles per hour

**(D)** 80 miles per hour

Sally drove 120 miles there and 120 miles back, for a total distance of 240 miles. Her first round was 1.75 hours and the second was 2.25 hours, for a total time of 4 hours. Divide 240 by 4 for her average speed:

$$\frac{240 \text{ miles}}{4 \text{ hours}} = \frac{60 \text{ miles}}{1 \text{ hour}}$$

She drove 60 miles per hour, so the answer is Choice (B).

## Defining the median and mode

The *median* is the middle number in a list, when the list is in numerical order. Say you have the numbers 5, 3, 8, 7, 2 and need the median. Put the numbers in order, 2, 3, 5, 7, 8, and the middle number, or median, is 5.

If there are two middle numbers (say with 2, 4, 5, 7, 8, 10), average the two middle numbers. In this example, the two middle numbers are 5 and 7, so the median is 6.

Finally there's the *mode*. In a mixed bag of numbers, the *mode* is the number or numbers that pop up most frequently. So with the numbers 3, 4, 4, 5, 8, 8, 9, there are two modes, 4 and 8. You can also have a set with no mode at all if everything shows up the same number of times, as with 3, 4, 5, 6.

**PLAY**

A certain set of numbers has a mean of 18, a median of 20, and a mode of 21. Which number *must* be in the data set?

**(A)** 18

**(B)** 20

**(C)** 21

**(D)** 22

The *mean* and *median* don't have to be in the set of numbers. The mean is calculated, and if the two middle numbers are, say, 19 and 21, you get the median of 20. But the mode *has* to be in the set, because it's the most commonly occurring number. So the correct answer is Choice (C).

Mode questions are rare, but median questions are more common:

**PLAY**

A student has a median score of 83 on five tests. If she scores 97 and 62 on her next two tests, her median score will

**(A)** increase to 90

**(B)** decrease to 82

**(C)** decrease to 79.5

**(D)** remain the same

The median is the score in the middle. If 83 is in the middle, placing 97 on one side and 62 on the other doesn't change the middle number. The correct answer is Choice (D).

Once again, the SAT takes a topic you know fairly well and introduces variations that may throw you the first time you see them.

## Defining the range

The *range* is the distance between the lowest and highest numbers. For example, if your lowest exam score is 82 and your highest is 110, because you got those bonus questions, the range is the difference between those scores: $110 - 82 = 28$.

The SAT doesn't make it that simple, but this book makes it that easy. On the SAT, the range represents something like sales tax, units per box, or something that you somehow have to calculate. So all you do is calculate it!

For example, if each volleyball team has either 4 or 6 players, and there are 12 teams at the tournament, what are the *lowest* and *highest* possible numbers of players? For the lowest number, use 4 players for each of the 12 teams: $4 \times 12 = 48$ For the highest number, use 6: $6 \times 12 = 72$.

PLAY

Try this one:

Mariama places between $\frac{1}{5}$ and $\frac{1}{4}$, inclusive, of her weekly paycheck into a savings account. If she placed $150 into her savings account last week, then how much, in dollars, *could* last week's paycheck have been? Disregard the dollar sign when gridding your answer.

First, find the amount of her paycheck with $150 as $\frac{1}{4}$ of it:

$$\frac{1}{4}x = \$150$$

$$x = \$600$$

Then find the amount of her paycheck with $150 as $\frac{1}{5}$ of of it:

$$\frac{1}{5}x = \$150$$

$$x = \$750$$

So her paycheck was between $600 and $750. Disregard the dollar sign, so any number you place between 600 and 750, (including those numbers because the question reads, *inclusive*,) is considered correct.

# Defining Probability

The *probability* of an event means how likely it is to occur. A 50 percent chance of rain means that the probability of rain is $\frac{1}{2}$. A probability can be defined as a fraction or a percent, and in rare cases (on the SAT), a decimal. Here's the equation:

$$\text{probability of an event } (p_e) = \frac{\text{the number that you want}}{\text{the number that is possible}}$$

Say that you have a jar of 18 marbles where 7 are blue. The probability of reaching in and grabbing a blue marble is $\frac{7}{18}$, because there are 7 that you want and 18 possible.

Probability is always between 0 and 1. If something will *definitely* happen, the probability is 1, or 100 percent. The probability that the sun will rise tomorrow is 100 percent. If something will definitely *not* happen, the probability is 0. The probability that Elvis will sing again is 0.

The probabilities of different outcomes where only one can happen always add up to 1. Say you took a history exam. Say also the probability of you getting an A is 60 percent, a B is 20 percent, a C is 10 percent, a D is 5 percent, and an F is 5 percent. There's only one possible outcome — you can't get two grades on one exam — and all the probabilities add up to 100 percent.

If there are two events, and you want the probability of one *or* the other, add the probabilities. After that history exam, your probability of earning an A *or* a B is 80 percent, which comes from adding the 60 percent chance of getting an A to the 20 percent probability of getting a B.

If there are two *separate* events, and you want the probability of *both* happening, multiply the probabilities. Here's an example:

**PLAY**

Jenny arranges interviews with three potential employers. If each employer has a 50 percent probability of offering her a job, what's the probability that she gets offered all three?

**(A)** 10%

**(B)** 12.5%

**(C)** 75%

**(D)** 100%

These are three separate events, each with a probability of 50 percent. The probability of Jenny being offered all three jobs is $50\% \times 50\% \times 50\%$, or $\frac{1}{2} \times \frac{1}{2} \times \frac{1}{2} = \frac{1}{8}$, which calculates to 12.5% for Choice (B).

**TIP**

Probability questions are lower on the list of common SAT Math questions, but they do appear, and they're simple enough if you've worked a few.

# Measuring Graph Data

Here are the three most common types of graphs you're likely to see on the SAT:

>> Bar graph

>> Circle or pie graph

>> Two-axes line graph

## Measuring bar graphs

A *bar graph* has vertical or horizontal bars.

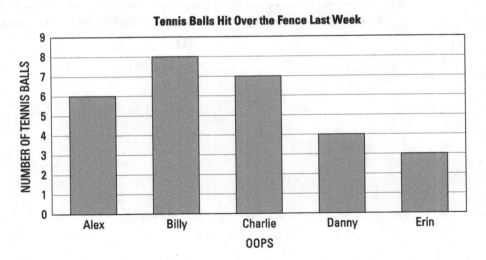

# Measuring circle or pie charts

A *circle* or *pie chart* represents the total, or 100 percent.

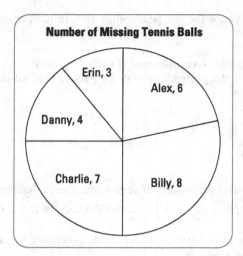

**Number of Missing Tennis Balls**

Erin, 3
Alex, 6
Danny, 4
Charlie, 7
Billy, 8

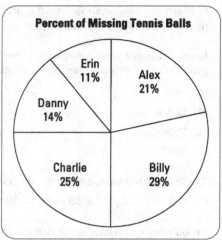

**Percent of Missing Tennis Balls**

Erin 11%
Alex 21%
Danny 14%
Charlie 25%
Billy 29%

# Measuring line graphs

A typical *line graph* has a bottom and a side axis.

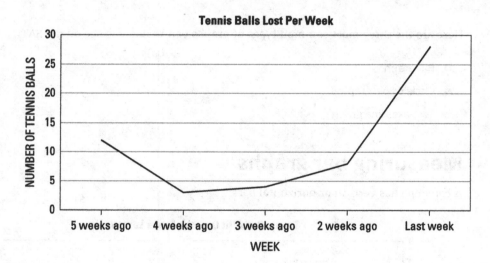

**Tennis Balls Lost Per Week**

NUMBER OF TENNIS BALLS

30
25
20
15
10
5
0

5 weeks ago    4 weeks ago    3 weeks ago    2 weeks ago    Last week

WEEK

# Measuring scatter plots

A special kind of two-axes graph is the *scatter plot*. A scatter plot contains a bunch of dots scattered in a pattern, like this:

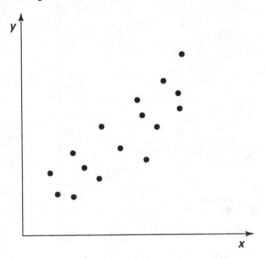

Notice how the points seem to follow a certain flow, going up and to the right. When you see this, you can draw a line that captures the flow. This line is known as a *trend line* or *correlation*. On the test, you may be given a scatter plot and have to estimate where the points are going based on the trend line, like this:

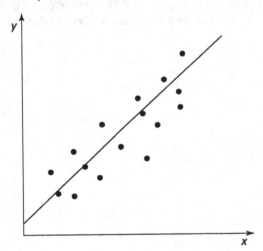

On the SAT, a correlation is always *linear*. When you read left to right, if the correlation goes *up*, it's positive, and if it goes *down*, it's negative, just like the slope of a graphed line.

**PLAY**

Which of the following best describes the data set?

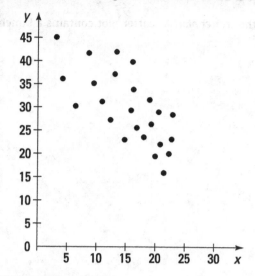

**(A)** A positive correlation

**(B)** A negative correlation

**(C)** An exponential correlation

**(D)** No correlation

There is clearly a correlation, which is never exponential (on the SAT), so out go Choices (C) and (D). Add the trend line to see whether the correlation is positive or negative:

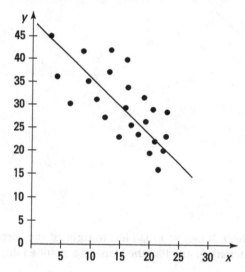

The trend line goes down, so the correlation is negative. Choice (B) it is.

# Measuring multiple graphs

Sometimes the SAT places two graphs of related data with two or three related questions on these graphs. In this example, the second graph is a bar graph going from 0 to 100 percent. Read the graph by subtracting to find the appropriate percentage. For example, in 2016, "Grandparents won't donate a building" begins at 20 percent and goes to 50 percent, a difference of 30 percent. You've fallen into a trap if you say that "Grandparents won't donate a building" was 50 percent.

In 2019, "Just felt like it" goes from 80 percent to 100 percent, which means it was actually 20 percent.

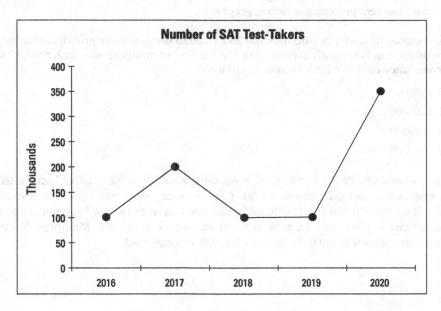

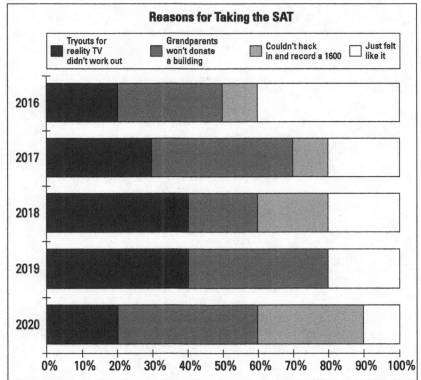

The first graph gives you the number of SAT test-takers in thousands. (By the way, these aren't real numbers.) Be sure to look at the labels of the axes. For example, *Thousands* along the side axis tells you that in 2016, there weren't 100 test-takers but 100,000. Using the two graphs together, you can find out the number of test-takers who took the SAT for a particular reason. For example, in 2017, 200,000 students took the test. Also in 2017, "Couldn't hack in and record a 1600" (from 70 to 80, or 10 percent) made up 10 percent of the reasons for taking the SAT. Multiply 10 percent or $0.10 \times 200{,}000 = 20{,}000$ test-takers.

The SAT may feature two or three questions about a particular graph or set of graphs. When you encounter these, start with the question, then go to the graphs. Answer the following question based on the two preceding practice graphs:

**PLAY**

The number of students who took the SAT in 2020 because their grandparents wouldn't donate a building was how much greater than the number of students who took the SAT in 2018 because they couldn't hack in and record a 1600?

(A) 250,000

(B) 140,000

(C) 120,000

(D) 100,000

The answer is Choice (C). In 2020, "Grandparents won't donate a building" accounted for 40 percent of test-taking reasons (from 20 to 60). Because 2020 had 350,000 test-takers, multiply $0.40 \times 350,000 = 140,000$. In 2018, "Couldn't hack in and record a 1600" counted for 20 percent of test-taking reasons (60 to 80). In 2018, 100,000 students took the test. Multiply $0.20 \times 100,000 = 20,000$. The correct answer is $140,000 - 20,000 = 120,000$, or Choice (C).

# 5

# It's All You: Taking Practice SAT Exams

Check your readiness for the SAT by taking full-length practice tests.

Improve your performance by reviewing the answer explanations for all the practice questions.

Convert your correct answers to an actual SAT score.

# Chapter **14**

# Practice Exam 1

**Y**ou're now ready to take a practice SAT. Like the actual SAT, the following practice exam consists of an exhaustive 65-minute Reading Test, a 35-minute Writing and Language Test, a 25-minute Math Test with no calculator allowed, a 55-minute Math Test with a calculator permitted, and an optional 50-minute Essay Test. If you can get through all that, you're in good shape.

Take this practice test under normal exam conditions and approach it as you would the real SAT:

>> **Work where you won't be interrupted.** Leave your cell phone in another room, and ask anyone living with you (parents, siblings, dog) not to disturb you for the next several hours. (Good luck with that.)

>> **Practice with someone else who is taking the SAT.** This allows you to get used to the feeling of working with another person in the room; plus, this person can keep you focused and provide a sense of competition.

>> **Answer as many questions as time allows.** Consider answering all the easier questions within each section first and then going back to the harder questions. Because you're not penalized for guessing, go ahead and guess on the remaining questions before time expires.

>> **Set a timer for each section.** If you have time left at the end, you may go back and review answers (within the section), continue and finish your test early, or pause and catch your mental breath before moving on to the next section.

>> **Use the answer sheet.** Practice bubbling your answers as you get them, not saving them for the end. We've seen plenty of points lost from bubbling mistakes — skipping lines, doubling some answers, running out of time and not filling in a bunch — and that's just a silly way to dent your score.

>> **Don't get up while the clock is running.** Though technically you're allowed to do this, it's not conducive to an effective time-management strategy.

>> **Take breaks between sections.** Take one minute after each section and a ten-minute break after the Writing and Language Test, and if you're writing the Essay, take another ten-minute break after the Math Test – Calculator Allowed.

» **Work through the entire exam, including the essay if you're signed up for it.** Get used to the experience of going through the entire exam in one setting. It's not easy the first time, but you'll build the strength to stay focused through the entire marathon session.

After completing this practice test, go to Chapter 15 to check your answers. Be sure to review the explanations for *all* the questions, not just the ones you miss. The answer explanations provide insight and a review of everything you went over in the previous chapters. This way, too, you review the explanations for questions that you weren't sure of.

REMEMBER

The exam is your scratch paper, so use that to note the reading, work the math, and circle questions to return to. The bubble sheet is *only* for bubbling answers.

Ready? Tear out the bubble answer sheet, grab a pencil and four sheets of loose-leaf paper (if you're writing the optional essay), and get a timer. Sit back, relax, and enjoy your trip through Practice Exam 1.

# Answer Sheets

For Sections 1 through 4, use the ovals and grid-ins provided with this practice exam to record your answers. Begin with Number 1 for each new section. For the essay, write on four sheets of loose-leaf or notebook paper. Or you can use the following blank pages.

## Section 1: Reading Test

1. Ⓐ Ⓑ Ⓒ Ⓓ
2. Ⓐ Ⓑ Ⓒ Ⓓ
3. Ⓐ Ⓑ Ⓒ Ⓓ
4. Ⓐ Ⓑ Ⓒ Ⓓ
5. Ⓐ Ⓑ Ⓒ Ⓓ
6. Ⓐ Ⓑ Ⓒ Ⓓ
7. Ⓐ Ⓑ Ⓒ Ⓓ
8. Ⓐ Ⓑ Ⓒ Ⓓ
9. Ⓐ Ⓑ Ⓒ Ⓓ
10. Ⓐ Ⓑ Ⓒ Ⓓ
11. Ⓐ Ⓑ Ⓒ Ⓓ

12. Ⓐ Ⓑ Ⓒ Ⓓ
13. Ⓐ Ⓑ Ⓒ Ⓓ
14. Ⓐ Ⓑ Ⓒ Ⓓ
15. Ⓐ Ⓑ Ⓒ Ⓓ
16. Ⓐ Ⓑ Ⓒ Ⓓ
17. Ⓐ Ⓑ Ⓒ Ⓓ
18. Ⓐ Ⓑ Ⓒ Ⓓ
19. Ⓐ Ⓑ Ⓒ Ⓓ
20. Ⓐ Ⓑ Ⓒ Ⓓ
21. Ⓐ Ⓑ Ⓒ Ⓓ
22. Ⓐ Ⓑ Ⓒ Ⓓ

23. Ⓐ Ⓑ Ⓒ Ⓓ
24. Ⓐ Ⓑ Ⓒ Ⓓ
25. Ⓐ Ⓑ Ⓒ Ⓓ
26. Ⓐ Ⓑ Ⓒ Ⓓ
27. Ⓐ Ⓑ Ⓒ Ⓓ
28. Ⓐ Ⓑ Ⓒ Ⓓ
29. Ⓐ Ⓑ Ⓒ Ⓓ
30. Ⓐ Ⓑ Ⓒ Ⓓ
31. Ⓐ Ⓑ Ⓒ Ⓓ
32. Ⓐ Ⓑ Ⓒ Ⓓ
33. Ⓐ Ⓑ Ⓒ Ⓓ

34. Ⓐ Ⓑ Ⓒ Ⓓ
35. Ⓐ Ⓑ Ⓒ Ⓓ
36. Ⓐ Ⓑ Ⓒ Ⓓ
37. Ⓐ Ⓑ Ⓒ Ⓓ
38. Ⓐ Ⓑ Ⓒ Ⓓ
39. Ⓐ Ⓑ Ⓒ Ⓓ
40. Ⓐ Ⓑ Ⓒ Ⓓ
41. Ⓐ Ⓑ Ⓒ Ⓓ
42. Ⓐ Ⓑ Ⓒ Ⓓ
43. Ⓐ Ⓑ Ⓒ Ⓓ
44. Ⓐ Ⓑ Ⓒ Ⓓ

45. Ⓐ Ⓑ Ⓒ Ⓓ
46. Ⓐ Ⓑ Ⓒ Ⓓ
47. Ⓐ Ⓑ Ⓒ Ⓓ
48. Ⓐ Ⓑ Ⓒ Ⓓ
49. Ⓐ Ⓑ Ⓒ Ⓓ
50. Ⓐ Ⓑ Ⓒ Ⓓ
51. Ⓐ Ⓑ Ⓒ Ⓓ
52. Ⓐ Ⓑ Ⓒ Ⓓ

## Section 2: Writing and Language Test

1. Ⓐ Ⓑ Ⓒ Ⓓ
2. Ⓐ Ⓑ Ⓒ Ⓓ
3. Ⓐ Ⓑ Ⓒ Ⓓ
4. Ⓐ Ⓑ Ⓒ Ⓓ
5. Ⓐ Ⓑ Ⓒ Ⓓ
6. Ⓐ Ⓑ Ⓒ Ⓓ
7. Ⓐ Ⓑ Ⓒ Ⓓ
8. Ⓐ Ⓑ Ⓒ Ⓓ
9. Ⓐ Ⓑ Ⓒ Ⓓ

10. Ⓐ Ⓑ Ⓒ Ⓓ
11. Ⓐ Ⓑ Ⓒ Ⓓ
12. Ⓐ Ⓑ Ⓒ Ⓓ
13. Ⓐ Ⓑ Ⓒ Ⓓ
14. Ⓐ Ⓑ Ⓒ Ⓓ
15. Ⓐ Ⓑ Ⓒ Ⓓ
16. Ⓐ Ⓑ Ⓒ Ⓓ
17. Ⓐ Ⓑ Ⓒ Ⓓ
18. Ⓐ Ⓑ Ⓒ Ⓓ

19. Ⓐ Ⓑ Ⓒ Ⓓ
20. Ⓐ Ⓑ Ⓒ Ⓓ
21. Ⓐ Ⓑ Ⓒ Ⓓ
22. Ⓐ Ⓑ Ⓒ Ⓓ
23. Ⓐ Ⓑ Ⓒ Ⓓ
24. Ⓐ Ⓑ Ⓒ Ⓓ
25. Ⓐ Ⓑ Ⓒ Ⓓ
26. Ⓐ Ⓑ Ⓒ Ⓓ
27. Ⓐ Ⓑ Ⓒ Ⓓ

28. Ⓐ Ⓑ Ⓒ Ⓓ
29. Ⓐ Ⓑ Ⓒ Ⓓ
30. Ⓐ Ⓑ Ⓒ Ⓓ
31. Ⓐ Ⓑ Ⓒ Ⓓ
32. Ⓐ Ⓑ Ⓒ Ⓓ
33. Ⓐ Ⓑ Ⓒ Ⓓ
34. Ⓐ Ⓑ Ⓒ Ⓓ
35. Ⓐ Ⓑ Ⓒ Ⓓ
36. Ⓐ Ⓑ Ⓒ Ⓓ

37. Ⓐ Ⓑ Ⓒ Ⓓ
38. Ⓐ Ⓑ Ⓒ Ⓓ
39. Ⓐ Ⓑ Ⓒ Ⓓ
40. Ⓐ Ⓑ Ⓒ Ⓓ
41. Ⓐ Ⓑ Ⓒ Ⓓ
42. Ⓐ Ⓑ Ⓒ Ⓓ
43. Ⓐ Ⓑ Ⓒ Ⓓ
44. Ⓐ Ⓑ Ⓒ Ⓓ

# Section 3: Math Test — No Calculator Allowed

1. Ⓐ Ⓑ Ⓒ Ⓓ    4. Ⓐ Ⓑ Ⓒ Ⓓ    7. Ⓐ Ⓑ Ⓒ Ⓓ    10. Ⓐ Ⓑ Ⓒ Ⓓ    13. Ⓐ Ⓑ Ⓒ Ⓓ
2. Ⓐ Ⓑ Ⓒ Ⓓ    5. Ⓐ Ⓑ Ⓒ Ⓓ    8. Ⓐ Ⓑ Ⓒ Ⓓ    11. Ⓐ Ⓑ Ⓒ Ⓓ    14. Ⓐ Ⓑ Ⓒ Ⓓ
3. Ⓐ Ⓑ Ⓒ Ⓓ    6. Ⓐ Ⓑ Ⓒ Ⓓ    9. Ⓐ Ⓑ Ⓒ Ⓓ    12. Ⓐ Ⓑ Ⓒ Ⓓ    15. Ⓐ Ⓑ Ⓒ Ⓓ

16.    17.    18.    19.    20.

# Section 4: Math Test — Calculator Allowed

1. Ⓐ Ⓑ Ⓒ Ⓓ    7. Ⓐ Ⓑ Ⓒ Ⓓ    13. Ⓐ Ⓑ Ⓒ Ⓓ    19. Ⓐ Ⓑ Ⓒ Ⓓ    25. Ⓐ Ⓑ Ⓒ Ⓓ
2. Ⓐ Ⓑ Ⓒ Ⓓ    8. Ⓐ Ⓑ Ⓒ Ⓓ    14. Ⓐ Ⓑ Ⓒ Ⓓ    20. Ⓐ Ⓑ Ⓒ Ⓓ    26. Ⓐ Ⓑ Ⓒ Ⓓ
3. Ⓐ Ⓑ Ⓒ Ⓓ    9. Ⓐ Ⓑ Ⓒ Ⓓ    15. Ⓐ Ⓑ Ⓒ Ⓓ    21. Ⓐ Ⓑ Ⓒ Ⓓ    27. Ⓐ Ⓑ Ⓒ Ⓓ
4. Ⓐ Ⓑ Ⓒ Ⓓ    10. Ⓐ Ⓑ Ⓒ Ⓓ    16. Ⓐ Ⓑ Ⓒ Ⓓ    22. Ⓐ Ⓑ Ⓒ Ⓓ    28. Ⓐ Ⓑ Ⓒ Ⓓ
5. Ⓐ Ⓑ Ⓒ Ⓓ    11. Ⓐ Ⓑ Ⓒ Ⓓ    17. Ⓐ Ⓑ Ⓒ Ⓓ    23. Ⓐ Ⓑ Ⓒ Ⓓ    29. Ⓐ Ⓑ Ⓒ Ⓓ
6. Ⓐ Ⓑ Ⓒ Ⓓ    12. Ⓐ Ⓑ Ⓒ Ⓓ    18. Ⓐ Ⓑ Ⓒ Ⓓ    24. Ⓐ Ⓑ Ⓒ Ⓓ    30. Ⓐ Ⓑ Ⓒ Ⓓ

31.    32.    33.    34.    35.

36.    37.    38.

# Section 1: Reading Test

**TIME:** 65 minutes for 52 questions

**DIRECTIONS:** Read these passages and answer the questions that follow based on what is stated or implied in the passages and accompanying diagrams, charts, or graphs.

*Questions 1–10 refer to the following excerpt from* **O Pioneers** *by Willa Cather.*

The Bergson homestead was easier to find than many another, because it overlooked a shallow, muddy stream. This creek gave a sort of identity to the farms that bordered upon it. Of all the bewil-
(5) dering things about a new country, the absence of human landmarks is one of the most depressing and disheartening. The houses were small and were usually tucked away in low places; you did not see them until you came directly upon them. Most
(10) of them were built of the sod itself, and were only the inescapable ground in another form. The roads were but faint tracks in the grass, and the fields were scarcely noticeable. The record of the plow was insignificant, like the feeble scratches on
(15) stone left by prehistoric races, so indeterminate that they may, after all, be only the markings of glaciers, and not a record of human strivings.

In eleven long years John Bergson had made but little impression upon the wild land he had
(20) come to tame. It was still a wild thing that had its ugly moods; and no one knew when they were likely to come, or why. Mischance hung over it. Its Genius was unfriendly to man. The sick man was feeling this as he lay looking out of the window,
(25) after the doctor had left him, on the day following his daughter Alexandra's trip to town. There it lay outside his door, the same land, the same lead-colored miles. He knew every ridge and draw and gully between him and the horizon. To the south,
(30) his plowed fields; to the east, the sod stables, the cattle corral, the pond — and then the grass.

Bergson went over in his mind the things that had held him back. One winter his cattle had perished in a blizzard. The next summer one of his
(35) plow horses broke its leg in a prairie dog hole and had to be shot. Another summer he lost his hogs from disease, and a valuable stallion died from a rattlesnake bite. Time and again his crops had failed. He had lost two children, boys, that came
(40) between Lou and Emil, and there had been the cost

of sickness and death. Now, when he had at last struggled out of debt, he was going to die himself. He was only forty-six, and had, of course, counted on more time.

(45) Bergson had spent his first five years getting into debt, and the last six getting out. He had paid off his mortgages and had ended pretty much where he began, with the land. He owned exactly six hundred and forty acres of what stretched
(50) outside his door; his own original homestead and timber claim, making three hundred and twenty acres, and the half-section adjoining, the home-stead of a younger brother who had given up the fight, gone back to Chicago to work in a fancy
(55) bakery and distinguish himself in a Swedish athletic club. So far John had not attempted to cultivate the second half-section, but used it for pasture land, and one of his sons rode herd there in open weather.

(60) John Bergson had the Old-World belief that land, in itself, is desirable. But this land was an enigma. It was like a horse that no one knows how to break to the harness, that runs wild and kicks things to pieces. He had an idea that no one
(65) understood how to farm it properly, and this he often discussed with Alexandra. Their neighbors, certainly, knew even less about farming than he did. Many of them had never worked on a farm until they took up their homesteads. They had been handworkers at home; tailors, locksmiths, joiners,
(70) cigar-makers, etc. Bergson himself had worked in a shipyard.

1. Which of the following statements best describes John Bergson's attitude toward nature?

   (A) Natural features are beautiful.

   (B) Human beings should not interfere with nature.

   (C) Nature is inferior to human construction.

   (D) Wilderness areas are preferable to cities and towns.

**GO ON TO NEXT PAGE**

**2.** Which choice provides the best evidence for the answer to the previous question?

(A) Lines 4–7 ("Of all . . . disheartening")

(B) Lines 18–20 ("In eleven . . . tame")

(C) Lines 23–26 ("The sick man . . . town")

(D) Lines 61–62 ("But this land . . . enigma")

**3.** What best fits the definition of "human strivings" in the context of Line 17?

(A) "shallow, muddy stream" (Lines 2–3)

(B) "bewildering things" (Lines 4–5)

(C) "new country" (Line 5)

(D) "faint tracks in the grass" (Line 12)

**4.** The comparison between the plowed fields and "the feeble scratches on stone left by prehistoric races" (Lines 14–15) serves to

(A) introduce the idea of human weakness

(B) show that this settlement has a long history

(C) emphasize the primitive quality of the farming

(D) describe the effects of glaciers

**5.** The "Genius" mentioned in Line 23 may best be defined as

(A) intelligence

(B) spirit

(C) brain

(D) type

**6.** Which of the following best explains the meaning of the pronoun "this" in Line 24?

(A) the amount of work Bergson had invested in his land

(B) the symptoms of Bergson's illness

(C) Bergson's bad mood

(D) the wild nature of Bergson's land

**7.** The list of events in the third paragraph (Lines 33–42) serve to

(A) illustrate Bergson's bad luck

(B) show that Bergson was unprepared for farming

(C) emphasize some hope for the future of Bergson's farm

(D) provide information about Bergson's character

**8.** In the context of the last paragraph (Lines 60–72), the land is "an enigma" (Line 62) because

(A) it differs from the land of the Old World

(B) the settlers don't know how to farm it

(C) it is too dry

(D) John Bergson planned poorly

**9.** John Bergson would most likely agree with which statement?

(A) No matter how prepared you are, you will not survive on the frontier.

(B) Life in the Old World is superior to life on the frontier.

(C) Survival on the frontier is dependent upon animals.

(D) Life on the frontier is not always easy.

**10.** Which choice provides the best evidence for the answer to the previous question?

(A) Lines 7–9 ("The houses were small . . . them")

(B) Lines 18–20 ("In eleven long . . . tame")

(C) Lines 33–41 ("One winter . . . sickness and death")

(D) Lines 64–68 ("He had an idea . . . than he did")

*Questions 11–20 refer to the following passage and diagram from* **A Brief History of the Olympics** *by David C. Young (Wiley).*

"Victory by speed of foot is honored above all." Those are the words of Xenophanes, a sixth century BCE philosopher who objected to athletes and their popularity. The phrase "speed of foot" may recall the words expressed in Homer's (5) Odyssey stressing the glory which an athlete may win "with his hands or with his feet." The shortest foot race, the stade, was one length of the stadium track, the practical equivalent of our 200-meter dash (actually, only 192.27 meters at (10) Olympia, the site of the original Olympic games). Greek tradition held that this 200-meter race was the first and only event held at the first Olympiad in 776 BCE.

The name of the winner of the 200 appears (15) first in all lists of victors in any Olympiad. Some people think that the stade winner had the year named after him. This is not really true. Most Greek states had other means of dating any given year, usually by the name of one or more political leaders. But when Hippias of Elis compiled his catalogue of victors, the stade victor obviously headed his list for each individual Olympiad. Perhaps because the Olympic festival was one of (25) the few truly international institutions in Greece, later Greeks found it convenient to use the sequence of Olympiads as a chronological reference. Thus an entry in Julius Africanus' text will read, for example, "Olympiad 77, Dandis of Argos (30) [won] the stade." Subsequent years within the Olympiad are simply viewed as Olympiad 77, years two, three, and four.

As one would expect, methods of running seem to be no different then from now. Several (35) vase paintings show a group of runners rather close to one another, their bodies pitched forward, their arms making large swings up and down. These are clearly runners in the 200, for modern sprinters look much the same. So also distance (40) runners can be easily identified. Like their modern counterparts, they can run upright, with less arc in their leg movements, and their arms dangle comfortably at their sides. Some of these ancient athletes developed the effective strategy of hanging (45) back with the rest of the pack, reserving some strength until near the end. Then they would suddenly break away from the rest and close with a strong spurt of speed, as if barely tired, passing

the leaders who became weak and faded. Ancient sources never specify the exact number of laps in (50) the distance race, and modern opinions vary greatly. The most widely accepted number is 20 laps, a distance of a little over 3845 meters (2.36 miles), more than double our classic distance race of 1500 meters. (55)

The ancient stadium was shaped very differently from the modern one. It was almost twice as long as ours, and about half as wide. There was no course around an infield, no infield at all, just adjacent lanes for the runners. The athletes had (60) therefore no gradual turns around a curve at each end, as in a modern stadium. Stephen Miller, excavator at Nemea, found a posthole not far from the north end of the stadium. He conjectures that it held a turning post. It is highly likely that, in (65) the distance race, such a single turning post for all athletes was probably used. But in the 400, down and back, the runner would need to turn sharply around the post. Most scholars think that each 400 runner would have had his own turning post. (70) Otherwise there would have been too much congestion at that only turn. A few vases show athletes not patently sprinters or distance runners going around a turning post. In one, a judge stands watch. But if each 400-meter runner had (75) his own turning post, the scene probably shows a distance race.

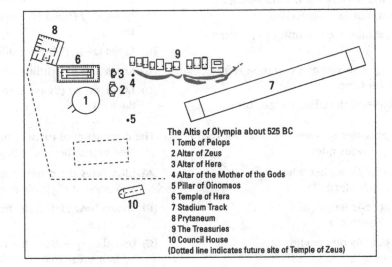

The Altis of Olympia about 525 BC
1 Tomb of Pelops
2 Altar of Zeus
3 Altar of Hera
4 Altar of the Mother of the Gods
5 Pillar of Oinomaos
6 Temple of Hera
7 Stadium Track
8 Prytaneum
9 The Treasuries
10 Council House
(Dotted line indicates future site of Temple of Zeus)

GO ON TO NEXT PAGE

11. The quotations in this passage primarily serve to

   (A) offer conflicting opinions
   (B) establish an authoritative tone
   (C) invite the reader to conduct further research
   (D) give a sense of Greek literary style

12. According to information presented in the passage and accompanying figure, the area where the Olympiad took place

   (A) devoted less space to athletic contests than to other activities
   (B) was consecrated to the gods
   (C) was rectangular in shape
   (D) fulfilled athletes' needs

13. In the context of Line 9, what is the best definition of "practical"?

   (A) hands-on
   (B) likely to succeed
   (C) working equivalent
   (D) pragmatic

14. According to the passage, which of the following statements is correct?

   (A) Winners earned glory for the states they represented, not for themselves.
   (B) The Greek stadium was similar to modern arenas.
   (C) The Olympiads served as a common reference point for time.
   (D) Running styles differed in ancient times.

15. Which choice provides the best evidence for the answer to the previous question?

   (A) Lines 3–4 ("philosopher who objected . . . popularity")
   (B) Lines 8–11 ("one length of the stadium . . . games")
   (C) Lines 33–34 ("As one would expect . . . now")
   (D) Lines 26–28 ("later Greeks . . . reference")

16. The author's comment "as one would expect" (Line 33) is probably based on

   (A) his own experience as a runner
   (B) the fact that human anatomy does not change
   (C) recent archeological discoveries
   (D) information from contemporary literature

17. In the context of Line 52, what is the best definition of "accepted"?

   (A) generally believed
   (B) taken from what is offered
   (C) approved
   (D) admitted

18. With which statement would the author of this passage most likely agree?

   (A) History is an accurate record of events.
   (B) The best historical evidence comes from literature.
   (C) Historians should access many sources of information.
   (D) Unless written records exist, history must remain unknown.

19. Which choice provides the best evidence for the answer to the previous question?

   (A) Lines 5–7 ("words expressed . . . with his feet")
   (B) Lines 12–14 ("Greek tradition . . . 776 BCE")
   (C) Lines 28–30 ("Julius Africanus . . . stade")
   (D) Lines 35–37 ("vase paintings . . . up and down")

20. The discussion of turning posts in Lines 72–77 ("A few vases show . . . distance race.")

   (A) illustrates the difference between modern and ancient Olympic events
   (B) shows how historians misinterpret evidence
   (C) reveals a question that can be solved only by more research
   (D) explains the limits of ancient athletes

*Questions 21–31 refer to the following passages. Passage I is an excerpt from* Novel Plant Bioresources *by Gurib Fakim (Wiley). Passage II is an excerpt from* Biology For Dummies, *2nd Edition, by Rene Kratz and Donna Siegfried (also published by Wiley).*

## Passage I

The world still faces tremendous challenges in securing adequate food that is healthy, safe, and of high nutritional quality for all and doing so in an environmentally sustainable manner. With the
(5) growing demand of an expected 9 billion people by 2050, it remains unclear how our current global food system will cope. Currently, 868 million people suffer from hunger, while micronutrient deficiencies, known as hidden hunger, undermine the
(10) development, health, and productivity of over 2 billion people. The estimation of plant species that exist in the world is between 250,000 and 400,000. As many as 80% of the world's people depend on traditional medicines, which involve the use of plant
(15) extracts or their active principles for their primary health care needs. Plant diversity has a critical role to play in addressing the food and nutrition security and medicinal needs of the people of this world. Plant diversity is not evenly distributed across the
(20) world and tends to be concentrated in specific, diversity-rich areas. It is generally known that most diversity of species occurs within the warm regions of the tropics and less diversity exists in temperate regions of the world.

(25) Plants are an intricate part of all our ecosystems. Besides the obvious provisioning of food in ensuring that people are food and nutritionally secured, many plants contribute directly to our agriculture by providing valuable traits and genes
(30) used by modern-day breeders for crop improvement, in particular those plants which are closely related to crop plants, the so-called "crop wild relatives," and restore health in an important human adaptation, as fundamental a feature of
(35) human culture as is use of fire, tools, and speech. Having evolved over millennia, the knowledge, cultural traditions, and medicinal resources of many human societies may be rapidly disappearing with the loss of cultural and biological diversity.

(40) In spite of this great diversity of plants on Earth and the fundamental role they play, the story of crops and humanity has shown an increasing reliance on a small proportion of plant species used by humans. The beginnings of exploitation of plant
(45) diversity for food and nutrition are as old as humankind, and early hunter gatherers in pre-agricultural times would have exploited their local environment for readily available fruits, berries, seeds, flowers, shoots, storage organs, and fleshy roots to comple-
(50) ment meat obtained from hunting.

Furthermore, crop plants have resulted in an even greater reliance by humans on much reduced plant diversity than was previously used for food by pre-agricultural human societies. More than 70,000
(55) plants are known to have edible parts. The world's food comes from about 100 plant species, based on calories, protein, and fat supply. However, only four crop species (maize, wheat, rice, and sugar) supply almost 60% of the calories and protein in the human
(60) diet. There are thousands of plant species with neglected potential utility.

Many studies show that plant diversity is globally threatened. Recently a group of international experts called for the development of a global
(65) program for the conservation of useful plants and associated knowledge.

## Passage II

The loss in biodiversity could have effects beyond just the loss of individual species. Living things are connected to each other and their
(70) environment in how they obtain food and other resources necessary for survival. If one species depends on another for food, for example, then the loss of a prey species can cause a decline in the predator species.

(75) Some species, called keystone species, are so connected with other organisms in their environment that their extinction changes the entire composition of species in the area. As biodiversity decreases, keystone species may die out, causing a
(80) ripple effect that leads to the loss of many more species. If biodiversity gets too low, then the future of life itself becomes threatened. An example of a keystone species is the purple seastar, which lives on the northwest Pacific coast of the United States.
(85) Purple seastars prey on mussels in the intertidal zone. When the seastars are present, they keep the mussel population in check, allowing a great diversity of other marine animals to live in the intertidal zone. If the seastars are removed from the
(90) intertidal zone, however, the mussels take over, and many species of marine animals disappear from the environment.

GO ON TO NEXT PAGE ▶

Biodiversity increases the chance that at least some living things will survive in the face of large changes in the environment, which is why protect-(95) ing it is crucial. The combined effect of various human actions in Earth's ecosystems is reducing the planet's biodiversity. In fact, the rate of extinctions is increasing along with the size of the human population. No one knows for certain how (100) extensive the loss of species due to human impacts will ultimately be, but there's no question that human practices such as hunting and farming have already caused numerous species to become extinct.

Percentage of Undernourished Persons in the World, 1990–2013

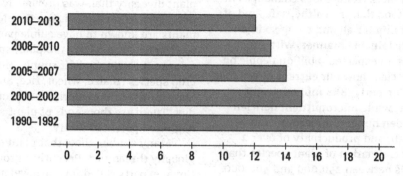

*United Nations Food and Agricultural Organization*

21. In the context of Line 5, what is the best definition of "demand"?

(A) command

(B) insistence

(C) popularity

(D) need

22. In the context of Line 20, which of the following best expresses the meaning of "concentrated"?

(A) distributed

(B) thought about

(C) given attention

(D) grouped

23. The author of Passage I presents statistics about the types of crops humans cultivate for food in order to

(A) highlight other possible sources of food

(B) explain why food resources are scarce

(C) show that food is harvested inefficiently

(D) reveal the shortcomings of the average person's diet

24. Which choice provides the best evidence for the answer to the previous question?

(A) Lines 4–7 ("With the growing . . . will cope")

(B) Lines 11–12 ("The estimation . . . and 400,000")

(C) Lines 36–39 ("Having evolved . . . biological diversity")

(D) Lines 60–61 ("There are thousands . . . potential utility")

25. Passage II implies that large populations of mussels

(A) become keystone species in their environment

(B) may displace other species

(C) do not compete for food with purple seastars

(D) are a major cause of extinctions

26. Which of the following would the author of Passage II most likely support?

(A) a drive to clean seashore areas

(B) a petition to ban the cultivation of mussels

(C) a program to preserve keystone species in forested areas

(D) a required course in marine biology

**27.** Which choice provides the best evidence for the answer to the previous question?

(A) Lines 68–70 ("Living things . . . their environment")

(B) Lines 75–78 ("Some species . . . the area")

(C) Lines 81–82 ("If biodiversity . . . becomes threatened")

(D) Lines 96–98 ("The combined . . . planet's biodiversity")

**28.** Taken together, these passages may best be characterized as

(A) an argument in favor of biodiversity

(B) a comparison of current and prehistoric food supplies

(C) a discussion of how ecosystems work

(D) an inventory of popular crops and endangered species

**29.** With which statement would the authors of both passages most likely agree?

(A) Human beings should not exploit plant and animal resources.

(B) Slowing the rate of extinctions is no longer possible.

(C) Reliance on a small number of food sources causes problems.

(D) Keystone species should be protected at all costs.

**30.** According to the passages and accompanying graph, which of these statements is true?

(I) The percentage of the population with an adequate amount of food rose from 1990 to 2013.

(II) The number of people who lack important nutrients is greater than the number of people who are considered "undernourished" in official surveys.

(III) The number of animal species providing food for human beings is decreasing.

(A) I only

(B) II only

(C) I and II

(D) II and III

**31.** In comparison to Passage I, Passage II is

(A) more focused on food supplies

(B) less concerned with plant diversity

(C) more focused on plants

(D) more focused on ecosystems

*Questions 32–42 refer to the following passage from President Abraham Lincoln's Second Inaugural Address, the speech he gave in 1865 when he took the oath of office for his second term as President. The Civil War between the North and the South was nearing its end as Lincoln spoke.*

Fellow Countrymen:

At this second appearing to take the oath of the presidential office, there is less occasion for an extended address than there was at the first. Then a statement, somewhat in detail, of a course to be (5) pursued, seemed fitting and proper. Now, at the expiration of four years, during which public declarations have been constantly called forth on every point and phase of the great contest which still absorbs the attention, and engrosses the (10) energies of the nation, little that is new could be presented. The progress of our arms, upon which all else chiefly depends, is as well known to the public as to myself; and it is, I trust, reasonably satisfactory and encouraging to all. With high hope (15) for the future, no prediction in regard to it is ventured.

On the occasion corresponding to this four years ago, all thoughts were anxiously directed to an impending civil-war. All dreaded it — all (20) sought to avert it. While the inaugural address was being delivered from this place, devoted altogether to saving the Union without war, insurgent agents were in the city seeking to destroy it without war — seeking to dissolve the Union, and divide (25) effects, by negotiation. Both parties deprecated war; but one of them would make war rather than let the nation survive; and the other would accept war rather than let it perish. And the war came.

One eighth of the whole population were (30) colored slaves, not distributed generally over the Union, but localized in the Southern part of it. These slaves constituted a peculiar and powerful interest. All knew that this interest was, somehow, the cause of the war. To strengthen, perpetuate, (35) and extend this interest was the object for which the insurgents would rend the Union, even by war;

GO ON TO NEXT PAGE

while the government claimed no right to do more than to restrict the territorial enlargement of it.

(40) Neither party expected for the war, the magnitude, or the duration, which it has already attained. Neither anticipated that the cause of the conflict might cease with, or even before, the conflict itself should cease. Each looked for an
(45) easier triumph, and a result less fundamental and astounding. Both read the same Bible, and pray to the same God; and each invokes His aid against the other. It may seem strange that any men should dare to ask a just God's assistance in wringing
(50) their bread from the sweat of other men's faces; but let us judge not that we be not judged. The prayers of both could not be answered; that of neither has been answered fully.

The Almighty has His own purposes. "Woe
(55) unto the world because of offences! for it must needs be that offences come; but woe to that man by whom the offence cometh!" If we shall suppose that American Slavery is one of those offences which, in the providence of God, must needs come,
(60) but which, having continued through His appointed time, He now wills to remove, and that He gives to both North and South, this terrible war, as the woe due to those by whom the offence came, shall we discern therein any departure from those divine
(65) attributes which the believers in a Living God always ascribe to Him? Fondly do we hope — fervently do we pray — that this mighty scourge of war may speedily pass away. Yet, if God wills that it continue, until all the wealth piled by the
(70) bond-man's two hundred and fifty years of unrequited toil shall be sunk, and until every drop of blood drawn with the lash, shall be paid by another drawn with the sword, as was said three thousand years ago, so still it must be said "the
(75) judgments of the Lord, are true and righteous altogether."

With malice toward none; with charity for all; with firmness in the right, as God gives us to see the right, let us strive on to finish the work we are
(80) in; to bind up the nation's wounds; to care for him who shall have borne the battle, and for his widow, and his orphan — to do all which may achieve and cherish a just, and a lasting peace, among ourselves, and with all nations.

**32.** In the context of Line 5, what is the best definition of "course"?

(A) study

(B) plan

(C) field

(D) lessons

**33.** In Paragraph 1 (Lines 2–17), what does Lincoln imply about the war?

(A) Too much has been said about the war.

(B) Politicians have paid too little attention to it.

(C) His side is winning.

(D) No one will be satisfied with the result.

**34.** Which choice provides the best evidence for the answer to the previous question?

(A) Lines 3–4 ("less occasion . . . at the first")

(B) Lines 5–6 ("course . . . proper")

(C) Lines 10–12 ("absorbs . . . presented")

(D) Lines 12–15 ("The progress . . . encouraging to all")

**35.** Lincoln most likely states that "little that is new could be presented" (Lines 11–12) because

(A) the war monopolizes the attention and resources of the nation

(B) he has no vision of a peaceful future

(C) the public's views are unknown

(D) his listeners are not ready for the future

**36.** According to Lincoln, during his first inauguration

(A) citizens generally agreed on a plan for his administration

(B) the movement to disband the nation had already begun

(C) there was unconditional support for war

(D) negotiations to avoid war had already ended

**37.** In the context of Line 34, what is the best definition of "interest"?

(A) attention

(B) issue

(C) benefit

(D) problem

38. In the fourth paragraph of Lincoln's speech (Lines 40–53) he

    (A) pleads for an end to war

    (B) emphasizes what both sides have in common

    (C) dismisses the concerns of his opponents

    (D) argues that the war was unavoidable

39. Which choice provides the best evidence for the answer to the previous question?

    (A) Lines 41–42 ("the magnitude . . . attained")

    (B) Lines 43–44 ("the conflict itself . . . cease")

    (C) Lines 46–47 ("Both read . . . same God")

    (D) Line 53 ("neither has . . . fully")

40. Throughout the speech, Lincoln uses the pronouns we, us, and our to refer to

    (A) Northerners

    (B) Southerners

    (C) those present during the speech

    (D) both Northerners and Southerners

41. Lincoln's purpose in giving this speech was most likely to

    (A) proclaim victory

    (B) condemn slavery

    (C) emphasize the idea of a united country

    (D) encourage his troops

42. The dominant strategy in this speech is

    (A) an appeal to logic

    (B) a reliance on religious principles

    (C) an appeal for personal support

    (D) a condemnation of opponents

*Questions 43–52 refer to the following information, excerpted and adapted from* **The Story of Eclipses,** *by George F. Chambers (London: George Newnes, Ltd.).*

The primary meaning of the word "eclipse" is a disappearance, the covering over of something by something else. This apparently crude definition will be found, on investigation, to represent precisely the facts of the case. (5)

As the Earth and the Moon are solid bodies, each must cast a shadow into space as the result of being illuminated by the Sun, a source of light. The various bodies which together make up the Solar System, the planets and their moons, are constantly in motion. Consequently, if we imagine a (10) line to be drawn between any two bodies at any given time, such a line will point in a different direction at another time, and so it may occasionally happen that three of these ever-moving bodies (15) will sometimes come into one and the same straight line. When one of the extremes of the series of three bodies in a common direction is the Sun, the intermediate body deprives the other extreme body, either wholly or partially, of (20) illumination. When one of the extremes is the Earth, the intermediate body intercepts, wholly or partially, the other extreme body from the view of observers situated at places on the Earth which are in the common line of direction, and the interme- (25) diate body is seen to pass over the other extreme body as it enters upon or leaves the common line of direction. The phenomena resulting from such contingencies of position and direction are variously called eclipses, transits, and occultations, (30) according to the relative apparent magnitudes of the interposing and obscured bodies, and according to the circumstances that attend them.

The Earth moves round the Sun once in every year; the Moon moves round the Earth once in (35) every lunar month (27 days). The Earth moves round the Sun in a certain plane, an imaginary surface on which a line drawn between any two points lies flat. If the Moon as the Earth's companion moved round the Earth in the same plane, an (40) eclipse of the Sun would happen regularly every month when the Moon was in "conjunction," the "New Moon," during which the Moon is not visible in the sky, and also every month at the intermediate period there would be a total eclipse of the (45) Moon on the occasion of every "opposition," or "Full Moon," when the Moon appears as a complete circle. But because the Moon's orbit does not lie in quite the same plane as the Earth's, but is inclined at an angle averaging about $5\frac{1}{8}°$, the (50) actual facts are different. Instead of there being in every year about 25 eclipses (of the sun and of the moon in nearly equal numbers), which there would be if the orbits had identical planes, there are only a very few eclipses in the year. Never, under the (55) most favorable circumstances, are there more than seven, and sometimes as few as two.

GO ON TO NEXT PAGE

Eclipses of the Sun are more numerous than those of the Moon in the proportion of about three (60) to two, yet at any given place on the Earth more lunar eclipses are visible than solar eclipses, because eclipses of the Moon, when they occur, are visible over the whole hemisphere, or half, of the Earth that is turned towards the Moon. The area over which a total eclipse of the Sun is visible is (65) just a belt of the Earth no more than about 150 to 170 miles wide.

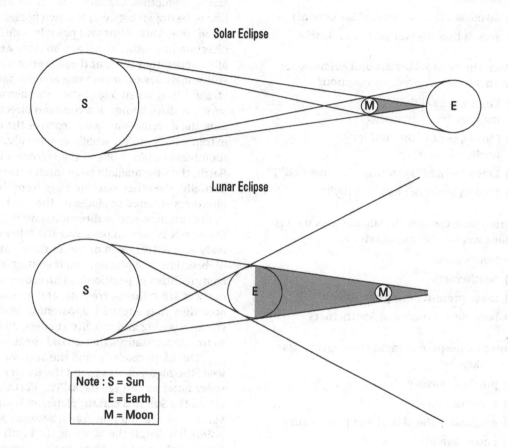

Solar Eclipse

Lunar Eclipse

Note : S = Sun
E = Earth
M = Moon

43. In the context of Line 1, the best meaning of "primary" is

(A) earliest

(B) most primitive

(C) most direct

(D) most basic

44. According to the explanation in this passage, which of the following could be considered "an eclipse"?

(A) a child who hides behind a car

(B) a car that moves and blocks the view of a child

(C) a child who enters a car and closes a window

(D) a child who emerges from a car

45. Which choice provides the best evidence for the answer to the previous question?

(A) Lines 2–3 ("disappearance . . . else")

(B) Lines 9–11 ("various bodies . . . motion")

(C) Lines 28–33 ("The phenomena result-ing . . . attend them")

(D) Line 48–51 ("the Moon's orbit . . . different")

46. The most common stylistic devices in this passage are

(A) definition and example

(B) narration and characterization

(C) description and figurative language

(D) analogies and implied comparison

**47.** In the context of Line 20, what is the best definition of "extreme"?

(A) exaggerated

(B) highest degree

(C) outer

(D) most advanced

**48.** Why does any line "drawn between any two bodies at any given time" (Lines 12–13) "point in a different direction at another time" (Lines 13–14)?

(A) The line is not real.

(B) The paths of the Sun, Moon, and Earth are unknown.

(C) The Moon and Earth are in constant motion.

(D) The Earth is larger than the Moon.

**49.** Which of the following supports the answer to Question 48?

(A) Lines 7–8 ("each must cast . . . source of light")

(B) Lines 14–17 ("occasionally happen . . . the same straight line")

(C) Lines 34–36 ("The Earth moves . . . 27 days.")

(D) Lines 62–64 ("when they occur . . . towards the Moon")

**50.** According to the diagram, which of the following is visible to a person standing on the unilluminated portion of the Earth during a lunar eclipse?

(A) a portion of the Moon

(B) the Moon's shadow

(C) the Sun's shadow

(D) the Earth's shadow

**51.** Information about the Moon's orbit being "inclined at an angle averaging about $5\frac{1}{8}°$" (Line 50) relative to the Earth

(A) illustrates the unimportance of the Moon

(B) emphasizes that eclipses of the Sun are more widely seen than eclipses of the Moon

(C) explains why the Earth, Moon, and Sun do not align more frequently

(D) shows that eclipses of the Sun and Moon occur in equal numbers

**52.** According to the passage, which statement is true?

(A) The Sun casts shadows on the Moon and on the Earth.

(B) More people see eclipses of the Moon than eclipses of the Sun.

(C) Our Solar System includes the Sun, stars, planets, and moons.

(D) Eclipses of the Sun cover a larger area than eclipses of the Moon.

# Section 2: Writing and Language Test

**TIME:** 35 minutes for 44 questions

**DIRECTIONS:** Some sentences or portions of sentences are underlined and identified with numbers. In the questions, you see differing versions of the underlined material. Choose the best answer to each question based on what is stated or implied in the passage and accompanying visual elements. Mark the corresponding oval on the answer sheet.

## Exploring Animal Self-Awareness

Dr. Vint Virga stares at Molly, a <u>Barbary sheep, Molly has been behaving</u> strangely since her tail was
**1**
amputated after an accident. Molly spends almost all of her time nervously checking for flies that she used to bat away easily with her tail. Dr. Virga decides that Molly has a phobia, an irrational fear. He prescribes medication and works to ease her fears by distracting her with food and <u>subtracting</u> her anxi-
**2**
ety level so that she can stand quietly when insects do approach. Virga travels from zoo to zoo, where he solves the problems of animals like Molly.☐3☐

Animal behaviorists may be veterinarians, as Dr. Virga is, or animal trainers, zoologists, college professors, zookeepers, and many other types of workers who specialize in animals. Animal behaviorists interpret how individuals or whole populations of animals eat, move, rest, play, and <u>relating to their environment</u>. Identifying prob-
**4**
lems, <u>the animals may be treated by the behaviorist</u>
**5**
with medicine or behavior modification techniques.

The field is new. In earlier times, what was going on inside an animal's mind was not a concern.

The Greek philosopher Aristotle (384 to 322 BCE) said that animals couldn't think. French philosopher Rene Descartes (1596 to 1650 CE) compared the cry of an animal to the squeak of a clock spring, a mechanical reaction. Even in the modern era, behaviorists are <u>now sometimes accused</u> of anthropomor-
**6**
phism, ascribing human traits to nonhuman beings. The danger of this approach is that animals won't be seen for who they are and their behavior may be misinterpreted. Scientist Philip Low says, "If you ask my colleagues whether animals have emotions and thoughts, many will drop their voices or change the subject."

Almost <u>anyone, who has pets, sees</u> evidence of
**7**
animals' inner life. Recent studies show that elephants recognize themselves <u>when they see themselves</u> in a
**8**
mirror, and many species, such as fruit flies, ants, and chimpanzees, cooperate. Zookeepers frequently report that animals grieve when others housed in the same enclosure die. In 2012, a number of scientists in Cambridge University signed a declaration asserting that animals probably have emotions and consciousness, <u>but they are self-aware</u>.
**9**

Animals behaviorism is a growing field, with a projected increase in jobs in its various subspecialties of <u>at least 11%</u>, according to the United States [10] Bureau of Labor Statistics. Pay for nonfarm animal caretakers, who do not need a college degree, averages around $20,000 per year, though veterinarians make about $85,000 a year. In general, higher paid careers <u>return</u> better education and training. [11]

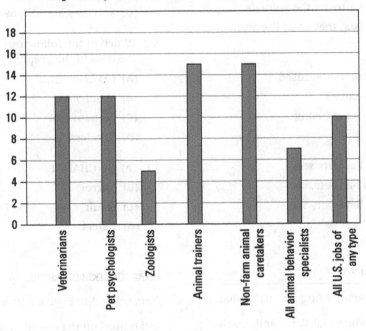

Percentage of Projected Job Growth : Animal Care and Service Workers

1. **(A)** NO CHANGE
   **(B)** Barbary sheep, and Molly has been behaving
   **(C)** Barbary sheep that has been behaving
   **(D)** Barbary sheep. Molly behaved

2. **(A)** NO CHANGE
   **(B)** lowering
   **(C)** draining
   **(D)** subordinating

3. Which of the following is the best improvement for the first paragraph?
   **(A)** Add this sentence to the end of the paragraph: "He is an animal behaviorist."
   **(B)** Delete this sentence: "Dr. Virga decides that Molly has a phobia, an irrational fear."
   **(C)** Add this sentence to the beginning of the paragraph: "Barbary sheep are also known as aoudads."
   **(D)** Delete "since her tail was amputated after an accident."

GO ON TO NEXT PAGE ➤

4. **(A)** NO CHANGE
   **(B)** environmental relation of animals
   **(C)** the way in which they relate to their environment
   **(D)** relate to their environment

5. **(A)** NO CHANGE
   **(B)** the animals, treat by the behaviorist
   **(C)** the behaviorist treats the animals
   **(D)** the behaviorists, they treat the animals

6. **(A)** NO CHANGE
   **(B)** sometimes are now accused
   **(C)** sometimes accused
   **(D)** now sometimes accusing

7. **(A)** NO CHANGE
   **(B)** anyone who has pets sees
   **(C)** anyone, who has pets, see
   **(D)** anyone who have pets see

8. **(A)** NO CHANGE
   **(B)** when one sees itself
   **(C)** seeing itself
   **(D)** when it sees itself

9. **(A)** NO CHANGE
   **(B)** being self-aware
   **(C)** though they are self-aware
   **(D)** and they are self-aware

10. Which of the following choices best supports the data in the graph:
    **(A)** NO CHANGE
    **(B)** about 7%
    **(C)** perhaps 11%
    **(D)** 15% less

11. **(A)** NO CHANGE
    **(B)** mirror
    **(C)** result
    **(D)** reflect

### Trenches in The Great War

About a century ago, in August, 1914, what participants called "The Great War" and, ironically, "The War to End All Wars," had begun . We know
<sub>12</sub>
this conflict as World War I, one of the bloodiest periods in human history. When it ended in 1918, about 9 million soldiers were dead and the health of 7 million more was permanently disabled. They
<sub>13</sub>
were never again healthy enough to return to their former way of life.

[1] About 25,000 miles of trenches — enough to circle the globe at the Equator — were dug to protect and shelter soldiers from enemy fire. [2] Trenches on both sides — the Allies and their foes, the Central Powers — were only a few hundred yards apart. 14 [3] A unique feature of World War
<sub>14</sub>

I was the trench system. [4] A typical trench, diagrammed in Figure 1, was about 6 to 8 feet deep and topped on the enemy side by sandbags.

The frontline trench had short protrusions designed for shooting machine guns or launching grenades. Listening to the enemy was also
<sub>15</sub>
done there. The frontline trenches were backed by
<sub>16</sub>
support trenches a few hundred yards away, where medical officers tended the wounded and where other, non-combat activities took place. Both were connected by a communication trench, which was
<sub>17</sub>
parallel to the others. Because fire could spread quickly in a straight line, the trenches, placed out
<sub>18</sub>
in a zigzag pattern, with fire breaks every few yards.

The trenches were not pleasant places. [19] Sandbags, thin iron sheets, or sticks supported the walls. The frontline trench was protected by a line of barbed wire, and the area in between was called "No Man's Land" because to be caught there was to risk instant death. Soldiers were stationed in the frontline trenches for 3 to 7 days and then rotated to support trenches for <u>they're</u> rest period, 20 eventually returning to the front line. Despite four years of war and huge numbers of deaths, neither side succeeded in moving its trenches more than a short distance into enemy territory. <u>The soldiers spent the day in a mixture of boredom and terror. They felt boredom waiting for an attack and terror</u> 21 <u>when one occurred.</u>

Few civilians understood the conditions the soldiers faced. A sample trench in a London park appeared comfortable. Soldiers who had seen the real trenches were often bitter when they saw the luxury of the sample trench, which did not resemble those on the front. [22]

### Trenches in World War I

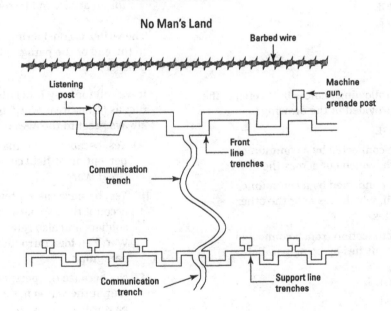

No Man's Land

Barbed wire

Listening post

Machine gun, grenade post

Front line trenches

Communication trench

Communication trench

Support line trenches

12. **(A)** NO CHANGE
 **(B)** began
 **(C)** will have begun
 **(D)** begun

13. **(A)** NO CHANGE
 **(B)** impaired
 **(C)** unfit
 **(D)** wounded

14. To make this paragraph most logical, Sentence 3 should be placed
 **(A)** where it is now
 **(B)** before Sentence 1
 **(C)** after Sentence 2
 **(D)** after Sentence 4

GO ON TO NEXT PAGE

15. Which of the following is the best way to combine the underlined sentences?

   (A) The frontline trench had short protrusions designed for shooting machine guns or launching grenades, listening to the enemy was also done there.

   (B) Listening to the enemy, the frontline trench had short protrusions designed for shooting machine guns or launching grenades.

   (C) The frontline trench had short protrusions designed for shooting machine guns or launching grenades, and they could listen to the enemy there.

   (D) The frontline trench had short protrusions designed for shooting machine guns, launching grenades, and listening to the enemy.

16. (A) NO CHANGE

   (B) supported by

   (C) beyond

   (D) backed to

17. Which of the following choices best reflects the information provided in the drawing?

   (A) NO CHANGE

   (B) Both were connected by a communication trench, which cut across the others.

   (C) Both were connected by a communication trench, which was near the other two trenches.

   (D) The communication trench connected the other trenches by being parallel.

18. (A) NO CHANGE

   (B) were placed

   (C) placing

   (D) were placing

19. To add emphasis, which of the following should be added at this point?

   (A) NO CHANGE

   (B) There were many trenches, and many soldiers.

   (C) Fire was a danger.

   (D) Wooden floorboards covered a drainage area, but the narrow trenches were never quite dry.

20. (A) NO CHANGE

   (B) there

   (C) their

   (D) soldier's

21. How may the underlined sentences best be combined?

   (A) The soldiers spent the day in a mixture of boredom, waiting for an attack, and terror, when one occurred.

   (B) Bored and terrified, the soldiers spent the day.

   (C) The soldiers spent the day in a mixture of boredom and terror, feeling boredom waiting for an attack and terror when one occurred.

   (D) The soldiers spent the day in a mixture of boredom and terror, boredom waiting for an attack and terror in an attack.

22. The writer is considering adding this sentence to the end of the paragraph to conclude the passage:

   It was all too easy for civilians to see this conflict as "The Great War," but the war was not always great in the eyes of those who fought it.

   (A) Yes, because it summarizes the public perception of field conditions during The Great War.

   (B) Yes, because the sentence takes into account the gap between civilians and soldiers and also refers to "The Great War," an idea introduced in the first paragraph.

   (C) No, because the perspective of those who fought the war is not a main topic of the passage.

   (D) No, because civilians and soldiers held The Great War in the same regard.

**Family Summer in Vermont**

Ten years old, hair in pigtails, <u>sitting</u> in the
23
back seat of our pink-and-white car, which is on
the way to Vermont. The elderly next door neighbors in our quiet suburb, the Hamiltons, have been
pressing my parents about a vacation rental near
their house on the shore of Lake Saint Catherine,
and <u>they've</u> finally given in. Mommy and Daddy
24
don't like the Hamiltons, restricting contact with
the couple to one dinner when we first <u>moved in,</u>
25
<u>which</u> Alfred Hammond served food for each of
us at the head of the table. When our family ate
dinner, platters circled the table, unless they were
in reach of long arms and serving spoons. In that
case everyone simply grabbed what <u>they wanted</u>
<u>and ate it</u>.
26

In Vermont, <u>we greeted the Hamiltons</u>. The
27
two-room cabin is made of fragrant wood (pine,
I think), and the air is blessedly cool. (Even at that
age I couldn't take heat.) Jimmy and I sleep in the
bedroom in bunks attached to the wall near our
parents' air mattress.

[28] [1] The water of Lake Saint Catherine is
pretty deep. [2] There's no beach, just a dock,
but we can both swim, so Jimmy and I jump off
the dock, paddle around until we reach the little
wooden ladder and then climb up to start all over
again. [3] My Daddy was on the swim team in
high school. [4] Once or twice Daddy rows across
the lake in a little wooden boat, <u>because</u> he clearly
29
doesn't relish the effort. [5] We also fish from the
dock. [6] I remember holding a dead, wriggling,
two-inch something that I throw back in the water
as soon as Daddy takes a picture of it.

On some days we go sightseeing. I remember a marble quarry at Barre. Mostly (typical of my
mother's priorities) we stay in the gift shop, <u>where</u>
<u>shards of marble are</u> on sale, as well as some
30
finished items. In my view the big slabs look like
tombstones, <u>and the tombstones make me nervous</u>
31
<u>and they make me glad when we</u> leave.

[32][1]We take another trip, at night, to a drive-
in movie. [2] All I remember of that evening is a
white-knuckle trip back to the cabin. [3] I can tell
from my parents' voices that they're scared, too.
[4] At each junction they <u>defer</u> rapidly, and we do
33
find the cottage, but I spend the time worrying that
we'll drive off the road and into a ditch, or worse,
that we'll just drive forever.

GO ON TO NEXT PAGE ▶

23. **(A)** NO CHANGE
    **(B)** sitting, I
    **(C)** I'm sitting
    **(D)** having sat

24. **(A)** NO CHANGE
    **(B)** the Hamiltons have
    **(C)** my parents have
    **(D)** they have

25. **(A)** NO CHANGE
    **(B)** moved in which
    **(C)** moved,
    **(D)** moved in, at which

26. **(A)** NO CHANGE
    **(B)** he or she wanted and ate
    **(C)** they wanted, and ate
    **(D)** was wanting and eating

27. **(A)** NO CHANGE
    **(B)** we were greeting the Hamiltons
    **(C)** we greet the Hamiltons
    **(D)** greeting the Hamiltons

28. What change, if any, should be made to the third paragraph?
    **(A)** NO CHANGE
    **(B)** Delete Sentence 1.
    **(C)** Delete Sentence 3.
    **(D)** Change Sentence 5 to "We also fish from the dock, which is made of wood."

29. **(A)** NO CHANGE
    **(B)** therefore
    **(C)** on the other hand
    **(D)** but

30. **(A)** NO CHANGE
    **(B)** which has shards of marble
    **(C)** with shards of marble
    **(D)** that has shards of marble

31. **(A)** NO CHANGE
    **(B)** which make me nervous and glad to
    **(C)** and the tombstones make me nervous and glad when we
    **(D)** nervous and glad when we

32. Which of the following would add the most emphasis to the last paragraph?
    **(A)** Before Sentence 1, add: "We take many trips throughout my childhood."
    **(B)** Delete sentence 1.
    **(C)** After Sentence 2, add: "Without street-lights, the country roads appear dark and dangerous to me, a city girl."
    **(D)** After Sentence 4, add: "I enjoyed the movie, though."

33. **(A)** NO CHANGE
    **(B)** refer
    **(C)** confer
    **(D)** relegate

## Interfering with Nature

In 1859, <u>Thomas Austin an Australian who</u>
<u>enjoyed hunting, released</u> 24 rabbits on his land.
_34_
The hunter stated that "introduction of a few
rabbits could do little harm" and "might provide a
touch of home." <u>He liked to hunt.</u> Before this time,
_35_
<u>there was</u> some domestic rabbits in Australia,
_36_
mostly in cages or other enclosures. With a moderate climate, the wild rabbits bred all year round.

<u>Soon Australia had a rabbit problem. More than</u>
_37_
<u>200 million rabbits were living there.</u> Farms and
wooded areas were overrun with <u>rabbits, and</u>
_38_
millions of dollars worth of crops were destroyed,
and many young trees died when the rabbits
chewed rings around the bark. Fewer trees led to
increased erosion and loss of topsoil. The hunter
never thought that 24 rabbits would become a
national problem. His action is an example of human <u>intervention</u> in a natural ecosystem that is too
_39_
complicated to understand completely.

The same kind of action has been taking place
in Arizona. Water is precious in Arizona's desert
environment. Tamarisk trees, a non-native species
that was imported about a century ago and planted
to fight soil erosion, <u>has</u> very deep roots. They soak
_40_
up a lot of water — up to 200 gallons a day for a
mature tree. Chopping down tamarisks or burning
them didn't solve the problem, as the trees quickly
grew back. So tamarisk beetles, which kill the
trees, were <u>initiated</u> into the environment.
_41_

The number of tamarisk trees <u>have decreased</u>
_42_
because of the beetles. The policy seems to be a
success. However, not all factors are known. What
about the birds that live in tamarisk trees? Will
they die as their habitat changes? When the
tamarisk trees are gone, will the beetles attack
other trees? If too many trees disappear, will the
soil erode, harming the habitat of still more
organisms?

No one knows the answer to these questions,
because nature is too complex for limited human
intelligence to understand completely. <u>One</u>
<u>answer that is known to humans</u> is that interfering
_43_
with the environment cannot be stopped, and some
unforeseen consequences will occur. It is what
human beings do when they plant crops, construct
cities, dam rivers, and tap into energy and
water supplies. The human effect on nature is
everywhere.

44 [1] The solution is not to stay away from
nature, but instead to be more careful in how we
interact with nature. [2] Studying how organisms
interact is important. [3] You should also check
consumption. [4] Scientists must provide information on the environment and the potential
consequences of changes to the environment. [5]
Citizens must tailor their behavior according to
that information.

34. **(A)** NO CHANGE
    **(B)** Thomas Austin an Australian, that enjoyed hunting, released
    **(C)** an Australian who enjoyed hunting and was named Thomas Austin released
    **(D)** Thomas Austin, an Australian who enjoyed hunting, released

35. **(A)** NO CHANGE
    **(B)** DELETE the underlined portion.
    **(C)** Thomas Austin liked to hunt.
    **(D)** Thomas Austin, he liked to hunt.

36. **(A)** NO CHANGE
    **(B)** their was
    **(C)** there were
    **(D)** their were

37. Which is the best way to combine the underlined sentences?
    **(A)** Soon Australia had a rabbit problem, but more than 200 million rabbits were living there.
    **(B)** More than 200 million rabbits were living there soon, and Australia had a rabbit problem.
    **(C)** More than 200 million rabbits soon lived in Australia, and they caused a problem.
    **(D)** Soon, with more than 200 million rabbits, Australia had a problem.

38. **(A)** NO CHANGE
    **(B)** rabbits;
    **(C)** rabbits; and
    **(D)** rabbits; while

39. **(A)** NO CHANGE
    **(B)** intercession
    **(C)** evocation
    **(D)** affectation

40. **(A)** NO CHANGE
    **(B)** have
    **(C)** had
    **(D)** did have

41. **(A)** NO CHANGE
    **(B)** started
    **(C)** commenced
    **(D)** introduced

42. **(A)** NO CHANGE
    **(B)** have been decreasing
    **(C)** has decreased
    **(D)** decreasing

43. **(A)** NO CHANGE
    **(B)** What we do know
    **(C)** One answer known to humans
    **(D)** Known

44. Which of the following changes makes the paragraph most logical?
    **(A)** Add before Sentence 1: "Everything changes."
    **(B)** Add after Sentence 2: "Interacting with nature should always be considered before acting."
    **(C)** Replace Sentence 3 with: "Monitoring consumption of water, energy, and other resources is also crucial."
    **(D)** Add this sentence after Sentence 5: "Nature is our most important resource."

DO NOT TURN THE PAGE UNTIL TOLD TO DO SO   STOP   DO NOT RETURN TO A PREVIOUS TEST

# Section 3: Math Test — No Calculator Allowed

TIME: 25 minutes for 20 questions

DIRECTIONS: This section contains two different types of questions. For Questions 1–15, choose the best answer to each question and darken the corresponding oval on the answer sheet. For Questions 16–20, follow the separate directions provided before those questions.

NOTES:

- You may *not* use a calculator.

- All numbers used in this exam are real numbers.

- All figures lie in a plane.

- All figures may be assumed to be to scale unless the problem specifically indicates otherwise.

- The domain of a given function *f* is the set of all real numbers *x* for which *f(x)* is a real number, unless the problem specifically indicates otherwise.

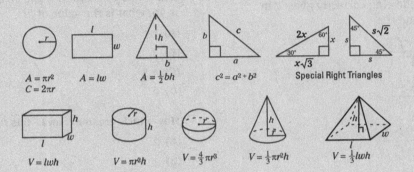

- The number of degrees in a circle is 360.

- The number of radians in a circle is $2\pi$.

- The sum of the measures of the angles of a triangle is 180.

1. In the *xy*-coordinate plane, what is the area of the rectangle with opposite vertices at $(-3, -1)$ and $(3, 1)$?

   (A) 3
   (B) 6
   (C) 9
   (D) 12

2. The following Venn diagram shows the ice-cream flavor choice of 36 children at an ice-cream party. Each child could choose vanilla ice cream, chocolate ice cream, both, or neither. What percent of the children had chocolate ice cream only?

   (A) 10%
   (B) 25%
   (C) 50%
   (D) 75%

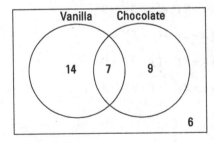

**3.** If $\frac{4}{5}$ of a number is 24, what is $\frac{1}{5}$ of the number?

(A) 5

(B) 6

(C) 8

(D) 18

**4.** The formula below is used in finance to compute $A$, the payment Amount per period, where $P$ is the initial Principal, or loan amount, $r$ is the interest rate per period, and $n$ is the total number of payments per period.

$$A = P\frac{r(1+r)^n}{(1+r)^n - 1}$$

Which of the following correctly gives $P$ in terms of $A$, $n$, and $r$?

(A) $P = A\dfrac{r(1+r)^n}{(1+r)^n - 1}$

(B) $P = A\dfrac{(1+r)^n - 1}{r(1+r)^n}$

(C) $P = A\dfrac{r(1+r)^n - 1}{(1+r)^n}$

(D) $P = A\dfrac{(1+r)^n}{r(1+r)^n - 1}$

**5.** A circle in the $xy$-coordinate plane has a center of $(2,5)$ and a radius of 3. Which of the following is an equation of the circle?

(A) $(x-2)^2 + (y-5)^2 = 9$

(B) $(x-2)^2 + (y-5)^2 = 3$

(C) $(x+2)^2 - (y+5)^2 = 9$

(D) $(x+2)^2 - (y+5)^2 = 3$

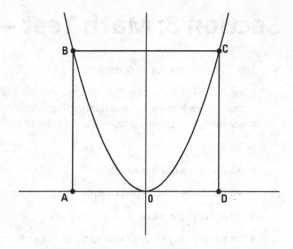

**6.** In the figure above, $ABCD$ is a square and points $B$, $C$, and $O$ lie on the graph of $y = \dfrac{x^2}{k}$, where $k$ is a constant. If the area of the square is 36, what is the value of $k$?

(A) 1.5

(B) 3

(C) 4.5

(D) 6

**7.** How much greater than $t-5$ is $t+2$?

(A) 2

(B) 4

(C) 5

(D) 7

**8.**
$$f(x) = x^3 - 4x$$
$$g(x) = x^2 + x - 2$$

Which of the following expressions is equivalent to $\dfrac{f(x)}{g(x)}$, for $x > 2$?

(A) $\dfrac{x-2}{x(x-1)}$

(B) $\dfrac{x-1}{x(x-2)}$

(C) $\dfrac{x(x-1)}{x-2}$

(D) $\dfrac{x(x-2)}{x-1}$

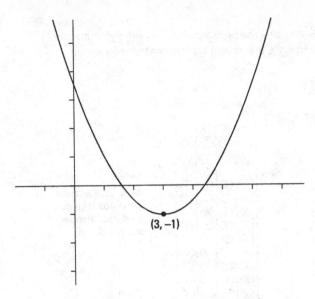

**9.** In the parabola above, the vertex is at $(3,-1)$. Which of the following are $x$-coordinates of two points on this parabola whose $y$-coordinates are equal?

(A) 1 and 5

(B) 1 and 6

(C) 2 and 5

(D) 2 and 6

**10.** The price of a television was first decreased by 10 percent and then increased by 20 percent. The final price was what percent of the initial price?

(A) 88%

(B) 90%

(C) 98%

(D) 108%

**11.** In the $xy$-plane, the center of a circle has coordinates $(-2,4)$. If one endpoint of a diameter of the circle is $(-2,1)$, what are the coordinates of the other endpoint of this diameter?

(A) $(-5,4)$

(B) $(-2,6)$

(C) $(-2,7)$

(D) $(1,4)$

**12.** If $\frac{3n}{2p}=\frac{4}{3}$, what is the value of $\frac{n}{p}$?

(A) 2

(B) 1

(C) $\frac{9}{8}$

(D) $\frac{8}{9}$

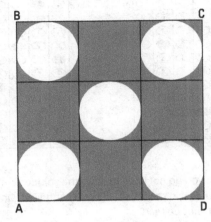

**13.** Square $ABCD$ is divided into nine equal squares, five of which have circles inscribed in them. If $AB = 6$, what is the total shaded area?

(A) $24-10\pi$

(B) $24-5\pi$

(C) $36-10\pi$

(D) $36-5\pi$

**14.** In the $xy$-plane, line $l$ passes through $(-1,3)$ and is parallel to the line $4x+2y=k$. If line $l$ passes through the point $(p,-p)$, what is the value of $p$?

(A) $-2$

(B) $-1$

(C) 1

(D) 2

**15.** $y = x^2 - 2x + 3$
$y = -3x + 5$

How many solutions are there to the system of equations above?

(A) The answer cannot be determined with the information given.

(B) There are no solutions.

(C) There is exactly one solution.

(D) There are exactly two solutions.

GO ON TO NEXT PAGE

Directions for student-produced response Questions 16–20: Solve the problem and then write your answer in the boxes on the answer sheet. Mark the ovals corresponding to the answers, as shown in the following example. Note the fraction line and the decimal point.

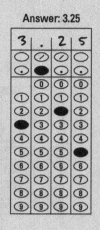

Answer: 7/2

Answer: 3.25

Answer: 853

Write your answer in the box. You may start your answer in any column.

Although you do not have to write the solutions in the boxes, you do have to blacken the corresponding ovals. You should fill in the boxes to avoid confusion. Only the blackened ovals will be scored. The numbers in the boxes will not be read.

There are no negative answers.

A mixed number, such as $3\frac{1}{2}$, may be gridded in as a decimal (3.5) or as a fraction ($\frac{7}{2}$). Do not grid in $3\frac{1}{2}$; it will be read as $\frac{31}{2}$.

Grid in a decimal as far as possible. Do not round your answer and leave some boxes empty.

A question may have more than one answer. Grid in one answer only.

**16.** Find the smallest even number that is divisible by 3, 5, and 7.

**17.** A certain fraction is equivalent to $\frac{2}{3}$. If the fraction's denominator is 12 less than twice its numerator, find the denominator of the fraction.

**18.** If $p > 0$ and $p^2 = 3p + 40$, what is the value of $p$?

**19.** If $x^2 - 3x = 50$ and $x^2 + 5x = 12$, what is the value of $x^2 + x$?

**20.** If $xy = 120$, and $\frac{1}{x} + \frac{1}{y} = \frac{1}{4}$, find $x + y$.

**STOP**

DO NOT TURN THE PAGE UNTIL TOLD TO DO SO     DO NOT RETURN TO A PREVIOUS TEST

# Section 4: Math Test — Calculator Allowed

**TIME:** 55 minutes for 38 questions

**DIRECTIONS:** This section contains two different types of questions. For Questions 1–30, choose the best answer to each question and darken the corresponding oval on the answer sheet. For Questions 31–38, follow the separate directions provided before those questions.

**NOTES:**

- You may use a calculator.

- All numbers used in this exam are real numbers.

- All figures lie in a plane.

- All figures may be assumed to be to scale unless the problem specifically indicates otherwise.

- The domain of a given function $f$ is the set of all real numbers $x$ for which $f(x)$ is a real number, unless the problem specifically indicates otherwise.

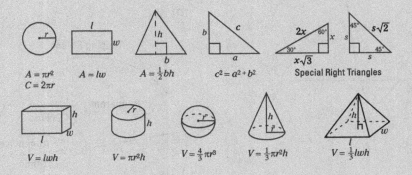

$A = \pi r^2$
$C = 2\pi r$

$A = lw$

$A = \frac{1}{2}bh$

$c^2 = a^2 + b^2$

Special Right Triangles

$V = lwh$

$V = \pi r^2 h$

$V = \frac{4}{3}\pi r^3$

$V = \frac{1}{3}\pi r^2 h$

$V = \frac{1}{3}lwh$

- The number of degrees in a circle is 360.

- The number of radians in a circle is $2\pi$.

- The sum of the measures of the angles of a triangle is 180.

---

**1.** In a random sample of 50 marbles, 11 are red. At this rate, how many of 2,000 marbles from the same lot will be red?

**(A)** 110

**(B)** 220

**(C)** 440

**(D)** 550

**2.** Three cars drove past a speed-limit sign on a highway. Car A was traveling twice as fast as Car B, and Car C was traveling 20 miles per hour faster than Car B. If Car C was traveling at 60 miles per hour, how fast was Car A going?

**(A)** 20 miles per hour

**(B)** 30 miles per hour

**(C)** 40 miles per hour

**(D)** 80 miles per hour

GO ON TO NEXT PAGE

**3.** *No two points on the graph have the same y-coordinate.* Which of the following graphs has this property?

**(A)**

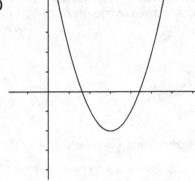

**(B)**

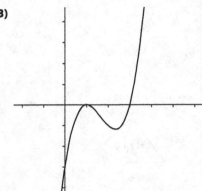

**(C)**

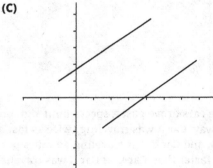

**(D)**

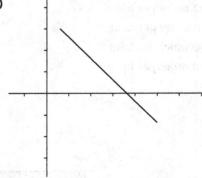

**4.** In the *xy*-plane, which of the following equations depicts a line perpendicular to the graph of $y = -\frac{2}{3}x + 2$?

(A) $y = -\frac{2}{3}x + -2$

(B) $y = \frac{2}{3}x + 2$

(C) $y = \frac{3}{2}x - 2$

(D) $y = -\frac{3}{2}x + 2$

**5.** If 3 less than twice a number is 13, what is 5 times the number?

(A) 8

(B) 30

(C) 40

(D) 50

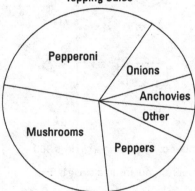

**6.** According to the circle graph, how many of the pizza toppings individually represent more than 25 percent of total sales?

(A) one

(B) two

(C) three

(D) four

**7.** If $|10 - 3y| < 3$, which of the following is a possible value of *y*?

(A) 0

(B) 1

(C) 2

(D) 3

**8.** If $2x = 4^{-\frac{1}{2}}$, what is the value of $x$?

(A) 2

(B) 1

(C) $\frac{1}{2}$

(D) $\frac{1}{4}$

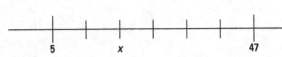

**9.** In the preceding figure, tick marks are equally spaced on the number line. What is the value of $x$?

(A) 6

(B) 17

(C) 19

(D) 25

**10.** If $a$ and $b$ are positive integers and $2^{3a} \times 2^{3b} = 64$, what is the value of $a + b$?

(A) 1

(B) $\frac{3}{2}$

(C) 2

(D) 4

**11.** If $(x - 4)^2 = 49$ and $x < 10$, what is the value of $x$?

(A) $-11$

(B) $-5$

(C) $-3$

(D) $-1$

**12.** If $2a^2 = 56$, what is the value of $8a^2$?

(A) 144

(B) 156

(C) 212

(D) 224

**13.** In the rectangular coordinate system, the line with equation $y = 2x + 4$ crosses the $x$-axis at the point with coordinates $(f, g)$. What is the value of $f$?

(A) $-4$

(B) $-2$

(C) 0

(D) 2

GO ON TO NEXT PAGE

**14.** Which of the following represents all values of $x$ that satisfy this inequality: $7 \geq -2x + 3$?

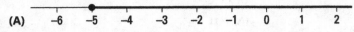

**(A)**

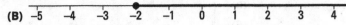

**(B)**

**(C)**

**(D)**

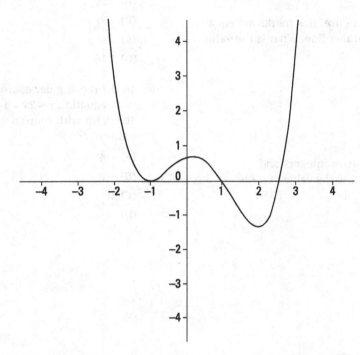

**15.** The preceding figure shows the graph of $y = f(x)$ from $x = -3$ to $x = 4$. For what value of $x$ in this interval does the function $f$ attain its minimum value?

**(A)** 2

**(B)** 1

**(C)** 0

**(D)** −2

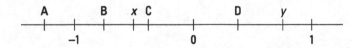

**16.** Which point on the preceding number line best represents the product of $x$ and $y$?

**(A)** A

**(B)** B

**(C)** C

**(D)** D

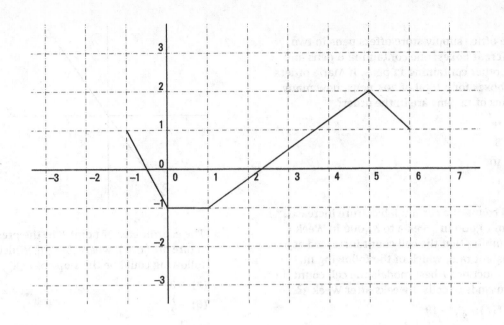

**17.** The graph of $y = f(x)$ is shown above. If $f(3) = k$, which of the following is the value of $f(k)$?

(A) $-1$

(B) $-\frac{1}{2}$

(C) $0$

(D) $\frac{1}{2}$

**18.** If $-1 < x < 0$, which of the following statements must be true?

(I) $x > \frac{x}{2}$

(II) $x^2 > x$

(III) $x^3 > x^2$

(A) I only

(B) II only

(C) I and II only

(D) II and III only

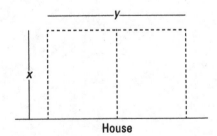

**19.** A gardener is building a fence to enclose her garden and divide it in half, as shown in the preceding figure. The fourth side of the garden is adjacent to her house, so it does not require fencing. The total area of the garden is 2,400 square feet. In terms of $x$, how many feet of fencing does the gardener require?

(A) $2,400 - 3x$

(B) $x + \dfrac{2,400}{x}$

(C) $3x + \dfrac{2,400}{x}$

(D) $3x + \dfrac{1,200}{x}$

**20.** An equilateral triangle has vertices at $(-1, 1)$ and $(5, 1)$. Which of the following *could* be the coordinates of the third vertex?

(A) $(2, -5)$

(B) $(2, 1 - 3\sqrt{3})$

(C) $(2, 3\sqrt{3})$

(D) $(3\sqrt{3}, 1)$

**21.** $x^2 + y^2 - 4x - 6y + 12 = 0$

In the $xy$-plane, the graph of the preceding equation is a circle. Which of the following is the radius of the circle?

(A) $4$

(B) $3$

(C) $2$

(D) $1$

GO ON TO NEXT PAGE

**22.** The office supply store offers pens in two different boxes: one containing 6 pens and the other containing 12 pens. If Maria orders 28 boxes for a total of 204 pens, how many boxes of 12 pens are in the order?

(A) 6

(B) 8

(C) 10

(D) 12

**23.** Cell count of a certain lab culture increased from 19,000 in Week 3 to 41,000 in Week 6. Assuming that the cell count increased at a constant rate, which of the following linear functions $f$ best models the cell count, in thousands of cells, $t$ weeks after Week 3?

(A) $f(t) = \frac{3}{22}t - 19$

(B) $f(t) = \frac{22}{3}t - 19$

(C) $f(t) = \frac{3}{22}t + 19$

(D) $f(t) = \frac{22}{3}t + 19$

| $k$ | 1 | 2 | 3 | 4 | 5 | 6 |
|-----|---|---|---|---|---|---|
| $f(k)$ | 15 | 11 | 7 | $n$ | −1 | −5 |

**24.** The preceding table defines a linear function. What is the value of $n$?

(A) 1

(B) 2

(C) 3

(D) 4

**25.** When the number $m$ is multiplied by 5, the result is the same as when 6 is subtracted from $m$. What is the value of $8m$?

(A) −12

(B) −6

(C) $-\frac{3}{2}$

(D) 3

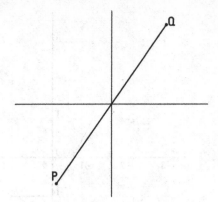

**26.** The coordinates of point $P$ in the preceding figure are $(a, b)$, where $|b| > |a|$. Which of the following could be the slope of $PQ$?

(A) −3

(B) $-\frac{1}{2}$

(C) $\frac{1}{2}$

(D) $\frac{3}{2}$

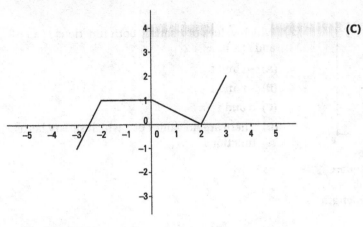

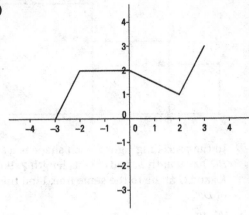

**(C)**

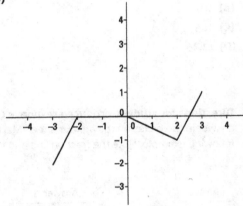

**(D)**

**27.** The graph of $y = g(x)$ is shown above. Which of the following could be the graph of $y = g(x-1)$?

**(A)**

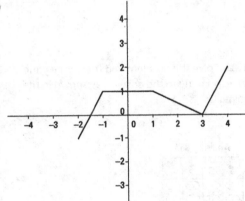

**(B)**

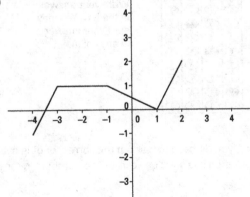

**28.** In the $xy$-plane, lines $p$ and $q$ are perpendicular. If line $p$ contains the points $(-2, 2)$ and $(2, 1)$, and line $q$ contains the points $(-2, 4)$ and $(k, 0)$, what is the value of $k$?

**(A)** $-3$

**(B)** $-2$

**(C)** $-1$

**(D)** $0$

GO ON TO NEXT PAGE

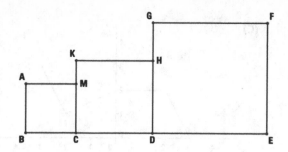

**30.** Which values of $x$ satisfy both functions $f(x) = 3$ and $f(x) = x^2 + 2$?

(A) −1 and 0

(B) −1 and 1

(C) 0 and 1

(D) There are no values of $x$ which satisfy both functions.

**29.** In the preceding figure, each shape is a square, $BC$ has length 4, and $CD$ has length 7. Points $A$, $K$, and $G$ all lie in the same line. Find the length of $DE$.

(A) 10

(B) 11

(C) 11.5

(D) 12.25

---

**Directions for student-produced response Questions 31–38:** Solve the problem and then write your answer in the boxes on the answer sheet. Mark the ovals corresponding to the answer, as shown in the following example. Note the fraction line and the decimal points.

Answer: $^7/_2$     Answer: 3.25     Answer: 853

Write your answer in the box. You may start your answer in any column.

Although you do not have to write the solutions in the boxes, you do have to blacken the corresponding ovals. You should fill in the boxes to avoid confusion. Only the blackened ovals will be scored. The numbers in the boxes will not be read.

There are no negative answers.

A mixed number, such as $3\frac{1}{2}$, may be gridded in as a decimal (3.5) or as a fraction ($\frac{7}{2}$). Do not grid in $3\frac{1}{2}$; it will be read as $\frac{31}{2}$.

Grid in a decimal as far as possible. Do not round your answer and leave some boxes empty.

A question may have more than one answer. Grid in one answer only.

**31.** If $x^2 - y^2 = 39$ and $x - y = 3$, what is the value of $y$?

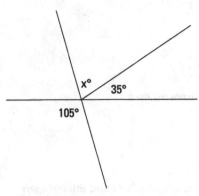

**32.** What is the value of $x$ in the preceding figure?

**33.** Six times a number is the same as the number added to 6. What is the number?

$$a - \frac{1}{2}b = -8$$

**34.** If $a = \frac{1}{2}$ in the preceding equation, what is the value of $b$?

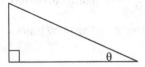

**35.** In the right triangle shown above, if angle $\theta = 30°$, what is $\sin\theta$?

**36.** A circle lies in the $xy$-coordinate plane. If the circle is centered at $(-3, 17)$ and touches the $y$-axis at one point only, what is the diameter of the circle?

**Questions 37 and 38 are based on the following information.** $1,000 invested at $i$ percent simple annual interest yields $200 over a 2-year period.

**37.** How much interest would the $1,000 investment yield if the $i$ percent interest were compounded annually over the 2-year period? Ignore the dollar sign when gridding your answer.

**38.** What dollar amount invested at $i$ percent simple annual interest will yield $1,000 interest over a 5-year period? Ignore the dollar sign when gridding your answer.

# Section 5: The Essay

TIME: 50 minutes

As you read this passage, consider how the author uses the following:

- Facts, examples, and other types of evidence to support his assertions

- Logical structure and reasoning to link ideas and evidence

- Elements of style, such as appeals to reason, word choice, and so forth, to make his case

The following is excerpted from The NOW Habit at Work by Neil Fiore (Wiley).

(1) In *Emotions Revealed: Recognizing Faces and Feelings to Improve Communication and Emotional Life,* Paul Ekman describes how to determine if people are lying by observing the universal microfacial expressions of anger, disgust, fear, joy, sadness, surprise, and contempt. Even if a person doesn't consciously know that you're lying or trying to cover up your true feelings, she will have a gut reaction that something isn't right. The hidden and often subconscious message embedded in your words, actions, facial expressions, and body movements reflects your true attitude and affects your energy level. Others may subconsciously notice the disconnection between your words and your nonverbal message and sense that you're not telling the whole truth.

(2) We all know how leaders often preach one thing and do the opposite, causing their actions to contradict their words and professed beliefs. Colleagues have said of Viktor Frankl, a Holocaust survivor and founder of logotherapy [a form of psychotherapy], that when he advocated that every life has meaning, there was a unity between his words, his actions, and the way he lived.

(3) Are your messages and actions integrated around your higher brain and executive self? You may want to examine how your actions and stated values are aligned with what you consciously and rationally believe. Then ask yourself, "Is my walk congruent with my talk? What underlying and overarching beliefs are revealed in the way I talk to myself and others? Is it all struggle and sacrifice?" Are you saying, "Life is tough and then you die" or "You have to work harder, but it will never be good enough"?

(4) Even more powerful than your actual words is the impact of what you think and expect from yourself and others. Research has repeatedly shown that teachers who are led to believe that certain children have high intelligence scores paid more attention to those children and encouraged them to do their best. As a result, the test scores and behaviors of those children improved significantly, even though these children actually had the lowest intelligence scores in their class. The teachers' beliefs and expectations influenced their behavior and had real, positive effects on the children they taught. The same is true of your beliefs about yourself and your employees.

(5) Beliefs and expectations influence much more than just your attitude. What you believe affects your brain and body the way a placebo pill — an inert substance presented as effective medicine — improves depression and physical symptoms in as many as 30% of patients. You might want to consider, therefore, telling yourself, your children, and your employees that you believe in them and their willingness to learn and do good work and that you are a firm supporter of their worth and truer, higher self. You may find it more effective to communicate to yourself and others that life is an interesting puzzle, a mystery that you were meant to solve and that you have the innate ability to do so. Your words and actions might communicate that you enjoy your life and are optimistic about your future. Pessimists tend to be more accurate about the odds of success but give up sooner, while optimists keep trying until they come up with a creative solution and are happier. You may want to communicate the message "You're going to make it, even though you don't know how. Something will come to you, and you will pick yourself up and stand on your own two feet."

(6) Being optimistic is one way to motivate yourself to keep taking another shot at success and face the inevitable challenges of life while hoping to turn lemons into lemonade. An optimistic view of life — and of yourself, your co-workers, and employees — will turn your mind toward what's going well and has the effect of lowering

depression. Research by Martin Seligman of the University of Pennsylvania's Positive Psychology Center found that those who wrote down three things that went well each day and their causes every night for one week had a significant increase in happiness and a decrease in depressive symptoms. Remarkably, the participants got so much value out of the exercise that they continued on their own for more than six months, and when tested again, they were found to be even happier. Other research points to the importance of meaning in life — interest in exploring a sense of purpose or mission for one's life — as contributing to happiness, healthy self-esteem, and effectiveness.

---

**DIRECTIONS:** Write an essay in which you analyze how Fiore makes an argument that one's true beliefs influence both self and others. In your essay, discuss how Fiore uses the elements of style listed before the passage, as well as other stylistic choices, to strengthen his argument. Focus your response on the most important aspects of the passage.

Do not explain whether you agree or disagree with Fiore. Instead, focus on how the author builds his argument.

---

# Chapter 15

# Practice Exam 1: Answers and Explanations

**A**fter you finish the practice test sections in Chapter 18, take some time to go through the answers and explanations in this chapter to find out which questions you missed and why. Even if you answered the question correctly, the explanation may offer a useful strategy that speeds up your performance on the next round. We also include additional information that'll be useful on the real SAT. If you're short on time, turn to the end of this chapter to find an abbreviated answer key.

## Answers for Section 1: Reading Test

1. **C.** Lines 5 through 7 state that "... the absence of human landmarks is one of the most depressing and disheartening." Lines 10 through 11 refer to "sod," or dirt, as "inescapable." "Inescapable," "depressing," and "disheartening" — all negative descriptions that apply to nature, in John Bergson's view. Did you select Choice (D) based on Lines 60 through 61, which mentions Bergson's "Old-World belief that land, in itself, is desirable"? That statement comes in a paragraph that laments the pioneers' inability to farm the land "properly" (Line 65). In the same paragraph, Bergson compares the land to a "horse . . . that runs wild and kicks things to pieces" (Lines 62 through 64), clearly implying that land tamed by human efforts would be better. Choice (C) is the correct answer.

2. **A.** Check out the explanation to Question 1. The land is "depressing and disheartening" because it lacks "human landmarks" (Lines 5 through 7). Choice (A) for Question 2 is the best evidence to support the answer to Question 1.

3. **D.** Choices (A), (B), and (C) refer to natural features. Only Choice (D) describes something made by human beings. Though the roads are primitive — "faint tracks in the grass" (Line 12) — they are the result of human effort, or "strivings" (Line 16).

4. **C.** The first paragraph (Lines 1 through 17) shows a land that has been settled only on the most basic level. Because the "record of the plow was insignificant" (Lines 13–14), the reader imagines shallow marks in the soil, which are similar to scratches made ages ago by primitive, or "prehistoric" people. Thus, Choice (C) is correct.

5. **B.** The usual meaning of *genius* is "supersmart." In this passage, though, a less common definition fits "the spirit or character" of a place or person or time period. In this case, *genius* refers to the inherent pattern of natural layout.

6. **D.** The first four sentences of Paragraph 2 (Lines 18–31) discuss the land in negative terms. Though Bergson had "come to tame" (Line 20) the land, he had not succeeded, because it was "still a wild thing" (Line 20) and cursed by bad luck ("mischance" [Line 22]). True, Bergson is ill, but the paragraph isn't about his symptoms; it's about the land, making Choice (D) the best answer.

7. **A.** The third paragraph lists what went wrong on Bergson's farm: weather, a broken leg, snakebite, disease, and death. The other choices may be true, but the purpose of this paragraph is purely the bad luck.

8. **B.** All the choices may be true, but in the context of the last paragraph (Lines 60–72), the land is an "enigma" (Line 62) because the neighbors were "tailors, locksmiths, joiners, cigar-makers" (Lines 70–71), but not farmers. These neighbors, not the land, are the problem, and to them, the land is an "enigma," or puzzle.

9. **D.** John Bergson has much to regret. The first paragraph (Lines 1 through 17) describes "depressing and disheartening" scenes. Lines 33 through 42 list the hardships Bergson endured, including the death of his animals, failure of his crops, and loss of two children to illness. After years on the homestead, John Bergson "had ended up pretty much where he began" (Line 47–48). Choice (D) fits nicely here, because the life you see in this passage is definitely not easy. A close second — but still incorrect answer — is Choice (A). Yes, Bergson was unprepared for the conditions in the New World (the logical term for his surroundings, as he left the "Old World" to go there). But he also faced bad luck (see the explanation to Questions 8). Therefore, Choice (A) is too extreme.

10. **C.** Reread the explanation to Question 9, and you see one bit of evidence — the hardships that Bergson endured — matches Choice (C). That's your answer!

11. **B.** Authoritative refers to "knowledgeable and reliable." Thus the author quotes ancient sources, including Xenophanes (Line 2), Homer (Line 5), and Julius Africanus (Line 28), to support his statements about the ancient games.

12. **A.** The figure accompanying this passage shows only one spot — the Stadium Track — devoted to athletic contests, while several others were allotted to other structures, such as treasuries, altars, the temple, and the council house. The Stadium Track occupied less space than these other structures for other activities.

13. **C.** The author compares the length of two races: the *stade*, the shortest race in ancient times (192.27 meters) and the 200-meter race of modern times. The modern race is nearly the same — the *working equivalent* of the older event.

14. **C.** Lines 26–28 tell you that "later Greeks found it convenient to use the sequence of Olympiads as a chronological reference" probably because the Olympics were "one of the few truly international institutions in Greece" (Lines 24–25). Choice (A), that winners earned glory for the states they represented, may have been true but is not alluded to in the passage.

15. **D.** Take a look back to the explanation to Question 14, and you see that "later Greeks found it convenient to use the sequence of Olympiads as a chronological reference," as Choice (D) states.

16. **B.** Paragraph 3 (Lines 33–55) discusses running styles as depicted on ancient vases. The runners are compared to modern sprinters and long-distance racers. However, the author never mentions anything about himself. He may be a runner, but he may also be a couch potato who watches football. Choice (B) is a good bet because human anatomy *doesn't* change.

17. **A.** According to Lines 49–52, "Ancient sources never specify the exact number of laps" and "modern opinions vary greatly". What do most historians think? The "most widely accepted" — *generally believed* — number is 20 laps.

18. **C.** In this passage, the author cites evidence from many sources, including vase paintings (Line 35) and literature (Homer's Odyssey [Lines 5–6]). He also quotes official documents (Hippias of Elis's catalogue of victors [Lines 21–22]) and mentions archeological discoveries (the posthole at Nemea [Line 63]). Though Choice (B) cites a source outside literature, tradition is not a historical record.

19. **D.** Scan the explanation to Question 18, and you see that the author refers to many types of evidence. Choice (D) provides reference to at least two, so it's the best choice here.

20. **C.** The athletes pictured on the vases might be either sprinters or long-distance runners. The author explains that "most scholars think" long-distance runners had to have their own turning posts to avoid "much congestion" (Lines 71–72). However, the passage ends with speculation ("But if each . . . probably shows" [Lines 75–77]). So was there one turning post or many? Only *more research*, as Choice (C) says, can determine the answer.

21. **D.** As usual in a vocabulary-in-context question, each answer is a definition of the word. In context though, only one choice fits. The 9 billion people who'll be living on Earth in 2050 will have a *need* for food, making Choice (D) the best answer here.

22. **D.** Some areas have more biodiversity and some have less, according to Lines 19–20. The areas with more diversity tend to be in specific areas — where they are *grouped*, or concentrated, making Choice (D) the answer you seek.

23. **A.** Passage I states that the world's food comes from about 100 plant species, while more than 70,000 plant species provide edible food. These remaining untapped plant species are other possible sources of food.

24. **D.** These lines speak directly to the untapped potential for these plants to produce food: "There are thousands of plant species with neglected potential utility."

25. **B.** Passage II tells you that when "mussels take over" (Line 90), other marine animals "disappear from the environment" (Lines 91–92). In other words, the mussels *displace* or remove other species — as Choice (B) states. Choice (D) may have tempted you, but that answer is too extreme. You know only that the other species "disappear," not that they become extinct. They could be thriving in another spot! Choice (B) is the best answer here.

26. **C.** Passage II describes keystone species as being so important that their decline wrecks entire ecosystems. Though the passage uses a marine environment as an example, the passage itself is about ecosystems in general, including forests. Choice (C) is the right one here.

**27. B.** Though each answer choice highlights a line that deals with the importance of biodiversity, only Choice (B) refers specifically to keystone species: "Some species, called keystone species, are so connected with other organisms in their environment that their extinction changes the entire composition of species in the area."

**28. A.** Passage I argues for biodiversity in several spots. "Plant diversity has a critical role to play" in food and medicine, according to Lines 16–17, and the world will lose "valuable *traits* [characteristics] and genes" (Line 29) and "knowledge, cultural traditions, and medicinal resources" (Lines 36–37) if biological diversity decreases. Passage I ends with a statement about "international experts" who want "a program for the conservation" (Lines 63–65) of plants.

Passage II goes even further, stating that if "biodiversity gets too low, then the future of life itself becomes threatened" (Lines 81–82). Passage II also calls protecting biodiversity "crucial" (Line 96) because doing so "increases the chance that at least some living things will survive in the face of large changes in the environment" (Lines 93–95). Sounds like *an argument in favor of biodiversity*, as Choice (A) states. The other choices represent information in the passages, but only Choice (A) applies to the main idea of both passages.

**29. C.** Both passages make a strong case for biodiversity, as you see in the explanation for Question 28. Therefore, reliance on a small number of crops isn't a good idea, as Choice (C) indicates. Passage I states that plant diversity, a subcategory of biodiversity, "has a critical role to play in addressing the food and nutrition security and medicinal needs of the people of this world" (Lines 16–18). Passage II explains that biodiversity "increases the chance that at least some living things will survive in the face of large changes in the environment" (Lines 93–95). Choice (A) doesn't work because the author of Passage I sees exploitation as a fact of life for as long as the Earth has supported human life, not a negative factor. Choice (B) doesn't make the cut because the call for "a global program of conservation" (Lines 64–65) implies that the rate of extinction can be slowed. Choice (D) drops out because Passage I doesn't address keystone species. Choice (C) is correct.

**30. C.** The graph tells you that the percentage of *undernourished persons* fell steadily from 1990 to 1992 (19 percent) to 2011 to 2013 (12 percent). Therefore, Statement I is true. According to Lines 8-9, more than 2 billion people *lack important nutrients,* but 868 million "suffer from hunger" (Lines 7-8), so Statement II works. Statement III falls apart because although the passage refers to an increasing rate of extinctions, you don't know whether the extinct species provided food for human beings. Because Statements I and II are true, the correct answer is Choice (C).

**31. D.** When you compare passages, be sure that you understand the answer choices. Both passages deal with diversity in the environment, but Passage I focuses on diversity in food supplies — the opposite of the answer given in Choices (A) and (B). Passage I is about plants, again the opposite of Choice (C). Choice (D) is the winner here because Passage II discusses the relationships between species in an ecosystem.

**32. B.** During Lincoln's first inaugural speech, he set out plans for his presidency and for the nation "to be pursued" (Line 5-6) or followed. Now, however, he can't, because of "the great contest" — the war — that is still going on. Therefore, he can't make a *plan,* the best meaning of *course* in this context.

**33. C.** Lincoln states that "the progress of our arms" (Line 12) is "reasonably satisfactory and encouraging to all" (Lines 14–15) and that there is "high hope for the future" (Line 15–16). Because he is speaking to his supporters, the pronoun *our* refers to those who agree with Lincoln — the Northern side of the conflict. What would be *satisfactory and encouraging?* Victory. Choice (C) is correct.

34. **D.** As you see in the explanation to Question 33, Lincoln finds "the progress of our arms" (Line 12) "reasonably satisfactory and encouraging to all" (Lines 14–15).

35. **A.** Lincoln is referring to his plan, or "course," that he had proposed four years earlier. Just before the statement that "little that is new could be presented" (Line 11–12), Lincoln speaks of "the great contest which still absorbs the attention, and engrosses the energies of the nation" (Line 9-11). In other words, *the war monopolizes the attention and resources of the nation,* as Choice (A) says. Choice (B) doesn't work because in the last paragraph Lincoln sets forth a vision of the future, where he and others will "bind up the nation's wounds" (Line 80) and achieve "lasting peace among ourselves, and with all nations" (Lines 83–84). The passage contains no evidence for Choices (C) and (D).

36. **B.** Lines 23–24 explains that during his first inaugural address, "insurgent agents were in the city" trying to "destroy" the Union "without war." Did you select Choice (C)? Lincoln carefully explains that neither side wanted war: "Both parties deprecated war" (Line 26–27). However, both sides were willing to go to war if necessary. That last phrase — *if necessary* — tells you that support for war was not *unconditional.*

37. **C.** The third paragraph (Lines 30–39) discusses the issue of slavery, so Choice (B) is tempting. However, Lincoln — who strongly opposed slavery — discusses it as an "interest" that is powerful enough to cause the war. In fact, he says that to "strengthen, perpetuate, and extend this interest," the South was willing to go to war. So in this context, Lincoln is using "interest" to describe the self-interest, or benefit, flowing to those who favored slavery.

38. **B.** Over and over, Lincoln looks for common ground: "Both sides deprecated war" (Line 26–27), "Neither party expected" (Line 40), "Neither anticipated" (Line 42), "Each looked" (Line 44), "Both read" (Line 46) and so forth. Choice (B) works perfectly here.

39. **C.** The explanation to Question 38 lists several possible supporting points, one of which appears as Choice (C), which is your answer.

40. **D.** A quick glance at the fourth paragraph (Lines 40–53) shows that Lincoln sees common ideas between both Northerners and Southerners. (Check out the explanation for Question 38 for examples.) The last paragraph of the speech underlines the same point, setting out tasks that both sides must accomplish: "bind up the nation's wounds . . . care for him who shall have borne the battle, and for his widow, and his orphan" (Lines 80–82). Both sides have soldiers, widows, and orphans. The best proof, though, is in Lines 82–84, where Lincoln calls for all to "achieve and cherish a just, and a lasting peace among ourselves." Peace comes when warring sides — both Northerners and Southerners — stop fighting. No doubt about it: Choice (D) is the answer.

41. **C.** From the first words — "Fellow countrymen" (Line 1) — to the last — "peace among ourselves" (Line 83–84) — Lincoln focuses on the union of both North and South. True, he does condemn slavery, so Choice (B) is appealing. However, the discussion of slavery occurs in the context of the war. Many portions of the speech refer to the importance of preserving the Union ("saving the Union" [Line 12], for example) and the speech emphasizes common ground between the warring sides, as in "he gives to both North and South" (Line 61–62). Therefore, Choice (C) is a better answer than Choice (B).

42. **B.** In several sentences, Lincoln refers to the Bible, sometimes with a direct quotation ("Woe unto the world" [Lines 54–55]) and sometimes with an indirect allusion ("let us judge not" [Line 51]). Specific references to God also appear in the fourth, fifth, and sixth paragraphs. For these reasons, Choice (B) is best.

43. **D.** The answer choices here, in typical SAT fashion, are definitions of *primary*. In the context of Line 1, however, only Choice (D) makes sense. Boil everything down to the essentials, and an eclipse occurs when something disappears.

44. **B.** The passage explains that if one thing is "covering over . . . something else" (Lines 2–3), you have an eclipse, as the "something else" disappears. If the car blocks the view of the child, you can't see the child. The child is *eclipsed.* Choice (B) fits the definition and is the correct answer.

45. **A.** The definition of an eclipse is "a disappearance, the covering over of something by something else" (Lines 2–3). The car "blocks" the child from view, so this line supports the answer to Question 44.

46. **A.** The passage begins with a definition of eclipse and moves on to the examples of eclipses of the sun and moon. You also see the definition of *plane* in Line 37, not to mention definitions of *new* and *full* moons.

47. **C.** Lines 17–28 asks the reader to imagine the Sun, Moon, and Earth arranged in a line. One of these is in the middle, and each of the other two is an "extreme" — the *outer* body. The drawing may help you with this one; it illustrates the position of the three bodies during an eclipse.

48. **C.** Line 15 refers to "ever-moving bodies," and the sentence containing the words the question is asking about ("drawn between any two bodies at any given time" [Lines 12–13]) begins with the word *consequently.* Right before *consequently,* you see *constantly in motion* (Lines 10–11).

49. **B.** In the explanation to Question 49, you see some lines that support Choice (C). One of those lines appears here, in Choice (B), which is your answer.

50. **D.** The Earth blocks the light of the Sun, casting a shadow on the Moon — the Earth's shadow, also known as Choice (D).

51. **C.** If the universe were flat — lying on a plane — there would be "in every year about 25 eclipses (of the sun and of the moon in nearly equal numbers)" — according to Lines 51–53. However, the passage explains that the Moon's orbit isn't on the same plane, so the three bodies line up less frequently. The correct answer is Choice (C).

52. **B.** Lines 62–64 tell you that "eclipses of the Moon, when they occur, are visible over the whole hemisphere, or half, of the Earth." Eclipses of the Sun, however, are visible in "just a belt of the Earth no more than about 150 to 170 miles wide" (Lines 66–67). Therefore, more people see eclipses of the Moon than of the Sun, as Choice (B) states. Choice (C) is out because the solar system does not include other stars: You may know this from your science classes, but just in case, Line 10 defines the solar system as "the planets and their moons."

# Answers for Section 2: Writing and Language Test

1. **C.** The original is a run-on sentence — that is, two complete sentences attached to each other by a comma — a huge no-no in the grammar world. Choices (B) and (D) correct the original problem, but Choice (B) adds *and,* resulting in a less mature expression. Choice (D) introduces a new mistake, changing the present-tense verb to past and breaking the pattern established in the paragraph, which is all in present tense. Choice (C) includes the necessary information in a grammatically correct way.

2. **B.** The sentence tells you that Molly's anxiety level should go down, because she is "nervously checking" and then, the vet hopes, she "can stand quietly." Okay, when you *subtract,* you do end up with a smaller number. However, anxiety isn't a number; it's a feeling. You can *lower* the intensity of a feeling, but you can't *subtract* it. Choice (B) is the word you seek here. Choice (C) doesn't apply to anxiety, and Choice (D) establishes a level of importance — not what you need in this sentence.

3. **A.** The first paragraph focuses on one patient, Molly, and Dr. Virga's treatment of her. The second paragraph explains what an animal behaviorist does. By adding "He is an animal behaviorist," you establish a strong transition from Paragraph 1 to Paragraph 2.

4. **D.** The original sentence has a list of activities that behaviorists study. Whenever you see a list, check that it's *parallel,* meaning each verb in the sentence is in the same form. You have *eat, move, rest, play,* and *relating:* Nope. Change *relating* to *relate* and read the list. Can you hear how everything matches? Now it's parallel and correct.

5. **C.** The sentence begins with a verb form, *identifying.* By the rules of grammar, the subject of the sentence must be doing the action expressed by an introductory verb form. The subject of the original sentence is *animals,* who are definitely not *identifying* problems. Switch the sentence around so that the behaviorist does the *identifying.* Both Choices (C) and (D) solve the problem. Choice (C) is better than Choice (D), though, because Choice (D) drags in an extra word, *they.*

6. **C.** Check the context of the underlined words. With the clarification of *Even in this modern era,* the word *now* is redundant. Delete that, and the sentence is fine.

7. **B.** When you place commas around a descriptive statement in a sentence, the commas act like little handles. You can lift out the words they surround and still say the same thing with just a bit less detail. In this sentence, though, removing *who has pets* changes the meaning of the sentence. Instead of talking about pet owners, you're talking about all people — *anyone.* To keep the intended meaning, dump the commas. Now you have to choose between Choices (B) and (D). *Anyone* is a singular pronoun. It must be matched with singular verbs. Choice (D) improperly introduces plural verbs (*have, see*). Go for Choice (B), and you're right.

8. **A.** *Elephants* is a plural word and should be matched with other plurals, as the original sentence does (*they see themselves*). This one needs no change, so Choice (A) is your answer.

9. **D.** If elephants recognize themselves in a mirror, they are self-aware, so the original makes no sense. *But* signals some sort of change, such as an exception to the first part of the sentence. However, you don't want to reverse course here; you want to continue, and the conjunction *and* fills the role nicely, making Choice (D) your answer.

10. **B.** Take a close look at the graph. The figure 11percent comes from the projected increase in *all United States jobs of any type*, not jobs solely in the field of animal behavior. Now look at the number for *all animal behavior specialists*. The number there is 7 percent, so Choice (B) is correct.

11. **D.** You study more, and you make more money. That's the gist of the last sentence, but *return* sounds like the higher paid career is before the education and training. Instead, because the education and training are first, the *higher paid careers reflect*, because they *show* the worth of *better education and training*. Choice (D) is the right answer.

12. **B.** The sentence focuses on a single point in the past, so simple past tense, *began*, is best here.

13. **B.** The underlined word describes *health*, not the wounded soldiers. Health may be *impaired* (weakened or damaged), but not *disabled*. That description, along with *unfit* and *wounded* — Choices (C) and (D) — may refer to people, but not to health.

14. **B.** The sentence establishes the topic of the paragraph: the trench system. Placed at the beginning of Paragraph 2, the topic sentence creates a link to the first paragraph, which is a general introduction to World War I, because the sentence mentions *World War I* and *the trench system*.

15. **D.** The three activities show up in a list in Choice (D), stated concisely and correctly. Choice (A) is a run-on sentence (two complete thoughts linked only by a comma, a gram-matical crime). Choice (B) creates what English teachers call a misplaced modifier, because an introductory verb form (*Listening to the enemy*) must describe the subject of the sentence. In Choice (B), the *frontline trench* is *listening to the enemy* — not the intended meaning. Choice (C) is wordy and introduces a pronoun, *they*, without telling you who *they* are.

16. **A.** Behind the frontline trenches were the support trenches. The original sentence uses *backed by*, which tells the reader both the location and the function, because when you *back* something, you also provide support. You could say *supported* by support trenches, but the use of the word *support* twice in one phrase is awkward writing.

17. **B.** Check out the figure. The communication trench isn't parallel to the others. How could it be when it was supposed to connect them? Parallel lines, like railroad tracks, never meet. Instead, the communication trench cuts across the other two, as you see in the figure.

18. **B.** The original sentence isn't a sentence at all. It's a fragment because it has no logical subject-verb pair. *The trenches placed* (the original wording) has the trenches placing themselves in the ground, which doesn't make sense. Instead, *the trenches were placed* by someone not named in the sentence.

19. **D.** The paragraph begins by telling the reader that the trenches *were not pleasant places*, but little else in the paragraph supports that statement except the information about the walls. Choice (D) provides emphasis (*narrow, never quite dry*).

20. **C.** The underlined word, *they're*, means "they are" — not the meaning you want here. Opt for the possessive pronoun *their*, Choice (C), for a grammatically correct expression.

21. **A.** Choice (A) combines the sentences concisely, and it correctly uses the idiom "mixture of *A* and *B*." Choice (B) is concise but says too little. Choice (C) is wordy, and Choice (D) is wrong because it's a run-on sentence — two complete sentences can't be joined with just a comma.

22. **B.** The passage needs the additional sentence as a conclusion, so Choices (C) and (D) are out, plus they're factually incorrect: the soldiers' perspective is a main topic, and soldiers saw the war differently from civilians. Choice (A) is true for the added sentence, but the passage conclusion needs to recap the entire passage, not just the last paragraphs. The correct answer is Choice (B), because the sentence takes into account the gap between civilians and soldiers along with "The Great War," introduced in the first paragraph. By returning to this idea, the added sentence sums up the last paragraph and links the first and last paragraphs, giving a sense of unity to the passage.

23. **C.** The original sentence has no subject, so you have to add one. The rest of the passage is in first person — the narrator uses *I, me, my,* and so forth. It makes sense to add the subject *I*. In Choice (B), the *I* doesn't work as a subject because it doesn't pair with the verb form *sitting*. Choice (C), on the other hand, is a perfect match, because *I'm* is a contraction of *I am*. Choice (D) has no subject, so it fails. Go for Choice (C), which corrects the error.

24. **C.** The problem with the original is that *they've* (the contraction for *they have*) can have two meanings, because the pronoun *they* may refer to either *the Hamiltons* or the *parents*. The passage is clear: The parents have given in and gone to Vermont; the Hamiltons haven't given in and withdrawn their suggestion for a vacation spot.

25. **D.** The pronoun *which* refers to *dinner,* but Standard English requires the preposition *at,* because the family is *at the dinner*. Go for Choice (D).

26. **B.** The pronoun *everyone* is singular: it has the word *one* in it. Because the next pronoun refers to *everyone,* it, too, must be singular, but *they* is plural. Change *they* to *he or she,* which is singular, and the pronouns match. Choice (B) is your answer.

27. **C.** Did you choose Choice (A)? If so, you fell for a common trap. Choice (A) by itself is grammatically correct, but it's in the past tense *(greeted)*. Because the whole passage is in the present tense, this sentence needs to be consistent: *greet.*

28. **C.** This question tests whether you can recognize or create focus in a paragraph. Most of the paragraph deals with that summer's activities — swimming, boating, and fishing. Sentence 3 veers off course into the father's experiences in high school. Because it has no relation to the rest of the ideas in the paragraph, Sentence 3 has to go, and Choice (C) is your answer.

29. **D.** Because Daddy doesn't enjoy rowing the boat, a contrast transition fits here, such as "however" or "otherwise." *On the other hand* almost works, but it needs to be preceded by *on one hand,* which the passage does not have.

30. **A.** Though the other answer choices are close, a place (gift shop) *where* something happens (shards on sale) is correct.

31. **B.** The original wording is like someone who eats 4,000 calories a day and does nothing but sit on the couch and watch television. Diet time! When you slim down (in real life or in writing), you must do so carefully. Choice (B) conveys the correct meaning more concisely than the original. Choice (C) keeps the meaning, but it has to lose a few more pounds . . . er, I mean words. Choice (D) changes the meaning, because the *tombstones* aren't *nervous and glad* — the narrator is.

32. **C.** Why is the trip home so frightening? The paragraph supplies a little evidence: The narrator is worried that they will *drive into a ditch* or fail to find the cabin. Choice (C) adds more support for the fear expressed, explaining the reaction of *a city girl* to unlighted roads.

33. **C.** *Defer* means to pass a question on to a superior, say your friend asks for homework help, and you need to bring the question to your teacher. *Refer* means to recommend someone, as you would refer a friend to a tutor. *Confer* is the correct choice here, as it means to discuss. Lastly, *relegate* means to dismiss to lower position, say you would relegate the chore of feeding the dog to your little brother. Answer Choice (C).

34. **D.** Commas surrounding a description make the description nonessential, or extra, to the meaning of the sentence. The original sentence identifies the rabbit-releaser by name. After you know the name, everything else — in this case, the fact that *Thomas Austin* was *an Australian* and someone *who enjoyed hunting* — is extra. The original sentence gets you halfway to the goal of correct punctuation by placing a comma after *hunting*. Halfway isn't good enough! Choice (D) isolates the description properly by inserting another comma after *Austin*.

35. **B.** The passage begins by explaining that *Thomas Austin . . . enjoyed hunting.* Why repeat the information? Delete this sentence, as Choice (B) indicates, and you create a more concise paragraph without sacrificing meaning.

36. **C.** In a sentence beginning with *there was* or *there were* (as well as *here was* or *here were*), the subject follows the verb. *There* (or *here*) can never be a subject. In this sentence, *some domestic rabbits* follows the verb. The subject, *rabbits*, is plural, so you need the plural verb *were*. Why Choice (C) and not Choice (D)? *Their* is a possessive pronoun, and the meaning of the sentence has nothing to do with possession.

37. **D.** Choice (D) is the most concise, yet it conveys the same information as the original. The other choices aren't incorrect, but they're too wordy.

38. **B.** The semicolon joins two complete sentences. Choices (A), (C), and (D) have the unnecessary conjunctions *and* and *while*.

39. **A.** Don't mess with Mother Nature! That's what you do in an *intervention*, a word that's correct in this context. An *intercession* takes place when one pleads on behalf of another. An *evocation* is the bringing a feeling, memory, or image to mind, and an *affectation* is a pretense or artificial expression. None of the other choices fit, so Choice (A) is your answer.

40. **B.** The subject of the sentence is *trees*, which is plural, not *erosion*, which is singular. Therefore, the correct verb is *have*, not *has*. Though the story takes place in the past, the trees still have deep roots, so neither *had* nor *did have* works here.

41. **D.** The usual meaning of *introduce* is to bring two strangers together (*Alice, this is George.*). In this context, the strangers are a species (the tamarisk beetle) and an ecosystem. *To initiate* (the original word), as well as *to start* and *to commence*, is to begin something new. None of these words fits the context.

42. **C.** *The number of* is a singular subject referring to a single number, no matter how big that number is. Therefore, you have to pair this singular expression with a singular verb, *has decreased*. Choice (C) is correct here.

43. **B.** The original is wordy. Choice (B) puts the original on a diet and slims it down correctly. True, Choice (D) is even shorter, but it leaves the sentence without a subject and isn't Standard English.

44. **C.** Choice (C) adds specific examples to the more general original (*You should also check consumption*), which also inappropriately shifts from third person (talking about the

subject) to second person (talking to the reader). The examples strengthen the writer's recommendation — that human interaction with nature should be accomplished carefully. Choices (A) and (D) are too general, and Choice (B) is repetitive. No doubt about it, Choice (C) is best.

# Answers for Section 3: Math Test — No Calculator Allowed

**1. D.** Sketch out this problem to help you solve it:

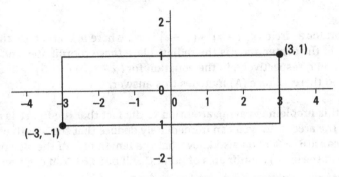

The length of the rectangle is 6, and the height is 2. The area of a rectangle is *length* times *width*, so the area of this rectangle is $(6)(2) = 12$.

**2. B.** Because you're interested in the children who had only chocolate ice cream, you want to look in the chocolate circle where it doesn't overlap with the vanilla circle; the number in that section is 9. That means 9 kids had only chocolate ice cream, out of the 36 kids at the party. To find the percent of children who had chocolate ice cream, simply divide the part that you're interested in (9) by the whole (36):

$$\frac{9}{36} = \frac{1}{4} = 25\%$$

**3. B.** Set up the equation with $x$ as the number and solve for $x$.

$$\frac{4}{5}x = 24$$
$$4x = 120$$
$$x = 30$$

Now find $\frac{1}{5}$ of 30, which is 6.

**4. B.** Don't let this one drive you mad. To transfer the clunky fraction from $P$ to $A$, simply multiply both sides by the reciprocal and cancel:

$$A = P \frac{r(1+r)^n}{(1+r)^n - 1}$$

$$\left(\frac{(1+r)^n - 1}{r(1+r)^n}\right) A = P \frac{r(1+r)^n}{(1+r)^n - 1}\left(\frac{(1+r)^n - 1}{r(1+r)^n}\right)$$

$$\left(\frac{(1+r)^n - 1}{r(1+r)^n}\right) A = P \frac{r(1+r)^n}{(1+r)^n - 1}\left(\frac{(1+r)^n - 1}{r(1+r)^n}\right)$$

$$\left(\frac{(1+r)^n - 1}{r(1+r)^n}\right) A = P$$

$$P = A \frac{(1+r)^n - 1}{r(1+r)^n}$$

5. **A.** The equation for a circle is $(x-h)^2 + (y-k)^2 = r^2$, where $h$, $k$, and $r$ are the $x$- and $y$-coordinates of the center and $r$ is the radius. Place these coordinates and radius 2, 5, and 3 for $h$, $k$, and $r$, respectively, in the equation for $(x-2)^2 + (y-5)^2 = 3^2$ and square the 3 on the end there. Choice (A) matches this answer.

6. **A.** The key to this problem is paying attention to the fact that the figure is a square. Knowing that the area is 36, you can immediately deduce that the length of a side of the square is 6 because $6^2 = 36$. You also know that the length of half the side of the square is 3. That means that the $(x,y)$ coordinates of point $C$ will be $(3,6)$. You can then plug those coordinates into the equation $y = \frac{x^2}{k}$ and solve for $k$:

$$6 = \frac{3^2}{k}$$
$$6 = \frac{9}{k}$$
$$6k = 9$$
$$k = \frac{3}{2} \text{ or } 1.5$$

7. **D.** Get rid of the $t$, and the question becomes, "How much greater than $-5$ is 2?" Well, that would be 7, so Choice (D) is the right answer.

8. **D.** If $f(x) = x^3 - 4x$ and $g(x) = x^2 + x - 2$, simply place $x^3 - 4x$ over $x^2 + x - 2$, factor the expressions, and cancel what you can:

$$\frac{x^3 - 4x}{x^2 + x - 2}$$
$$\frac{x(x-2)(x+2)}{(x-1)(x+2)}$$
$$\frac{x(x-2)}{x-1}$$

9. **A.** The key to this problem is remembering that parabolas are symmetrical along the line that passes vertically through the vertex (known as the *axis of symmetry*). That means that if you were to fold the parabola along that line, both sides would line up. For the purpose of this problem, it means that $x$-values with the same $y$-coordinates must be the same distance from the axis of symmetry, which is at $x = 3$ in this case. Both values in Choice (A) are two away from 3, so that looks like a great option. In Choice (B), 1 is two away from 3, but 6 is three away, so that option doesn't work. For Choice (C), 2 is one away from 3, but 5 is two away; again they're not the same distance from the axis of symmetry. Choice (D)

keeps 2, which is still one away from 3, and moves the other point further away, to 6. Choice (A) it is!

10. **D.** Whenever you're working on percentage problems, it's a great idea to start with $100. So if the TV cost $100, and then the price was decreased by 10 percent ($10), the reduced price is $90. You add 20 percent on to 90 by finding 20 percent of 90 and adding it to $90: $0.20(90) = 18$; $90 + $18 = $108$. It's easy to see that $108 is 108 percent of $100:

$$\frac{$108}{$100} = 1.08 = 108\%.$$

11. **C.** It's always a great idea to sketch problems where you're told the coordinates but not given a picture.

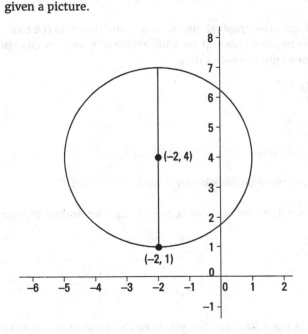

Looking at your picture, it's easy to see that the other endpoint of the diameter is also going to have −2 as its $x$-coordinate. Now all you need to do is determine the radius of the circle so you can figure out the $y$-coordinate. Looking at the two points that were given in the problem, you can see that the radius is 3 $(4 - 1 = 3)$. That means that the $y$-coordinate of the other endpoint will be 3 away from the center: $(-2, 4 + 3) = (-2, 7)$.

12. **D.** To isolate $\frac{n}{p}$, multiply both sides by the reciprocal of the coefficient, or $\frac{2}{3}$:

$$\frac{3n}{2p} = \frac{4}{3}$$

$$\left(\frac{2}{3}\right)\frac{3n}{2p} = \frac{4}{3}\left(\frac{2}{3}\right)$$

$$\frac{n}{p} = \frac{8}{9}$$

13. **D.** The first step is to find the area of square $ABCD$. You know the length of one of the sides, so you know that the area is that length squared: $6^2 = 36$. Now you just need to subtract off the area of the five circles. You can see that each of the nine smaller squares has a side length equal to one-third of the length of the big square: $\frac{1}{3}(6) = 2$. This means that each circle has a diameter of 2 and a radius of 1. The area of a circle is $A = \pi r^2$, so the area of each circle is $A = \pi(1)^2 = \pi$. Now you can find the area of the shaded part of the diagram. The area will be the total square area minus the area of five circles: $36 - 5\pi$, or Choice (D).

**14.** **C.** The first step is to find the slope of the given line by solving for $y$:

$$2y = -4x + k$$
$$y = -2x + \frac{k}{2}$$

The slope of this line is $-2$. Because you know that line $l$ is parallel to this line, you now know that line $l$ has a slope of $-2$. Now you can use the point $(-1, 3)$ and $y = mx + b$ to determine the equation of $l$. Substitute $-2$ for $m$, $-1$ in for $x$, and $3$ in for $y$, and then solve for $b$: $3 = -2(-1) + b$, so $b = 1$. Now you know the equation for $l$ is $y = -2x + 1$. You can substitute $p$ and $-p$ in for $x$ and $y$, respectively, to solve the problem: $-p = -2(p) + 1$. Simplifying, $-p = -2p + 1$, or $p = 1$.

**15.** **D.** The number of solutions as graphed means how many times do the two functions cross, but in algebra it refers to the number of possible values of $x$. Since each expression is equal to $y$, set the expressions equal to each other:

$$x^2 - 2x + 3 = -3x + 5$$
$$x^2 + x - 2 = 0$$
$$(x + 2)(x - 1) = 0$$

Looks like $x$ has two solutions.

**16.** **210.** Every even number must be divisible by 2, so $2 \times 3 \times 5 \times 7 = 210$.

**17.** **36.** If the numerator is $n$, the denominator is $2n - 12$. Start by finding the numerator:

$$\frac{2}{3} = \frac{n}{2n - 12}$$
$$2(2n - 12) = 3n$$
$$4n - 24 = 3n$$
$$n = 24$$

Hold on though — $n$ is the *numerator*, but you need the *denominator*. You know that the fraction is equivalent to $\frac{2}{3}$, so set up the equation with $d$ as the denominator:

$$\frac{2}{3} = \frac{24}{d}$$
$$2d = 72$$
$$d = 36$$

**18.** **8.** Although you could use trial and error, without answer choices to try it may be better to factor it. To factor a *quadratic equation* (that is, an equation with something "squared" in it), first set the equation equal to 0 with the squared term positive:

$$p^2 = 3p + 40$$
$$p^2 - 3p - 40 = 0$$
$$(p - 8)(p + 5) = 0$$
$$p = -5, 8$$

Because $p > 0$, $p = 8$.

**19.** **31.** Don't math it out. You *could* solve for $x$ and place the value into $x^2 + x$, but because this is the SAT, you know there's an easier way. First add the two equations:

$$x^2 - 3x = 50$$
$$+\left(x^2 + 5x = 12\right)$$
$$\overline{\phantom{xxx}2x^2 + 2x = 62\phantom{xxx}}$$

Divide both sides by 2, and $x^2 + x = 31$.

20. **30.** This question is all about working with fractions. Consider the following:

$$\frac{1}{x} + \frac{1}{y} = \frac{1}{4}$$

When you're working with fractions, getting a common denominator on each side is a good idea. Here's how it works out:

$$\left(\frac{y}{y}\right)\frac{1}{x} + \left(\frac{x}{x}\right)\frac{1}{y} = \frac{1}{4}$$
$$\frac{y}{xy} + \frac{x}{xy} = \frac{1}{4}$$
$$\frac{x+y}{xy} = \frac{1}{4}$$

You know that $xy = 120$, so plug that in and solve for $x + y$ as a single unit (in other words, not $x$ and $y$ separately).

$$\frac{x+y}{xy} = \frac{1}{4}$$
$$\frac{x+y}{(120)} = \frac{1}{4}$$
$$4(x+y) = 120$$
$$x + y = 30$$

# Answers for Section 4: Math Test — Calculator Allowed

1. **C.** Set up a ratio with $x$ as your target:

$$\frac{11}{50} = \frac{x}{2,000}$$
$$50x = 22,000$$
$$x = 440$$

2. **D.** You know that Car C is traveling at 60 miles per hour. Because Car C is going 20 miles per hour faster than Car B, you can determine that Car B is traveling 40 miles per hour ($60 - 20 = 40$). Finally, because Car A is traveling twice as fast as Car B, Car A's speed is $2 \times 40 = 80$ miles per hour.

3. **D.** Because no two points on the correct graph have the same $y$-coordinate, you know that for any $y$-value you pick, a horizontal line drawn at that $y$-value will cross the graph only once. The only option where that is true is Choice (D), because all the other answers have parts where a horizontal line could cross the graph more than once.

4. **C.** Two graphed lines are perpendicular when the slopes are negative reciprocals. The target line has a slope of $-\frac{2}{3}$, so any line with a slope of $\frac{3}{2}$ is perpendicular.

5. **C.** Call the unknown number in the question $x$. You know that 3 less than twice $x$ is 13. Turning that into math: $2x - 3 = 13$. You can solve that equation by adding 3 to both sides and then dividing by 2 to get $x = 8$. Make sure that you don't get fooled here and think that 8 is the answer! The question asks for what five times the number ($x$) is, so $5x = 5(8) = 40$, Choice (C).

6. **B.** In this problem, see which pizza topping alone represents more than a quarter of the circle. Any topping with a central angle bigger than 90 degrees is part of a sector that is more than 25 percent. Pepperoni and mushroom seem to be the only toppings that take up more than a quarter, so your answer is *two*, Choice (B).

7. **D.** A great idea here is to simply plug in the answer choices and see which one works out. When you plug in 0, Choice (A), you quickly see that $|10 - 3(0)| = |10 - 0| = 10$, which is bigger than 3. Plugging in 1, you end up with 7, which is also bigger than 3. Plug in 2, and the result is 4, which is still bigger than 3 (though you're getting closer!). Now try plugging in 3: $|10 - 3(3)| = |10 - 9| = 1$, and $1 < 3$! Choice (D) must be the right answer.

8. **D.** Remember that a negative exponent is just the reciprocal of the term with the exponent, and an exponent of $\frac{1}{2}$ is the same as a square root. Convert the expression accordingly and solve for $x$:

$$2x = 4^{-\frac{1}{2}}$$
$$= \frac{1}{4^{\frac{1}{2}}}$$
$$= \frac{1}{\sqrt{4}}$$
$$= \frac{1}{2}$$
$$2x = \frac{1}{2}$$
$$x = \frac{1}{4}$$

9. **C.** There are six spaces that are 42 apart (because $47 - 5 = 42$). Because each space is the same size, you can find the length of each space by dividing 42 by 6, for a space length of 7. The unknown number is two spaces away from 5, so if each space is 7, find $x$ by adding $2 \times 7$ to 5, $2(7) + 5 = 19$, for an answer of Choice (C).

10. **C.** Here's a problem where you need to remember the rules of exponents. Do you recall that $x^a \cdot x^b = x^{a+b}$? That means that, in this case, you can simplify: $2^{3a} \cdot 2^{3b} = 2^{3a+3b}$. Hopefully, you also saw that 64 is a power of 2 — $2^6$ to be exact. Rewriting the equation gives you $2^{3a+3b} = 2^6$. Because the base is the same on each side, 2, you can set the powers equal to each other so that $3a + 3b = 6$. You're looking for the value of $a + b$, so divide both sides by 3 and you get that $a + b = 2$, Choice (C).

11. **C.** Take the square root of both sides and remember that both 7 and −7 square to 49.

$$(x - 4)^2 = 49$$
$$x - 4 = 7, -7$$
$$x = 11, -3$$

Because $x < 10$, it must be −3.

**12.** **D.** Don't bother solving for $a$. You know that $2a^2 = 56$, and you're looking for $8a^2$, which is $4(2a^2) = 4(56) = 224$.

**13.** **B.** When a line crosses the $x$-axis, you know that the $y$-value at that point has to be 0. That means you can plug 0 into the equation for $y$ and solve for the $x$:

$$0 = 2x + 4$$
$$-4 = 2x$$
$$x = -2$$

**14.** **B.** Simplify the expression. Just remember that when you divide both sides by a negative (in this case, –2), switch the inequality sign — then swap the $x$ and the value, meaning you switch the inequality sign again:

$$7 \geq -2x + 3$$
$$4 \geq -2x$$
$$-2 \leq x$$
$$x \geq -2$$

Both Choices (B) and (D) include numbers greater than –2, but Choice (B) has the circle at –2 filled in, meaning that –2 is included in the solution set, which is exactly what you want because you're looking for all numbers greater than or *equal to* –2.

**15.** **A.** The minimum value of a function is where the $y$-value is the lowest. Find the lowest point of the curve, and check the $x$ value: the $y$-value is lowest where $x$ is 2.

**16.** **C.** Pick approximate numbers for $x$ and $y$, such as –0.5 for $x$ and 0.75 for $y$. Multiply these together for $(-0.5)(0.75) = -0.375$. The only points between 0 and –1 are B and C, and you want one between 0 and –0.5, so the answer is Choice (C).

**17.** **A.** Remember that the number in parentheses is the $x$-value. In this chart, $f(3) = k$ tells you that then when $x = 3$, $y$ is $\frac{1}{2}$, so if $f(3) = k$, then $k = \frac{1}{2}$. To find the value of $f(k)$, same as $f\left(\frac{1}{2}\right)$, go to where $x = \frac{1}{2}$, and $y = -1$.

**18.** **B.** This problem is easier if you pick a number for $x$, such as –0.5 or $-\frac{1}{2}$, and try out each statement. Try the first statement:

$$-0.5 > \frac{-0.5}{2}$$
$$-0.5 > -0.25$$

This is false, so eliminate Choices (A) and (C). Choices (B) and (D) both claim that Statement II is true, but try it just to be sure:

$$(-0.5)^2 > -0.5$$
$$0.25 > -0.5$$

This is true, so now check Statement III for the tiebreaker:

$$(-0.5)^3 > (-0.5)^2$$
$$-0.125 > 0.25$$

And it's not true. Choice (B) is the answer.

**19. C.** The fence that the gardener needs is equal to $3x + y$, so what you really need to do is figure out a way to represent $y$ in terms of $x$. Because the area of the garden is 2,400 square feet, you can use your knowledge of the area of a rectangle to see that $2,400 = xy$. Divide both sides by $x$ to solve for $y$ for $y = \dfrac{2,400}{x}$, and then place that back in to the original expression for the total fencing needed: $3x + y = 3x + \dfrac{2,400}{x}$, Choice (C).

**20. B.** To help solve this problem, sketch a picture. Keep in mind that the triangle can point upward or downward.

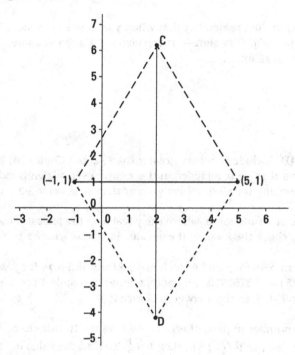

The third vertex of the triangle will lie along the line that cuts through the midpoint between the two given vertices. You can find the coordinates of that midpoint by finding the average of the $x$'s and the average of the $y$'s: $\left(\dfrac{-1+5}{2}, \dfrac{1+1}{2}\right) = (2,1)$. So the $x$-coordinate of the third vertex will be 2, which eliminates Choice (D). Because equilateral triangles have 60-degree angles in them, you can drop an altitude from the unknown vertex to make a 30-60-90 triangle. You know that the leg connecting a vertex to the 90-degree angle is going to be 3 units long, and from there, you can use your knowledge of common right triangles to see that the unknown altitude is $3\sqrt{3}$. That means that the unknown vertex is $3\sqrt{3}$ away from1, so it's either at $\left(2, 1+3\sqrt{3}\right)$ or $\left(2, 1-3\sqrt{3}\right)$. Choice (B) is the only choice that fits.

**21. D.** Convert the equation of the circle to the center-radius form, where the center is $(h, k)$ and the radius is $r$: $(x-h)^2 + (y-k)^2 = r^2$.

$$x^2 + y^2 - 4x - 6y + 12 = 0$$
$$x^2 + y^2 - 4x - 6y = -12$$
$$\left[x^2 - 4x\right] + \left[y^2 - 6y\right] = -12$$
$$\left[(x-2)^2 - 4\right] + \left[(y-3)^2 - 9\right] = -12$$
$$(x-2)^2 + (y-3)^2 = 1$$

Because $r^2 = 1$, $r = 1$ and the answer is Choice (D).

**22. A.** If $x$ boxes each hold 12 pens, then that group has $12x$ pens. If there are 28 boxes total, then $28 - x$ boxes each hold 6 pens, and that group has $6(28 - x)$ pens. Set up the equation for the total of 204 pens:

$$12x + 6(28 - x) = 204$$
$$12x + (168 - 6x) = 204$$
$$6x = 36$$
$$x = 6$$

**23. D.** In the third week after Week 3, $t = 3$, so plug 3 in for $t$ in each answer and see which one yields 41. The answer is in thousands, so 41 refers to 41,000:

$$f(t) = \frac{22}{3}t + 19$$
$$f(3) = \frac{22}{3}(3) + 19$$
$$= 22 + 19$$
$$= 41$$

**24. C.** Looking at the chart, you can see that the top row increases by one in each box. In the bottom row, each box is four fewer than the previous one. That means that $n$ will be four fewer than 7, or $n$ is $7 - 4 = 3$.

**25. A.** When $m$ is multiplied by 5, or $5m$, the result equals when 6 is subtracted from $m$, or $m - 6$. Set up the equation and solve for $m$:

$$5m = m - 6$$
$$4m = -6$$
$$m = -\frac{6}{4}$$
$$= -\frac{3}{2}$$

Now multiply this result by 8 for $8m$:

$$-\frac{3}{2} \times 8 = -12$$

**26. D.** Looking at the picture, you can see that the line has a positive slope (as you read left to right, the line goes up). Already you can eliminate Choices (A) and (B). To find the slope of the line, use the points $(a, b)$ and $(0, 0)$:

$$m = \frac{b - 0}{a - 0} = \frac{b}{a}$$

You know from $|b| > |a|$ that the fraction will be larger than 1, making Choice (D) the only viable choice.

**27. A.** When you change the $x$-value in a function, the graph changes horizontally. In this case, you're subtracting 1 from $x$ before plugging it into the function $g$, so the graph shifts either left or right. Knowing this narrows your choices down to Choices (A) and (B). You can look at the original graph and see that $g(2) = 0$. To get $y = g(x - 1)$ to equal 0, you need $x - 1$ to equal 2: $x - 1 = 2$, $x = 3$. That means that $(3, 0)$ will be a point on the transformed graph. Choice (A) is the only graph with that point on it.

**28. A.** Your first step is to find the slope of line $p$.

$$m = \frac{2-1}{-2-2} = \frac{1}{-4} = -\frac{1}{4}$$

Because perpendicular lines have opposite (negative) reciprocal slopes, the slope of line $q$ must be 4. So far, you know that line $q$ has a slope of 4 and passes through the point $(-2,4)$. You can use the equation $y = 4x + b$ and substitute in the point to figure out what $b$ is: $4 = 4(-2) + b$ becomes $b = 12$ when you solve it. Now you have the equation of line $q$: $y = 4x + 12$. Substitute in the point $(k,0)$ and solve for $k$: $0 = 4k + 12$, $-12 = 4k$, and $k = -3$.

**29. D.** This is a tricky one. The key is that points $A$, $K$, and $G$ are on the same line, because it tells you that the side-length ratio of the medium-to-small squares is the same as the side-length ratio of the large-to-medium squares. Look at this drawing to see the pattern:

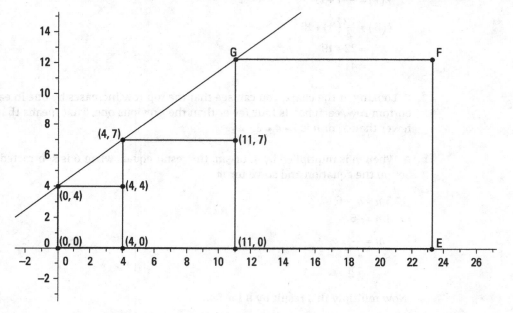

You know from the question that the medium-square side length is 7 and the small-square side length is 4, making the ratio 7 to 4. Multiply this ratio by the medium-square side length to find the large-square side length:

$$7\left(\frac{7}{4}\right) = \frac{49}{4} = 12.25$$

**30. B.** You know that $f(x)$ equals both 3 and $x^2 + 2$, so set those expressions equal to each other and solve for $x$:

$$3 = x^2 + 2$$
$$1 = x^2$$
$$x = 1, -1$$

And this matches answer Choice (B).

**31. 5.** For this problem, you need to factor a difference of perfect squares: $x^2 - y^2 = (x - y)(x + y)$. Substitute in the numbers that you know, $39 = (3)(x + y)$, and then divide both sides by 3 to get $x + y = 13$. Because you know both $x + y$ and $x - y$, you can add the two together: $(x + y) + (x - y) = 2x = 13 + 3 = 16$. Now you know that $x$ is 8. If $x$ is 8 and $x + y = 13$, $y$ is 5.

**32. 70.** The trick is to see that 105° is a vertical angle to $35° + x°$. Because vertical angles are equal, you know that $105 = 35 + x$.

**33. 1.2 or 6/5.** Call the number $x$. Translating the words into math: "Six times $x$ is the same as $x$ added to 6" becomes $6x = 6 + x$. Now solve for $x$:

$$6x = 6 + x$$
$$5x = 6$$
$$x = 1.2$$

**34. 17.** Place $\frac{1}{2}$ for $a$ and solve for $b$:

$$a - \frac{1}{2}b = -8$$
$$\left(\frac{1}{2}\right) - \frac{1}{2}b = -8$$
$$-\frac{1}{2}b = -8\frac{1}{2}$$
$$b = 17$$

**35. 1/2 or .5.** If one angle is 90° and angle $\theta = 30°$, then the third angle is 60°, making this a 30-60-90 triangle with a side ratio of $1 : \sqrt{3} : 2$. The sin of an angle is the angle's opposite side, which in this case is the triangle's smallest side, over the triangle's hypotenuse. From the ratio, you know that the smallest side is half the length of the hypotenuse, for an answer of $\frac{1}{2}$ or 0.5. When you grid in your answer, either 1/2 or .5 is considered correct.

**36. 6.** Sketch out the problem to help you solve:

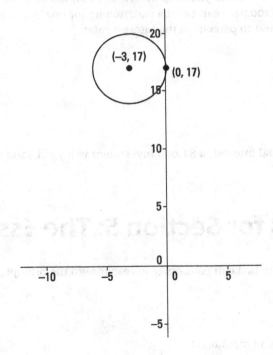

For the circle to touch the $y$-axis in only one place, it must touch the $y$-axis at (0, 17). That point is three units away from the center of the circle, meaning that the radius of the circle is 3 and the diameter is 6.

**37. 210.** If $1,000 invested at *i* percent simple annual interest yields $200 over a two-year period, you can deduce that it earns $100 over one year. To find *i*, the interest rate, yielding $100 simple annual interest on $1,000, divide the amount of interest by the amount of the investment:

$$\frac{100}{1,000} = 0.1 = 10\%$$

Now you know that $i = 10$, for an interest rate of 10 percent.

To calculate compound interest, you can use the compound interest formula. However, for only two cycles, you can find the answer without the formula. Simply calculate the simple interest twice: once for the first year, and once for the second year. Start with the original $1,000 investment, and increase it 10 percent:

$$\$1,000 + (10\% \times \$1,000) = \$1,000 + \$100 = \$1,100$$

The investment is worth $1,100 at the end of the first year. To find its value at the end of the second year, increase $1,100 by 10 percent:

$$\$1,100 + (10\% \times \$1,100) = \$1,100 + \$110 = \$1,210$$

The question asks for the amount of interest yielded, not the final value. To find the amount of interest, subtract the original value from the final value:

$$\$1,210 - \$1,000 = \$210$$

**38. 2,000.** Knowing the interest rate is 10 percent simple annual interest, how much should be invested at this rate for five years to yield $1,000? To yield $1,000 over five years, the investment should yield $200 per year. Set the equation up for one year's worth of interest with *x* as the investment and 10 percent as the interest rate:

$$10\%x = \$200$$
$$\frac{10x}{100} = \$200$$
$$\frac{x}{10} = \$200$$
$$x = \$2,000$$

At 10 percent simple annual interest, a $2,000 investment will yield $200 per year and $1,000 over five years.

# Answer Guidelines for Section 5: The Essay

Here are some possible points to make in your essay in response to the prompt.

## Reading

Note how many of these ideas you mentioned:

» The main argument is that everyone gives "messages" to others, either through words or body language and facial expression.

» Positive messages create positive results, and negative messages do the opposite.

- Immediately after the reference to Ekman, the author elaborates on the main point by explaining that even unconscious lies have an effect on the listener.

- The passage explains some steps that the reader can take to nurture a positive attitude.

- The conclusion also reinforces the main idea, that one can achieve greater "happiness, self-esteem, and effectiveness."

How did you do? If you covered all these points in your essay, give yourself a 4. If you discussed three or four, award yourself 3 points. Only two? Take 2 points. If you mentioned the main idea and nothing else, give yourself 1 point.

## Analysis

The most important part of your essay is analysis of the writer's technique. Here are some possible points:

- The passage begins with a reference to the views of an expert witness, Paul Ekman. Although Ekman's credentials don't appear in the passage, the implication is that the book is an authoritative source.

- At the end of Paragraph 1, the author appeals to fear by warning: "Others may subconsciously notice the disconnection between your words and your nonverbal message" and sense the lie.

- The example of Viktor Frankl in Paragraph 2 contrasts Frankl's honesty ("unity between his words, his actions, and the way he lived") with the warning about lying at the end of Paragraph 1.

- Also countering the fear are the recommendations in Paragraphs 6 and 7, which suggest positive messages the reader can give to him- or herself and to others. The passage ends with a practical method — a journal exercise — for nurturing a positive attitude.

- Personal pronouns — *we* and *you* (as in *We all know* and *What are you communicating to yourself*) create a bond between the author and reader.

- In the third and fourth paragraphs, a series of rhetorical questions (asked for effect, with no answer from the author) draw the reader into the discussion and provoke reflection on the topic.

- Sophisticated vocabulary choices, such as *executive, aligned,* and *congruent,* create a serious, businesslike tone. These words imply that the reader (even one who has to look up the definitions!) is serious and businesslike. That impression, flattery or not, may make the reader more open to the writer's argument.

- The research experiment on teachers' attitudes and the information about placebos discussed in Paragraphs 5 and 6 provide scientific backing for the author's ideas.

- The conclusion refers to "meaning in life" and unifies the passage by taking the reader back to the example of Viktor Frankl.

How were your analytical skills? If you mentioned seven or more of the ideas, you earned 4 points. If you discussed four, five, or six of the techniques, take 3 points. Only two or three? You earned 2 points. Just one? Take 1 point.

# Writing

Your final category is writing and applies to your own essay. Evaluating your own writing may be difficult. If you can find a friendly teacher or a helpful adult, ask for assistance in checking your grammar and style. Pay attention to these factors:

» **Structure:** Does your essay have a solid, logical structure? One possibility is to work in order from the first paragraph of the passage, where the author states the thesis (idea to be proved), and then move through paragraph after paragraph until you reach the end of the passage. Another possibility is to examine writing techniques in separate paragraphs. For example, you may have one paragraph on Eckman and Frankl, one on word choice (including personal pronouns), and one on rhetorical questions.

» **Evidence:** Do you back up every statement you make with quotations or specific references to the passage? Count how many times you zeroed in on details. You should have at least two in every paragraph you write and maybe more.

» **Language:** Does your essay sound formal, as if a teacher were explaining the passage? If you lapsed into slang or informal word choice, your essay is weaker.

» **Mechanics:** English teachers group grammar, spelling, and punctuation in this category. As you reread, underline any sentence fragments or run-ons, misspelled words, and faulty commas or quotation marks.

Adding up points to evaluate your writing is tricky. In general, give yourself 2 points (up to a total of 8) for each category in the bulleted list in which you excelled. If you stumbled slightly in a category (say, three or four grammar or spelling mistakes), give yourself 1 point. If you feel your performance in one of these categories was poor (perhaps you drifted off topic or made seven or eight grammar errors), take again only 1 point.

# Scoring your essay

To get a fair idea of how your essay measures up to College Board standards, fill in this grid.

| Category | Reading | Analysis | Writing |
|---|---|---|---|
| Number of Points | | | |

These results are your essay scores in Reading, Analysis, and Writing. For more guidance on scoring your essay, check Chapters 7 and 8.

# Answer Key

## Section 1: Reading Test

| | | | | | | | |
|---|---|---|---|---|---|---|---|
| 1. | C | 14. | C | 27. | B | 40. | D |
| 2. | A | 15. | D | 28. | A | 41. | C |
| 3. | D | 16. | B | 29. | C | 42. | B |
| 4. | C | 17. | A | 30. | C | 43. | D |
| 5. | B | 18. | C | 31. | D | 44. | B |
| 6. | D | 19. | D | 32. | B | 45. | A |
| 7. | A | 20. | C | 33. | C | 46. | A |
| 8. | B | 21. | D | 34. | D | 47. | C |
| 9. | D | 22. | D | 35. | A | 48. | C |
| 10. | C | 23. | A | 36. | B | 49. | B |
| 11. | B | 24. | D | 37. | C | 50. | D |
| 12. | A | 25. | B | 38. | B | 51. | C |
| 13. | C | 26. | C | 39. | C | 52. | B |

## Section 2: Writing and Language Test

| | | | | | | | |
|---|---|---|---|---|---|---|---|
| 1. | C | 13. | B | 25. | D | 37. | D |
| 2. | B | 14. | B | 26. | B | 38. | B |
| 3. | A | 15. | D | 27. | C | 39. | A |
| 4. | D | 16. | A | 28. | C | 40. | B |
| 5. | C | 17. | B | 29. | D | 41. | D |
| 6. | C | 18. | B | 30. | A | 42. | C |
| 7. | B | 19. | D | 31. | B | 43. | B |
| 8. | A | 20. | C | 32. | C | 44. | C |
| 9. | D | 21. | A | 33. | C | | |
| 10. | B | 22. | B | 34. | D | | |
| 11. | D | 23. | C | 35. | B | | |
| 12. | B | 24. | C | 36. | C | | |

## Section 3: Math Test — No Calculator Allowed

| | | | | | | | |
|---|---|---|---|---|---|---|---|
| 1. | D | 6. | A | 11. | C | 16. | 210 |
| 2. | B | 7. | D | 12. | D | 17. | 36 |
| 3. | B | 8. | D | 13. | D | 18. | 8 |
| 4. | B | 9. | A | 14. | C | 19. | 31 |
| 5. | A | 10. | D | 15. | D | 20. | 30 |

## Section 4: Math Test – Calculator Allowed

| | | | | | | | |
|---|---|---|---|---|---|---|---|
| 1. | C | 11. | C | 21. | D | 31. | 5 |
| 2. | D | 12. | D | 22. | A | 32. | 70 |
| 3. | D | 13. | B | 23. | D | 33. | 1.2 or 6/5 |
| 4. | C | 14. | B | 24. | C | 34. | 17 |
| 5. | C | 15. | A | 25. | A | 35. | 1/2 or .5 |
| 6. | B | 16. | C | 26. | D | 36. | 6 |
| 7. | D | 17. | A | 27. | A | 37. | 210 |
| 8. | D | 18. | B | 28. | A | 38. | 2,000 |
| 9. | C | 19. | C | 29. | D | | |
| 10. | C | 20. | B | 30. | B | | |

# Chapter 16

# Practice Exam 2

Now for another. Like the actual SAT — and the other practice exam in Chapter 14 — the following practice exam consists of a marathon 65-minute Reading Test, a 35-minute Writing and Language Test, a 25-minute Math Test with no calculator allowed, a 55-minute Math Test with a calculator permitted, and an optional 50-minute Essay Test. If you can get through all that, you're in good shape.

Take this practice test under normal exam conditions and approach it as you would the real SAT:

>> **Work where you won't be interrupted.** Leave your cell phone in another room, and ask anyone living with you (parents, siblings, dog) not to disturb you for the next several hours. (Good luck with that.)

>> **Practice with someone else who is taking the SAT.** Get used to the feeling of working with another person in the room. This person can also help keep you focused and provide a sense of competition.

>> **Answer as many questions as time allows.** Consider answering all the easier questions within each section first and then going back to the harder questions. Because you're not penalized for guessing, go ahead and guess on the remaining questions before time expires.

>> **Set a timer for each section.** If you have time left at the end, you may go back and review answers (within the section), continue and finish your test early, or pause and catch your mental breath before moving on to the next section.

>> **Use the answer sheet.** Practice bubbling your answers as you get them, not saving them for the end. We've seen plenty of points lost from bubbling mistakes — skipping lines, doubling some answers, running out of time and not filling in a bunch — and that's just a silly way to dent your score.

>> **Don't get up while the clock is running.** Though technically you're allowed to do this, it's not conducive to an effective time-management strategy.

>> **Take breaks between sections.** Take one minute after each section and a ten-minute break after the Writing and Language Test.

>> **Work through the entire exam, including the essay if you're signed up for it.** Get used to the experience of going through the entire exam in one sitting. It's not easy the first time, but you'll build the strength to stay focused through the entire marathon session.

After completing this practice test, go to Chapter 17 to check your answers. Be sure to review the explanations for *all* the questions, not just the ones you miss. The answer explanations provide insight and a review of everything you went over in the previous chapters. This way, too, you review the explanations for questions that you weren't sure of.

**REMEMBER**

The exam is your scratch paper, so use that to note the reading, work the math, and circle questions to return to. The bubble sheet is *only* for bubbling answers.

Ready? Tear out the bubble answer sheet, grab a pencil and four sheets of loose-leaf paper (if you're writing the optional essay), and get a timer. Sit back, relax, and enjoy your trip through Practice Exam 2.

# Answer Sheets

For Sections 1 through 4, use the ovals and grid-ins provided with this practice exam to record your answers. Begin with Number 1 for each new section. For the essay, write on four sheets of loose-leaf or notebook paper. Or you can use the following blank pages.

## Section 1: Reading Test

1. Ⓐ Ⓑ Ⓒ Ⓓ
2. Ⓐ Ⓑ Ⓒ Ⓓ
3. Ⓐ Ⓑ Ⓒ Ⓓ
4. Ⓐ Ⓑ Ⓒ Ⓓ
5. Ⓐ Ⓑ Ⓒ Ⓓ
6. Ⓐ Ⓑ Ⓒ Ⓓ
7. Ⓐ Ⓑ Ⓒ Ⓓ
8. Ⓐ Ⓑ Ⓒ Ⓓ
9. Ⓐ Ⓑ Ⓒ Ⓓ
10. Ⓐ Ⓑ Ⓒ Ⓓ
11. Ⓐ Ⓑ Ⓒ Ⓓ

12. Ⓐ Ⓑ Ⓒ Ⓓ
13. Ⓐ Ⓑ Ⓒ Ⓓ
14. Ⓐ Ⓑ Ⓒ Ⓓ
15. Ⓐ Ⓑ Ⓒ Ⓓ
16. Ⓐ Ⓑ Ⓒ Ⓓ
17. Ⓐ Ⓑ Ⓒ Ⓓ
18. Ⓐ Ⓑ Ⓒ Ⓓ
19. Ⓐ Ⓑ Ⓒ Ⓓ
20. Ⓐ Ⓑ Ⓒ Ⓓ
21. Ⓐ Ⓑ Ⓒ Ⓓ
22. Ⓐ Ⓑ Ⓒ Ⓓ

23. Ⓐ Ⓑ Ⓒ Ⓓ
24. Ⓐ Ⓑ Ⓒ Ⓓ
25. Ⓐ Ⓑ Ⓒ Ⓓ
26. Ⓐ Ⓑ Ⓒ Ⓓ
27. Ⓐ Ⓑ Ⓒ Ⓓ
28. Ⓐ Ⓑ Ⓒ Ⓓ
29. Ⓐ Ⓑ Ⓒ Ⓓ
30. Ⓐ Ⓑ Ⓒ Ⓓ
31. Ⓐ Ⓑ Ⓒ Ⓓ
32. Ⓐ Ⓑ Ⓒ Ⓓ
33. Ⓐ Ⓑ Ⓒ Ⓓ

34. Ⓐ Ⓑ Ⓒ Ⓓ
35. Ⓐ Ⓑ Ⓒ Ⓓ
36. Ⓐ Ⓑ Ⓒ Ⓓ
37. Ⓐ Ⓑ Ⓒ Ⓓ
38. Ⓐ Ⓑ Ⓒ Ⓓ
39. Ⓐ Ⓑ Ⓒ Ⓓ
40. Ⓐ Ⓑ Ⓒ Ⓓ
41. Ⓐ Ⓑ Ⓒ Ⓓ
42. Ⓐ Ⓑ Ⓒ Ⓓ
43. Ⓐ Ⓑ Ⓒ Ⓓ
44. Ⓐ Ⓑ Ⓒ Ⓓ

45. Ⓐ Ⓑ Ⓒ Ⓓ
46. Ⓐ Ⓑ Ⓒ Ⓓ
47. Ⓐ Ⓑ Ⓒ Ⓓ
48. Ⓐ Ⓑ Ⓒ Ⓓ
49. Ⓐ Ⓑ Ⓒ Ⓓ
50. Ⓐ Ⓑ Ⓒ Ⓓ
51. Ⓐ Ⓑ Ⓒ Ⓓ
52. Ⓐ Ⓑ Ⓒ Ⓓ

## Section 2: Writing and Language Test

1. Ⓐ Ⓑ Ⓒ Ⓓ
2. Ⓐ Ⓑ Ⓒ Ⓓ
3. Ⓐ Ⓑ Ⓒ Ⓓ
4. Ⓐ Ⓑ Ⓒ Ⓓ
5. Ⓐ Ⓑ Ⓒ Ⓓ
6. Ⓐ Ⓑ Ⓒ Ⓓ
7. Ⓐ Ⓑ Ⓒ Ⓓ
8. Ⓐ Ⓑ Ⓒ Ⓓ
9. Ⓐ Ⓑ Ⓒ Ⓓ

10. Ⓐ Ⓑ Ⓒ Ⓓ
11. Ⓐ Ⓑ Ⓒ Ⓓ
12. Ⓐ Ⓑ Ⓒ Ⓓ
13. Ⓐ Ⓑ Ⓒ Ⓓ
14. Ⓐ Ⓑ Ⓒ Ⓓ
15. Ⓐ Ⓑ Ⓒ Ⓓ
16. Ⓐ Ⓑ Ⓒ Ⓓ
17. Ⓐ Ⓑ Ⓒ Ⓓ
18. Ⓐ Ⓑ Ⓒ Ⓓ

19. Ⓐ Ⓑ Ⓒ Ⓓ
20. Ⓐ Ⓑ Ⓒ Ⓓ
21. Ⓐ Ⓑ Ⓒ Ⓓ
22. Ⓐ Ⓑ Ⓒ Ⓓ
23. Ⓐ Ⓑ Ⓒ Ⓓ
24. Ⓐ Ⓑ Ⓒ Ⓓ
25. Ⓐ Ⓑ Ⓒ Ⓓ
26. Ⓐ Ⓑ Ⓒ Ⓓ
27. Ⓐ Ⓑ Ⓒ Ⓓ

28. Ⓐ Ⓑ Ⓒ Ⓓ
29. Ⓐ Ⓑ Ⓒ Ⓓ
30. Ⓐ Ⓑ Ⓒ Ⓓ
31. Ⓐ Ⓑ Ⓒ Ⓓ
32. Ⓐ Ⓑ Ⓒ Ⓓ
33. Ⓐ Ⓑ Ⓒ Ⓓ
34. Ⓐ Ⓑ Ⓒ Ⓓ
35. Ⓐ Ⓑ Ⓒ Ⓓ
36. Ⓐ Ⓑ Ⓒ Ⓓ

37. Ⓐ Ⓑ Ⓒ Ⓓ
38. Ⓐ Ⓑ Ⓒ Ⓓ
39. Ⓐ Ⓑ Ⓒ Ⓓ
40. Ⓐ Ⓑ Ⓒ Ⓓ
41. Ⓐ Ⓑ Ⓒ Ⓓ
42. Ⓐ Ⓑ Ⓒ Ⓓ
43. Ⓐ Ⓑ Ⓒ Ⓓ
44. Ⓐ Ⓑ Ⓒ Ⓓ

# Section 3: Math Test — No Calculator Allowed

1. Ⓐ Ⓑ Ⓒ Ⓓ    4. Ⓐ Ⓑ Ⓒ Ⓓ    7. Ⓐ Ⓑ Ⓒ Ⓓ    10. Ⓐ Ⓑ Ⓒ Ⓓ    13. Ⓐ Ⓑ Ⓒ Ⓓ
2. Ⓐ Ⓑ Ⓒ Ⓓ    5. Ⓐ Ⓑ Ⓒ Ⓓ    8. Ⓐ Ⓑ Ⓒ Ⓓ    11. Ⓐ Ⓑ Ⓒ Ⓓ    14. Ⓐ Ⓑ Ⓒ Ⓓ
3. Ⓐ Ⓑ Ⓒ Ⓓ    6. Ⓐ Ⓑ Ⓒ Ⓓ    9. Ⓐ Ⓑ Ⓒ Ⓓ    12. Ⓐ Ⓑ Ⓒ Ⓓ    15. Ⓐ Ⓑ Ⓒ Ⓓ

16.    17.    18.    19.    20.

# Section 4: Math Test — Calculator Allowed

1. Ⓐ Ⓑ Ⓒ Ⓓ    7. Ⓐ Ⓑ Ⓒ Ⓓ    13. Ⓐ Ⓑ Ⓒ Ⓓ    19. Ⓐ Ⓑ Ⓒ Ⓓ    25. Ⓐ Ⓑ Ⓒ Ⓓ
2. Ⓐ Ⓑ Ⓒ Ⓓ    8. Ⓐ Ⓑ Ⓒ Ⓓ    14. Ⓐ Ⓑ Ⓒ Ⓓ    20. Ⓐ Ⓑ Ⓒ Ⓓ    26. Ⓐ Ⓑ Ⓒ Ⓓ
3. Ⓐ Ⓑ Ⓒ Ⓓ    9. Ⓐ Ⓑ Ⓒ Ⓓ    15. Ⓐ Ⓑ Ⓒ Ⓓ    21. Ⓐ Ⓑ Ⓒ Ⓓ    27. Ⓐ Ⓑ Ⓒ Ⓓ
4. Ⓐ Ⓑ Ⓒ Ⓓ    10. Ⓐ Ⓑ Ⓒ Ⓓ    16. Ⓐ Ⓑ Ⓒ Ⓓ    22. Ⓐ Ⓑ Ⓒ Ⓓ    28. Ⓐ Ⓑ Ⓒ Ⓓ
5. Ⓐ Ⓑ Ⓒ Ⓓ    11. Ⓐ Ⓑ Ⓒ Ⓓ    17. Ⓐ Ⓑ Ⓒ Ⓓ    23. Ⓐ Ⓑ Ⓒ Ⓓ    29. Ⓐ Ⓑ Ⓒ Ⓓ
6. Ⓐ Ⓑ Ⓒ Ⓓ    12. Ⓐ Ⓑ Ⓒ Ⓓ    18. Ⓐ Ⓑ Ⓒ Ⓓ    24. Ⓐ Ⓑ Ⓒ Ⓓ    30. Ⓐ Ⓑ Ⓒ Ⓓ

31.    32.    33.    34.    35.

36.    37.    38.

# Section 1: Reading Test

TIME: 65 minutes for 52 questions

DIRECTIONS: Read these passages and answer the questions that follow based on what is stated or implied in the passages and accompanying diagrams, charts, or graphs.

*Questions 1-10 refer to the following excerpt from* **David Copperfield,** *by Charles Dickens.*

It was Miss Murdstone who was arrived, and a gloomy-looking lady she was; dark, like her brother, whom she greatly resembled in face and voice; and with very heavy eyebrows, nearly meet-
(5) ing over her large nose, as if, being disabled by the wrongs of her sex from wearing whiskers, she had carried them to that account. She brought with her two uncompromising hard black boxes, with her initials on the lids in hard brass nails. When she
(10) paid the coachman she took her money out of a hard steel purse, and she kept the purse in a very jail of a bag which hung upon her arm by a heavy chain, and shut up like a bite. I had never, at that time, seen such a metallic lady altogether as Miss
(15) Murdstone was.

She was brought into the parlour with many tokens of welcome, and there formally recognized my mother as a new and near relation. Then she looked at me, and said, "Is that your boy, sister-
(20) in-law?" My mother acknowledged me. "Generally speaking," said Miss Murdstone, "I don't like boys. How d'ye do¹, boy?" Under these encouraging cir-cumstances, I replied that I was very well, and that I hoped she was the same; with such an indifferent
(25) grace, that Miss Murdstone disposed of me in two words: "Wants manners!"

Having uttered which, with great distinctness, she begged the favour of being shown to her room, which became to me from that time forth a place of
(30) awe and dread, wherein the two black boxes were never seen open or known to be left unlocked, and where (for I peeped in once or twice when she was out) numerous little steel fetters and rivets, with which Miss Murdstone embellished herself when
(35) she was dressed, generally hung upon the looking-glass in formidable array.

As well as I could make out, she had come for good, and had no intention of ever going again. She began to "help" my mother next morning, and
(40) was in and out of the store-closet all day, putt-ing things to rights, and making havoc in the old arrangements. Almost the first remarkable thing I

observed in Miss Murdstone was, her being con-stantly haunted by a suspicion that the servants had a man secreted somewhere on the premises.
(45) Under the influence of this delusion, she dived into the coal-cellar at the most untimely hours, and scarcely ever opened the door of a dark cupboard without clapping it to again, in the belief that she had got him. Though there was nothing very airy
(50) about Miss Murdstone, she was a perfect Lark in point of getting up. She was up (and, as I believe to this hour, looking for that man) before anybody in the house was stirring. Peggotty gave it as her opinion that she even slept with one eye open; but
(55) I could not concur in this idea; for I tried it myself after hearing the suggestion thrown out, and found it couldn't be done.

*1. A shortened form of "How do you do?"*

1. The narrator compares Miss Murdstone's eyebrows to
   (A) her brother
   (B) overweight people
   (C) boxes
   (D) men's whiskers

2. In Lines 13–14, the narrator had never "seen such a metallic lady" as Miss Murdstone for all of the following reasons except
   (A) her nasty disposition
   (B) her black boxes
   (C) her purse
   (D) her handbag

3. In the context of Line 7, "account" may best be defined as
   (A) story
   (B) version
   (C) reason
   (D) sum

**GO ON TO NEXT PAGE**

**4.** In the context of Line 24, "indifferent" may best be defined as

(A) uncaring

(B) mediocre

(C) exceptional

(D) unconventional

**5.** The narrator implies that in the future his relationship with Miss Murdstone

(A) becomes more loving

(B) pleases his mother

(C) revolves around her search for a hidden man

(D) is characterized by fear

**6.** Which choice provides the best evidence for the answer to the previous question?

(A) Lines 16–18 ("She was brought . . . new and near relation")

(B) Lines 22–25 ("Under these encouraging . . . indifferent grace")

(C) Lines 29–30 ("which became to me . . . dread")

(D) Lines 39–42 ("She began to 'help' . . . old arrangements")

**7.** The word "help" is in quotation marks in Line 39 because

(A) the author wants to add emphasis to the word

(B) the word is a direct quotation from the narrator

(C) the word is a direct quotation from Miss Murdstone

(D) Miss Murdstone's actions aren't helpful

**8.** The interaction between the narrator and Peggotty

(A) shows the ignorance of the narrator

(B) characterizes Peggotty as ignorant

(C) reveals antagonism between the narrator and Peggotty

(D) exemplifies the narrator's inquisitive nature

**9.** Which lines provide the best evidence for the answer to Question 8?

(A) Lines 37–38 ("As well as I could make out . . . going again")

(B) Lines 44–50 ("a suspicion that the servants . . . had got him")

(C) Lines 50–52 ("Though there was nothing airy . . . getting up.")

(D) Lines 56–58 ("I tried it myself . . . couldn't be done")

**10.** The tone of this passage may best be described as

(A) nostalgic

(B) authoritative

(C) critical

(D) regretful

*Questions 11–21 refer to the following excerpt from a 1910 article entitled "Negro 'Suffrage' in a Democracy," by Ray Stannard Baker.* **Note:** *"Suffrage" is the right to vote.*

Upon this question, we, as free citizens, have the absolute right to agree or disagree with the present laws regulating suffrage; and if we want more people brought in as partakers in government, or some people who are already in, barred out, we have a right to organize, to agitate, to do our best to change the laws. Powerful organizations of women are now agitating for the right to vote; there is an organization which demands suffrage for Chinese and Japanese who wish to become citizens. It is even conceivable that a society might be founded to lower the suffrage age-limit from twenty-one to nineteen years, thereby endowing a large number of young men with the privileges, and therefore the educational responsibilities, of political power. On the other hand, a large number of people, chiefly in our Southern States, earnestly believe that the right of the Negro to vote should be curtailed, or even abolished. (5) (10) (15)

Thus we disagree, and government is the resultant of all these diverse views and forces. No one can say dogmatically how far democracy should go in distributing the enormously important powers of active government. Democracy is not a dogma[1]; it is not even a dogma of free suffrage. Democracy is a life, a spirit, a growth. The primal necessity of any sort of government, democracy or otherwise, whether it be more unjust or less unjust toward special groups of its citizens, is to exist, to be a going concern, to maintain upon the whole a stable (20) (25) (30)

and peaceful administration of affairs. If a democracy cannot provide such stability, then the people go back to some form of oligarchy². Having secured a fair measure of stability, a democracy proceeds
(35) with caution toward the extension of the suffrage to more and more people — trying foreigners, trying women, trying Negroes.

And no one can prophesy how far a democracy will ultimately go in the matter of suffrage.
(40) We know only the tendency. We know that in the beginning, even in America, the right to vote was a very limited matter. In the early years, in New England, only church-members voted; then the franchise³ was extended to include property-
(45) owners; then it was enlarged to include all white adults; then to include Negroes; then, in several Western States, to include women.

Thus the line has been constantly advancing, but with many fluctuations, eddies, and back-
(50) currents — like any other stream of progress. At the present time the fundamental principles which underlie popular government, and especially the whole matter of popular suffrage, are much in the public mind. The tendency of government through-
(55) out the entire civilized world is strongly in the direction of placing more and more power in the hands of the people. In our own country we are enacting a remarkable group of laws providing for
(60) direct primaries in the nomination of public officials, for direct election of United States Senators, and for direct legislation by means of the initiative and referendum; and we are even going to the point, in many cities, of permitting the people to
(65) recall an elected official who is unsatisfactory. The principle of local option, which is nothing but that of direct government by the people, is being everywhere accepted.

*1. System of belief not open to discussion. 2. Rule by a small group. 3. Right to vote.*

**11.** What is the purpose of the first paragraph?

(A) to demand the right to vote for non-white citizens

(B) to explain the constitution

(C) to assert the right to criticize laws

(D) to condemn organized protests

**12.** When the passage was written, all of the following were barred from voting except

(A) non-citizens

(B) 20-year-old men

(C) citizens of Chinese background

(D) African American men

**13.** Which choice provides the best evidence for the answer to the previous question?

(A) Lines 1–7 ("we, as free citizens . . . change the laws")

(B) Lines 7–8 ("Powerful organizations . . . right to vote")

(C) Lines 9–19 ("demands the suffrage . . . abolished")

(D) Lines 33–37 ("Having secured . . . Negroes")

**14.** According to the author of this passage, which expression describes democracy?

(A) a system in which all voices are equal

(B) a process that allows disagreement

(C) a peaceful government

(D) the right to vote

**15.** With which of these statements would the author probably agree?

(A) Power brings responsibility.

(B) Laws should rarely be changed.

(C) Voting restrictions are always wrong.

(D) State officials are more important than ordinary citizens.

**16.** Which choice provides the best evidence for the answer to the previous question?

(A) Lines 3–6 ("if we want more people brought in . . . barred out")

(B) Lines 12–16 ("lower the suffrage age-limit . . . political power")

(C) Lines 20–24: ("Thus we disagree . . . active government")

(D) Lines 55–58: ("The tendency of government . . . power in the hands of the people")

GO ON TO NEXT PAGE ➤

**17.** In the context of Lines 33–37 ("Having secured . . . trying Negroes"), which is the best definition of "trying"?

(A) experimenting with

(B) attempting to reach

(C) placing on trial

(D) striving for

**18.** In the context of Line 40, which of the following best defines "tendency"?

(A) way

(B) goal

(C) ability

(D) trend

**19.** The extended metaphor of a "stream" in Lines 48–50 ("Thus the line . . . stream of progress") serves to

(A) show that setbacks are a natural part of the process

(B) criticize opposition to voting rights

(C) praise those who work for voting rights

(D) reveal the boundaries of voting rights

**20.** The author of this passage would most likely support which of the following?

(A) required permits for protests against the government

(B) strict rules for absentee ballots

(C) petitions directed at elected officials

(D) campaign finance laws

**21.** Which is most likely the intended audience for this passage?

(A) those who want to expand voting rights

(B) those who question the suffrage movement

(C) women

(D) noncitizens

*Questions 22–32 refer to the following passages and the accompanying chart. Passage I is excerpted from* **Bacteria: The Benign, the Bad, and the Beautiful** *by Trudy M. Wassenaar (Wiley). Passage II is excerpted from an interview with Colleen Cavanaugh, a scientist who researches the partnerships between animals and bacteria on the ocean floor (from* **Talking Science**, *edited by Adam Hart-Davis and published by Wiley).*

**Passage I**

Every surface around us is covered with bacteria. One drop of seawater contains a minimum of one million bacterial cells, at least up to a depth of 200 meters; the number decreases by a factor of ten as one dives deeper. Bacteria live in all depths of (5) the water column, all the way down to the bottom of the ocean. One gram of soil also contains roughly 10 million bacterial cells, of types different from those found in seawater. Deeper soil will hold fewer bacteria, but no surface on earth is naturally sterile, (10) apart from places where temperatures soar, such as volcanoes. Add to the marine and soil bacteria those living in submerged sediments, another major habitat full of life, and one can estimate the total number of all bacteria on earth at a given time. It (15) results in a number written with 30 digits, give or take a digit.

If only we could see them without the necessity of a microscope! How practical it would be to be able to see the bacteria growing in a freshly made (20) dessert that had raw egg whites and sugar as the key ingredients and is now standing on the kitchen counter to set. One egg contained Salmonella bacteria, which feed on the sugar and start multiplying at the ambient temperature to reach critical (25) numbers in only a few hours, and which will make half of the dinner party guests ill. If only we could learn to recognize the dangerous ones, to avoid or kill them, and to leave the others alone. No longer would we need the soaps, cleansers, toothbrushes, (30) dishwashing or laundry detergents, hand lotions, and all the other products that the advertisements make us believe would be unsafe to use without the addition of antibacterial agents. Imagine we were able to check the bacteria added to a health drink (35) and they were all dead, and possibly useless, by the time the product was bought. Being able to see and recognize bacteria would tell us that, in most cases, such additions are completely unnecessary, even ineffective, or useless. (40)

**Passage II**

Some giant worms living near deep-sea vents in the ocean floor can grow up to two meters (about six feet) long. They look like long, very white tubes with red tips. They're made of material similar to your fingernails. The scientists had already (45) established that the food chain was supported by bacteria living on pure chemicals. But these tubeworms were bizarre. Not only were they huge, but they also completely lacked mouths and guts. They had cousins the size of a piece of hair that had been shown to take up organic molecules as food through their skin. So that's what the scientists assumed the tube-worms were doing.

(50)

I saw a slide of a trophosome, brown spongy tissue, from a tube-worm. . . . When a scientist was dissecting the tissue, he discovered a lot of white crystals, which turned out to be pure, elemental sulphur. This is where I jumped up and said, "Whoa! It's perfectly clear. There must be sulphur-oxidizing bacteria that can use the hydrogen sulphide that's in the water from the vents, and react it with oxygen, and get energy from that reaction." In other words, there must be symbiotic[1] bacteria within the tissue that are feeding the animals." They would be similar to algae — the photosynthetic organisms[2] that live in coral and feed the coral internally. But the scientist said, "No, no. Sit down, kid. We think it's a detoxifying organ. Hydrogen sulphide is a potent toxin. It binds to your hemoglobin.[3] Hydrogen sulphide is as toxic as cyanide[4]."

(55)

(60)

(65)

(70)

He continued, "We think it's a detoxifying organ, and it's oxidizing sulphide to elemental sulphur, which is nontoxic." And I said, "Well, that's fine. But if you have bacteria doing the sulphide oxidation, they can detoxify the sulphide, make energy, and fix carbon dioxide, and feed this mouthless, gutless animal." Eventually I was able to convince him, and he sent me a small piece of tissue to examine for the presence of bacteria.

(75)

(80)

[Another scientist] found a substance that is only known to occur in organisms that are autotrophic — that is, self-feeding. They can take carbon dioxide out of water or the air and fix it into organic molecules to be used as food. So to me, finding it in the animal tissue was a clincher. And together we wrote a series of papers establishing that there was this symbiosis — interdependence — between bacteria and these giant tube-worms.

(85)

(90)

*1. Organisms in interdependent relationships. 2. Organisms that combine water, carbon dioxide, and sunlight and convert them into oxygen and food. 3. A substance in red blood cells that transports oxygen. 4. A deadly poison.*

**United States: Bacterial Infections from Food Sources, rate per 100,000 population**

| Bacteria | 2011 | 2012 | 2013 | Goal for 2020 |
|---|---|---|---|---|
| Salmonella | 16.47 | 16.42 | 15.9 | 11.4 |
| E-coli | 0.98 | 1.12 | 1.15 | 0.6 |
| Campylobacter | 14.31 | 14.30 | 13.82 | 8.5 |

*Source: US Centers for Disease Control (http://www.cdc.gov)*

22. According to Passage I, which statement is true?

(A) Bacteria are present in nearly every part of the earth.

(B) The number of bacteria present under the earth increases as the distance from the surface increases.

(C) Bacteria exist on every surface on earth.

(D) The number of bacteria on earth can be counted accurately.

23. Which choice provides the best evidence for the answer to the previous question?

(A) Lines 1–2 ("Every surface . . . with bacteria")

(B) Lines 9–10 ("Deeper soil will hold fewer bacteria. . . .")

(C) Lines 10–12 ("no surface . . . such as volcanoes")

(D) Lines 16–17 ("It results in a number . . . take a digit")

GO ON TO NEXT PAGE ➔

24. In the context of Lines 13–14, what example does the passage give of "another major habitat"?

(A) the ocean

(B) dirt

(C) all underwater areas

(D) soil that is underwater

25. According to the information in Passage I and the graph, which statement is not true?

(A) Salmonella may be present in raw eggs.

(B) Salmonella-related infections have been increasing.

(C) Anti-bacterial cleaners may kill Salmonella.

(D) Salmonella bacteria grow at room temperature.

26. With which statement would the author of Passage I most likely agree?

(A) Antibacterial household products are not really necessary.

(B) Harmful bacteria cannot be identified.

(C) Homeowners should buy microscopes.

(D) Eggs are not safe.

27. According to Passage II, tube-worms are "bizarre" (Line 48) because they

(A) live on pure chemicals

(B) are found in extreme conditions

(C) have no digestive organs

(D) take in food through their skin

28. According to Passage II, living beings receive nourishment in all of these ways except

(A) through the skin

(B) by mouth

(C) from chemicals

(D) directly from oxygen

29. In the context of Line 62, what is the best definition of "react"?

(A) mix

(B) behave as

(C) process

(D) answer

30. According to Passage II, bacteria in tube-worms are similar to the algae mentioned in Line 65 because both

(A) create nourishment within other organisms

(B) need sunlight to survive

(C) nourish coral

(D) detoxify oxygen

31. With which statement would the authors of both passages probably agree?

(A) Bacteria should be destroyed whenever possible.

(B) Bacteria can be easily managed.

(C) Bacteria are sometimes beneficial.

(D) No one understands much about bacteria.

32. Which choice provides the best evidence for the answer to the previous question?

(A) Line 49 ("also completely lacked mouths and guts")

(B) Lines 71–72 ("Hydrogen sulphide is as toxic as cyanide")

(C) Lines 89–90 ("this symbiosis . . . giant tube-worms")

(D) Lines 84–86 ("They can take carbon dioxide out of the air . . . used as food")

*Questions 33–42 refer to the following excerpt and chart from* **Small Loans, Big Dreams** *by Alex Counts (Wiley). This passage focuses on the work of Mohammed Yunus, an economist and banker from Bangladesh who created the Grameen Bank to give small loans to those too poor to qualify for traditional loans.*

The genius of Muhammed Yunus's work is not that he figured out how to empower poor people with loans, but that he was able to develop a model that he could replicate more than a thousand times while maintaining control over the quality of the (05) enterprise. The difference is critical to understanding the implications of what he has accomplished. One branch can serve 2,000 people, whereas a thousand branches can serve 2 million. It takes an entirely different set of skills to start a pilot project (10) than it does to successfully franchise it. Pilot projects reach hundreds of poor people; franchises can touch millions.

In circles where poverty and environmental issues are discussed, one often hears the comment "Small is beautiful." Tiny programs tailored to local needs are romanticized, while anything big — governments, corporations, even large nonprofit organizations — is distrusted. Rarely is it considered that while small may often be beautiful, small is, after all, still small. A world in which thousands of successful pilot projects reach a tiny percentage of the world's poor, and leave the vast majority untouched, is a world where mass poverty is destined to persist and deepen.

It is hardly an exaggeration to say that nearly every major problem facing the world has several solutions that have been proven effective on a small scale. But only if the best of those projects can be replicated or franchised, and expanded while maintaining reasonably high quality, will there be hope for resolving the interconnected mesh of social, environmental, and economic injustices that are tearing at the insides of humanity.

Muhammed Yunus has demonstrated that large-scale replication of an effective antipoverty strategy can be both successful and profitable. He resisted the temptation to keep Grameen small (and easily controlled by him), and in the process reached 2 million borrowers, created a decentralized management structure, and trained a workforce of 11,000 people. Doing so has not always been easy. Striking the right balance between keeping all Grameen branches similar while allowing for innovation and experimentation came after years of trial and error. The conditions that gave rise to widespread employee discontent in 1991 were a result of bigness, and so was the gradual decline in the zealousness with which some employees carried out their duties.

Fueling the aggressive expansion program was the managing director's faith in the ability of people to use credit well even when they were not directly supervised by him. Many Grameen critics predicted disaster when Yunus was not there to monitor everything, but their fears have proven largely unfounded. Bangladeshis, long portrayed as lacking the skills for middle management and business ownership, have demonstrated those abilities as Grameen staff and borrowers.

Other poverty-focused credit programs in Bangladesh, many of them Grameen imitators, now reach 2.5 million additional families. Furthermore, Grameen replication programs in other Third World countries now reach tens of thousands of people, and many projects are growing rapidly. Each month, dozens of people from other developing countries come to Bangladesh to learn how Grameen works so that they can start similar projects after returning home.

For many years, one of the most serious criticisms of Grameen was that credit was not the magic bullet that some accused Yunus as touting it to be. The problem of poverty, critics argued, was complex, and needed a solution that took into account not only its financial dimensions, but also things like ignorance, political powerlessness, and ill health. Other programs that provided credit, for example, required that borrowers undergo a six-month course on literacy and political organizing before they were allowed to take a loan. Experts scoffed at Grameen's requiring as little as seven hours of training before releasing loans to borrowers. The conventional wisdom questioned whether poor, uneducated people knew what to do with small loans without more guidance from above.

Yunus rejected these ideas. He admitted that poverty was a multifaceted problem, but he did not believe it necessarily needed a multifaceted solution. The poor, he argued, already had skills, were already politically conscious, and were already aware of the need for schooling and taking care of their health. It was first and foremost their lack of income that made using their skills impossible. Providing investment capital for additional income generation, he asserted, would unlock the capacity of poor people to solve many, if not all, of the manifestations of poverty that affected their lives.

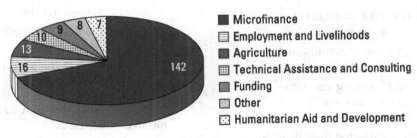

- Microfinance
- Employment and Livelihoods
- Agriculture
- Technical Assistance and Consulting
- Funding
- Other
- Humanitarian Aid and Development

This chart shows types of organizations that use a statistical tool created by the Grameen Foundation called the "Progress out of Poverty Index" to measure the effectiveness of antipoverty initiatives.

GO ON TO NEXT PAGE

33. As used in Line 10, "pilot project" is best defined by which other phrase from the passage?

   (A) "a model that he could replicate more than a thousand times" (Lines 3–4)

   (B) "Tiny programs tailored to local needs" (Lines 16–17)

   (C) "a tiny percentage of the world's poor" (Lines 22–23)

   (D) "solutions that have been proven effective on a small scale" (Lines 28–29)

34. The author's objections to pilot projects include all of the following EXCEPT that they

   (A) involve too few people

   (B) often apply only to a specific situation

   (C) can't be reproduced

   (D) are too expensive

35. The comment that "Tiny programs . . . are romanticized" (Lines 16–17) implies that such programs

   (A) aren't evaluated fairly

   (B) bring people together

   (C) are seen as impractical

   (D) can accomplish more than programs with more limited goals

36. With which statement would the author of the passage most likely agree?

   (A) Poverty causes environmental problems.

   (B) Poor people are unjustly deprived in several different ways.

   (C) Wealthy people look down upon the poor.

   (D) Economic troubles should be solved through the justice system.

37. Which choice provides the best evidence for the answer to the previous question?

   (A) Lines 11–13 ("Pilot projects reach hundreds . . . touch millions")

   (B) Lines 32–33 ("the interconnected mesh . . . injustices")

   (C) Lines 43–46 ("Striking the right balance . . . trial and error")

   (D) Lines 95–98 ("Providing investment . . . affected their lives")

38. The passage and the chart most support the idea that

   (A) Progress in antipoverty programs is nearly impossible.

   (B) Only microfinance data is relevant to antipoverty work.

   (C) Antipoverty work is too complex to be measured.

   (D) Successful interventions to reduce poverty can be measured.

39. The purpose of Lines 46–50 ("the conditions that gave rise to . . . their duties") is mostly to

   (A) indicate that Yunus's critics were correct when they "predicted disaster" (Line 55)

   (B) show an example of the "trial and error" mentioned in Line 46

   (C) show that the "managing director's faith in the ability of people to use credit well" (Lines 52–53) was misplaced

   (D) reveal the need for Yunus "to monitor everything" (Line 56)

40. The critics of the Grameen Bank most likely favor programs that focus on which of the following?

   I. Better education

   II. Universal health care

   III. Political power for the poor

   (A) I only

   (B) II only

   (C) III only

   (D) all of the above

41. Which choice provides the best evidence for the answer to the previous question?

   (A) Lines 26–28 ("It is hardly an exaggeration . . . have been proven effective")

   (B) Lines 46–50 ("The conditions that gave rise . . . carried out their duties")

   (C) Lines 74–78 ("The problem of poverty . . . and ill health")

   (D) Lines 90–93 ("The poor, he argued . . . health")

42. In the context of Line 91, what is the best definition of "conscious"?

   (A) aware

   (B) alert

   (C) awake

   (D) deliberate

Questions 43–52 refer to the following passage from
**Freud: Darkness in the Midst of Vision** *by Louis Breger
(Wiley). It discusses the work of psychologist Jean-Marie
Charcot and the condition of hysteria.*

By the late 1880s, Charcot had turned his
attention to hysteria, and it was here that his need
for power and control most interfered with his
scientific aims. Hysteria — from the Greek word for
(05) "womb" — was a little understood condition,
sometimes believed to be no more than malingering. It was stigmatized by the medical establish-
ment and associated with witchcraft and medieval
states of possession. Hysterical patients displayed a
(10) variety of symptoms including amnesias, paralyses,
spasms, involuntary movements, and anesthesias.
Closely related were cases of so-called neurasthe-
nia, characterized by weakness and lassitude.
Unlike the neurological conditions that Charcot had
(15) previously studied, no anatomical basis could be
found for these syndromes. Looking back from
today's vantage point, it is doubtful if there ever
was a single entity that could be described as
hysteria. The diagnosis was, rather, a grab bag for a
(20) variety of conditions whose common feature was
that they were "psychological," that no discernable
physical causes could be found for them. From a
modern standpoint, the so-called hysterics com-
prised a diverse group: some probably had medical
(25) conditions that were undiagnosable at the time,
others psychotic and borderline disorders, and
many — it seems clear from the descriptions —
suffered from severe anxiety, depression, the
effects of a variety of traumas, and dissociated
(30) states.

Charcot made crucial contributions to
the understanding of hysteria, clarifying the
psychological-traumatic nature of symptoms and
conducting convincing hypnotic demonstrations. In
(35) addition to the so-called hysterical women on the
wards of the [hospital], there were a number of
persons of both sexes who had been involved in
accidents — for example, train wrecks — who
displayed symptoms such as paralyses after the
(40) accident. Some of them were classified as cases of
"railway spine" and "railway brain" because their
symptoms mimicked those found after spinal cord

or brain injuries. Physicians debated, with much
fervor, whether these conditions had a physical
basis. Charcot studied several such patients and (45)
was able to demonstrate the absence of damage to
the nervous system, hence proving the psychological nature of the symptoms. His most convincing
demonstration relied on the use of hypnosis, a
procedure which he had rehabilitated and made (50)
scientifically respectable. He was able to hypnotize
subjects and suggest that when they awoke from
their trances their limbs would be paralyzed. These
hypnotically induced symptoms were exactly the
same as those of both hysterical patients and the (55)
victims of accidents. He was also able to remove
such symptoms with hypnotic suggestion. In a
related demonstration, he was able to distinguish
between hysterical and organic amnesia, using
hypnosis to help patients recover lost memories, (60)
which was not possible, of course, when the
amnesia was based on the destruction of brain
tissue. While these demonstrations established the
psychological nature of hysterical symptoms, it was
a psychology without awareness. The patients were (65)
not conscious, either of the origin and nature of
their symptoms — they were not malingering or
deliberately faking — or of their reactions to the
hypnotic suggestions. Charcot spoke of a post-
traumatic "hypnoid state" — what today would be (70)
called dissociation — the blotting out of consciousness of events and emotions associated with
traumatic events.

Charcot's genuine contributions were several.
He made hysteria a respectable subject of scientific (75)
study, described and classified syndromes on the
basis of symptoms, and differentiated the condition
from known neurological diseases. By documenting
a number of cases of male hysteria, he disproved
the old link between the condition and the organs (80)
of female sexuality. He reestablished hypnotism as
a research tool and showed how it could be
employed to induce and remove hysterical and
post-traumatic symptoms. Finally, and perhaps
most significant in terms of its long-range impor- (85)
tance for Freud, all these findings and demonstrations gave evidence of an unconscious mind.

GO ON TO NEXT PAGE ▶

43. The author cites all the following conditions as hysterical except

 (A) amnesia

 (B) inability to move

 (C) uncontrolled bodily activity

 (D) wild laughter

44. The meaning of "psychological" (Line 47) in this context may best be described as

 (A) mentally ill

 (B) requiring psychotherapy

 (C) not arising from a physical condition

 (D) the result of childhood events

45. According to the passage, Charcot

 (A) linked hysteria to disturbing events in the patient's life

 (B) cured hysteria

 (C) understood that hysteria was actually a group of illnesses, not one condition

 (D) relied primarily on drug therapy for his patients

46. Which choice provides the best evidence for the answer to the previous question?

 (A) Lines 4–7 ("Hysteria — from the Greek word . . . malingering.")

 (B) Lines 19–22 ("The diagnosis was . . . found for them.")

 (C) Lines 36–48 ("a number of persons . . . nature of the symptoms")

 (D) Lines 75–78 ("He made hysteria . . . neurological diseases.")

47. The author probably mentions patients "of both sexes" (Line 37)

 (A) to counter the idea that only females become hysterical

 (B) to be fair to both male and female patients

 (C) to indicate that Charcot treated only women

 (D) to show that Charcot treated everyone who asked

48. "Railway spine" and "railway brain" (Line 41) are

 (A) injuries resulting from train accidents

 (B) terms once used for conditions resembling paralysis and head injuries

 (C) physical injuries that take a psychological toll

 (D) states displayed only under hypnosis

49. Charcot used hypnosis for all the following EXCEPT

 (A) to distinguish between physical and psychological symptoms

 (B) to enable a patient to move body parts that were previously immobile

 (C) to restore memories to some patients

 (D) to retrieve memories from brain-damaged patients

50. In the context of Line 59, what is the best definition of "organic"?

 (A) physical

 (B) natural

 (C) mental

 (D) psychological

51. Based on information in the passage, the author of this passage would probably agree with which of the following statements?

 (A) Hysteria is best treated with hypnosis.

 (B) Hysterics should not be treated medically.

 (C) Hysteria is always linked to severe physical danger, such as a train wreck.

 (D) To scientists today, hysteria is a meaningless term.

52. Which choice provides the best evidence for the answer to the previous question?

 (A) Lines 1–4 ("By the late 1880s . . . his scientific aims.")

 (B) Lines 22–30 ("From a modern . . . dissociated states.")

 (C) Lines 53–56 ("These hypnotically . . . victims of accidents.")

 (D) Lines 78–81 ("By documenting . . . female sexuality.")

DO NOT TURN THE PAGE UNTIL TOLD TO DO SO **STOP** DO NOT RETURN TO A PREVIOUS TEST

# Section 2: Writing and Language Test

**TIME:** 35 minutes for 44 questions

**DIRECTIONS:** Some sentences or portions of sentences are underlined and identified with numbers. In the questions, you see differing versions of the underlined material. Choose the best answer to each question based on what is stated or implied in the passage and accompanying visual elements. Mark the corresponding oval on the answer sheet.

## Endangered Coral Reefs

Coral reefs are large underwater structures, usually in shallow water near <u>coastlines, they are</u> [1] made up of thousands upon thousands of tiny marine animals. A single coral, which is known as a polyp, ingests still smaller marine creatures. A coral has no internal bones but rather an exoskeleton, <u>which is</u> [2] a hard structure outside its body. <u>Analysis of a coral reef shows that</u> [3] you're looking at a colony that may be centuries old.

More than 10% of the coral reefs on earth <u>had died</u> [4] in the last few decades. About 30% more are so damaged that they may also <u>conclude</u> [5] within ten or twenty years. If we do nothing to slow the destruction of coral, by 2050 about 60% of the earth's coral will be dead. Who should care about the death of a coral reef? Just scientists, environmental activists, or scuba divers? <u>However</u>, [6] all of us should care. Coral reefs cover less than 0.2% of the oceans, <u>but they contain fish species.</u> [7] Reefs

protect the coastline from storms. Worldwide, about 450 million people live near coral reefs, and most make their living or are supplied with food directly or indirectly <u>stemming from</u> [8] coral reefs.

[1] Dr. David Vaughan, a scientist at the Mote Tropical Research Laboratory in Key West, Florida, discovered a technique called microfragmenting. [2] By "seeding" small stone or ceramic disks with 1.5 inch fragments of coral cut from a healthy reef and <u>then he was adding</u> [9] nutrients, Dr. Vaughan has been able to coax the fragments to grow about 25 times faster than they would in the wild. [3] Massive coral that usually makes up the bulk of a reef usually grows about two inches a year. [4] With microfragmentation, some species of coral have grown at 50 times their normal rate! [5] Returned to the ocean, these bits of coral spread across a dead or dying reef and continue to grow there, reviving the reef. [10]

Of course, the destruction of coral must be addressed in other ways, mainly by changing conditions that kill coral in the first place. Global warming has raised the average temperature of the ocean and helped to increase the water's acidity; furthermore, seawater is increasingly polluted by run-off from coastal settlements. Species of fish that are beneficial to a reef's ecosystem have been overfished. Dr. Vaughan's discovery is part of the answer. <u>Every nation must also address overfishing, because damage to coral is spread [11] evenly around the globe</u>.

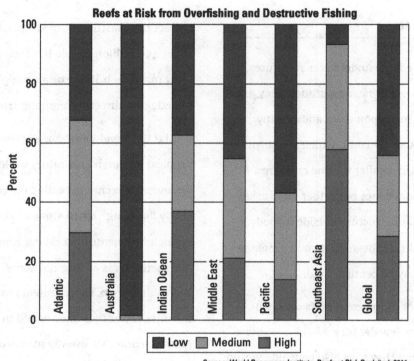

**Reefs at Risk from Overfishing and Destructive Fishing**

Legend: Low, Medium, High

Source: World Resources Institute, Reefs at Risk Revisited, 2011

1. **(A)** NO CHANGE
   **(B)** coastlines,
   **(C)** coastlines. They are
   **(D)** coastlines which are

2. **(A)** NO CHANGE
   **(B)** which an exoskeleton is
   **(C)** being that is a
   **(D)** defined as being a

3. Which of the following is consistent with the friendly tone of the passage?
   **(A)** NO CHANGE
   **(B)** When you see a coral reef,
   **(C)** Scientists speculate that looking at a coral reef,
   **(D)** Upon encountering a coral reef,

4. **(A)** NO CHANGE
   **(B)** were dying
   **(C)** has died
   **(D)** have died

5. **(A)** NO CHANGE
   **(B)** terminate
   **(C)** expire
   **(D)** become void

6. **(A)** NO CHANGE
   **(B)** Actually
   **(C)** Furthermore
   **(D)** Therefore

7. Which of the following most effectively emphasizes the role that coral plays in the marine ecosystem?

(A) NO CHANGE

(B) but they play a significant role in the underwater environment

(C) but they are home to about 4,000 fish species

(D) delete the underlined portion and end the sentence with a period

8. (A) NO CHANGE

(B) coming out of

(C) originating by way of

(D) from

9. (A) NO CHANGE

(B) then adding

(C) having added then

(D) then he added

10. To best maintain the logic and flow of the paragraph, Sentence 3 should be

(A) placed where it is now

(B) placed after Sentence 5

(C) placed before Sentence 1

(D) deleted

11. Which of the following best interprets the evidence provided in the graph?

(A) NO CHANGE

(B) Because damage to coral is spread evenly around the globe, every nation must also address overfishing.

(C) Although damage to coral from improper fishing is not spread evenly around the globe, every nation must address this destructive practice.

(D) With the fact that damage to coral is worldwide, every nation must also address overfishing.

## Separatism and Catalonia

To separate and to join, these two things are
                    12
the impulses that drive human behavior on an in-dividual level and on a national level. On a personal level, people are drawn to form groups and part-nerships as well as to create a unique identity and personality. On a global stage, throughout history, countries and empires have formed, broken apart, and then sometimes reconsolidated. Recently, separatism seems to be on the rise. The former Soviet Union fell apart in 1991, what had been one
                              13
country changed into fifteen independent nations.

In the same time period in Eastern Europe, some nations, such as Czechoslovakia and Yugoslavia, divided into smaller units. The Czech Republic and Slovakia were created from the former Czecho-slovakia, and Yugoslavia dissolved into Croatia, Slovenia, Montenegro, and other countries.

It's now in the news. In 2014, residents of two
              14
different countries voted on the question of staying as part of a larger entity or to form an independent
                                          15
nation. In September, Scottish citizens voted to retain themselves as part of Great Britain,
        16
furthermore the vote was a close call.
   17

Two months later, <u>citizens of</u> Catalonia, an
18
autonomous region of Spain, overwhelmingly
favored independence. Catalonia, which has a
population of 7.6 million, has a strong economy
based on industry, tourism, and agriculture. From
1939 to 1975, Catalonia's language and culture
<u>was</u> suppressed by the dictatorship then in power.
19
The central Spanish government banned Catalan,
Catalonia's language, in government and public
institutions. In 1978, though, the new Spanish
constitution returned some independence to the
region. These changes did not completely quiet the
call for a separate identity and sovereign political power in Catalonia. The region has had many
elections in which independence for Catalonia was
a major issue.

However, the 2014 vote was merely
<u>symbolic;</u> days earlier the Spanish Constitutional
20
Court had ruled that the vote was not binding.
About 2.25 million votes were cast, out of 5.4 million eligible voters. More than 80% of the votes
were for independence. <u>The poll accomplished
little practical change. It was a huge victory for</u>
21
<u>Catalonians. It was very emotional.</u> Because it
was not a legal vote, no government officials
<u>had been involved.</u> About 40,000 volunteers
22
worked at the polls and counted the ballots. During
the last regional elections in 2012, the secession-
ist party received about 1.8 million votes of the 3.7
million cast. There is no doubt that independence
for Catalonia and other areas will continue to be
an issue.

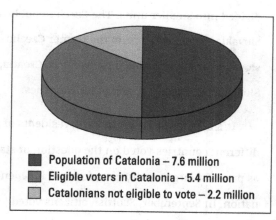

- ■ Population of Catalonia – 7.6 million
- ■ Eligible voters in Catalonia – 5.4 million
- ■ Catalonians not eligible to vote – 2.2 million

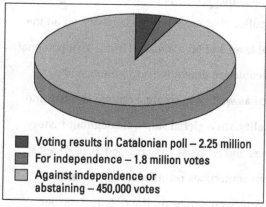

- ■ Voting results in Catalonian poll – 2.25 million
- ■ For independence – 1.8 million votes
- ■ Against independence or abstaining – 450,000 votes

12. **(A)** NO CHANGE
    **(B)** Separating and to join, these
    **(C)** To separate and to join
    **(D)** To separate and to join;

13. **(A)** NO CHANGE
    **(B)** fell apart in 1991. What had been
    **(C)** falling apart in 1991, and what was
    **(D)** fell apart in 1991 because what had been

14. **(A)** NO CHANGE
    **(B)** Separatism is still in the news.
    **(C)** Currently, separatism is now in the news.
    **(D)** Now in the news.

15. **(A)** NO CHANGE
    **(B)** to be formed
    **(C)** to have formed
    **(D)** forming

16. (A) NO CHANGE
    (B) guard
    (C) keep
    (D) remain

17. (A) NO CHANGE
    (B) consequently
    (C) as a result
    (D) but

18. (A) NO CHANGE
    (B) interested parties in
    (C) voters in
    (D) those who live in

19. (A) NO CHANGE
    (B) were
    (C) had been
    (D) is

20. (A) NO CHANGE
    (B) figurative
    (C) imaginary
    (D) illusory

21. (A) NO CHANGE
    (B) The poll accomplished little practical change. It was a huge victory for Catalonians, but it was very emotional.
    (C) The poll accomplished little practical change. And it was a huge victory for Catalonians. It was very emotional.
    (D) The poll accomplished little practical change, but it was a huge, emotional victory for Catalonians.

22. (A) NO CHANGE
    (B) was involved
    (C) were involved
    (D) had been themselves involved

## The Life and Career of P. D. James

[1]

Author Virginia Woolf wrote that wannabe 23 writers need financial independence and "a room of one's own" in order to create art. This state-ment is seen as a truth. It is believed to be true by many who struggle to become writers, painters, 24 and musicians. Phyllis Dorothy James White had reason to disagree with Woolf. Under the name "P. D. James," she wrote more than 20 highly 25 acclaimed novels, most featuring a character, Adam Dalgleish, who was simultaneously a poet and a detective for Scotland Yard. James's brooding hero, as well as her clear sense of the psychology and effects of violent behavior, gave unusual depth to her work.

[2]

James was born in 1920 in Oxford, England. Her father, Sidney James, believed that educa-tion was not necessary for women, and Phyllis left school at 16. She was always interested in creating mysteries. She claimed that when she 26 first heard about Humpty Dumpty, she wanted to know whether he fell or was pushed! James always wanted to be a mystery writer; she was hampered 27                                                          28 by World War II. She was a nurse during the war, and afterwards, when her husband returned from combat with a mental illness, she had to work to support her family. She studied hospital adminis-tration and labored for Britain's National Health Service. For years, she arose very early in the morning and wrote for several hours before

GO ON TO NEXT PAGE ➡

heading off to her job. With this schedule, James needed three years to complete her first book, *Cover Her Face*, which was published in 1962. That novel was successful, <u>even though</u> James continued
29
to work while writing in her off hours. She served as an administrator in the forensic science and criminal law departments of the Department of Home <u>Affairs, that experience gave</u> realistic details
30
to her novels. She was famous for her thorough research. She said that ideas for her work nearly always came from "a particular place." 31

[3]

James did not retire from her job until 1979, whereupon she was able to write full time. Instead

of money and a private room, she accomplished much while raising two children, caring for an ill husband, and holding a job. When she <u>had died</u> in
32
late 2014, James was praised as a unique and talented author who made a lasting contribution not just to the mystery genre but to literature itself.

[4]

James's work has been translated into dozens of languages and often appeared on the bestseller list. Her last novel, *Death Comes to Pemberley*, was a sequel to Jane Austen's famous novel *Pride and Prejudice*, with Austen's characters acting as suspects and detectives. 33

23. **(A)** NO CHANGE
    **(B)** possible
    **(C)** aspiring
    **(D)** hopeful

24. Which of the following best combines the two underlined sentences?
    **(A)** This statement is seen as a truth, believed to be true by many who struggle to become writers, painters, and musicians.
    **(B)** Many who struggle to become writers, painters, and musicians believe this statement is true.
    **(C)** Struggling to become writers, painters, and musicians, this statement is seen as true.
    **(D)** A truth, believed by many who struggle to become writers, painters, and musicians, is this statement.

25. Which of the following best emphasizes the success that James had as an author?

    (A) NO CHANGE

    (B) more than 20 novels

    (C) novels

    (D) highly acclaimed novels

26. (A) NO CHANGE

    (B) bringing

    (C) writing

    (D) finding

27. (A) NO CHANGE

    (B) omit the underlined words and capitalize the following word

    (C) Always wanting to be a mystery writer,

    (D) James had always wanted to be a mystery writer,

28. (A) NO CHANGE

    (B) disadvantaged

    (C) banned

    (D) barred

29. (A) NO CHANGE

    (B) so

    (C) however

    (D) but

30. (A) NO CHANGE

    (B) Affairs; that experience gave

    (C) Affairs, gave

    (D) Affairs, that experience had given

31. At this point, the author is considering adding the following sentence:

She added that she liked to "create in books some kind of opposition between places and characters." Should the author make this change?

    (A) Yes, because reading James' own words brings depth to the passage.

    (B) Yes, because the quote describes the context in which James liked to write.

    (C) No, because the sentence is not within scope of the topic of the passage.

    (D) No, because places and characters cannot be opposite.

32. (A) NO CHANGE

    (B) died

    (C) dies

    (D) was dead

33. To make the passage flow most consistently, Paragraph 4 should be placed

    (A) Where it is now

    (B) Before Paragraph 1

    (C) After Paragraph 1

    (D) After Paragraph 2

## Exploring the Career Path

Those with creative spirits too often think in limited terms when it comes to careers. Writers may consider novels or film scripts, and visual art-
33
ists envision their paintings or drawings in museum shows. However, creativity is a job requirement in many lesser-known fields. Sometimes those

fields give applicants a greater chance at success in job-finding than highly-profile positions.
35
Someone interested in fashion, for example, may think about television reality shows that focus on careers designing clothing or modeling it. Besides those jobs are many other fashion-related positions. Magazine editors, pattern makers, and

GO ON TO NEXT PAGE →

photographers are only a few of the many posts that maintain a connection with fashion. A multimedia artist, who creates websites or advertisements for fashion lines using sound and visuals, has a much better chance of <u>hiring than a fashion designer</u>. A graphic designer — someone who
      36
concentrates on visuals for magazines, television, websites, and <u>media</u> — can have as fulfilling
                            37
a career as a clothing designer. A novelist may be struck by the lightning of fame and achieve a spot on the bestseller list, but technical writers are more likely to find steadier work writing instruction manuals for computers and communicating advanced technical information in journals and reports. <u>Those who work in creative fields have a better outlook for employment than the projected</u>
                                                  38
<u>average increase in all jobs.</u> Architects, who design homes and commercial structures, have an especially <u>robust</u> job outlook.
         39

To explore these jobs and <u>finding out about</u>
                              40
many others, the United States government publishes the *Occupational Outlook Handbook,* online and in print. In this handbook, thousands upon thousands of occupations <u>are being described</u>.
                                           41
The <u>medium</u> salaries are listed; furthermore, the
     42

handbook gives you the entry-level education requirement. Each occupation is cross-referenced to "similar occupations," so a person can find <u>their other</u> potential careers. The handbook also
      43
discusses duties associated with the job, the working conditions, and training.

Even in high school, students should begin to consider how to enter the workforce and in what capacity. Of course, the future always presents some unknown factors, and people change as they experience life. It's possible for someone interested in, for example, chemistry, to decide that law is more appealing after taking courses in political science or criminal justice. Still, planning can pay off. It's not impossible to change majors in college or to jump from one field to another after graduating, but sometimes catching up is harder than starting out with a goal in mind. The key is to maintain an open mind when thinking about careers, <u>and balancing it with</u> solid preparation.
                   44
This preparation may be classes in an area of interest, summer or afterschool employment, or internships.

| Field | Ten-Year Job Outlook (2012–2022) |
|---|---|
| fashion designers | − 3% |
| graphic designers | + 7% |
| art directors | + 3% |
| crafts and fine artists | + 3% |
| architects | + 17% |
| multimedia artists and designers | + 6% |
| writers (literary) | + 3% |
| technical writers | + 17% |
| all US jobs, in any field | + 10.8% |

*Source: US Bureau of Labor Statistics*

**34.** (A) NO CHANGE
   (B) considering
   (C) consider
   (D) have considered

**35.** (A) NO CHANGE
   (B) high-profile
   (C) large-profile
   (D) high-profiled

**36.** (A) NO CHANGE
   (B) hiring than a fashion designer does
   (C) having been hired than a fashion designer
   (D) being hired than a fashion designer

**37.** (A) NO CHANGE
   (B) other media
   (C) other mediums
   (D) other medias

**38.** Which of the following best represents the information depicted in the table?
   (A) NO CHANGE
   (B) The projected outlook for creative fields is slightly better than the outlook for employment in all United States jobs.
   (C) The projected outlook for creative fields is not as good as the outlook for employment in all United States jobs.
   (D) Those who work in creative fields have good outlook for employment than the projected average increase in all jobs.

**39.** (A) NO CHANGE
   (B) full
   (C) complete
   (D) hearty

**40.** (A) NO CHANGE
   (B) to find out about
   (C) to find out on
   (D) finding out for

**41.** (A) NO CHANGE
   (B) have been described
   (C) describe
   (D) are described

**42.** (A) NO CHANGE
   (B) median
   (C) media
   (D) medial

**43.** (A) NO CHANGE
   (B) their
   (C) other
   (D) the other

**44.** (A) NO CHANGE
   (B) balancing by
   (C) and balanced with
   (D) balanced with

GO ON TO NEXT PAGE

# Section 3: Math Test — No Calculator Allowed

TIME: 25 minutes for 20 questions

DIRECTIONS: This section contains two different types of questions. For Questions 1–15, choose the best answer to each question and darken the corresponding oval on the answer sheet. For Questions 16–20, follow the separate directions provided before those questions.

**Notes:**

- You may not use a calculator.

- All numbers used in this exam are real numbers.

- All figures lie in a plane.

- All figures may be assumed to be to scale unless the problem specifically indicates otherwise.

- The domain of a given function $f$ is the set of all real numbers $x$ for which $f(x)$ is a real number, unless the problem specifically indicates otherwise.

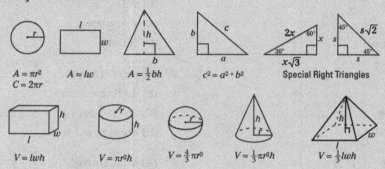

$A = \pi r^2$
$C = 2\pi r$
$A = lw$
$A = \frac{1}{2}bh$
$c^2 = a^2 + b^2$
Special Right Triangles

$V = lwh$
$V = \pi r^2 h$
$V = \frac{4}{3}\pi r^3$
$V = \frac{1}{3}\pi r^2 h$
$V = \frac{1}{3}lwh$

- The number of degrees in a circle is 360.

- The number of radians in a circle is $2\pi$.

- The sum of the measures of the angles of a triangle is 180.

---

**1.** If $2a + 3b = 17$ and $2a + b = 3$, then $a + b =$

(A) 1

(B) 5

(C) 7

(D) 10

**2.** A bicycle has a front wheel radius of 15 inches. If the bicycle wheel travels 10 revolutions, how far has a point on the outside of the wheel traveled, in inches?

(A) $10\pi$

(B) $30\pi$

(C) $300\pi$

(D) $450\pi$

**3.** If $p$ and $q$ are positive integers, then $\left(5^{-p}\right)\left(5^{q+1}\right)^{p}$ is equivalent to

(A) $5^{pq+p}$

(B) $5^{pq}$

(C) $5^{pq-p}$

(D) $5^{q+1}$

**4.** In a set of five positive whole numbers, the mode is 90 and the average (arithmetic mean) is 80. Which of the following statements is false?

(A) The number 90 appears two, three, or four times in the set.

(B) The number 240 cannot appear in the set.

(C) The number 80 must appear exactly once in the set.

(D) The five numbers must have a sum of 400.

**5.** In a triangle, the second side is 3 centimeters longer than the first side. The length of the third side is 5 centimeters less than twice the length of the first side. If the perimeter is 34 centimeters, find the length, in centimeters, of the longest side.

(A) 3

(B) 9

(C) 12

(D) 13

**6.** Melvin, Chris, Enoch, Dave, Carey, Mike, Dan, and Peter are choosing dorm rooms for college. Each room holds four people. They have the following requirements:

  I. Mike and Melvin refuse to live together.

  II. Enoch will live with Chris or Carey (or possibly both).

  III. If Dave and Dan live together, Peter will live with them.

When rooms are chosen, Melvin, Carey, and Dan live together. Which of the following groups must live in the other room?

(A) Chris, Dave, and Mike

(B) Chris, Mike, and Peter

(C) Dave, Enoch, and Peter

(D) Dave, Mike, and Peter

**7.** If the distance from Springfield to Watertown is 13 miles and the distance from Watertown to Pleasantville is 24 miles, then the distance from Pleasantville to Springfield in miles could not be

(A) 10

(B) 11

(C) 13

(D) 24

**8.** In a certain game, there are only two ways to score points; one way is worth 3 points, and the other is worth 5 points. If Brandon's total score is 61, which of the following could be the number of 3-point scores that Brandon had?

(A) 10

(B) 11

(C) 12

(D) 13

**9.** Which of the following complex numbers is equal to $(2-3i)-(4i^2+5i)$ for $i^2=-1$?

(A) $6+2i$

(B) $6-2i$

(C) $6-8i$

(D) $6-12i$

**10.** If the square of $x$ is 12 less than the product of $x$ and 5, which of the following expressions could be used to solve for $x$?

(A) $x^2=5x-12$

(B) $x^2=12-5x$

(C) $2x=12-5x$

(D) $2x=5x-12$

**11.** If $2y-c=3c$, then $y=$

(A) $\frac{c}{2}$

(B) $c$

(C) $\frac{3c}{2}$

(D) $2c$

**12.** The solution set to the equation $|3x-1|=7$ is

(A) $\{2\}$

(B) $\left\{2,\frac{2}{3}\right\}$

(C) $\left\{-2,\frac{2}{3}\right\}$

(D) $\left\{-2,\frac{8}{3}\right\}$

GO ON TO NEXT PAGE ➤

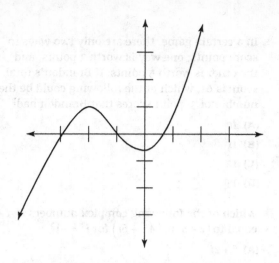

**13.** If this graph represents $f(x)$, then the number of solutions to the equation $f(x) = 1$ is

(A) zero

(B) one

(C) two

(D) three

**14.** A square with an area of 25 is changed into a rectangle with an area of 24 by increasing the width and reducing the length. If the length was reduced by 2, by how much was the width increased?

(A) 2

(B) 3

(C) 4

(D) 5

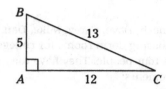

**15.** In triangle ABC above, if $\sin B = \frac{12}{13}$ and $\cos B = \frac{5}{13}$, what is $\tan C$?

(A) $\frac{5}{13}$

(B) $\frac{12}{13}$

(C) $\frac{5}{12}$

(D) $\frac{12}{5}$

**Directions for Questions 16–20:** Solve the problem and then write your answer in the box provided on the answer sheet. Mark the ovals corresponding to the answer, as shown in the following example. Note the fraction line and the decimal points.

Answer: 7/2  Answer: 3.25  Answer: 853

Write your answer in the box. You may start your answer in any column.

Although you do not have to write the solutions in the boxes, you do have to blacken the corresponding ovals. You should fill in the boxes to avoid confusion. Only the blackened ovals will be scored. The numbers in the boxes will not be read.

There are no negative answers.

A mixed number, such as $3\frac{1}{2}$, may be gridded in as a decimal (3.5) or as a fraction ($\frac{7}{2}$). Do not grid in $3\frac{1}{2}$; it will be read as $\frac{31}{2}$.

Grid in a decimal as far as possible. Do not round your answer and leave some boxes empty. Also, do not place a leading zero before the decimal; for example, grid .5 not 0.5.

A question may have more than one answer. Grid in one answer only.

16. Lauren took four exams. Her scores on the first three were 89, 85, and 90. If her average (arithmetic mean) on all four exams was 90, what did she get on the fourth exam?

17. If $p > 0$ and the distance between the points $(4, -1)$ and $(-2, p)$ is 10, find $p$.

18. If $a - b = 8$ and $ab = 10$, find $a^2 + b^2$.

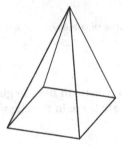

19. The preceding pyramid has a square base of length 10 centimeters and a height of 12 centimeters. Determine the total surface area of all five faces, in square centimeters.

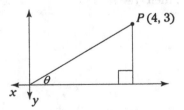

20. In the preceding drawing, what is $5(\sin\theta)$?

# Section 4: Math Test — Calculator Allowed

**TIME:** 55 minutes for 38 questions

**DIRECTIONS:** This section contains two different types of questions. For Questions 1–30, choose the best answer to each question and darken the corresponding oval on the answer sheet. For Questions 31–38, follow the separate directions provided before those questions.

**Notes:**

- You may use a calculator.
- All numbers used in this exam are real numbers.
- All figures lie in a plane.
- All figures may be assumed to be to scale unless the problem specifically indicates otherwise.
- The domain of a given function $f$ is the set of all real numbers $x$ for which $f(x)$ is a real number, unless the problem specifically indicates otherwise.

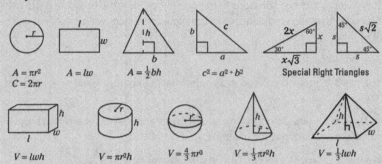

$A = \pi r^2$
$C = 2\pi r$

$A = lw$

$A = \frac{1}{2}bh$

$c^2 = a^2 + b^2$

**Special Right Triangles**

$V = lwh$

$V = \pi r^2 h$

$V = \frac{4}{3}\pi r^3$

$V = \frac{1}{3}\pi r^2 h$

$V = \frac{1}{3}lwh$

- The number of degrees in a circle is 360.
- The number of radians in a circle is $2\pi$.
- The sum of the measures of the angles of a triangle is 180.

1. In a 28-student class, the ratio of boys to girls is 3:4. How many girls are there in the class?

   (A) 4
   (B) 9
   (C) 12
   (D) 16

2. If $f(x) = 2x^4$, then $f(-2) =$

   (A) −256
   (B) −32
   (C) 32
   (D) 256

3. In a drawer are seven pairs of white socks, nine pairs of black socks, and six pairs of brown socks. Getting dressed in a hurry, Josh pulls out a pair at a time and tosses them on the floor if they are not the color he wants. Looking for a brown pair, Josh pulls out and discards a white pair, a black pair, another black pair, and another white pair. What is the probability that on his next reach into the drawer he will pull out a brown pair of socks?

   (A) $\frac{1}{3}$
   (B) $\frac{3}{11}$
   (C) $\frac{6}{17}$
   (D) $\frac{7}{18}$

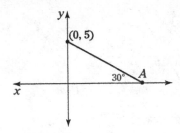

**4.** What are the coordinates of Point A in the diagram above?

(A) $(0,10)$

(B) $(5,0)$

(C) $(5\sqrt{3},0)$

(D) $(10\sqrt{3},0)$

**5.** Evaluate $\left(4^{0}+64^{1/2}\right)^{-2}$

(A) $-81$

(B) $\dfrac{1}{81}$

(C) $\dfrac{1}{6}$

(D) $3$

**6.** The ratio of Dora's money to Lisa's money is 7:5. If Dora has $24 more than Lisa, how much does Dora have?

(A) $10

(B) $14

(C) $60

(D) $84

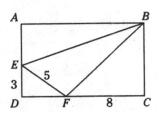

**7.** Given that *ABCD* is a rectangle, and triangle *BCF* is isosceles, find the length of the line segment *BE* in this diagram.

(A) 10

(B) 11

(C) 12

(D) 13

**8.** On a number line, Point A is at −4, and Point B is at 8. Where would a point be placed $\frac{1}{4}$ of the distance from A to B?

(A) −2

(B) −1

(C) 1

(D) 2

**9.** A batch of mixed nuts was created by adding 5 pounds of peanuts, costing $5.50 per pound, to 2 pounds of cashews, costing $12.50 per pound. What would be the cost, per pound, of the resulting mixture?

(A) $7.35

(B) $7.50

(C) $9.00

(D) $10.50

**10.** If $\dfrac{x-1}{x-2}=\dfrac{x+7}{x+2}$, then $x$ equals:

(A) 1

(B) 2

(C) 3

(D) 4

$$\sqrt{2bx-2c}+5=7$$

**11.** Based on the preceding equation, what is the value of $bx-c$?

(A) $\dfrac{1}{4}$

(B) $\dfrac{1}{2}$

(C) 1

(D) 2

GO ON TO NEXT PAGE

**12.** The volume of a gas, V, in cubic centimeters (cc), is directly proportional to its temperature, T, in Kelvins (K). If a gas has a volume of 31.5 cc at 210 K, then its volume at 300 K would be

(A) 121.5 cc

(B) 49 cc

(C) 45 cc

(D) 22.05 cc

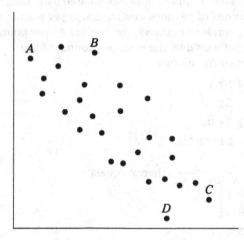

**13.** If the data in the preceding scatter plot were approximated by a linear function, the line would come closest to which pair of points?

(A) A and B

(B) A and C

(C) B and C

(D) C and D

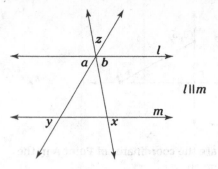

$l \parallel m$

**14.** In the preceding diagram, $x = 70°$ and $y = 30°$. The sum $a + b + z$ equals

(A) 90°

(B) 100°

(C) 120°

(D) 180°

$$y = 20x + 25$$

**15.** The preceding equation models the total cost $y$, in dollars, that a sports shop charges a customer to rent a pair of skis for $x$ days. The total cost consists of a flat fee plus a charge per day. When the equation is graphed in the $xy$-plane, what does the $y$-intercept of the graph represent in terms of the model?

(A) Total daily charges of $45

(B) A flat fee of $25

(C) A charge per day of $20

(D) A charge per day of $25

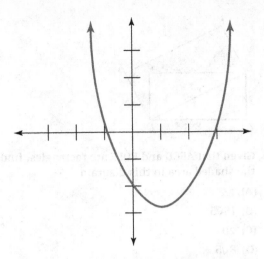

**16.** The above graph represents a function, $f(x)$. Which of the following graphs could represent $f(x+4)$?

(A)

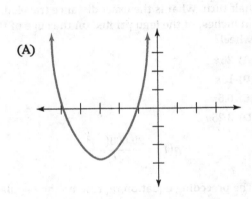

(B)

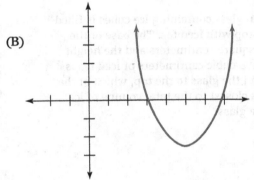

(C)

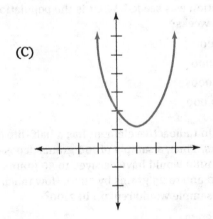

(D)

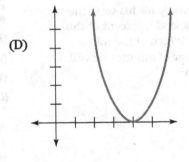

GO ON TO NEXT PAGE

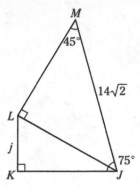

**17.** In this diagram, the measure of side $j$ is

(A) 7

(B) $7\sqrt{2}$

(C) $7\sqrt{3}$

(D) 14

**18.** A cylindrical glass containing ice cubes is filled to the very top with iced tea. The base of the glass is 20 square centimeters and the height is 10 cm. If 78 cubic centimeters of iced tea is needed to fill the glass to the top, which of the following is closest to the total volume of ice cubes in the glass?

(A) 22

(B) 78

(C) 122

(D) 145

**19.** Max has three hours to study for his tests the next day. He decides to spend $k$ percent of this time studying for math. Which of the following represents the number of minutes he will spend studying for math?

(A) $\frac{k}{300}$

(B) $\frac{3k}{100}$

(C) $\frac{100k}{180}$

(D) $\frac{180k}{100}$

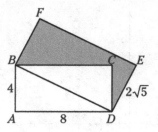

**20.** Given that $ABCD$ and $BDEF$ are rectangles, find the shaded area in this diagram.

(A) 24

(B) $16\sqrt{5}$

(C) 20

(D) $8\sqrt{5}$

**21.** A 26-inch-diameter bicycle wheel rotates a half turn. What is the exact distance traveled, in inches, of the logo printed on the edge of the wheel?

(A) $26\pi$

(B) $13\pi$

(C) $6.5\pi$

(D) $3.25\pi$

$$p(t) = \frac{20{,}000(2)^{\frac{t}{4}}}{t}$$

**22.** The preceding equation represents the population of a yeast culture, $p$, for $t$ weeks after the population was seeded. What is the population after 8 weeks?

(A) 10,000

(B) 20,000

(C) 40,000

(D) 160,000

**23.** A certain radioactive element has a half-life of 20 years. Thus, a sample of 100 grams deposited in 1980 would have decayed to 50 grams by 2000 and to 25 grams by 2020. How much of this sample would remain in 2100?

(A) $\frac{25}{16}$ grams

(B) $\frac{25}{8}$ grams

(C) $\frac{25}{4}$ grams

(D) $\frac{25}{2}$ grams

**24.** Set $S$ contains the numbers 20 to 40, inclusive. If a number is chosen at random from $S$, what is the probability that the number is even?

**(A)** $\frac{1}{2}$

**(B)** $\frac{10}{21}$

**(C)** $\frac{11}{21}$

**(D)** $\frac{11}{20}$

**25.** A circle in the $xy$-plane has the equation $(x-4)^2+(y-1)^2=9$. Which of the following points lies in the interior of the circle?

**(A)** $(-4,1)$

**(B)** $(-1,1)$

**(C)** $(0,0)$

**(D)** $(4,-1)$

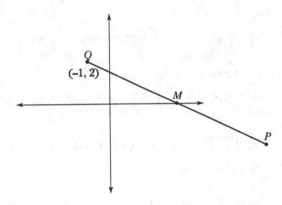

**26.** In this figure, the slope of line $\ell$ is $-\frac{1}{3}$, and $M$ is the midpoint of the line $PQ$. What are the coordinates of Point $P$?

**(A)** $(8,-1)$

**(B)** $(9,-1)$

**(C)** $(10,-2)$

**(D)** $(11,-2)$

**27.** If $ab=n$, $b+c=x$, and $n\neq 0$, which of the following must equal $n$?

**(A)** $ax+c$

**(B)** $ax-c$

**(C)** $a(x-c)$

**(D)** $x(a-c)$

**28.** The number $g$ is divisible by 3 but not by 9. Which of the following could be the remainder when $7g$ is divided by 9?

**(A)** 0

**(B)** 2

**(C)** 4

**(D)** 6

**29.** If $a>0$, which of the following statements must be true?

**(A)** $a^2>a$

**(B)** $a>\frac{1}{a}$

**(C)** $2a>a$

**(D)** $\frac{1}{a}<1$

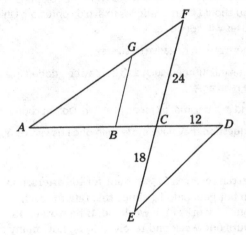

**30.** In this diagram, $AF \parallel ED$, $GB \parallel EF$, and $AG=GF$. What is the length of $AB$?

(*Note:* Figure not drawn to scale.)

**(A)** 18

**(B)** 16

**(C)** 12

**(D)** 8

GO ON TO NEXT PAGE

**Directions for student-produced response questions 31-38:** Solve the problem and then write your answer in the boxes on the answer sheet. Mark the ovals corresponding to the answer, as shown in the following example. Note the fraction line and the decimal points.

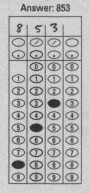

Answer: 7/2     Answer: 3.25     Answer: 853

Write your answer in the box. You may start your answer in any column.

Although you do not have to write the solutions in the boxes, you do have to blacken the corresponding ovals. You should fill in the boxes to avoid confusion. Only the blackened ovals will be scored. The numbers in the boxes will not be read.

There are no negative answers.

A mixed number, such as $3\frac{1}{2}$, may be gridded in as a decimal (3.5) or as a fraction ($\frac{7}{2}$). Do not grid in $3\frac{1}{2}$; it will be read as $\frac{31}{2}$.

Grid in a decimal as far as possible. Do not round your answer and leave some boxes empty.

A question may have more than one answer. Grid in one answer only.

31. Darren receives $15 an hour for his afterschool job but gets paid $1\frac{1}{2}$ times this rate for each hour he works on a weekend. If he worked 18 hours one week and received $315, how many of these hours did he work during the weekends?

32. In a school survey, 40% of all students chose history as their favorite subject; 25% chose English; and 14 students chose some other subject as their favorite. How many students were surveyed?

33. Find the value of $x$ that satisfies $\sqrt{4x-8}+1=7$.

34. If $\sqrt{|x+3|}=3$ and $x \geq 0$, what is the value of $x$?

35. $y = x^2 - 2x + 6$
    $y = 2x + 3$

If the ordered pair $(x,y)$ satisfies the preceding system of equations, what is one possible value of $x$?

36. To rent a private party room in a restaurant, there is a fixed cost plus an additional fee per person. If the cost of a party of 8 is $270 and the cost of a party of 10 is $320, find the cost, in dollars, of a party of 18.

**Questions 37 and 38 are based on the following information.** Tom invested $1,200 into two accounts. One account yields 5 percent simple annual interest, and the other yields 7 percent simple annual interest.

37. If after exactly one year, the two investments yielded a total of $74 in interest, how much, in dollars, was invested into the account earning 5 percent interest? Ignore the dollar sign when gridding your answer.

38. If Tom wants his investment to yield a total of $160 in interest over a period of exactly two years, how much, in dollars, must he transfer from the account yielding 5 percent to the account yielding 7 percent? Ignore the dollar sign when gridding your answer.

**STOP**

DO NOT TURN THE PAGE UNTIL TOLD TO DO SO     DO NOT RETURN TO A PREVIOUS TEST

# Section 5: The Essay

**TIME:** 50 minutes

As you read this passage, consider how the author uses the following:

- Facts, examples, and other types of evidence to support his assertions

- Logical structure and reasoning to link ideas and evidence

- Elements of style, such as figurative language, word choice, and so forth, to make his case

*This passage is excerpted from* **Content Nation** *by John Blossom (Wiley).*

(1)     If you use technology to create information and experiences that can be shared with others, you're a publisher. Some of your personal activities may seem to be too small in scope to put under the banner of a word like "publishing." After all, not everything that we publish has a huge audience or seems to be very important, but if others find that what you've shared is valuable, then you've achieved what every publisher in the world tries to achieve.

(2)     With the advent of the Internet and other advanced communication networks, though, the scale of what one person can do with publishing tools has changed radically. Affordable computers, mobile phones, and many other types of devices connected to communications networks have enabled billions of people to share content with one another locally and globally as never before. Technology now allows any person on the planet to publish things to virtually any number of people in any place at any time at little or no cost — without their knowing in great detail how it happens. Worldwide publishing, once the pursuit of a handful of wealthy and powerful people, is now a tool in the hands of the world. Students, farmers, business professionals, teachers, researchers, politicians, homemakers, and anyone else who can access our global communications networks are now engaging with other people who have similar interests and establishing appreciation for one another through their common publishing capabilities. Much of this publishing takes place on social media.

(3)     Because of its publishing capability, social media offers us the opportunity to consider what it is to be human in ways that humankind has not been able to explore effectively for thousands of years. When the people with whom we build close bonds and upon whom we rely for success in life could be anywhere in the world from any way of life, the potential for our future as a species of life on this planet takes on a new and startling form. Instead of the organism of centralized civilization, we have been handed back the keys to create our own new civilizations as we please. Many will choose to enhance very traditional forms of human existence through social media, with many rapidly evolving and shifting points of highly valuable collaboration and production, which can scale to mass goods and services very efficiently.

(4)     In enabling major shifts in where value is produced in human society, we will not be throwing away the advantages and legacies of modern civilization. Instead, we will be leveraging them to support new forms of value, allowing mass production and mass culture to benefit us when and where it pleases us, but being able to produce more value independent of the highly centralized distribution and control mechanisms of traditional civilization. The culture of artificial scarcity, encouraged by highly centralized publishing and marketing mechanisms, will give way through social media to a culture more focused on identifying and exploiting the natural abundance of human insight and innovation rapidly and efficiently, enabling more people to collaborate on projects large and small that respond to the threats and opportunities in a changing world more effectively.

(5)     In the process of becoming a society focused on exploiting the abundance found in human abilities, we are likely to see political changes as well. It will become ever harder to communicate political themes and objectives that don't have authentic support from everyday people. If the era of television ushered in mass communications that enabled the selling of politicians like tubes of toothpaste, social media ushers in the era of politics in which most facts impacting politics and policies are

**GO ON TO NEXT PAGE** ➡

known instantly and openly. Political victories go to politicians who know how to influence grass-roots political conversations most effectively. Like many things in social media, the transformation that can come in political circles is less about technologies than it is about the ability of those technologies to scale rapidly and effectively to any level of human organization to build effective bonds between people.

The impact of social media's influence can be deceptively simple depending on the scale you use to apply it, just like the changes that a piece of ice can make may be deceptively simple based on scale. Let a small cube of ice melt on a table, and something simple has changed. Put a mile of ice over a continent and life is changed forever. So it will be with the scale and depth of Content Nation's influential impact as it begins to reach into the lives of every person on the planet. (6)

---

**DIRECTIONS:** Write an essay in which you explain how Blossom builds an argument to persuade his audience that social media has created a fundamental change in the way human beings relate to one another. In your essay, analyze how Blossom uses elements of style to persuade readers to agree with his argument. Concentrate your analysis on the most important features of the passage.

Do not state whether you agree with Blossom's claims. Instead, show how Blossom argues his point.

---

DO NOT TURN THE PAGE UNTIL TOLD TO DO SO  **STOP**  DO NOT RETURN TO A PREVIOUS TEST

# Chapter 17

# Practice Exam 2: Answers and Explanations

After you finish taking Practice Exam 2 in Chapter 16, spend some time going through the answers and explanations in this chapter to find out which questions you missed and why. Even if you answered every question correctly, read the explanations in this chapter because you'll find some tips and warnings in the explanations that will help you be ready-set-go for the actual SAT. If you're short on time, you can quickly check your answers with the abbreviated answer key at the end of the chapter.

Once you've counted the correct answers for each test, refer to Chapter 18 to get your score! If it didn't go so hot, don't worry: check *each* wrong answer for *why* you got it wrong. Most times it's a simple mistake or oversight that's easy to fix — but you need to know about it in order to fix it.

## Answers for Section 1: Reading

1. **D.** This passage displays Dickens's famous ability to create a character with just a few words. Miss Murdstone's "very heavy eyebrows" (Line 4) are described as the whiskers (facial hair) she would have on her chin and cheeks if she were a man. The wording is a little confusing, so this question is really testing whether you can decode old-fashioned and complicated expressions. Here's the translation: Miss Murdstone is "disabled by the wrongs of her sex" (women don't, in general, have whiskers!), and she "carried" (Line 6), or wore, the eyebrows "to that account," which in modern terms would be *on account of that fact* or *because of that fact.*

2. **A.** Miss Murdstone is literally covered with metal. Choice (B) is wrong because her "hard black boxes" have "her initials on the lids in hard brass nails" (Lines 8–9). Choice (C) is out because her purse is made of "hard steel" (Line 11). You can eliminate Choice (D) because the purse is kept in a "jail of a bag" (Line 12) and suspended by a "chain"

(Line 13). Jails are characterized by metal bars, and chains are usually made of metal. All that's left is her *disposition*, or tendency, which is certainly nasty but not made of metal.

3. **C.** Miss Murdstone is described as having a version of men's whiskers as eyebrows, because women can't grow whiskers. She wore her eyebrows "to that account" (Line 7), or for that reason. Choice (C) is correct.

4. **B.** The narrator has just heard Miss Murdstone say, "Generally speaking . . . I don't like boys" (Lines 20–21), followed by the social formula, "How d'ye do" (Line 22), which is "How do you do?" in modern terms. It's not surprising that the narrator's response doesn't have a lot of sincerity, and instead has *mediocre* (medium, so-so) grace to it.

5. **D.** According to the narrator, Miss Murdstone's room is "from that time forth a place of awe and dread" (Lines 29–30). *Dread* is another word for extreme fear, so Choice (D) wins the gold medal for this question. Did Choice (B) catch your eye? The SAT-makers like to throw in an answer that appears in the passage but doesn't answer the question they're asking. Miss Murdstone is supposed to "help" (Line 39) the narrator's mother, but the narrator's relationship with Miss Murdstone isn't included in that statement.

6. **C.** As you see in the explanation to Question 5, the room of "awe and dread" supports the correct answer — Choice (D) — *is characterized by fear.*

7. **D.** Quotation marks can indicate a quote, or they can indicate a gap between intention and reality. Miss Murdstone is supposed to be helping, and she may even have used that word in describing her own actions. But later in the sentence, the narrator says that she made *havoc in the old arrangements* by moving things around. *Havoc* means "chaos," and creating chaos doesn't help anyone. Thus, Choice (D) is the best answer.

8. **A.** When Peggotty says that Miss Murdstone "slept with one eye open" (Line 55), Peggotty is using a figure of speech to describe Murdstone's *vigilance*, or watchfulness. The narrator says that he "tried it" (Line 56) and "found it couldn't be done" (Lines 57–58) because he accepted Peggotty's words as the *literal*, or actual, truth. His confusion comes from his ignorance; he's just too young to separate a figure of speech from reality. The only other possibility is Choice (D) because the narrator does experiment with his own sleep. However, Choice (A) is better because the narrator isn't questioning Peggotty's comment (and *inquisitive* means "tending to ask questions"). Instead, he's trying to duplicate what he believes is Miss Murdstone's habit.

9. **D.** You probably thought you'd need a line about Peggotty here, but in fact the best evidence shows the narrator's reaction to Peggotty. As you see in the explanation to Question 8, the narrator reveals his ignorance by trying to sleep with "one eye open" (Line 55).

10. **C.** The narrator is *not* a fan of Miss Murdstone; he criticizes her harsh nature (all those references to metal in the first paragraph!) and her behavior toward him (she says that she doesn't like boys). She turns her room into a place of "awe and dread" (Line 30). Sounds critical, don't you think? Choice (C) is correct.

11. **C.** The passage begins with the statement that citizens "have the absolute right to agree or disagree with the present laws" (Lines 1–3). Later, the author says that people have the right "to organize, to agitate, to do our best to change the laws" (Lines 6–7). Although the passage as a whole discusses who has the right to vote, the more *fundamental* (basic) message is that citizens can protest and work to change laws that they believe are unjust. Choice (C) fits perfectly here.

12. **D.** The passage refers to an age limit of 21, so Choice (B) doesn't work. Because an organization "demands suffrage for Chinese and Japanese who wish to become citizens" (Lines 9–11), you can deduce that Choices (A) and (C) are out. The passage refers to "a large number of people . . . [who] earnestly believe that the right of the Negro to vote should be curtailed, or even abolished" (Lines 16–19). *Curtail* is "to restrict," and *abolish* is "to do away with." You can't curtail something unless it exists. Furthermore, the third paragraph describes the gradual extension of the right to vote from the original small group of church members to "all white adults, then to include Negroes" (Lines 45–46). No doubt about it, Choice (D) is your answer.

13. **C.** The explanation to Question 12 includes the lines cited in Choice (C), which is your answer.

14. **B.** The author favors the expansion of voting rights and equality, but those are only part of what the author discusses. In Line 24, he states that democracy is not "a dogma." The footnote explains that a *dogma* is a "system of belief not open to discussion." Therefore, democracy is open to discussion, or, as Choice (B) puts it, *a process that allows disagreement.* This question illustrates a typical SAT trap — answer choices that refer only to parts of the passage and that miss the big picture. Because the passage is about voting rights, Choices (A) and (D) are appealing — but wrong!

15. **A.** Decades before Spider-Man's uncle explains that "great power brings great responsibility," the author of this passage grasped that concept. In Lines 12–15, he states that lowering the voting age would give "a large number of young men with the privileges, and therefore the educational responsibilities" of exercising that right. Choice (A) rules!

16. **B.** Check out the explanation to Question 15, and you see the lines cited in Choice (B), which is your answer.

17. **A.** Lines 34–35 state that "democracy proceeds with caution toward the extension" of the right to vote to "more and more people." The phrase "with caution" is key here, because the extension is an experiment. If one step works, the next step seems possible. Choice (A) is the answer.

18. **D.** Lines 38–39 say that "no one can prophesy how far a democracy will ultimately go," so the endpoint is unclear. The paragraph describes a gradual expansion of voting rights, which is a direction of, as Choice (D) states, a *trend.*

19. **A.** The "line" referred to in Line 48 is the limit of voting rights. It's been "constantly advancing, but with many fluctuations, eddies, and back-currents" (Lines 48–50). *Fluctuations* are changes, which can be in any direction. Similarly, *eddies* are little swirls of water, stuck for a while in one place. The "back-currents" occur when the water in the stream moves backward. All these elements are what you expect to encounter when you look at a stream — not a constant, steady move forward, but a messy flow with setbacks. Because water is part of nature, its movement is natural. Put these ideas together and you end up with Choice (A).

20. **C.** The passage *advocates* (pushes for) activism, for "more people . . . as partakers in government" (Line 4). The passage mentions the "right to organize" (Line 6), which includes petitions. How does the author feel about absentee ballots and campaign finance? No hints appear in the passage, so Choices (B) and (D) don't work. Choice (C) is the correct answer.

21. **B.** The passage argues that democracy involves discussion and disagreement, so *those who question* are participating in democracy. Choice (A) is tempting, but you don't have to argue with someone who agrees with you. Choice (B) is the best answer.

22. **A.** This question is a bit tricky because one of the answers is *almost* correct. *Almost* isn't good enough, though, on the SAT. Line 1 states that "Every surface *around us* is covered with bacteria," so you may have jumped on Choice (C). The catch is *around us*, because no one lives in a volcano, which is bacteria-free, according to Lines 10–12. Those lines cite volcanoes as exceptions to the rule that "no surface on earth is naturally sterile." So bacteria are present nearly everywhere — as Choice (A) states. Choice (B), by the way, is the direct opposite of the what the author says, and you can rule out Choice (D) because that answer choice says that the "number of bacteria on earth can be counted accurately." If the number is accurate, it is specific. The author's statement about "30 digits, give or take a digit" is vague and implies that an accurate count cannot be made.

23. **C.** As you see in the explanation to Question 22, volcanoes are the exception to the "naturally sterile" rule where bacteria do not exist, and Choice (C) is correct.

24. **D.** This question tests your ability to read carefully. The phrase "submerged sediments" comes just before "another major habitat," and defines that habitat. What are *submerged sediments*? The adjective *submerged* means "underwater," and *sediment* is "matter, mostly soil, that settles to the bottom of a body of water." Choice (D) is your answer here.

25. **B.** The chart shows that the rate of infection from Salmonella has dropped each year from 2011 to 2013.

26. **A.** Lines 30–34 refer to advertisements that "make us believe" we are not safe without "the soaps, cleansers, toothbrushes, dishwashing or laundry detergents, hand lotions" and other products. Because the ads have to "make us believe," the implication is that this idea is not true. In other words, such products aren't necessary, as Choice (A) says. Choices (B) and (C) are too general. Passage I states, "If only we could see them . . ." but doesn't say that *harmful bacteria cannot be identified* or that *homeowners should buy microscopes.* Choice (D) doesn't work because the passage refers to "raw egg whites" (Line 21) sitting on a counter, not to eggs in general.

27. **C.** This question checks whether you read carefully. The author of Passage II first discusses other organisms that live on bacteria that in turn live on "pure chemicals" (Line 47). Tube-worms, then, are part of a group. Then comes the description of these worms as "bizarre" (Line 48), followed by a statement that tube-worms are "not only huge, but they also completely lacked mouth and guts." "Guts" is another word for *digestive organs,* and Choice (C) is therefore correct.

28. **D.** Lines 60–62 refer to "sulphur-oxidizing bacteria that can use hydrogen sulphide" to react with oxygen to "get energy." The oxygen itself isn't a direct source of nourishment; it's part of a process. Because Choice (D) is not true, it's your answer.

29. **C.** In science, *react* means "to change as a result of a chemical process" — the definition best suited to the sentence, in which bacteria "use the hydrogen sulphide that's in the water" (Lines 60–61) and "react it with oxygen" (Line 62). Choice (C) is a good fit here. The runner-up is Choice (A), but *mix* is too general a word for a much more complicated process.

**30. A.** Photosynthetic organisms, the footnote tells you, combine water, carbon dioxide, and sunlight into oxygen and food. Lines 66–67 refer to organisms of this type that "live in coral and feed the coral internally." Okay, that definition fits Choice (A), because the organisms live inside the coral and supply "feed the coral internally" (Line 67). The bacteria in tube-worms use "hydrogen sulphide that's in the water" and convert it and feed the worms. Another (somewhat gross) example of food arriving from the inside, not from the supermarket! Choice (A) is best here.

**31. C.** The author of Passage I talks about "bacteria added to a health drink" (Line 35). If the health-food crowd wants to eat some types of bacteria, at least a few types are *benign* (a word meaning "harmless," with an added hint of goodness). The word *benign*, by the way, appears in the subtitle of the book. (You read the subtitle in the introduction, right?) The author of Passage II discusses the interaction between bacteria and tube-worms — a situation that is definitely beneficial to the worms. Choice (C) is your answer.

**32. C.** Reread the explanation to Question 31, and you see that these lines support the idea that bacteria aren't always the bad guys. In this case, Choice (C) is the way to go.

**33. B.** A pilot project leads the way, much as the pilot of a plane leads the passengers to their destination. (The luggage, however, is another story.) The passage tells you that not all pilot projects can be replicated, so Choice (A) can't be correct. Choice (C) doesn't apply to the term *pilot project* at all. You're left with Choices (B) and (D). Of the two, Choice (B) is better because the passage refers to *successful* pilot projects (Lines 10–11), implying that not all succeed, and Choice (D) assumes that the projects have been *proven effective.* Choice (B) is your answer.

**34. D.** The passage concerns what the author sees as the best quality of the Grameen Bank — that its model can be replicated and adapted easily, thus reaching many more poor people. The author contrasts this success with pilot projects, which, as he explains in Line 12, reach *hundreds of people* instead of the millions affected by the Grameen Bank. Choices (A), (B), and (C) deal with this limitation. Nowhere does the passage address funding, so Choice (D) is clearly the best answer.

**35. A.** Something *romanticized* is not judged fairly, because the viewer has a *romantic* bias. You know this description is true from the passage, which states that "circles where poverty and environmental issues are discussed" (Lines 14–15) — small projects are seen with a romantic eye and thus aren't evaluated fairly, as Choice (A) states. A tiny program may bring people together, as in Choice (B), but this has nothing to do with it being romanticized. Choice (C) is the opposite of what the author says in the passage. Choice (D) doesn't cut it because tiny programs by nature have limited goals.

**36. B.** A *mesh* is a net, woven from threads. Lines 32–33 refer to "the interconnected mesh" of three types of problems — "social, environmental, and economic injustices." Thus, poverty, which is the topic discussed in the passage as a whole and in this paragraph in particular, affects its victims in several ways, as Choice (B) states.

**37. B.** As you see in the explanation to Question 36, "the interconnected mesh" is the best evidence for the idea that the poor are *deprived in several different ways.* Choice (B) is your answer.

**38. D.** The caption and the graph are your clues to the correct answer here. The passage makes clear that progress is not rare, so you can rule out Choice (A). The chart shows that the Progress out of Poverty Index (the PPI) is used by many different types of organizations, so Choice (B) doesn't work. Similarly, the fact that the PPI exists shows that progress can be measured. Goodbye, Choice (C). What's left is the correct answer, Choice (D) — because the PPI measures real progress from many types of antipoverty initiatives.

**39. B.** The lines cited in the question show that Grameen Bank had some growing pains. The right formula wasn't immediately present, though the passage as a whole makes clear that the bank has succeeded. In 1991, some employees experienced "discontent" and some "carried out their duties" badly (Lines 47–50). These troubles fall into the category of *trial and error* because when you try things, you fail until you happen upon the road to success. Thus, Choice (B) is the one you seek. Choice (A) may have tempted you, but the eventual success of the Grameen Bank shows that the critics were wrong. Choice (C) flops because Bangladeshis "demonstrated those abilities as Grameen staff and borrowers" (Lines 59–60). The successful "decentralized management structure" (Lines 40–41) contradicts Choice (D). Choice (B) is the correct answer.

**40. D.** Lines 75–78 tell you that critics see the problem of poverty as complex, one needing "a solution that [takes] into account . . . ignorance, political powerlessness, and ill health." Ignorance is cured by *better education*, ill health is alleviated by *universal healthcare*, and political powerlessness is reduced by giving *political power to the poor*. Therefore, all three options are correct, and the right answer is Choice (D).

**41. C.** Check out the answer to Question 40. As you see, Lines 78 through 81 take care of all three items (education, healthcare, and political power). Choice (C) is the correct answer.

**42. A.** All the answer choices are a possible meaning of the word *conscious*, but the poor are *aware* of politics, not *alert, awake,* or *deliberate.*

**43. D.** When you think of *hysteria*, you probably picture out-of-control laughter, but the passage describes hysteria (in Lines 9–11) as Choice (A), *amnesia,* Choice (B), *paralyses,* and Choice (C), *spasms* or *involuntary movements.* Only *laughter* is missing, so Choice (D) is your answer.

**REMEMBER**

Real-world knowledge helps on the SAT Reading, but the final answer must always make sense in the context of the reading material provided.

**44. C.** The passage defines *psychological* as a state with "no discernable physical causes." Choice (C) comes the closest to this definition.

**45. A.** The second paragraph says that Charcot clarified the "psychological-traumatic nature of symptoms" and mentions survivors of train wrecks, so you can choose Choice (A) with confidence.

**WARNING**

Choice (C) is an SAT trap: It contains a statement that appears in the passage but doesn't fit the question. Hysteria was recognized as a group of illnesses after the fact, not by Charcot. Make sure the answer is specific to the question!

**46. C.** The answer to Question 45 clearly relates to these lines, which link hysteria to train wrecks and other trauma.

**47. A.** The passage implies that hysteria was once thought to be only a female disease, and Line 36 references the "so-called hysterical women on the wards of the [hospital]", therefore "of both sexes" counters that idea. Choice (A) is the right one. Also, Line 80 mentions "the old link" between hysteria and women.

**48. B.** According to Lines 41–43, Charcot says the "railway spine" and "railway brain" were cases in which "symptoms mimicked those found after spinal cord or brain injuries." This question is chock-full of little traps. Choice (A) tempts you because it mentions trains, and Choice (D) may grab your attention because Charcot did use hypnosis. Choice (C) makes sense in the real world, because when you're hurt, you have to cope with stress. But Choice (B) fits the passage and the question best.

**49. D.** Lines 59–63 tell you that memories blotted out by physical injuries to the brain couldn't be retrieved by hypnosis, so you know Choice (D) is the right answer.

**50. A.** The cited line separates amnesia, or memory loss, resulting from "hysterical and organic" causes. Lines 57–63 tell you that hypnosis helped those who were suffering from hysteria recover memories, but not those whose "amnesia was based on the destruction of brain tissue" — in other words, a physical condition. Choice (A) fits perfectly here.

**51. D.** To answer this question properly, you have to distinguish between Charcot and *the author of the passage,* a phrase that appears in the question stem. If you chose Choice (A), you fell into a trap. Charcot did treat hysteria with hypnosis, but Charcot worked in the late 19th century, and the author of the passage is writing in the 21st century. (You read the introduction to the passage, we presume. If not, resolve to read every introduction, every time. Great information can pop up there!) Choice (A) contains a present-tense verb (is). Medicine has certainly changed in the last hundred years or so, and for this reason, Choice (A) doesn't measure up. Choice (D), on the other hand, is supported by Line 23, which refers to "so-called hysterics."

**52. B.** Charcot contributed much to the understanding of hysteria, but he couldn't reach into the future and understand "medical conditions that were undiagnosable at the time" (Lines 24–25) and psychological conditions defined much later, including "severe anxiety, depression, the effects of a variety of traumas, and dissociated states" (Lines 28–30). Choice (B) is your best evidence here.

# Answers for Section 2: Writing and Language Test

**1. C.** A comma isn't strong enough to glue two complete sentences together, so the original has to change. Choices (B) and (D), however, trade one error for another because they imply that the coastlines are made of marine animals, not the coral reefs. Choice (C) takes care of the run-on sentence without losing the intended meaning.

**2. A.** The definition of *exoskeleton* is nicely tucked into the original sentence, set off by a proper comma. Choice (A) is your answer.

**TIP**

Set off a description with a comma (or two commas, if the sentence continues) if it adds extra information to the sentence. Think of the commas as little handles that can lift the description out of the sentence. If the meaning doesn't change, the commas are necessary. If you remove the description and the meaning is different, the commas have to go.

**3. B.** Each answer choice is grammatically correct, but the question wants a phrase that is consistent with the friendly tone of the passage. *Analysis, speculate,* and *encountering* are not as friendly as *when you see.*

4. **D.** The passage makes a big deal (and rightfully so!) about the past, present, and probable future death of coral reefs. To link past and present, present perfect tense is best. To match the plural subject, *10% of the coral reefs,* you need a plural verb form, *have died.*

5. **C.** This vocabulary-in-context question throws four synonyms for *end* or *die* at you. The only one appropriate for the end of a living being is *expire.* Choice (C) is correct.

6. **B.** *Actually* is the best transition to connect "all of us" to the scientists and others mentioned earlier in the sentence. It suggests that we're all in the same group. *However* implies a contrast, which isn't the case here, while *furthermore* suggests additional logic and *therefore* implies the result of the argument.

7. **C.** The sentence includes the word *but,* which implies a change in direction. You know that coral reefs cover only a small portion of the earth. The most obvious need here is a statement about their relative importance as a habitat. Stating that "they contain fish species" is a start but a fairly weak one. Choice (B) states the point but does not provide emphasis.

8. **D.** This question tests your ear for Standard English expression and vocabulary in context. Salaries and food come *from* coral reefs, either directly or indirectly. No other verb form works in this sentence. Choice (D) is simplest and best.

9. **B.** If you "say" the original sentence in your mind, you hear the preposition *by,* followed by two things — *seeding* and *then he added.* Mismatch! Go for *seeding* and *then adding* and the sentence is parallel — and correct.

10. **C.** Two sentences praise the quick growth of coral obtained by microfragmentation. Placing information on the normal growth rate between those two sentences makes no sense. The most logical spot for this information is at the beginning of the paragraph, where it serves as an introduction to the work of Dr. Vaughan. Choice (C) is better than Choice (D) because deleting the sentence deprives the reader of informative detail — an essential technique of argument.

11. **C.** The chart shows that coral suffers more from overfishing and destructive fishing in some parts of the world (Southeast Asia, for example) than in others (such as Australia). Choice (C) correctly interprets the visual evidence.

12. **C.** The original version is wordy. Why label "to separate and to join" as "things"? Choice (C) cuts unnecessary words and expresses the meaning clearly. Did you select Choice (B)? If so, you eliminated wordiness but created another problem. *Separating* and *to join* don't match, so, in grammar terms, they aren't parallel. Choice (D) inserts a semicolon, but that punctuation mark joins two complete sentences, which you don't have here. Choice (C) is the best answer.

13. **B.** The problem with the original is the comma. Two complete sentences can't be joined with just a comma. You need a semicolon (;) or a period. Choice (B) provides the period, creating two grammatically correct sentences. Choices (C) and (D) address the comma issue, but Choice (C) creates a fragment by changing *fell* to *falling,* and Choice (D) changes the meaning by introducing *because.* Go for Choice (B), the right answer.

14. **B.** You need a transition from older separatist events (the breakup of the Soviet Union and Eastern European nations) to the discussion of Scotland and Catalonia. Choice (B) creates a good bridge from the late '90s to more recent votes and is specific about *separatism* instead of *it* as in Choice (A). Choices (C) and (D) are also attempts at transitions, but Choice (C) is repetitive (*currently* and *now* say the same thing), and Choice (D) is not a complete sentence.

15. **D.** The sentence links two ideas — *staying* and, in the original version, *to form*. Mismatch! Change *to form* to *forming* and the ideas become parallel, and therefore, correct.

16. **D.** This question tests vocabulary in context. To *retain* is "to keep," but you can't *keep as* part of something. You can, however, *remain as*, which is the answer here.

17. **D.** A contrast transition is best. The Scottish referendum didn't pass, and the point that it was close is a contrast to highlight the interest in independence.

18. **C.** The pie charts show that not everyone in Catalonia was eligible to vote, and of those eligible, not all voted. The statement in the passage, therefore, needs to indicate *those who voted*. Choice (C) does this.

19. **B.** *Language* and *culture* are two things, so the plural verb *were* fits here.

20. **A.** The vote wasn't legally binding, so its value was as a symbol of discontent with the *status quo* (things as they are). The other words aren't appropriate in this context. *Figurative* refers to imaginative use of language, and *imaginary* labels something that isn't real. *Illusory* creates an illusion.

21. **D.** Mature writers eliminate short, choppy sentences by combining them. Choice (D) does so efficiently and correctly.

22. **C.** The first part of the sentence tips you off to the correct choice here. It contains the simple past-tense verb *was*. The meaning of the sentence provides no reason to switch to *had been involved* (the past perfect tense). The subject (*officials*) is plural, so you need a plural verb. Add all this together and you get the plural past tense, *were involved*, Choice (C).

23. **C.** The word *wannabe* has the right meaning, but it's too informal to match the tone of this passage. Go for *aspiring*, a formal word with the same definition.

24. **B.** When you're faced with a choice between active and passive voice (*believe* or *believed by*), go for active voice. Also, always cut unnecessary words. Choice (A) repeats *truth* and *believed to be true*. Choice (B) is active, concise, and correct.

25. **A.** When it comes to evidence, more detail is nearly always better than less. The original gives two specific facts: the number of novels James wrote and the fact that her work was "highly acclaimed." Both of these details add to the strength of the paragraph.

26. **C.** James was a writer, so her interest is in *writing* mysteries. The other choices, while grammatically correct, don't support the narrative of the passage.

27. **B.** Earlier in the paragraph, you find out that James "was always interested in writing mysteries." Repetition isn't necessary. Choice (B) is your answer.

28. **A.** To *hamper* is to "slow down" or to "place an obstacle in the way." This word nicely fits the context here. The war slowed James's plans for writing, but she eventually became an author.

29. **D.** The conjunction *even though* implies a limitation or a contradictory thought. You might say that *she went to the mall, even though she had no interest in shopping*. The meaning of this sentence doesn't fit the conjunction. Choices (C) and (D) do, but *however* isn't a conjunction and isn't allowed to link two complete sentences. Go for Choice (D) and you're correct.

30. **B.** The original sentence is a run-on, with two complete sentences linked only by a comma. A semicolon joins complete sentences, but a comma alone doesn't. Go for Choice (B).

31. **B.** The additional sentence concludes the paragraph by summing up the style and aim of James' writing, so the author should add it, making Choice (B) correct. Choice (A) is out because the purpose of the passage is to describe James' life and career, in which it succeeds without decorative quotes. Choice (C) is wrong because James' writing style is definitely within scope of the passage, and Choice (D) is wrong because the places and characters were opposite in a figurative, not literal, sense.

32. **B.** The past perfect tense, *had died,* places one event before another when the sequence of events matters. Here, the timing of James's death isn't particularly relevant to the meaning of the paragraph, so the simple past, *died,* is better. Choice (D) is correct.

33. **D.** Paragraph 4 describes James's continued success as an author, so it belongs after Paragraph 2, which describes her initial success. Paragraph 3 belongs at the end for two reasons. First, it refers to the introductory paragraph by mentioning "money and a private room," which rebuts Woolf's idea of what a writer needs and brings the passage to a full circle. Second, it discusses James's retirement and passing, which is a good way to conclude the brief biography.

34. **C.** Only *consider* is parallel to the other verbs nearby, including *think* and *envision.*

35. **B.** Two words, *high* and *profile,* combine with a hyphen to form one adjective that describes the noun *positions. Highly* is an adverb and doesn't work as a description of a noun. The correct answer is Choice (B).

36. **D.** The *artist* doesn't have a chance of *hiring* but of *being hired.* (The employer does the *hiring.*) You can therefore eliminate Choices (A) and (B). Choice (C) incorrectly places the action in the past *(having been hired).* Choice (D) is just what you need here.

**TIP**

Comparisons with *than* often omit a word. In Question 36, the word *does* is implied. Because the implied word is obvious, the meaning isn't affected and the sentence is properly constructed.

37. **B.** Magazines, television, and websites are media. To correct the logic of this comparison, add *other* to the correct plural form, *media.* Choice (B) is the right answer.

38. **C.** The chart tells you that the Bureau of Labor Statistics expects a 10.8 percent growth in all jobs. The creative jobs don't rise to that number, with the exception of architects. Choice (C) corrects the mistake.

39. **A.** The word *robust* can describe someone who has a strong, healthy body, but it also applies to *intangibles* (things that are abstract, not concrete). Here, the word correctly describes the *job outlook.*

40. **B.** This question tests two concepts: parallel structure (everything doing the same job in the sentence has the same grammatical identity) and prepositions (*about, on,* or *for* in this example). The original sentence isn't parallel because *to explore* can't pair up with *finding.* When *finding* becomes *to find,* the problem of parallel structure is solved. Next up, prepositions: In Standard English, you *find out about,* not *on* or *for.* Add these together and you arrive at Choice (B).

41. **D.** Simple present tense (*are described*) is best here. You don't need progressive tense, which puts you in the midst of an ongoing action. Nor should you connect to the past, as Choice (B) does. The *Occupational Outlook Handbook* is a book, and traditionally, present tense is best for explaining what a book contains. (Past tense works when you're talking about how the book was written or published.) Choice (C) is wrong because the *occupations* don't *describe*; they *are described*. No doubt about it, Choice (D) is the best answer.

42. **B.** *Median* is the middle value, like an average, which is the meaning you want here. *Medium* is a size, *media* refers to means of communication, and *medial* is a description of something in the middle. Here a description doesn't work, but the noun *median* does.

43. **C.** The sentence refers to *a person*, a singular noun. The plural pronoun *their* is a bad match, because singular and plural don't play nicely together in the world of grammar. You can change *their* to *his or her*, but that's not an option offered. The easiest fix is to drop the pronoun entirely, as Choice (C) does.

44. **D.** The original sentence isn't parallel, because *to keep* doesn't pair well with *and balancing it*. The simplest fix is to drop the *and* so that the verbs don't need to be parallel. Then the description *balanced with* works nicely. Choice (D) is correct.

# Answers for Section 3: Math Test — No Calculator Allowed

1. **B.** Add the two expressions:

$$2a + 3b = 17$$
$$+(2a + b = 3)$$
$$\overline{4a + 4b = 20}$$
$$a + b = 5$$

2. **C.** Ah, yes, an SAT classic. (The SAT should have its own YouTube channel. Oh wait, it does.) If the wheel has a radius of 15 inches, it has a circumference of $30\pi$ (because circumference is $2\pi r$). Ten revolutions carry a point on the outside of the wheel 10 times the circumference for $10 \times 30\pi = 300\pi$.

3. **B.** Start with $\left(5^{q+1}\right)^p$. When you take a power of a power, such as $\left(5^{q+1}\right)^p$, you multiply the powers: $\left(5^{q+1}\right)^p = \left(5^{pq+p}\right)$. Next, multiply this by the other part of the question, $\left(5^{-p}\right)$. When you multiply the same numbers with exponents, you add the exponents, so leave the 5 and just add the exponents. In this case, the $p$ and $-p$ cancel out, leaving the $pq$: $\left(5^{pq+p}\right)\left(5^{-p}\right) = 5^{pq}$.

4. **C.** Look at the statements one at a time. Choice (A) is true. The mode appears most often, so there will be two, three, or four 90s. Choice (B) requires you to remember the formula *total = number × mean*. In this case, the five numbers must add up to $5 \times 80 = 400$. Because you know there are at least two 90s, which add up to 180, the other three numbers must add up to 220. But because the numbers are all positive, and 240 is greater than 220, there is no room in the set for 240 and 2 additional values. However, for Choice (C), you can make a list that averages 80 but doesn't have 80 in it. The list *could* have 80 but doesn't *have to* have 80. Choice (D) is definitely true; you used this fact already when you checked Choice (A).

**5. D.** Draw the triangle with $x$ as the first side, $x+3$ as the second side, and $2x-5$ as the third side. The finished triangle looks like this:

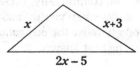

The perimeter, 34, is the sum of all the sides. Solve for $x$; then place that value for $x$ to get the side lengths:

$$(x)+(x+3)+(2x-5)=34$$
$$4x-2=34$$
$$4x=36$$
$$x=9$$
$$(9)+(9+3)+(2\cdot9-5)=34$$
$$9+12+13=34$$

**6. A.** Call the room shared by Melvin, Carey, and Dan room X, and the other room Y. Because Mike and Melvin won't live together, Mike must be in room Y. Now, if Dave and Dan live together, Peter will live with them, but you can't fit two more people into room X, so Dave and Dan must live apart, which puts Dave in room Y also. Similarly, you know that Enoch will live with Chris or Carey, so Chris can't be in room X, either. That puts Chris, Dave, and Mike in room Y.

**7. A.** Make a quick drawing of the situation. (Remember, the towns don't have to be in a straight line.)

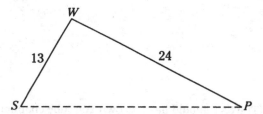

The distance you're interested in is the dotted line. Use the triangle inequality, which tells you that the sum of any two sides of a triangle must be greater than the third side. The number 10 doesn't satisfy the inequality, because $10+13=23$, which is less than 24.

**8. C.** If you multiply each of the choices by 3 points, you get 30, 33, 36, and 39. Because all the other scores are worth 5 points, you must be able to add a multiple of 5 to one of these numbers to get 61. The only one that works is 36, because $36+25=61$.

**9. C.** Distribute the negative and simplify the expression:

$$(2-3i)-(4i^2+5i)$$
$$2-3i-4i^2-5i$$
$$2-8i-4(-1)$$
$$2-8i+4$$
$$6-8i$$

**10.**  **A.** Twelve less than something is the thing minus 12, not the other way around. So you want an expression that says "$x$ squared equals 5 times $x$ minus 12," and that's Choice (A).

**11.**  **D.** To solve for $y$, isolate $y$ on one side of the equation:

$$2y - c = 3c$$
$$2y = 4c$$
$$y = 2c$$

**12.**  **D.** Solve the equation using the positive and negative values of the expression:

$$|3x - 1| = 7$$
$$3x - 1 = 7, -7$$
$$3x = 8, -6$$
$$x = \frac{8}{3}, -2$$

**13.**  **C.** The number of solutions to the equation $f(x) = 1$ is just the number of times that the graph has a height of 1, as shown here.

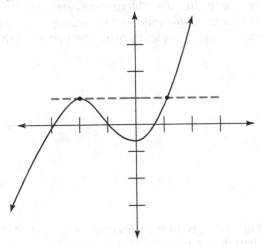

**14.**  **B.** The length and width of the square are 5 (because $5 \times 5 = 25$), so the new length, being narrower by 2, is 3. And 3 times the new width is 24 (the area of the rectangle), so the new width is 8 (because $24 \div 3 = 8$). The width went from 5 to 8, for an increase of 3.

**15.**  **C.** Using ol' SOH-CAH-TOA, because $\sin B = \dfrac{\text{opposite}}{\text{hypotenuse}} = \dfrac{12}{13}$ and $\cos B = \dfrac{\text{adjacent}}{\text{hypotenuse}} = \dfrac{5}{13}$, you can label the sides of the triangle like this:

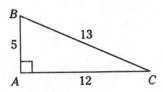

The tangent is of a different angle, but the principle is the same:

$$\tan C = \frac{\text{opposite}}{\text{adjacent}} = \frac{5}{12}$$

**16.**  **96.** This problem is easy if you remember an easy trick: *total = number × average*. In this case, the total must equal $4 \times 90 = 360$. Adding up Lauren's first three scores gives you 264, and $360 - 264 = 96$.

**17.** **7.** Remember the distance formula? It tells you that the distance between two points, $(x_1, y_1)$ and $(x_2, y_2)$ is $\sqrt{(x_2 - x_1)^2 + (y_2 - y_1)^2}$. Substituting your numbers, you get

$$10 = \sqrt{([-2]-[4])^2 + (p - [-1])^2} = \sqrt{(-6)^2 + (p+1)^2} = \sqrt{36 + (p+1)^2}$$

Square both sides, and $100 = 36 + (p+1)^2$. Now solve for $p$:

$$64 = (p+1)^2$$
$$8 = p + 1$$
$$7 = p$$

**18.** **84.** You could try to figure out what $a$ and $b$ equal, but you don't need to. The key to getting this question right is remembering the formulas discussed in Chapter 12 — specifically, the one that says that $(a - b)^2 = a^2 - 2ab + b^2$. You know that $a - b = 8$, so $(a - b)^2 = a^2 - 2ab + b^2 = 64$. You're being asked for $a^2 + b^2$, which is $(a^2 - 2ab + b^2) + 2ab$, or $64 + 2(10) = 84$.

**19.** **360.** The total surface area is the sum of the area of the square and the area of the four triangles. The square is easy: It's $10 \times 10 = 100$. The triangles are tougher. They don't have a height of 12. Twelve is the height of the pyramid, but the triangles are slanted. However, you can find the height of the slanted triangles by using the Pythagorean theorem, as shown in the following diagram:

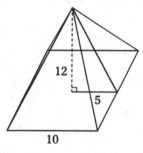

That little triangle in the diagram is a right triangle. One leg is 12, the height of the pyramid. The second leg is half the width of the square, or 5. This is a common right triangle, the 5-12-13 triangle. (If you didn't remember this one, you could have figured it out with the Pythagorean theorem.)

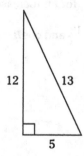

The hypotenuse, 13, is the altitude of each of the tilted triangles that make up the sides of the pyramid. Because the triangle's area is $\frac{1}{2} \times base \times height$, each triangle's area is $\frac{1}{2} \times 10 \times 13 = 65$. The four triangles together have an area of $4 \times 65 = 260$. Adding in the 100 from the base gives you 360.

**20.** **3.** Find the value of sinθ and multiply it by 5. If the coordinates of point $P$ are $(4,3)$, the diagonal is 5 (as in, 3-4-5 right triangle). Use the SOH from SOH-CAH-TOA to get that sine $\theta = \dfrac{opposite}{hypotenuse}$, which in this case is $\dfrac{3}{5}$. Multiply this by 5 for an answer of 3.

# Answers for Section 4: Math Test — Calculator Allowed

**1.** **D.** Let $3x$ equal the number of boys and $4x$ equal the number of girls. With 28 students, solve for $x$:

$$3x + 4x = 28$$
$$7x = 28$$
$$x = 4$$

Place 4 for $x$ to find the answer:

$$3x + 4x = 28$$
$$3(4) + 4(4) = 28$$
$$12 + 16 = 28$$

And there are 16 girls for an answer of Choice (D).

**2.** **C.** Plugging in the numbers gives you $2(-2)^4$. Per PEMDAS (see Chapter 10), start with the exponents:

$$2(-2)^4$$
$$2(16)$$
$$32 \text{, and } 2(16) = 32$$

**3.** **A.** The drawer had 22 pairs of socks originally. However, Josh has thrown four pairs on the floor (and you can bet his mom's going to have something to say about that). So there are now 18 pairs to choose from, of which 6 are brown. His probability of success is therefore $\dfrac{6}{18} = \dfrac{1}{3}$.

**4.** **C.** There is no shortage of 30-60-90 triangles, where the hypotenuse is always twice the shorter leg, while the longer leg equals the shorter leg times $\sqrt{3}$. Because you know the shorter leg equals 5, the longer leg is $5\sqrt{3}$, and the coordinates are $(5\sqrt{3}, 0)$.

**5.** **B.** You did fine on this one if you remembered your exponent rules: $4^0 = 1$ by definition (because anything to the 0 power equals 1), and $64^{1/2}$ is the square root of 64, which is 8. So the expression in parentheses equals $1 + 8 = 9$. And $9^{-2}$ is the reciprocal of $9^2$, which is $\dfrac{1}{81}$.

**6.** **D.** To find two numbers in the ratio 7:5 with a difference of 24, set it up with algebra: Call Dora's money $7x$ and Lisa's money $5x$, so $7x = 5x + 24$. Thus, $2x = 24$, and $x = 12$. Plugging the numbers back in (always an important step) tells you that Lisa's money is $5(12) = \$60$, and Dora's is $7(12) = \$84$.

Thus, D/(D-24) = 7/5. Cross multiply and 5D = 7D − 168, 2D = 168, so D = 84.

**7.** **D.** Because triangle $BCF$ is isosceles, $BC = CF = 8$. Because angle $D$ is a right angle, triangle $DEF$ is the world-famous 3-4-5 right triangle, and $DF = 4$. Because $DC = 4 + 8 = 12$, $AB$ is also 12. And, because $AD = BC = 8$, $AE = 8 - 3 = 5$. Now you're ready to find $EB$, the hypotenuse of the right triangle *ABE*. You can, of course, use the Pythagorean theorem, but you'll save time if you realize that you're face to face with a 5-12-13 right triangle, and *BE* = 13.

8. **B.** You can draw the line and count spaces to determine that the points are 12 units apart, or you can simply subtract: $8 - (-4) = 12$ (distance always involves a difference). Because $\frac{1}{4}$ of 12 is 3, you're looking for the point 3 units to the right of −4, and $-4 + 3 = -1$.

9. **B.** Five pounds of peanuts times $5.50 per pound is $27.50, and 2 pounds of cashews times $12.50 per pound is $25.00, so the total cost is $52.50 for 7 pounds. Divide $52.50 by 7 pounds to get $7.50 per pound.

10. **C.** You could solve for *x* by cross-multiplying or plugging in answers. Pick your poison. Cross-multiplying is probably more straightforward and saves you the risk of having to go through the process four times. It looks messy but everything cancels out.

$$\frac{x-1}{x-2} = \frac{x+7}{x+2}$$
$$(x-1)(x+2) = (x-2)(x+7)$$
$$x^2 + x - 2 = x^2 + 5x - 14$$
$$x - 2 = 5x - 14$$
$$-4x = -12$$
$$x = 3$$

11. **B.** Simplify the equation. Subtract 5, square both sides, and divide by 2 — like this:

$$\sqrt{2bx - 2c} + 5 = 7$$
$$\sqrt{2bx - 2c} = 2$$
$$2bx - 2c = 4$$
$$bx - c = 2$$

12. **C.** Direct proportion problems require a ratio — in this case, the ratio of volume to temperature. Thus, you can write $\frac{cc_1}{K_1} = \frac{cc_2}{K_2}$ and $\frac{31.5}{210} = \frac{x}{300}$. Cross-multiply to get $210x = 9,450$, and divide by 210 to get $x = 45$.

13. **B.** This scatter plot shows a negative trend, so the line of best fit would go roughly from the top left to the bottom right. However, point *D* is significantly lower than the rest of the points. If you try drawing a line between *A* and *D*, or *B* and *D*, you'll see that it's really not that close to a lot of the points. However, the line from *A* to *C* is a good approximation of the scatter plot as a whole, as you can see in this diagram.

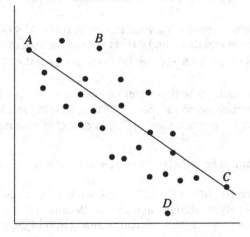

**14. D.** You don't even need to know what $x$ and $y$ equal in this problem. Look at the angle marked $c$ in the following diagram. $c$ and $z$ are vertical angles, which means that their measures are equal. Also, $a$, $c$, and $b$ form a straight line, so $a + c + b = 180°$. Therefore, $a + b + z = 180°$.

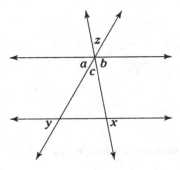

**15. B.** Walking out the door with skis, the customer is charged $25. That is the $y$-intercept of the graphed line. Each day the customer holds the skis (whether they're used or not) is another $20 charge, but that's represented by the slope of the line, not the $y$-intercept.

**16. A.** This question is based on the rules of graphed figures. $f(x)$ is another name for the $y$-value based on $x$. A higher $x$-value moves the point farther to the right. $f(x + 4)$ reads the value inside the parentheses (usually $x$, but in this case $x + 4$) as four spaces farther to the right than it actually is, so the graph moves four spaces to the left to compensate.

**17. A.** Do you remember your special triangle ratios? If not, it's okay: They're at the top of each Math section of the SAT. First, spot the common right triangles by breaking up the 75° angle at the bottom right into 45° and 30° angles. The top right triangle is a 45-45-90 triangle, which makes both of its legs equal to 14. The bottom leg is also the hypotenuse of the 30-60-90 triangle at the bottom. In a 30-60-90 triangle, the hypotenuse must be twice the shortest leg, which is $j$. Therefore, $j$ is 7.

**18. C.** If you forgot the equation for the volume of a cylinder, check the start of the SAT math section: It's right there for everyone else who forgot also. This formula, $V = \pi r^2 h$, is basically that volume is the base times the height — in this case, 20 square centimeters times 10 centimeters, for a volume of 200 cubic centimeters. Subtract the 78 cubic centimeters of iced tea, and the 122 cubic centimeters of ice cubes make up the remaining volume.

**19. D.** Because the answer is supposed to be in minutes, start by turning 3 hours into 180 minutes. You know that $k$ percent of these 180 minutes is going to be used for math. Remember that $k$ percent means $\frac{k}{100}$. Taking a percent of a number involves multiplication, so your answer is $180 \times \frac{k}{100}$, or $\frac{180k}{100}$.

**20. A.** You need the areas of rectangle $BDEF$ and triangle $BCD$. For the rectangle, you need the length of segment $BD$, which is also part of triangle $ABD$. Because you have two sides of right triangle $ABD$, use the Pythagorean theorem to find the length of the third side, which is your target $BD$: $4^2 + 8^2 = (BD)^2$, so $BD = \sqrt{80}$, or $4\sqrt{5}$. The area of the rectangle is $4\sqrt{5} \times 2\sqrt{5} = 8 \times 5 = 40$. The area of triangle $BCD$ is $\frac{8 \times 4}{2} = 16$. Subtract the two, and $40 - 16 = 24$.

**21. B.** The circumference of the wheel is $\pi d$, where $d$ is the diameter of the wheel. Because $d = 26$ inches, the circumference is $26\pi$ inches. The logo traveled half this distance, so divide the circumference by 2, for an answer of $13\pi$ inches.

**22.** **A.** Put your calculator away — this one is easy. Just plug in 8 for $t$ and the numbers work themselves out:

$$p(8) = \frac{20,000(2)^{\frac{8}{4}}}{8}$$
$$= \frac{20,000(2)^2}{8}$$
$$= \frac{20,000(4)}{8}$$
$$= \frac{80,000}{8}$$
$$= 10,000$$

**23.** **A.** Make a table for this one, dividing the sample by 2 for every 20 years:

| Year | 2000 | 2020 | 2040 | 2060 | 2080 | 2100 |
|---|---|---|---|---|---|---|
| Sample | 50 | 25 | $\frac{25}{2}$ | $\frac{25}{4}$ | $\frac{25}{8}$ | $\frac{25}{16}$ |

The final answer is $\frac{25}{16}$ grams.

**24.** **C.** First of all, there are 21 numbers, not 20, to choose from, because the set includes both 20 and 40. (You can count them to be sure.) Now, the even numbers are 20, 22, . . . and so on, up to 40, which makes five numbers in the 20s, five in the 30s, and 40, which is 11 numbers out of 21.

**25.** **D.** A circle with the equation $(x-4)^2 + (y-1)^2 = 9$ has a center of $(4,1)$ and a radius of 3, so it certainly extends down 2 from the center and covers point $(4,-1)$. However, it is entirely to the right of the $y$-axis, placing Choices (A), (B), and (C) outside the circle.

**26.** **D.** A slope of $-\frac{1}{3}$ means that the line goes down 1 unit for every 3 units it moves to the right. Because $M$ is on the $x$-axis, the line has gone down 2 units by the time it reaches $M$, so it must have moved 6 units to the right. That means that $M$ is at $(5,0)$. $M$ is the mid-point, which means that it's halfway to $P$. So, to get to $P$, move another 2 units down and 6 units right, which puts you at $(11,-2)$.

**27.** **C.** Because $b + c = x$, $b = x - c$. Substitute $(x - c)$ for $b$ in the first equation, and write $a(x - c) = n$, which is Choice (C).

**28.** **D.** Possible numbers for $g$ are numbers like 3, 6, 12, 15, 21, and so on. If you try multiplying these numbers by 7 and then dividing by 9, you discover that the remainder is always 3 or 6. Because 3 isn't one of the answer choices, the correct answer is 6. Note that the problem asks for which *could* be the remainder.

**29.** **C.** If $a$ equals 2 or more, then all the answer choices are true. However, if $a$ equals 1, or a number less than 1, such as $\frac{1}{2}$, most of answer choices become false. This question is an old SAT trap: Numbers between 0 and 1 (such as fractions) behave in funny ways. The only statement that is true for all positive numbers, whether fraction or whole, is Choice (C): Twice any positive number must be bigger than the original number.

**30.** **D.** Because there are parallel lines in this problem, you need to look for angles that are congruent. You can find them by looking for lines that make a $Z$ or a backward $Z$. Looking first at the bigger triangles, you can mark the diagram as follows:

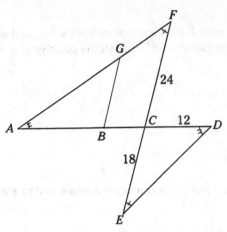

Notice that the two angles in the middle are vertical, so they're also equal. This is a picture of similar triangles: Angle F matches angle E, angle A matches angle D, and angle C is the same for both triangles. Therefore, you can use a ratio to figure out the length of AC:

$\frac{AC}{CD} = \frac{CF}{CE}$ and $\frac{AC}{12} = \frac{24}{18}$, which reduces to $\frac{AC}{12} = \frac{4}{3}$

Be careful that you match up the right parts when writing a ratio. Anyway, cross-multiplying your ratio tells you that $3(AC) = 48$, and $AC = 16$. Now, because $GB \parallel EF$, triangle ABG is similar to ACF as well. And, because $AG = GF$, the line GB cuts triangle ACF in half. That means that AB is half of AC, or 8.

31. **6.** Trial and error can work, but algebra is more reliable. Darren earns 15 dollars per hour on weekdays and $1\frac{1}{2} \times 15 = 22.50$ dollars per hour on weekends. If $d$ equals his weekday hours and $e$ equals his weekend hours, then $15d + 22.5e = 315$. Because $d + e = 18$ (his total hours), use substitution: $d = 18 - e$, so place $(18 - e)$ for $d$ in the other equation:

$$15d + 22.5e = 315$$
$$15(18 - e) + 22.5e =$$
$$270 - 15e + 22.5e =$$
$$270 + 7.5e = 315$$
$$7.5e = 45$$
$$e = 6$$

He worked 6 hours during the weekends. Just like that.

32. **40.** Sixty-five percent chose history or English, leaving 35 percent for other subjects. This 35 percent represents 14 students, so the question is, "35 percent of $x$ is 14?" Set it up like this and solve for $x$:

$$\frac{14}{x} = \frac{35}{100}$$
$$35x = 1,400$$
$$x = 40$$

33. **11.** In a radical problem, first isolate the radical, then square both sides to solve:

$$\sqrt{4x - 8} + 1 = 7$$
$$\sqrt{4x - 8} = 6$$
$$4x - 8 = 36$$
$$4x = 44$$
$$x = 11$$

**34. 6.** Copy down the equation and solve for $x$. First square both sides, and when you remove the absolute value, remember the expression has both the positive and negative values:

$$\sqrt{|x+3|} = 3$$
$$|x+3| = 9$$
$$x+3 = 9, -9$$
$$x = 6, -12$$

Because $x \geq 0$, it can only be 6.

**35. 1 or 3.** Because both expressions equal $y$, set the expressions equal to each other and solve for $x$:

$$x^2 - 2x + 6 = 2x + 3$$
$$x^2 - 4x + 3 = 0$$
$$(x-3)(x-1) = 0$$
$$x = 1, 3$$

Because $x$ could equal 1 or 3, grid in either 1 or 3, and either answer is considered correct.

**36. 520.** If the fee for each person is the same amount, and the difference in the total cost between eight people and ten people is $50 (because $320 - 270 = 50$), then each addition of two people adds $50 to the total price, and each person costs an extra $25. So 10 people cost $320, and the additional these 8 people add $200 to the price (because $8 \times 25 = 200$). Add the new $200 to the existing $320 for 10 people, and 18 people cost $520.

**37. 500.** Tom's two investments total $1,200, so set $x$ as the amount earning 5 percent and $(1,200 - x)$ as the amount earning 7 percent. Five percent of $x$ plus 7 percent of $(1,200 - x)$ equals $74, so set the equation up like this:

$$5\%(x) + 7\%(1,200 - x) = 74$$

Turn 5% and 7% into decimals 0.05 and 0.07, respectively, and solve for $x$:

Because $x$ represents the number of dollars earning 5 percent, the answer is 500.

**38. 200.** An investment that yields $160 simple interest over a period of two years yields $80 over a period of one year. Start by calculating the investment amounts needed to earn 5 percent and 7 percent. Just as in Question 37, because Tom's two investments total $1,200, set $x$ as the amount earning 5 percent and $(1,200 - x)$ as the amount earning 7 percent. Five percent of $x$ plus 7 percent of $(1,200 - x)$ equals $80 (for one year), so set the equation up like this:

$$5\%(x) + 7\%(1,200 - x) = 80$$

Turn 5% and 7% into 0.05 and 0.07 and solve for $x$:

$$0.05(x) + 0.07(1,200 - x) = 80$$
$$0.05x + 84 - 0.07x = 80$$
$$-0.02x = -4$$
$$x = 200$$

To earn $80 per year (totaling $160 over two years), Tom would need to have $200 in the account yielding 5 percent and the remaining $1,000 in the account yielding 7 percent. The question asks for the amount to be transferred from the 5 percent account to the 7 percent account. You know from Question 37 that the 5 percent account currently has $500, so Tom needs to transfer $300 to the other account, because $500 - $200 = $300.

# Answer Guidelines for Section 5: The Essay

Here are some possible points to make in your essay in response to the prompt.

## Reading

John Blossom tackles the issue of "publishing" over the internet and on social media to create what he calls a "content nation." (When you pronounce the word, the emphasis is on the first syllable, *con-*, because he refers to information.) Showing that you grasped these points contributes to your reading score:

» Blossom begins by redefining publishing, a term which he views broadly. The traditional meaning, printing and distributing through an established company, now means communicating ideas over the internet and other electronic media.

» Blossom acknowledges the power of technology to spread ideas but concedes that the audience for some "published" work is very small.

» Blossom sees new media as a force that levels the playing field. Not only the elite or traditional power structures can spread ideas but also "students, farmers, business professionals, teachers, researchers, politicians, homemakers, and anyone else" with access to the internet.

» New ways to communicate are actually redefining what it is to be human and form bonds with others.

» Marketing of goods is changing because of mass media. Again, power is spread out. Not only do stores or companies market through the internet, but individuals may also buy and sell goods.

» Politics is changing, too. Blossom refers to "authentic support from everyday people." In this sense, social media and other electronic means of communication strengthens democracy.

» Everything is a question of scale to Blossom. One person can make a difference by speaking to a small group, but electronic media allows messages to reach millions of people throughout the globe.

How did you do? If you mentioned five or six of the seven bullet points, give yourself 8 points for reading. If you hit three or four, take 6 points for reading. Only two? Award yourself 4 points. If you stayed on the main idea, take 2 points for reading.

**REMEMBER**

These guidelines are flexible. If you discussed these ideas in different terms, or if you came up with something we didn't mention, take credit — and points — for reading.

## Analysis

Now consider Blossom's writing style. All these ideas (and some not listed here) may be part of your analysis score:

» The second-person pronoun *you* immediately connects to the reader. The reader has probably used technology, so the connection becomes stronger because the reader has a stake in what Blossom is going to say.

» The first paragraph begins with a dramatic assertion: You're a publisher. (That's news to you, right?) The reader may begin to argue with Blossom at that point, but he's ready with an answer. He concedes that your "personal activities may be small in scope" but replies that "if others find that what you've shared is valuable," you have achieved what traditional publishers do. This technique is called "concession and reply." Blossom uses the same technique in Paragraph 4, when he says that "we will not be throwing away the advantages and legacies" civilization already has. You don't need to name this literary technique, but you should point out what Blossom does.

>> In the second paragraph, Blossom gives several examples of new publishing tools: the internet, affordable computers, mobile phones, and "other types of devices." These examples make his argument real to the reader, who probably owns or uses at least one of the listed tools.

>> The third paragraph employs figurative language (language that moves away from reality into the world of imagination). Civilization is "an organism" — a living creature — a metaphor that gives a sense of natural growth and development as well as human interdependence. (After all, an organism can't survive without all its parts, which work together to sustain life.) Figurative language also pops up in the statement that "we have been handed back the keys" to make a new society. The keys aren't literal (real); they are a metaphor for the transfer of power. The simile in the last paragraph, comparing the influence of social media to an ice cube, serves to illustrate large and small changes.

**TIP**

Don't obsess over technical vocabulary. Pointing out the effect of comparisons is more important than saying that one phrase is a metaphor (a comparison without *like* or *as*) and another is a simile (a comparison made with *like* or *as*). If you know the terms, use them, but don't omit an idea because you're unsure of the proper label.

>> Blossom tends to pair off ideas, often to illustrate opposites. The ice cube/ice sheet example in the last paragraph is one spot where he creates a pair. In Paragraph 2, he contrasts the past ("once the pursuit of a handful of wealthy and powerful people") to the present ("now a tool in the hands of the world").

>> Many contrasting pairs refer to scale. You find several references to small, such as in Paragraph 1, and large ("huge" in the same paragraph). In the third paragraph, you see "scale to mass goods and services," an implied comparison with smaller markets.

>> Often, the pairs referred to in the preceding bullet point appear in parallel sentences or portions of sentences. Check out where the contrast between past and present appears. Can you "hear" that the ideas are presented in parallel structure? Parallel structure links the ideas grammatically, matching the link Blossom sees in meaning.

>> The diction is formal but accessible. You don't see slang or friendly references (apart from *you* in Paragraph 1), but you don't have to swallow a dictionary to understand what Blossom is trying to say, either.

Evaluate your analysis. If you mentioned six or more of the eight bullet points, give yourself 8 points for analysis. If you hit four or five, take 6 points for analysis. Only two or three? Award yourself 4 points. If you discussed only one technique, take 2 points for analysis.

**REMEMBER**

These guidelines are flexible. If you discussed other style points or grouped several together, adjust your analysis score.

## Writing

Your final category is writing and applies to your own essay. Check these factors:

>> **Structure:** Does your essay have a solid, logical structure? One possibility is to work in order from the first paragraph of the passage, where the author states the thesis (idea to be proved), and then move through paragraph after paragraph until you reach the end of the passage.

Another possibility is first to examine Blossom's ideas on publishing, mass production, politics, and the shift of power to a larger mass of people. Then you might discuss Blossom's style, with a paragraph on his use of parallel pairs and second-person connection. Finally, examples of his diction and figurative language create a third paragraph.

» **Evidence:** Do you back up every statement you make with quotations or specific references to the passage? Count how many times you zeroed in on details. You should have at least two in every paragraph you write, and maybe more.

» **Language:** Does your essay sound formal, as if a teacher were explaining the passage? If you lapsed into slang or informal word choice, your essay is weaker.

» **Mechanics:** English teachers group grammar, spelling, and punctuation in this category. As you reread, underline any sentence fragments or run-ons, misspelled words, and faulty commas or quotation marks.

Adding up points to evaluate your writing is tricky. In general, give yourself 2 points (up to a total of 8) for each category in the bulleted list in which you excelled. If you stumbled slightly in a category (say, three or four grammar or spelling mistakes), give yourself 1 point. If you feel your performance in one of these categories was poor (perhaps you drifted off topic or made seven or eight grammar errors), take again only 1 point.

To help you evaluate your essay, take a look at the sample essays in Chapter 7. They give you a model of a poor, medium, and great essay. You can compare your work to those graded essays.

To get a fair idea of how your essay measures up to College Board standards, fill in the scoring grid in Chapter 15.

# Answer Key

## Section 1: Reading

| | | | | | | | |
|---|---|---|---|---|---|---|---|
| 1. | D | 14. | B | 27. | C | 40. | D |
| 2. | A | 15. | A | 28. | D | 41. | C |
| 3. | C | 16. | B | 29. | C | 42. | A |
| 4. | B | 17. | A | 30. | A | 43. | D |
| 5. | D | 18. | D | 31. | C | 44. | C |
| 6. | C | 19. | A | 32. | C | 45. | A |
| 7. | D | 20. | C | 33. | B | 46. | C |
| 8. | A | 21. | B | 34. | D | 47. | A |
| 9. | D | 22. | A | 35. | A | 48. | B |
| 10. | C | 23. | C | 36. | B | 49. | D |
| 11. | C | 24. | D | 37. | B | 50. | A |
| 12. | D | 25. | B | 38. | D | 51. | D |
| 13. | C | 26. | A | 39. | B | 52. | B |

## Section 2: Writing and Language

| | | | | | | | |
|---|---|---|---|---|---|---|---|
| 1. | C | 12. | C | 23. | C | 34. | C |
| 2. | A | 13. | B | 24. | B | 35. | B |
| 3. | B | 14. | B | 25. | A | 36. | D |
| 4. | D | 15. | D | 26. | C | 37. | B |
| 5. | C | 16. | D | 27. | B | 38. | C |
| 6. | B | 17. | D | 28. | A | 39. | A |
| 7. | C | 18. | C | 29. | D | 40. | B |
| 8. | D | 19. | B | 30. | B | 41. | D |
| 9. | B | 20. | A | 31. | B | 42. | B |
| 10. | C | 21. | D | 32. | B | 43. | C |
| 11. | C | 22. | C | 33. | D | 44. | D |

## Section 3: Mathematics — No-Calculator Section

| | | | | | | | |
|---|---|---|---|---|---|---|---|
| 1. | B | 6. | A | 11. | D | 16. | 96 |
| 2. | C | 7. | A | 12. | D | 17. | 7 |
| 3. | B | 8. | C | 13. | C | 18. | 84 |
| 4. | C | 9. | C | 14. | B | 19. | 360 |
| 5. | D | 10. | A | 15. | C | 20. | 3 |

## Section 4: Mathematics — Calculator Section

| | | | | | | | |
|---|---|---|---|---|---|---|---|
| 1. | D | 11. | B | 21. | B | 31. | 6 |
| 2. | C | 12. | C | 22. | A | 32. | 40 |
| 3. | A | 13. | B | 23. | A | 33. | 11 |
| 4. | C | 14. | D | 24. | C | 34. | 6 |
| 5. | B | 15. | B | 25. | D | 35. | 1 or 3 |
| 6. | D | 16. | A | 26. | D | 36. | 520 |
| 7. | D | 17. | A | 27. | C | 37. | 500 |
| 8. | B | 18. | C | 28. | D | 38. | 200 |
| 9. | B | 19. | D | 29. | C | | |
| 10. | C | 20. | A | 30. | D | | |

# Chapter **18**

# How Did You Do? Scoring Your Practice SAT

**F**our hours of work (five with the essay), and you're still not finished! After each practice SAT, calculate your scores with the steps that follow.

**TIP**

On the actual SAT, the algorithm varies slightly per exam, so 110 correct answers on one exam may yield a slightly different score from 110 correct answers on another exam.

## Finding Your Reading and Writing Score

Here's how you convert the number of questions you answered correctly to your SAT Reading and Writing score:

1.  **Count up the number of Reading Test questions that you answered correctly.**

    This is your "Reading Raw Score."

2.  **Convert your Reading Raw Score to your Reading Test Score.**

    Use this table for the conversion:

| Reading Raw Score | Reading Test Score |
| --- | --- |
| 0 | 100 |
| 1 | 100 |
| 2 | 100 |
| 3 | 100 |
| 4 | 110 |

| Reading Raw Score | Reading Test Score |
|---|---|
| 5 | 120 |
| 6 | 130 |
| 7 | 130 |
| 8 | 140 |
| 9 | 150 |
| 10 | 160 |
| 11 | 160 |
| 12 | 170 |
| 13 | 170 |
| 14 | 180 |
| 15 | 180 |
| 16 | 190 |
| 17 | 190 |
| 18 | 200 |
| 19 | 200 |
| 20 | 210 |
| 21 | 210 |
| 22 | 220 |
| 23 | 220 |
| 24 | 230 |
| 25 | 230 |
| 26 | 240 |
| 27 | 240 |
| 28 | 250 |
| 29 | 250 |
| 30 | 260 |
| 31 | 260 |
| 32 | 270 |
| 33 | 280 |
| 34 | 280 |
| 35 | 290 |
| 36 | 290 |
| 37 | 300 |
| 38 | 300 |

| Reading Raw Score | Reading Test Score |
|---|---|
| 39 | 310 |
| 40 | 310 |
| 41 | 310 |
| 42 | 320 |
| 43 | 320 |
| 44 | 330 |
| 45 | 330 |
| 46 | 340 |
| 47 | 350 |
| 48 | 360 |
| 49 | 360 |
| 50 | 370 |
| 51 | 390 |
| 52 | 400 |

**3.** **Count up the number of Writing and Language Multiple-Choice Test questions that you answered correctly.**

This is your "Writing Raw Score."

**4.** **Convert your Writing Raw Score to your Writing Test Score.**

Use this table for the conversion:

| Writing Raw Score | Writing Test Score |
|---|---|
| 0 | 100 |
| 1 | 100 |
| 2 | 100 |
| 3 | 110 |
| 4 | 110 |
| 5 | 120 |
| 6 | 130 |
| 7 | 140 |
| 8 | 140 |
| 9 | 150 |
| 10 | 160 |
| 11 | 160 |
| 12 | 170 |
| 13 | 170 |
| 14 | 180 |

| Writing Raw Score | Writing Test Score |
| --- | --- |
| 15 | 180 |
| 16 | 180 |
| 17 | 190 |
| 18 | 190 |
| 19 | 200 |
| 20 | 200 |
| 21 | 210 |
| 22 | 210 |
| 23 | 220 |
| 24 | 230 |
| 25 | 230 |
| 26 | 240 |
| 27 | 240 |
| 28 | 250 |
| 29 | 250 |
| 30 | 260 |
| 31 | 270 |
| 32 | 270 |
| 33 | 280 |
| 34 | 290 |
| 35 | 290 |
| 36 | 300 |
| 37 | 310 |
| 38 | 310 |
| 39 | 320 |
| 40 | 330 |
| 41 | 340 |
| 42 | 360 |
| 43 | 380 |
| 44 | 400 |

**5.  Add the two Test Scores.**

This is your SAT Reading and Writing score. Nice! Write the number down. Note that your essay is scored separately.

# Finding Your Math Test Score

Here's how you convert the number of questions you answered correctly to your SAT Math Test score:

1. **Count up the number of Math Test questions that you answered correctly for both Math sections.**

   Count up the questions from both the No Calc Allowed and the Calc Allowed tests for your "Math Raw Score."

2. **Convert your Math Raw Score to your Math Test Score.**

   Use this table for the conversion:

   | Math Raw Score | Math Test Score |
   | --- | --- |
   | 0 | 200 |
   | 1 | 200 |
   | 2 | 210 |
   | 3 | 220 |
   | 4 | 230 |
   | 5 | 250 |
   | 6 | 270 |
   | 7 | 280 |
   | 8 | 300 |
   | 9 | 310 |
   | 10 | 320 |
   | 11 | 340 |
   | 12 | 350 |
   | 13 | 360 |
   | 14 | 370 |
   | 15 | 380 |
   | 16 | 390 |
   | 17 | 400 |
   | 18 | 410 |
   | 19 | 420 |
   | 20 | 430 |
   | 21 | 440 |
   | 22 | 450 |
   | 23 | 460 |
   | 24 | 470 |
   | 25 | 480 |

| Math Raw Score | Math Test Score |
| --- | --- |
| 26 | 490 |
| 27 | 500 |
| 28 | 500 |
| 29 | 510 |
| 30 | 520 |
| 31 | 520 |
| 32 | 530 |
| 33 | 540 |
| 34 | 540 |
| 35 | 550 |
| 36 | 560 |
| 37 | 570 |
| 38 | 580 |
| 39 | 580 |
| 40 | 590 |
| 41 | 600 |
| 42 | 610 |
| 43 | 610 |
| 44 | 620 |
| 45 | 630 |
| 46 | 640 |
| 47 | 650 |
| 48 | 660 |
| 49 | 670 |
| 50 | 680 |
| 51 | 690 |
| 52 | 700 |
| 53 | 710 |
| 54 | 730 |
| 55 | 750 |
| 56 | 770 |
| 57 | 790 |
| 58 | 800 |

**3.** **Note the Test Score.**

This is your SAT Math score. Excellent! Write the number down.

# Finding Your Killer Essay Score

**If you wrote the essay,** your essay should have three scores, each from 2 to 8: Reading (whether you understood the passage), Analysis (how well you picked apart the arguments and writing style of the passage), and Writing (your own grammar and ability to express your thoughts). Each essay is a little different, so a general set of instructions doesn't apply. The answer chapters provide specific guidelines for the essay question(s) you worked on. Read those guidelines carefully. To see some sample graded responses, turn to Chapter 7.

# Recording Your Final Scores

Now you know your strengths and weaknesses. Resolve to work on any problem areas, so your next attempt at the SAT will result in a higher score.

**TIP**

Don't worry so much about one score! Take two or three practice exams, and you'll see your scores improving! Usually all the mistakes happen in the first practice, so check your mistakes, see what happened, and skip that mistake on the next round.

Like anything in the world that you do, you get better with practice. Get that practice out of the way here, now, so you improve *before* the real exam.

## First practice exam

**Reading and Writing Test Score** _____ (200–800)

**Math Test Score** _____ (200–800)

**Composite Test Score** _____ (400–1600)

**Essay:**

**Reading** _____ (2–8)

**Analysis** _____ (2–8)

**Writing** _____ (2–8)

**Composite Essay Score** _____ (6–24)

## Second practice exam

**Reading and Writing Test Score** _____ (200–800)

**Math Test Score** _____ (200–800)

Composite Test Score _____ (400–1600)

Essay:

Reading _____ (2–8)

Analysis _____ (2–8)

Writing _____ (2–8)

Composite Essay Score _____ (6–24)

# Third practice exam

Reading and Writing Test Score _____ (200–800)

Math Test Score _____ (200–800)

Composite Test Score _____ (400–1600)

Essay:

Reading _____ (2–8)

Analysis _____ (2–8)

Writing _____ (2–8)

Composite Essay Score _____ (6–24)

# Fourth practice exam

Reading and Writing Test Score _____ (200–800)

Math Test Score _____ (200–800)

Composite Test Score _____ (400–1600)

Essay:

Reading _____ (2–8)

Analysis _____ (2–8)

Writing _____ (2–8)

Composite Essay Score _____ (6–24)

# 6

# The Part of Tens

Avoid mistakes that other test takers make.

Discover ways to get the most from the practice exams.

# Chapter **19**

# Ten Mistakes Other Test-Takers Make That You Won't

E veryone does these. Everyone except you, that is. Most test-takers make these mistakes, look back on them, think about them, learn, try again, and finally get things right. That's *them*. You, however, can skip over most of that by knowing in advance what *not* to do.

## You Won't Forget Your Wristwatch

Who wears a watch these days? Well, *you* do if you want that scholarship. You *have* to manage your time. You need to know when you're halfway through, have 10 minutes to go, or at what point you are in each test. And don't forget about your breaks! You can't be late coming back to your seat.

Students who practice with a wristwatch tell me that they feel so much more in control of the experience. There's no panic that the time will suddenly run out, and that's just in practice! Try it on the real thing.

Note that your wristwatch has to be *simple*. It can't have smart functionality, which means it can't read your biorhythms and it especially can't connect to your phone. Also: *If your watch beeps during the exam, the proctors will take it.* So if you don't have anything that simple, go online or to the store and buy one! The cheaper the better.

# You Won't Bubble Everything at the End

Too many students are in the habit of circling the correct answers in the exam booklet and then quickly bubbling all 52 or so answers at the end of the hour. What could possibly go wrong? I had one student tell me that on his actual exam, when he reached Question 52 on the booklet, he was only on number 51 on the answer sheet! Oops. Then the time ran out.

You, however, won't miss half the questions — and blow 300 points — from a silly mistake like this. Get used to bubbling as you go. Make this a part of your practice!

# You Won't Let Your Calculator Batteries Die

If your calculator plugs in to charge, be sure it's plugged in the night before, and *don't forget to pack it*. If your calculator swaps batteries, put fresh ones in the night before and *test them out*. Even new batteries can be duds.

# You Won't Run Out of Steam

The SAT tests your stamina as much as anything else. Most students can't maintain these levels of concentration for four or five straight hours, so they burn out halfway through. Students have told me that by the third hour of a practice exam, they're just bubbling C, C, C. Obviously, this isn't an effective strategy — but at least it's on a practice test.

Like preparing for a marathon, preparing for the long SAT is a slow process to build yourself up. Practice for a few hours at a time and stop when you get tired. Do this a few times, and eventually you'll go the full distance without fail.

# You Won't Forget Snacks and Water

Pack some water bottles and snacks to keep in a locker for your breaks. Water is best — not soda or juice — and the snacks shouldn't be too sugary. Nutrition bars or sandwiches are good, as long as they don't have to go in the fridge. Your breaks are short, and you won't have time to buy something or wait in line for water.

# You Won't Work the Reading Test Straight On

The Reading Test in particular is arranged in the worst way for you to do well. It starts with the Literature passage, which takes the most time, and most passages have the main idea and inference questions early, with the line-number and detail questions last. If you work the Reading Test straight on, you run out of time about halfway through — and you wear yourself out!

Don't fall for this trap. Instead, take control. Work the passages and questions in an order that lets you get the most questions right! (This is covered in Chapter 3, so go there again.) Save the Literature passage for last, even though the SAT hands it to you first. For each passage, go straight to the line-number and detail questions (where the line number is in the question, *not* in the answer choices — those are different). Then, read the passage and answer the inference and main idea questions. Finally, go back to the Literature passage, where you may get stuck, but by then it doesn't matter because you've already finished the other passages.

Be sure to practice this out-of-order strategy ahead of time so it's smooth on test day.

# You Won't Rush Through the Questions

Some students think that they need to rush through the questions to make the time limit. This is true, if you want to get them all wrong by missing key details and making careless mistakes. I'd rather you get half the questions right and run out of time for the other half than miss them all by rushing through them. But that won't happen anyway: The SAT gives you enough time to answer all the questions correctly and calmly — if you don't get stuck.

**REMEMBER**

Remember the Other Golden Rule: *The secret to working fast and getting the answers right isn't rushing — it's knowing what you're doing.* The way you know what you're doing is by learning what's on the exam and practicing it.

# You Won't Get Stuck on a Question

You get roughly one minute per multiple-choice question. Imagine this: You encounter a tricky question that takes you five minutes, but you get it *right! Yes!* Then you run out of time before getting to the last four questions. So who won: you or that tricky question? Probably that question.

Don't let this happen. Instead, after about a minute, move on. Bubble a guess on your answer sheet, circle the question in your test booklet, fold the corner of the booklet page, and *move on.* You can come back to it later, or if you don't get the chance to, at least you took a guess. This way you don't miss out on questions at the end.

# You Won't Choke on the Essay

Choking, by definition (on the SAT), means getting stuck on something and becoming so flustered that you can't focus. This can happen at any point on the test, but because you know better than to get stuck on a question, you're unlikely to choke on one.

The essay, however, is another story. On the SAT, you have to write an introspective essay within 50 minutes, after a four-hour cognitive marathon. What's worse, you know that schools can see your essay, so no pressure there!

Of course, choking won't happen to you, because you learned how to write the essay in Chapter 7 and practiced it in Chapter 8. You *did* go through these chapters, right? Like any skill, writing the essay takes practice, and you don't want to be at the start of the learning curve on test day. This way, writer's block — and choking — is something that happens to other students, but not you.

# You Won't Change Your Morning Routine

The SAT is stressful enough. The last thing you need is to add more anxiety to the whole nerve-racking experience by changing your morning routine. If you normally have one glass of juice, should you have an extra glass for more vitamins or only half a glass so you don't have to get up? Should you have eggs for more protein or just toast to avoid the food crash? Here's a suggestion. *Do what you normally do.* It works every other day, and it'll work today. Don't change your routine.

If you're tempted to try an energy drink or something unusual for an enhanced test-taking experience, *try it first on a practice test!* Make sure this new mix doesn't upset your stomach or give you a headache. You don't need that distraction.

# Chapter 20

# Ten Ways to Get the Most from the Practice SATs

Sitting through the actual SAT is like being on stage. No matter how well you know the song or the routine, the first time you get up there it's a new experience and your performance goes south. However, the second time is *always* much better. Students tell me again and again that the second time they took the SAT went much better than the first time, partly because they had more practice, but also because the second time they were *used* to it.

This may be how the testing process goes, but you can close that gap and make your first SAT go much better by using the practice exams to prepare for the testing experience. Here are ten ways to get the most from the practice SATs.

## Practice an Entire SAT in One Sitting

How well you can answer the questions doesn't matter if you can't maintain your energy for the length of the exam. When you're in a pressure cooker like the actual exam, your brain is in over-drive. Whether you're omitting the essay (for a four-hour exam) or including it (for five hours), you need to become used to working intensely for these hours in one stretch so you can go the distance on exam day.

## Practice Not Making Mistakes Under Pressure

Did you get stuck on an early question and not finish the Writing and Language Test? Did you skip a line on the bubble sheet? Did you get lost in the pages, unable to find the question that you wanted to return to? Did you know better than to make these mistakes? Of course you did, but this happens to everyone, especially under pressure.

Only by falling into a trap do you learn out how to avoid it. Work out the bugs on a practice SAT. Make these mistakes at home, where it doesn't matter, instead of on the actual exam, where it's life or death (or a scholarship).

## Practice with Others in the Room

Nothing is more distracting on your SAT than hearing someone using scratch paper, sighing, turning pages, cursing, or (if she used *SAT For Dummies*) chuckling confidently while she works her exam. Get used to distractions by taking your practice SAT with friends or others who are also taking the SAT and therefore need to practice. The sounds as they work and sigh and groan or pat themselves on the back (because they also used *SAT For Dummies*) become less of a distraction as you get used to the noises and the now-present feeling of competition. This also helps your friends improve their scores while they help you improve yours.

## Practice as a Dress Rehearsal

Play by the rules of the testing center. No phone, hat, drink, snack, neck brace, or anything that brings a modicum of comfort is allowed within reach in the exam room. Your breaks are short, and your scratch paper is your test booklet. If this is not something that you're used to, it will drive you nuts on exam day, so make sure it's a road that you've been down before, and it won't be as bad.

Do you get thirsty? Hungry? Uncomfortable? Chilly? What do you wish you had: water, a sandwich, a power bar, coffee, aspirin? Keep these thoughts in mind and plan accordingly on test day. You have access to your personal belongings during the breaks, so bring these things in a bag and grab a quick refreshment during your break.

## Practice Your Competitive Edge

The practice test doesn't matter, so why try hard? In the third hour of the practice, you're exhausted, and you just want to get through it — and that's okay because it's a practice test, right?

Wrong. If you've never tried as hard as you can for four or five hours, you won't do it easily on exam day. You may intend to, but working at half effort on the practice exam is a hard habit to break, and it carries to the real thing.

It's like running a race by yourself versus running a race against someone else: You try harder when others are in the game. One way to get around this is by recording your scores and trying to beat your last performance. Another way is to try to beat a friend's score. The best way, though, is to take the practice exam with a friend in the room also taking the same exam. Try to beat this person: This makes it real and competitive, and you'll bring this edge to the actual exam.

# Practice Your Test-Taking Strategies

As you study and practice, you develop strategies for taking the exam. Maybe you work all the easy math questions first and then go back to the tougher questions. Maybe you try different ways to take on the Reading Test. These strategies give you control over the exam, but different strategies work for different test-takers. What works for you? What doesn't? What does it depend on? You should know the answers to these questions before you take the actual exam.

As you take the practice SATs, focus on your strategies. You will find things that work and things that don't, or you'll find your own take on an established strategy. Finding and honing your strategies that work is a very important part of your prep process, but *do this before test day*.

One thing you could do is go through a practice SAT that you've already worked. Because the questions are familiar to you, you can focus more on the test-taking strategies.

# Practice Using the Bubble Sheet

Students hate the bubble sheet. They practice and circle the answers in the test booklet, and they stop right there. Like it or not, the bubble sheet is part of the exam, and I've seen enough practice exams where the math or English question is answered correctly in the booklet but bubbled incorrectly on the sheet. It counts just as wrong, and the student is *mad*.

One student refused to practice with a bubble sheet. Then he took the actual SAT, and he told me after that he had somehow bubbled two answers on a single line! I think he had also lost count of which line he was on, so he missed a lot of questions. This was a top-scoring student who consistently answered 19 out of 20 questions correctly in practice, but *he bombed the exam because he wasn't used to the bubble sheet*. This didn't have to happen.

# Practice Finding Your Areas of Focus

Do you struggle more with reading Science or Social Studies passages? Do you handle triangles better than you do exponents? Do you lose steam (causing your performance to drop) by the third hour? Do you run out of time? With these practice SATs, you can get a sense of how you work and where you need to focus, and *then* you can close those gaps. *You cannot fix your gaps unless you find them first*. There are no truer words.

# Review the Practice SAT Answers and Explanations

After taking a four- or five-hour practice SAT, the last thing you probably want to do is spend time reviewing answers and explanations, so take a well-deserved break and save the answers and explanations for later. But be sure to review them.

After you're rested, take the following steps to review:

1. Identify which questions you answered incorrectly.

2. Read the answer explanations and review any relevant material so you're prepared for a similar question next time.

3. Fully close that gap by practicing similar questions from coauthor Ron's book *1,001 SAT Practice Questions For Dummies* (also published by Wiley).

4. If you wrote the essay, have a friend review it based on the rubric described in Chapters 7 and 8.

**TIP**

Here's another thing you can do. While you're taking the exam, mark any questions you're not sure of, and read the explanations for those answers after the practice. This way, even if you guessed correctly, you'll review that question along with the ones that you missed.

# Review the Practice SAT with Other Students

After taking a practice SAT along with your friends who are also taking the practice SAT, or even if your friends took the practice SAT separately, review your practice exam along with them. For each question that you miss, your friend can explain it to you; or if your friend also missed it, you can seek the answer together. Your friend will also have missed questions that you got right, so you can explain those to them! You boost their scores while they boost yours. After reviewing the entire exam, keep track of the missed questions so that you can review them in this book. Then get a pizza.

# Index

scoring, 92–94, 101, 357

structure, 348–349

style, 93

tone, 96

*200% of Nothing*

   answer, 110–112

   question, 109–110

   scoring essay, 110–112

   writing, 95

essay scores, 13

ethos, 96, 101, 107

evidence, essays, 101, 108, 112, 115

evidence questions

   passage-based questions, 80, 87

   Practice Exam 1, 288

   science passages, 47, 48

   social studies passages, 41

evocation, defined, 274

examining graded responses, essays, 101–104

exponents, 133–134, 133–138

expressions

   defined, 159

   solving, 159–160

## F

factoring, 155

factors, 125

facts, 34

factual questions

   science passages, 48

   social studies passages, 41

Fakim, Gurib, 233–235

farther versus further, 69

fee waiver, 11, 14

feminism, 113

*fewer* versus *less*, 69

figurative, defined, 335

figurative language, 97

financial assistance, 11

Fine, Allison, 105–109

Fiore, Neil, 262–263

fluctuations, defined, 329

foreign language students, 11–12

formulas, 120

45-45-90 triangle, 192

fractions. *See also* rational numbers

   improper, 126

   proper, 126

   reciprocal, 151–152

solving for x, 149–151

French language, 12

*Freud: Darkness in the Midst of Vision* (Breger), 303–304

Fulton, Frances I. Sims, 33–34

functions

   defined, 181

   graphing, 181–183

   minimum value, 281

   overview, 122

   quadratic, 154–157

fundamental, defined, 328

furthermore, proper use of term, 334

future value, 163

## G

gender-neutral words, 113

generate, defined, 71

genius, defined, 266

geometry

   angles

      acute, 186

      complementary, 187

      drawing, 186

      obtuse, 187

      right, 186

      supplementary, 187

      transversal, 188–189

      vertical, 187–188

   circles

      arc, 199–200

      area, 197

      chord, 197

      circumference, 197

      diameter, 197

      equation of, 179–181, 276, 282

      graphing, 179–181

      pi, 197

      radius, 197

      tangent, 198

   overview, 123

   polygons

      hexagon, 195

      octagon, 195

      parallelograms, 194–196

      pentagon, 195

      rectangles, 194

      squares, 194

      trapezoid, 194–196

## K

## L

## M

triangles
   30-60-90, 192–193
   3:4:5, 192
   45-45-90, 192
   area, 191
   equilateral, 189, 193
   hypotenuse, 190, 340
   inequality, 338
   isosceles, 189, 192, 193
   perimeter, 338
   Pythagorean theorem, 191, 340
   right, 190
   right triangle, 192
   similar, 191
   vertex, 282
trigonometry
   cosine, 206
   overview, 123, 205
   radians, 208–211
   right triangles with SOH CAH TOA, 206–208
   sine, 206
   solving equations, 211–212
   tangent, 206
   unit circles, 208–211
TTY Customer Service, 9
200% of Nothing (Dewdney)
   answer, 110–112
   question, 109–110
   scoring essay, 110–112
2-part passages, Reading Test, 25

# U

undefined numbers, 127
unit circles, 208–211

# V

variable, defined, 35
verbs
   defined, 65–66
   subject-verb agreement, 65–66
   wrong-tense, 61
verb tense questions, 335
   passage-based questions, 75, 79, 83, 87
vertex, 175, 282
vertical angles, 187–188
vigilance, defined, 328
visual element questions, passage-based questions, 87

vocabulary, level of, 93
vocabulary in context, grammar review, 68–69
vocabulary in context questions
   passage-based questions, 75, 80, 83, 84
   science passages, 48
   social studies passages, 42
   Writing and Language Test, 62–63, 63
volume
   cone, 203–204
   cube, 202
   cylinder, 203
   of pyramid, 201
   rectangular solid, 201

# W

Wall Street Journal, 25
Wassenaar, Trudy, 298–300
water bottles, 19, 362
were, proper use of term, 335
whole numbers, 125
Woldoff, Ron
   1,001 SAT Practice Questions For Dummies, 2, 17, 73
Woods, Geraldine
   1,001 Grammar Practice Questions For Dummies, 62, 73
   College Admission Essays For Dummies, 12
   English Grammar For Dummies, 62, 73
   English Grammar Workbook For Dummies, 62, 73
Woolf, Virginia, 36–37
word choice questions
   literary passages, 36
   passage-based questions, 81, 88
wristwatch
   getting, 17
   wearing, 19, 361
writing, 348
   fluency, 93
Writing and Language Test
   columns, 62
   composite scores, 13
   cross-test scores, 13
   focusing during, 20
   foreign students, 12
   grammar review
      case, 67
      noun-pronoun agreement, 66
      parallelism, 67
      punctuations, 68
      subject-verb agreement, 65–66

# About the Authors

**Ron Woldoff** completed his dual master's degrees at Arizona State University and San Diego State University, where he studied the culmination of business and technology. After several years as a corporate consultant, Ron opened his own company, National Test Prep, where he has helped students reach their goals on the GMAT, GRE, SAT, ACT, and PSAT. He created the programs and curricula for these tests from scratch, using his own observations of the tests and feedback from students. Ron has also taught his own GMAT and GRE programs as an adjunct instructor at both Northern Arizona University and the internationally acclaimed Thunderbird School of Global Management, as well as SAT and ACT at various high schools. Ron lives in Phoenix, Arizona, with his lovely wife, Leisah, and their three amazing boys, Zachary, Jadon, and Adam. You can find Ron on the web at testprepaz.com.

**Geraldine Woods** has prepared students for the SAT, both academically and emotionally, for the past four decades. She is the author of more than 50 books, including *English Grammar For Dummies*, *English Grammar Workbook For Dummies*, *1,001 Grammar Practice Questions For Dummies*, and earlier editions of *SAT For Dummies*, all published by Wiley. She blogs on grammar at www.grammarianinthecity.com

# Dedication

This book is humbly dedicated to the thousands of students whom we have helped reach their goals. You have taught us as much as we have taught you.

# Authors' Acknowledgments

**Ron Woldoff:** I would like to thank my friends Lionel Hummel and Jaime Abromovitz, who helped me get things started when I had this wild notion of helping people prepare for standardized college-admissions tests. I would like to thank my friend and former high-school teacher Ken Krueger, who guided me through the business side of test prep. And more than anyone else, I would like to thank my best friend and wife, Leisah, for her continuing support and for always being there for me.

**Geraldine Woods:** I'd like to thank Peter Bonfanti and Kristin Josephson, whose earlier work on SAT math has been enormously helpful. I appreciate the efforts of Carmen Krikorian, Erin Calligan Mooney, Tim Gallan, and Sophia Seidner — professionals who never let me down.

## Publisher's Acknowledgments

**Executive Editor:** Lindsay Lefevere

**Project Editor:** Tim Gallan

**Copy Editor:** Christine Pingleton

**Technical Editor:** Cindy Kaplan

**Production Editor:** Siddique Shaik

**Cover Image:** © George Rudy/Shutterstock